6016882

||||| ||| |||| ||| || ||| || |||
D1609264

WITHDRAWN

BEYOND SIGNIFICANCE TESTING

BEYOND SIGNIFICANCE TESTING

REFORMING DATA ANALYSIS METHODS IN BEHAVIORAL RESEARCH

REX B. KLINE

American Psychological Association • Washington, DC

Published by
American Psychological Association
750 First Street, NE
Washington, DC 20002
www.apa.org

To order
APA Order Department
P.O. Box 92984
Washington, DC 20090-2984
Tel: (800) 374-2721
Direct: (202) 336-5510
Fax: (202) 336-5502
TDD/TTY: (202) 336-6123
Online: www.apa.org/books/
E-mail: order@apa.org

In the U.K., Europe, Africa, and the Middle East, copies may be ordered from
American Psychological Association
3 Henrietta Street
Covent Garden, London
WC2E 8LU England

Typeset in Goudy by World Composition Services, Inc., Sterling, VA

Printer: Edwards Brothers, Ann Arbor, MI
Cover Designer: Naylor Design, Washington, DC
Project Manager: Debbie Hardin, Carlsbad, CA

The opinions and statements published are the responsibility of the authors, and such opinions and statements do not necessarily represent the policies of the American Psychological Association.

Library of Congress Cataloging-in-Publication Data

Kline, Rex B.
    Beyond significance testing: reforming data analysis methods in behavioral research / by Rex B. Kline.—1st ed.
        p. cm.
    Includes bibliographical references and index.
    ISBN 1-59147-118-4 (alk. paper)
    1. Psychometrics—Textbooks. I. Title.

BF39.K59 2004
150'.72'4—dc22

2003022594

British Library Cataloguing-in-Publication Data
A CIP record is available from the British Library.

Printed in the United States of America
First Edition

For my family,
Joanna, Julia Anne, and Luke Christopher,
bright angels all.

It's late. Time to make up your mind. Which will it be?
The reality of dreams or the dream of reality?
—Alfred Bester

CONTENTS

Preface .... *xi*

I. Introductory Concepts 1

Chapter 1.   Changing Times 3

Chapter 2.   Fundamental Concepts 19

Chapter 3.   What's Wrong With Statistical Tests—
And Where We Go From Here 61

II. Effect Size Estimation in Comparative Studies 93

Chapter 4.   Parametric Effect Size Indexes 95

Chapter 5.   Nonparametric Effect Size Indexes 143

Chapter 6.   Effect Size Estimation in One-Way Designs 163

Chapter 7.   Effect Size Estimation in Multifactor Designs 203

III. Alternatives to Statistical Tests 245

Chapter 8.   Replication and Meta-Analysis 247

Chapter 9.   Resampling and Bayesian Estimation 273

References 295

Index 313

About the Author 325

PREFACE

The goals of this book are to (a) review the now-large literature across many different disciplines about shortcomings of statistical tests; (b) explain why these criticisms have sufficient merit to justify change in data-analysis practices; (c) help readers acquire new skills concerning effect size estimation and interval estimation for effect sizes; and (d) review additional alternatives to statistical tests, including bootstrapping and Bayesian statistics.

This book is a follow-up to the report of Leland Wilkinson and the Task Force on Statistical Inference (TFSI; 1999) of the American Psychological Association (APA) and the fifth edition of the *Publication Manual of the American Psychological Association* (APA, 2001). Both the report of the TFSI and the most recent *Publication Manual* call for changes in the way data are analyzed for psychology research journals, including rhe reporting of effect sizes and confidence intervals for primary results. The reporting of effect sizes is now also required by increasing numbers of research journals in psychology and other disciplines. In addition, the reforms mentioned imply a reduced role for traditional statistical tests, which reflects decades of increasing criticism of the use of statistical tests in the behavioral and other sciences.

An additional goal is related to the criticism that the most recent *Publication Manual* calls for change in data analysis practices but does not give examples. Numerous examples with actual research results are presented throughout this volume.

This book is written for researchers and students in psychology and related areas who may not have strong quantitative backgrounds. It assumes that the reader has had at least one undergraduate-level course in behavioral science statistics. Each substantive chapter begins with a review of fundamental statistical issues but does not get into the minutia of statistical theory.

Works that do so are cited in the text, and such works can be consulted for more information. This book is suitable as a textbook for an introductory course in behavioral science statistics at the graduate level. It can also be used in a senior undergraduate-level course that considers modern methods of data analysis. Coverage of some of the more advanced topics in this book, such as noncentrality interval estimation and effect size estimation for random factors, could be skipped in such a class. Especially useful for all readers is chapter 3, which considers common misinterpretations of the results of statistical tests. These misinterpretations are widespread among students and researchers alike, and such false beliefs may have hindered the development of psychology and related areas as cumulative sciences.

It was a pleasure to work with the development and production staff at the APA. Their work is first-rate. The two anonymous reviews of an earlier version of this work were extraordinarily helpful. This kind of feedback is invaluable to an author, and any remaining shortcomings in the book reflect my own limitations. Special thanks to Debbie Hardin, the project manager for this book, who did a super job of dealing with the original (and technically complicated) manuscript. Finally, I greatly appreciate the support of my wife while working on this project and the delightful company of our two wonderful children, to whom this book is dedicated.

I

INTRODUCTORY CONCEPTS

1

CHANGING TIMES

Somehow the wondrous promise of the earth is that there are things beautiful in it, things wondrous and alluring, and by virtue of your trade you want to understand them.

—Mitchell Feigenbaum, Chaos theorist
(quoted in Gleick, 1988, p. 187)

This book has a home page on the Internet; its address is

http://www.apa.org/books/resources/kline

From the home page, readers can find supplemental readings about advanced topics, exercises with answers, resources for instructors and students, and links to related Web sites. Readers can also download data files for some of the research examples discussed later.

In 1996, the Board of Scientific Affairs of the American Psychological Association (APA) convened the Task Force on Statistical Inference (TFSI). The TFSI was asked to respond to the long-standing controversy about statistical significance tests and elucidate alternative methods (Wilkinson & TFSI, 1999). Some hoped that the TFSI would recommend a ban on statistical tests in psychology journals. Such a ban was also discussed in recent special sections or issues of *Psychological Science* (Harris, 1997a), *Research in the Schools* (McLean & Kaufman, 1998), and an edited book by Harlow, Mulaik, and Steiger (1997), the title of which asks the question, "What if there were no significance tests?" Problems with and alternatives to statistical tests were also discussed in a special issue of the *Journal of Experimental Education* (B. Thompson, 1993a).

Serious discussion of such a ban reflects the culmination of many years of disenchantment with statistical tests. In fact, this controversy has escalated decade by decade and has crossed various disciplines as diverse as psychology and wildlife sciences (e.g., D. Anderson, Burnham, & W. Thompson, 2000).

Talk of a ban on statistical tests would probably come as a surprise to a casual observer, to whom it would be plain that results of statistical tests are reported in most empirical articles published in psychology and related disciplines in the past 50 years (Hubbard & Ryan, 2000). The same observer stepping into almost any university classroom for courses in behavioral science statistics at either the undergraduate or graduate level would find that these tests have been the main subject matter for the past 20 years or more (Aiken, West, Sechrest, & Reno, 1990; Frederich, Buday, & Kerr, 2000).

Nevertheless, by the late 1990s the number of voices in the behavioral sciences decrying the limitations of statistical tests started to reach a critical mass. This was apparent in the formation of the TFSI by the APA to look at this controversy. It is also obvious in the fact that about two dozen research journals in psychology, education, counseling, and other areas now require the reporting of effect sizes in submitted manuscripts (Fidler & B. Thompson, 2001).[1] Two of these are flagship journals of associations (American Counseling Association, Council for Exceptional Children), each with more than 50,000 members. One of the most recent APA journals to make this requirement is the *Journal of Educational Psychology*. The requirement to report effect sizes sends a powerful message to potential contributors to these journals that use of statistical tests alone is insufficient, and the number of journals making it is bound to increase. Editorial policies in prominent journals can be an important bellwether for reform (Sedlmeier & Gigerenzer, 1989; Vacha-Haase, 2001). Indeed, Kaufman (1998) noted that the controversy over the use of statistical tests is the major methodological issue of our generation. So perhaps a casual observer might sense that change is coming after all.

GOALS AND PLAN OF THE BOOK

This book aims to help readers stay abreast of ongoing changes in the ways we analyze our data and report our findings in the behavioral sciences. These readers may be educators, applied researchers, reviewers of manuscripts for journals, or undergraduate or graduate students in psychology or related disciplines. It is assumed that many readers (like the author) were trained in traditional methods of data analysis—that is, the use of statistical tests as the primary (if not only) way to evaluate hypotheses. Readers who are currently students are perhaps at some advantage because their views and skills may not yet be so narrow. However, even very experienced researchers

---

[1] B. Thompson keeps a list of journals that require the reporting of effect sizes at http://www.coe.tamu.edu/~bthompson/journals.htm

who have published many articles may have wondered whether there are not better ways to evaluate research hypotheses, or whether it is actually necessary to include results of statistical tests in articles (e.g., Kaufman, 1998). Readers already convinced of the limitations of statistical tests should find in this book useful arguments to reinforce their viewpoint. Readers not sharing this view will, it is hoped, find some interesting ideas to ponder.

This book does not debate whether we in the psychological community should change the way we use statistical tests. Tryon (2001) and others have noted that more than 50 years of trying to remediate misuses of statistical tests by discussing their technical merits has not been productive. This book assumes instead that developments in the field already point toward a diminishing role for statistical tests. As a consequence, the goals of this book are to help readers understand (a) the controversy about and limitations of statistical tests, (b) strengths and weakness of some proposed alternatives to statistical tests, and (c) other methods related to a reduced role for statistical tests, such as meta-analysis. Of primary importance for the second and third points is effect size estimation which, as mentioned, is now required by many journals. The estimation of average effect size across a set of studies in the same general area is also a key part of most meta-analyses. Another major focus of this book involves interval estimation, especially the construction of confidence intervals based on observed effect sizes.

Part I of the book is concerned with fundamental concepts and summarizes the debate about statistical tests. Chapter 2 reviews principles of sampling and estimation that underlie confidence intervals and statistical tests. Chapter 3 outlines arguments against the continued use of statistical tests as our primary means to evaluate hypotheses. This discussion assumes that although there is nothing inherently wrong with statistical tests, what they actually do makes them unsuitable for perhaps most types of behavioral research. It is also argued that research progress in psychology has been hindered by our preoccupation with statistical tests.

Part II comprises four chapters that emphasize effect size estimation in *comparative studies* that compare at least two different groups or conditions. Chapter 4 reviews the general rationale of effect size estimation and introduces basic parametric effect size indexes for continuous outcome variables, including standardized mean differences and measures of association. Also considered is the comparison of groups at the case level with relatively simple statistics based on proportions of scores above or below certain reference points. The critical problem of evaluating substantive (theoretical, clinical, or practical) significance versus statistical significance is also discussed. Chapter 5 introduces nonparametric effect size indexes for comparing groups on categorical outcomes, such as relapsed versus not relapsed. Chapters 6 and 7 concern effect size estimation in one-way designs with at least three conditions and factorial designs with two or more independent variables. Many empirical examples are presented in chapters 4 to 7.

Presentations about effect size estimation are often chock full of equations. This is because many effect size indexes can be computed in more than one way, such as from group descriptive statistics or test statistics. To reduce the overall number, only the most essential equations are given in chapters 4 to 7. Some of these equations are for primary researchers who have access to the original data, but others are also handy in secondary analyses based on summary statistics often reported in printed or on-line documents. Information about additional ways to compute effect size indexes is available in technical books about meta-analysis, such as Cooper and Hedges (1994b).

Part III includes two chapters that cover topics related to reform of methods of data analysis in the social sciences. Chapter 8 deals with principles of replication and meta-analysis. The latter has become an increasingly important tool in both the social and health sciences for synthesizing results across a research literature. Its emphasis on effect sizes in primary studies instead of results of statistical tests avoids some of the limitations of the latter. Researchers working in areas with sufficient numbers of studies for meta-analysis thus need to understand its potential strengths and limitations. Chapter 9 surveys two other alternatives to traditional statistical tests that are often overlooked in psychology, statistical resampling—which includes the method of bootstrapping—and Bayesian estimation.

RETROSPECTIVE

Comprehensive historical accounts of the long-standing controversy about statistical significance tests can be found in Gigerenzer (1993), Huberty and Pike (1999), and Oakes (1986).

Hybrid Logic of Statistical Tests (1920–1960)

The basic logical elements of what is today often referred to as null hypothesis significance testing (NHST) were present in scientific papers as early as the 1700s (Stigler, 1986). These elements were not formally organized into a systematic method until the early 1900s, however. The method of NHST in its contemporary form is actually a hybrid of two different schools of thought, one from the 1920s associated with R. Fisher (e.g., 1925) and another from the 1930s called the Neyman–Pearson approach, after Neyman and E. S. Pearson (e.g., Neyman & E. S. Pearson, 1933). Other individuals contributed to these schools, such as K. Pearson and

A. Wald (Hogben, 1957), but the work of the three principals listed first forms the genesis of NHST.

The Neyman–Pearson model is an extension of the Fisher model. Fisher's approach featured only a null hypothesis and subsequent estimation of the conditional probability of the data under it with statistical tests. The probabilities generated by statistical tests are commonly called p values. There was no alternative hypothesis in Fisher's model. The conventional levels of statistical significance used today, .05 and .01, are generally attributed to Fisher, but he apparently did not advocate that these values be applied across all studies (Cowles & Davis, 1982). Anyhow, for its focus on p values under the null hypothesis, Fisher's model has been called the p-value approach (Huberty, 1993).

The addition of the alternative hypothesis to the basic Fisher model, the attendant specification of one- or two-tailed regions of rejection, and the application of fixed levels of α across all studies characterize the Neyman–Pearson model. The last characteristic listed is perhaps the main source of the rigid application of the .05 or .01 levels of statistical significance that is today's practice. For the same reason, the Neyman–Pearson model has been described as the fixed-p approach (Huberty, 1993). The Neyman–Pearson model also brought with it the conceptual framework of power and associated decision errors, Type I and Type II. A modern power analysis is in spirit and fact based on the Neyman–Pearson model, not the Fisher model.

To say that advocates of the Fisher model and the Neyman–Pearson model exchanged few kind words about each other's approach is an understatement. Their long-running debate was acrimonious. Nevertheless, the integration of the two models by statisticians and authors other than Fisher, Neyman, and E. S. Pearson into what makes up contemporary NHST took place roughly between 1935 and 1950 (Huberty, 1993). Gigerenzer (1993) referred to this integrated model as the *hybrid logic of scientific inference,* and P. Dixon and O'Reilly (1999) called it the "Intro Stats" method because this is the approach outlined in virtually all contemporary textbooks for introductory statistics in the behavioral sciences. Many authors have noted that (a) the hybrid logic that underlies modern NHST would have been rejected by Fisher, Neyman, and E. S. Pearson, although for different reasons; and (b) its composite nature may be a source of confusion about what results from statistical tests really mean.

Institutionalization of the "Intro Stats" Method (1940–1960)

Before 1940, statistical tests were used in relatively few published articles in psychology. Authors of works from this time instead used in nonstandard ways a variety of descriptive statistics or rudimentary test statistics. However, from roughly 1940 to 1960 during what Gigerenzer and

D. Murray (1987) called the *inference revolution* in psychology, the Intro Stats method was widely adopted in textbooks, university curricula, and journal editorial practice as *the* method to test hypotheses. Gigerenzer (1993) identified two factors that contributed to this shift. One is the move in psychology away from the study of single cases, such as in operant conditioning studies of individual animals, to the study of groups. This change occurred roughly from 1920 to 1950. Another is what Gigerenzer (1993) and others called the *probabilistic revolution* in science, which introduced indeterminism as a major theoretical concept in areas such as quantum mechanics and genetics to better understand the subject matter. In psychology, though, it was used to mechanize the inference process through NHST, a critical difference, as it turns out.

After the widespread adoption of the Intro Stats method, there was a dramatic increase in the reporting of statistical tests in journal articles in psychology and related fields. This trend is obvious in Figure 1.1, reproduced from Hubbard and Ryan. These authors sampled about 8,000 articles published between 1911 and 1998 in randomly selected issues of 12 different APA journals. Summarized in the figure are the percentages of articles in which statistical tests were used in the data analysis. This percentage is about 17% from 1911 to 1929. It increases to around 50% in 1940, continues to rise to about 85% by 1960, and exceeds 90% since the 1970s. The time period of the most rapid increase in use of NHST, about 1940 to 1960, corresponds to the inference revolution in psychology.

Some advantages to the institutionalization of NHST were noted by Gigerenzer (1993). The behavioral sciences grew rapidly after 1945, and its administration was made easier by the near-universal use of statistical tests. For example, journal editors could use NHST outcomes to decide which studies to publish or reject, respectively, those with or without statistically significant results, among other considerations. The method of NHST is mechanically applied, and thus seemed to remove subjective judgment from the inference process. That this objectivity is more apparent than real is another matter (more about this point later). The method of NHST also gave behavioral researchers a common language and perhaps identity as members of the same grand research enterprise. It also distinguished them from their counterparts in the natural sciences, who may use statistical tests to detect outliers but not typically to test hypotheses (Gigerenzer, 1993). The elevation of any method to dogma has potential costs, some of which are considered next.

Increasing Criticism of Statistical Tests (1940–Present)

There has been controversy about statistical tests for more than 70 years, or as long as they have been around (Kirk, 1996). Some examples of

Figure 1.1. Percentage of articles reporting results of statistical tests in 12 journals of the American Psychological Association from 1911 to 1998. From "The Historical Growth of Statistical Significance Testing in Psychology—And Its Future Prospects," by R. Hubbard and P. A. Ryan, 2000, *Educational and Psychological Measurement, 60*, p. 665. Copyright 2001 by Sage Publications. Reprinted with permission.

early critical works include Boring (1919), Berkson (1942), Rozeboom (1960), a book by Hogben (1957), and edited books by Morrison and Henkel (1970) and Kirk (1972). Overall, the numbers of published works critical of NHST has been increasing exponentially since the 1940s. D. Anderson et al. searched the research literature in ecology, medicine, business/economics, statistics, and the social sciences for works that questioned the scientific utility of statistical tests. Presented in Figure 1.2 are the total numbers of such works across all surveyed disciplines. Relatively small numbers were published from 1940 to 1960. However, the numbers of critical articles has increased rapidly since the 1970s, and just about 200 were published in the 1990s in psychology and the other disciplines surveyed by D. Anderson et al.

Summarized next are some of the major arguments against the continued widespread use of statistical tests in the behavioral sciences; they are considered in more detail in later chapters.

1. The p values generated by statistical tests are widely misunderstood. These misunderstandings include the belief that p values measure the likelihood of sampling error, replication, and the truth of the null or alternative hypothesis. These false beliefs may not be solely the fault of users of statistical tests, however. This is because the logical underpinnings of contemporary NHST are not entirely consistent.

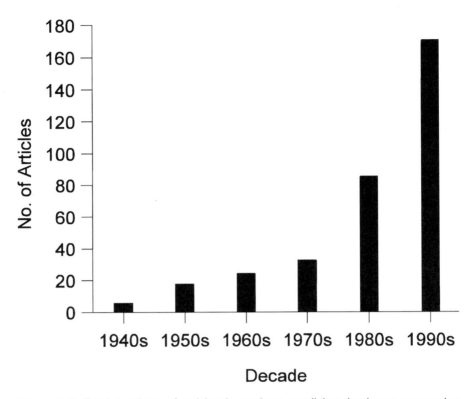

Figure 1.2. Total numbers of articles in ecology, medicine, business–economics, statistics, and the social sciences that question the utility of statistical tests. From "Null Hypothesis Testing: Problems, Prevalence, and an Alternative," by D. R. Anderson, K. P. Burnham, and W. L. Thompson, 2000, *Journal of Wildlife Management, 64,* p. 913. Copyright 2000 by The Wildlife Society. Adapted with permission.

2. Mistaken beliefs about what statistical tests tell us act as a collective form of cognitive distortion that has hindered research progress in the behavioral sciences. This is apparent by the failure to develop a stronger tradition of replication compared to the natural sciences, a lack of relevance of much of our research, and wasted research effort and resources. Critics do not generally suggest that statistical tests are the sole cause, but their excessive use exacerbates these problems.

3. It is likely that p values from statistical tests in many (if not most) behavioral studies are not very meaningful, especially when implausible null hypotheses are tested or distributional assumptions do not hold. If p values are suspect, so are decisions based on them.

4. The information actually provided by a statistical test is very specific, so much so that statistical tests do not typically tell researchers what they really want to know.

5. Statistical significance says nothing directly about the size of an effect or whether it has theoretical, practical, or clinical import. Effect size magnitude, substantive significance, and whether a result replicates are what we really want (and need) to know.

6. For all the problems of statistical tests, however, there is no magical alternative (J. Cohen, 1994). That is, proposed alternatives, such as effect size estimation and interval estimation in individual studies and the use of meta-analysis to synthesize these results across studies, have their own potential problems. Thus, alternatives to statistical tests should not be uncritically endorsed.

The Failure of Early "Suggestions" to Report Effect Sizes (1994–Present)

One way to compensate for some of the limitations of statistical tests is to report supplemental information, such as a measure of effect size magnitude. Kirk (1996) noted that the idea of effect size estimation is hardly new: It can found in the work by K. Pearson in the early 1900s, and one of most widely used effect size statistics in the analysis of variance—estimated eta-squared ($\hat{\eta}^2$), also called the correlation ratio (R^2)—is attributed to R. Fisher. The reporting of effect sizes is also generally advocated by contemporary critics of statistical tests.

The fourth edition of the APA's publication manual (APA, 1994) for the first time encouraged but did not require authors to report effect sizes along with results of statistical tests. Unfortunately, results of several empirical surveys of post-1994 volumes in more than 20 different journals indicate that this encouragement has had relatively little impact (Vacha-Haase, Nilsson, Reetz, Lance, & B. Thompson, 2000). For example, Kirk (1996) examined the 1995 volumes of four different APA journals. The proportions of empirical articles reporting effect sizes across the four journals ranged from 12 to 77%. The figure of 77% seems impressive, but Kirk (1996) noted that authors in this particular journal were more likely to use regression techniques, which automatically generate correlation effect sizes such as R^2. Rates of effect sizes in empirical articles in other journals are about 25%, but authors did not always interpret the effect sizes that they reported (e.g., B. Thompson & Snyder, 1998; Vacha-Haase & Ness, 1999). In a broader survey of reporting practices of articles published in the *Journal of Applied*

Psychology, Finch, Cumming, and Thomason (2001) found little evidence of reform in the reporting of results of statistical tests over the years 1940 to 1999. That there would be so little change in reporting practices since the inference revolution in psychology is surprising, especially given that relatively inexpensive personal computers have made available to applied researchers many sophisticated statistical methods. An analogy would be putting the engine from a modern car in the body of a car from the 1940s: Because of limitations of its dated chassis, the car may not actually go any faster.

The Rise of Meta-Analysis and Meta-Analytic Thinking (1976–Present)

Since its introduction in the late 1970s (Glass, 1976; R. Rosenthal, 1976), meta-analysis has become an important tool for research synthesis in several disciplines. Meta-analysis is described in chapter 8, so only its impact on the controversy about statistical tests is outlined in this chapter. The typical meta-analysis in the social sciences estimates the central tendency and variability in standardized effect sizes across a set of studies of the same phenomenon, such as the relative effectiveness of treatment over control. This focus on effect size and not statistical significance in individual studies encourages the reader of a meta-analytic article to think outside of the limitations of the latter. There are also now several examples in which meta-analytic results show that conclusions based on whether null hypotheses are rejected in individual studies have been wrong (e.g., Rossi, 1997).

The increasing use of meta-analysis has also encouraged *meta-analytic thinking*, to which Cumming and Finch (2001, p. 555) and B. Thompson (2002b) attributed the following characteristics:

1. An accurate appreciation of the results of previous studies is seen as essential.
2. A researcher should view his or her own study as making a modest contribution to that body of previous research.
3. A researcher should report results so that they can be easily incorporated into a future meta-analysis. This includes the reporting of effect sizes and confidence intervals.
4. Retrospective interpretation of new results, once collected, are called for via direct comparison with previous effect sizes.

Meta-analytic thinking is likely to become ever more predominate. It is also incompatible with using statistical tests as the primary inference tool.

Report of the TFSI and the APA's Fifth Edition of the *Publication Manual* (1999–Present)

The report of the TFSI dealt with a wide range of methodological and statistical issues (Wilkinson & TFSI, 1999). It also offered suggestions for the then-upcoming fifth edition of the APA's *Publication Manual* (APA, 2001). Some of the TFSI's main recommendations concerning data analyses are summarized next:

1. Use minimally sufficient analyses (simpler is better).
2. Do not report statistics from computer output without knowing what they mean.
3. Document assumptions about population effect sizes, sample sizes, or measurement behind a priori estimates of the statistical power of the study. Use confidence intervals about observed results instead of estimating the observed (post hoc) power.
4. Report observed effect sizes for primary outcomes or whenever p values are reported. This makes for better research and informs subsequent meta-analyses.
5. Report confidence intervals about observed effect sizes.
6. Give assurances to a reasonable degree that the data meet statistical assumptions.

However, the TFSI decided not to recommend a ban on statistical tests in psychology journals. In its view, such a ban would be a too extreme way to curb abuses of statistical tests (Wilkinson & TFSI, 1999, pp. 602–603).

The fifth edition of the APA's *Publication Manual* (APA, 2001) takes a similar stand. That is, it acknowledges the controversy about statistical tests, but it also states that it is not a proper role of the *Publication Manual* to resolve this debate (pp. 21–22). It goes on to recommend the complete reporting of the results of statistical tests, which would include the value of the test statistic, its degrees of freedom, and either the level of α applied across all tests, such as $p < .05$, or the exact p value from the output of a computer program, such as $p = .012$. Other recommendations about the statistical analyses (pp. 21–26) include the following:

1. Report adequate descriptive statistics, such as means, variances, and sizes of each group and a pooled within-groups variance–covariance in a comparative study or a correlation matrix in a regression analysis. This information is necessary for later meta-analyses or secondary analyses by other researchers.

2. Effect sizes should "almost always" be reported (p. 25). Several examples of effect size indexes are listed, many of which are discussed later in this book and by Kirk (1996) and Borenstein (1998), among others. The absence of effect sizes is also cited as an example of a study defect (p. 5). However, authors are still not required to report them.
3. The use of confidence intervals is "strongly recommended," but not required (p. 22).

Predictably, not everyone is happy with the report of the TFSI or the fifth edition of the *Publication Manual*. For example, B. Thompson (1999) noted that only encouraging the reporting of effect sizes or confidence intervals presents a self-canceling mixed message. Sohn (2000) lamented the lack of clear guidelines in the report of the TFSI for changing data analysis practices that may improve the relevance of psychology research. Finch et al. (2001) welcomed the TFSI report, but contrasted the somewhat ambiguous recommendations about statistical analyses in the APA's current *Publication Manual* against the relatively simple set of guidelines for manuscripts submitted to biomedical journals by the International Committee of Medical Journal Editors (1997). Kirk (2001) also welcomed the TFSI report but suggested that the next (sixth) edition of the *Publication Manual* should contain a much more detailed section on the recommendations of the TFSI. He also noted the relative absence of examples in the current *Publication Manual* (fifth edition) of how to appropriately report statistics. See TFSI (2000) for responses to some of these criticisms.

Interviews by Fidler (2002) with some of the principals shed light on why the fifth edition of the *Publication Manual* does not require reporting of effect sizes. There are some situations where it is difficult or impossible to compute effect sizes. This is especially true for some complex repeated-measures designs or multivariate designs. Thus, there was a reluctance to mandate a requirement that in some research contexts could not be met. However, it is possible to calculate effect sizes in perhaps most behavioral studies. It is also true that the effect size estimation void for some kinds of designs is being filled by ongoing research, and is or soon will be filled.

PROSPECTIVE

I believe the events just described indicate a future in which the role of traditional statistical tests in behavioral research will get smaller and smaller. This change will not happen overnight, and statistical tests are not about to disappear in the short term. Indeed, it is expected in the meantime that researchers will still have to report the results of statistical tests in their manuscripts. This is because, to be frank, their manuscripts may be rejected if they contain no statistical tests. However, researchers should give much less interpretive weight to outcomes of statistical tests than in the past. Specific recommendations follow.

1. Researchers should not view a statistically significant result as particularly informative. For example, they should not conclude that such results are automatically noteworthy or that they are likely to replicate.
2. Researchers should also not discount a statistically nonsignificant result. For example, they should not conclude that failing to reject the null hypothesis means that the population effect size is zero. This false belief may be responsible for the overlooking of possibly beneficial effects in health research (R. Rosenthal, 1994).
3. Effect sizes should always be reported, and confidence intervals should be constructed about them whenever possible. However, real reform does *not* involve computing effect sizes only for statistically significant results. This would amount to "business as usual" where the statistical test is still at center stage (Sohn, 2000). Real reform also means that effect sizes are interpreted and evaluated for their substantive significance, not just reported.

Other recommendations are given later in the book, many of which do not involve the use of statistical tests at all. This is consistent with a vision of the future in behavioral research that I and others advocate (e.g., B. Thompson, 2002b): Most studies in the future will *not* use statistical tests as the primary decision criterion, and those that do will concern only very specific problems for which variations of NHST may be appropriate, such as equivalence testing or inferential confidence intervals (chap. 3, this volume). It is also envisioned that the social sciences will become more like the natural sciences. That is, we will report the directions and magnitudes of our effects, determine whether they replicate, and evaluate them for their theoretical, clinical, or practical significance, not just their statistical significance (Kirk, 1996).

VOICES FROM THE FUTURE

As mentioned, it may be easier for younger researchers who are not as set in their ways to respond to the call for reform in methods of data analysis and inference. However, some journal editors—who are typically accomplished and experienced researchers—are taking the lead in reform.

So are the authors of many of the works cited in this book. Students are also promising prospects for reform because they are, in my experience and that of others (Hyde, 2001), eager to learn about limitations of traditional statistical tests. They can also understand, with proper instruction, ideas such as effect size and confidence intervals, even in introductory statistics courses. In fact, it is my experience that it is easier to teach undergraduates these concepts than the convoluted logic of NHST. Other basics of reform are even easier to teach, such as the need for replication.

Presented next are some example responses to the question, "What is the most important thing you learned in this class?" on a recent final examination in introductory psychology statistics I gave. These words from future behavioral researchers also reiterate some of the major goals of this book. May we all be so wise.

- Null hypothesis significance testing is not the only or necessarily the best way to test hypotheses.
- Just because a finding is statistically significant doesn't mean that it's important or reliable.
- If you increase the sample size enough, any result will be statistically significant. This is scary.
- To be skeptical of research papers that put a large emphasis on statistical significance.
- Statistical significance does not mean practical significance. Effect size, power, means, and standard deviations should be included in research reports. There needs to be in the social sciences a better understanding of statistical tests so that we can make better, more informed choices.

It has been said that if we do not make the future, others will do it for us. It is time to start building our future by moving beyond statistical tests and leaving behind other, old ways of doing things. We need to explore other possibilities for testing our hypotheses, ones that may lead to a more productive future for research in psychology and related disciplines. I hope this book will challenge, encourage, and support readers to think and act along these lines.

CONCLUSION

The controversy about statistical tests in psychology was briefly described, as were the events leading up to it. This history gives the context for the 1999 report of the Task Force on Statistical Inference and the 2001 fifth edition of the *Publication Manual* of the APA. It also indicates that the continued use of statistical tests as the sole way to test hypotheses and make inferential decisions in the behavioral sciences is unlikely. The points raised set the stage for reviewing in the next chapter some fundamental statistical concepts. These concepts are also crucial for understanding the limitations of statistical tests and characteristics of some proposed alternatives, such as interval estimation and effect size estimation.

RECOMMENDED READINGS

Gigerenzer, G. (1993). The superego, the ego, and the id in statistical reasoning. In G. Keren & C. Lewis (Eds.), *A handbook for data analysis in the behavioral sciences: Vol. 1. Methodological issues* (pp. 311–339). Hillsdale, NJ: Erlbaum.

Kirk, R. E. (2001). Promoting good statistical practices: Some suggestions. *Educational and Psychological Measurement, 61,* 213–218.

Wilkinson, L., & the Task Force on Statistical Inference. (1999). Statistical methods in psychology journals: Guidelines and explanations. *American Psychologist, 54,* 594–604.

2

FUNDAMENTAL CONCEPTS

When we are self-indulgent and uncritical, when we confuse hopes and facts, we slide into pseudoscience and superstition.

—Carl Sagan (1996, p. 27)

This chapter prepares readers for learning about alternatives to statistical tests through survey of fundamental concepts about research designs, variables, and estimation. Also reviewed are characteristics of statistical tests in general and those of three of the most widely used tests in comparative studies, the t test and F test for means and the chi-square (χ^2) test for two-way contingency tables. We will see in the next chapter that there are many misunderstandings about statistical tests, so readers should pay close attention to the discussions that follow. Exercises with answers for this chapter are available on this book's Web site.

TERMS AND IDEAS ABOUT COMPARATIVE STUDIES

Essential ideas about study design and the nature of independent or dependent variables are reviewed in this section. It is hoped that this presentation will build a common vocabulary for later chapters.

Independent Samples Designs and Correlated Designs

An independent variable (factor) has at least two levels. In an *independent samples (between-subjects) design*, each level is studied with an unrelated sample (group), and every case is measured once on the dependent (outcome) variable. If cases are randomly assigned to samples, the factor is a *manipulated* or *experimental variable* and the design is a *randomized-groups* or *completely randomized design*. If cases are classified into groups based on an intrinsic characteristic such as gender, the factor is a *nonexperimental* or *individual-difference variable*. Studies in which all factors are individual-difference variables are referred to as *nonexperimental, correlational,* or *observational studies*.

The samples are related in a *dependent-samples* or *correlated design*. There are two kinds. In a *repeated-measures* or *within-subjects design*, each case is measured at every level of the factor, such as pretest and posttest. This means that the "samples" are actually identical across the levels of the factor. R. Rosenthal, Rosnow, and Rubin (2000) distinguished between *intrinsically* and *nonintrinsically repeated-measures designs*. The logic of the former requires multiple assessments of each case, such as when maturational change is studied in individuals. The rationale of a nonintrinsically repeated-measures design does not require multiple testing of each case because the same factor could theoretically be studied with independent samples. For instance, the effect of caffeine versus no caffeine on athletic performance could be studied with unrelated groups in a completely randomized design or with just one group in a repeated-measures design. In the second kind of correlated design, a *matched-groups design*, a separate group corresponds to each level of the factor, just as in between-subjects designs. The difference is that each case in a matched-groups design is explicitly paired with a case in every other sample on at least one matching variable, which controls for this variable.

Compared to designs with independent samples, correlated designs may reduce error variance and increase statistical power. For these reasons, a correlated design may be chosen over an independent samples design even though the research question does not require dependent samples. These advantages have potential costs, though. Repeated-measures designs may require controls for order effects, and matched-groups designs are subject to regression effects if cases come from the extremes of their respective populations. See Ellis (1999) for a clear discussion of these and other design issues when studying dependent samples.

Balanced and Unbalanced Designs

An independent samples design is *balanced* if the number of cases in each group (n) is the same. If any two groups are of different size, the design is *unbalanced*. With no missing data, correlated designs are inherently balanced. Although there is no general statistical requirement for balanced designs, there are some potential drawbacks to unbalanced designs. One is loss of statistical power even if the total number of cases is the same for a balanced versus an unbalanced design. Suppose that $n_1 = n_2 = 50$ for a balanced two-group design. R. Rosenthal et al. (pp. 30–32) showed that the relative loss of power for an unbalanced design where $n_1 = 70$ and $n_2 = 30$ is equivalent to losing 16 cases (16% of the sample size) from the balanced design. The relative power loss increases as the group size disparity increases.

A critical issue concerns the reason why the group sizes are unequal. For example, an unbalanced design may arise because of randomly missing data from a design intended as balanced, such as when equipment fails and scores are not recorded. A handful of missing observations is probably of no great concern, such as if $n_1 = 100$ and $n_2 = 97$ as a result of three randomly missing scores. A more serious problem occurs when unbalanced designs are a result of nonrandomly missing data, such as when higher proportions of participants drop out of the study under one condition than another. Nonrandomly missing observations in this instance may cause a bias: Study participants who withdrew may differ systematically from those who remain, and the results may not generalize to the intended population. Unfortunately, there is no simple statistical "fix" for bias because of nonrandomly missing data. About all that can be done is to understand the nature of the data loss and how it affects the results; see West (2001) for more information.

Sometimes unbalanced designs are intentional—that is, based on a specific sampling plan. Standardization samples of contemporary ability tests are often stratified by demographic or other variables to match recent census data about the population of the United States. Because sizes of groups based on demographic variables such as gender or age are not usually equal in the population, samples so stratified may be unbalanced. Unequal group sizes in this case is actually an asset because it helps to ensure the representativeness of the sample in terms of relative group sizes. There are also times when groups with relatively low population base rates are intentionally oversampled. This is a common practice in research with special populations. Suppose that the base rate of clinical depression in the general population is 5%. In a particular study, a group of $n_1 = 50$ depressed patients is compared with $n_2 = 50$ control cases. This design is balanced, which maximizes the power of the group contrast. However, the base rate of depression in the sample is 10 times higher than in the population. Because sample base rates affect statistical tests and some types of effect size estimates, the results may not generalize if the population base rates are very different.

Schultz and Grimes (2002) made the point that equal group sizes are not always an asset even in randomized trials. Specifically, they show that forcing equal group sizes through restricted forms of random assignment, such as permuted-blocks randomization, may introduce bias compared to simple randomization, which does not guarantee equal group sizes. Thus, whether unequal group size is a problem depends on the research context.

Multiple Independent or Dependent Variables

Studies with just one independent variable are called *single-factor* or *one-way designs*. However, many behaviors studied by social scientists are affected by more than one variable. One of the goals of a *multifactor design* is to model this complexity by including two or more factors in the design. The terms *higher order, factorial,* or *blocking design,* among others, describe various kinds of multifactor designs. Blocking designs involve partitioning the total sample into groups based on an individual-difference variable (e.g., age) believed to affect outcome. If cases within each block are randomly assigned to levels of a manipulated factor, the resulting two-way design is a *randomized-blocks design.* Effect size estimation in single-factor designs is covered in chapters 4 through 6, and chapter 7 deals with this topic for multifactor designs.

Regardless of the number of factors, comparative studies with just one dependent variable are *univariate designs.* Many common statistical tests such as the t and F tests for means are generally univariate tests. *Multivariate designs* have at least two dependent variables, which allows measurement of outcome in more than one area. This book deals only with univariate designs. Because entire volumes are devoted to the basics of multivariate methods (e.g., Grimm & Yarnold, 1995, 2000), it is beyond the scope of this book to deal with them in detail. Also, multivariate analyses often wind up as a series of univariate analyses conducted with individual outcomes. This book's Web site has a supplemental chapter about multivariate effect size estimation in designs with independent samples and fixed factors.

Fixed-Effects and Random-Effects Factors

This distinction affects how the results are to be generalized and how effect size magnitude should be estimated. It is introduced by example: Suppose that the independent variable is dosage of a drug. There are theoretically an infinite number of dosages. If, say, five different dosages are randomly selected for study, the drug factor is a *random-effects factor*. Selecting dosages at random may give a representative sample from all possible levels. If so, the results of the study may generalize to the whole population of dosages. However, if the particular dosages for study are selected by some other means, the drug factor is probably a *fixed-effects factor*. For instance, a researcher may intentionally select five different dosages that form an equal-interval scale, such as 0 (control), 3, 6, 9, and 12 mg $\cdot$ kg^{-1}. Because these dosages are not randomly selected, the results may not generalize to other dosages not included in the original study, such as 15 mg · kg^{-1}.

Qualitative factors are usually treated as fixed factors. This is especially true for individual-difference variables such as gender where all possible levels may be included in the study. Quantitative variables can be analyzed as either fixed or random factors. A *control factor* is a special kind of random factor that is not of interest in itself but is included for the sake of generality (Keppel, 1991). Suppose that participants are required to learn a list of words. If only a single word list is used, it is possible that the results are specific to the particular words on that list. Using several different lists matched on characteristics such as relative word frequency and treating word list as a random factor may enhance generalizability. Repeated-measures factors that involve trials or measurement at specific times, such as three and six months after treatment, are usually considered fixed. If there are many repeated measures and only some are randomly selected for analysis, the repeated-measures factor is considered random.

Designs with random factors may require special considerations in statistical testing and effect size estimation. Thus, it may be better to consider a factor as fixed instead of random if in doubt. Chapters 6 and 7 deal with designs in which there is at least one random factor. Please note that the *subjects factor* is almost always seen as random because its levels—the individual cases—are usually different from study to study.

Covariate Analyses

Both correlated and blocking designs may reduce error variance compared to independent samples and one-way designs, respectively. Another way is covariate analysis. A *covariate* is a variable that predicts outcome but is ideally unrelated to the independent variable. The variance explained by the covariate is removed, which reduces error variance. Suppose a basic math skills pretest is given to students before they are randomly assigned to different instructional conditions for introductory statistics. Outcome is measured with a common final examination. It is likely that the pretest will covary with exam scores. In an analysis of covariance (ANCOVA), the effect of the pretest is statistically removed from the outcome variable. With enough reduction in error variance, the power of the test of instructional condition may be increased. Because ANCOVA is a statistical method, it can be incorporated into any of the designs mentioned earlier. However, ANCOVA is usually appropriate only for randomly assigned groups, and it is critical to meet the statistical assumptions of this method. These points are elaborated in chapter 6 when effect size estimation in covariate analyses is discussed.

SAMPLING AND ESTIMATION

Basic issues in sampling and estimation are reviewed next, including types of samples, statistics as estimators of population parameters, and interval estimation (i.e., the construction of confidence intervals based on sample statistics).

Types of Samples

One of the hallmarks of behavioral research is the distinction between populations and samples. It is rare that whole populations are studied. If the population is large, vast resources may be needed to study it. For example, the budget for the 2000 census of the population of the United States was about $4.5 billion, and almost a million temporary workers were hired for the endeavor (U.S. Census Bureau, 2002). It may be practically impossible to study even much smaller populations. For example, the base rate of autism is about 4 in 10,000 children (.04%). If autistic children are dispersed over a large geographic area or live in remote regions, studying all of them may be impracticable.

Behavioral scientists must usually make do with small subsets of populations or samples. There are three general kinds of samples: random, systematic, and ad hoc. *Random samples* are selected by a chance-based method that gives all observations an equal probability of appearing in the sample, which may yield a representative sample. Observations in *systematic samples* are selected using some orderly sampling plan that *may* yield a representative sample, but this is not guaranteed. Suppose that an alphabetical list of every household is available for some area. A random number between 10 and 20 is generated and turns out to be 17. Every 17th household from the list is contacted for an interview, which yields a 6% (1/17) sample in that area.

Most samples in social science research are neither random nor systematic but rather *ad hoc samples*, also called *samples of convenience, locally available samples*, or *accidental samples*. All of these terms imply the study of samples that happen to be available. A group of undergraduate students in a particular class who volunteer as research participants is an example of a convenience sample. There are two problems with such samples. First, they are probably not representative. For instance, it is known that volunteers differ systematically from nonvolunteers. Second, distributional theories that underlie statistical tests generally assume random sampling. If the data are from ad hoc samples, there is a conceptual mismatch with the test's distributional theory. This is a criticism of statistical tests among others considered in the next chapter.

Despite the potential problems of ad hoc samples, it is often difficult or impossible to collect random or even systematic samples. True random sampling requires a list of all observations in the population, but such lists rarely exist. Also, the notion of random or systematic sampling does not apply to animal research: Samples in this area are almost never randomly selected from known populations of animals. Perhaps the best way to mitigate the influence of bias in ad hoc samples is to follow what is now a fairly standard practice: Measure a posteriori a variety of sample characteristics and report them along with the rest of the results, which allows readers of the study to compare its sample with those of other studies in the same area. Another option is to compare the sample demographic profile with that of the population (if such a profile exists) to show that the sample is not obviously unrepresentative.

Sample Statistics as Estimators

Values of *population parameters*, such as means (μ), variances (σ^2), or correlations (ρ), are usually unknown. They are instead estimated with *sample statistics*, such as M (means), s^2 (variances), or r (correlations). These statistics are subject to *sampling error*, which refers to the difference between an estimator and the corresponding population value. These differences arise because the values of statistics from random samples tend to vary around that of the population parameter. Some of these statistics will be too high and others too low (i.e., they over- or underestimate the population parameter), and only a relatively small number will exactly equal the population value. This variability among estimators from different samples is a statistical phenomenon akin to background (natural) radiation: It's always there, sometimes more or less, fluctuating randomly from sample to sample. The amount of sampling error is generally affected by the variability of population observations, how the samples are selected, and their size. If the population is heterogenous (e.g., σ^2 is large), values of sample statistics may also be quite variable. Obviously, values of estimators from biased samples may differ substantially from that of the corresponding parameter. Given reasonably representative sampling and constant variability among population observations, sampling error varies inversely with sample size. This implies that statistics in larger samples tend to be closer on average to the population parameter than in smaller samples. This property describes the *law of large numbers*, and it says that one is more likely to get more accurate estimates from larger samples than smaller samples.

Sample statistics are either biased or unbiased estimators of the corresponding population parameter. The sample mean is an *unbiased estimator* because its average (expected) value across all possible random samples equals the population mean. The sample variance—also called a *mean square*—is an unbiased estimator of population variance if computed as the ratio of the sum of squares over the degrees of freedom, or

$$s^2 = \frac{SS}{df} = \frac{\sum\limits_{i=1}^{N} (X_i - M)^2}{N - 1} \tag{2.1}$$

where X is an individual score. In contrast, a sample variance derived as $S^2 = SS/N$ is a *negatively biased estimator* because its values are on average less than σ^2. All references to sample variances that follow assume Equation 2.1 unless otherwise indicated. Expected values of statistics that are *positively biased estimators* generally exceed that of the corresponding parameter.

There are ways to correct some statistics for bias. For example, although s^2 is an unbiased estimator of σ^2, the sample standard deviation s is a negatively biased estimator of σ. However, multiplication of s by the correction factor in parentheses that follows

$$\hat{\sigma} = \left(1 + \frac{1}{4(N-1)}\right)s \tag{2.2}$$

yields the statistic $\hat{\sigma}$, which is a numerical approximation to the unbiased estimator of σ. Because the value of the correction factor in Equation 2.2 is larger than 1.00, $\hat{\sigma} > s$. There is also greater correction for negative bias in smaller samples than in larger samples. If $N = 5$, for instance, the unbiased estimate of σ is

$$\hat{\sigma} = \{1 + 1/[4\ (5-1)]\}\ s = (1.0625)s$$

but for $N = 50$, the unbiased estimate is

$$\hat{\sigma} = \{1 + 1/[4\ (50-1)]\}\ s = (1.0051)s$$

which shows relatively less adjustment for bias in the larger sample. In even larger samples, the value of the correction factor in the previous equation is essentially 1.00; that is, there is practically no adjustment for bias. This is another instance of the law of large numbers: Averages of even-biased statistics from large samples tend to closely estimate the corresponding parameter.

Point and Interval Estimation

Sample statistics are used for two types of estimation. *Point estimation* is when the value of a sample statistic (e.g., M) is taken as the sole estimate of a parameter (e.g., μ). Because of sampling error, however, it is quite unlikely that the two will be equal. *Interval estimation* recognizes this reality by constructing a *confidence interval* about a point estimate. A confidence interval reflects the amount of sampling error associated with that estimate within a specified level of uncertainty. A confidence interval can also be seen as a range of plausible values for the corresponding parameter. In graphical displays, confidence intervals may be represented as error bars around a single point. Carl Sagan (1996) called error bars "a quiet but insistent reminder that no knowledge is complete or perfect" (pp. 27–28). Wider reporting of confidence intervals is also part of suggested reform of statistical practice in the social sciences (see chapter 1).

We need a more precise definition of a confidence interval. The following is based on Steiger and Fouladi (1997, pp. 229–230):

1. A $1 - \alpha$ confidence interval for (on) a parameter is a pair of statistics yielding an interval that, over repeated samples, includes the parameter with probability $1 - \alpha$. (The symbol α is the level of statistical significance.)
2. A $100 (1 - \alpha)\%$ confidence interval for a parameter is a pair of statistics yielding an interval that, over repeated samples, includes the parameter $100 (1 - \alpha)\%$ of the time.

The value of $1 - \alpha$ is selected by the researcher to reflect the degree of statistical uncertainty. The lower bound of a confidence interval is the *lower confidence limit*, and the upper bound is the *upper confidence limit*. Because the most common levels of statistical significance in NHST are $\alpha = .05$ or $\alpha = .01$, one usually sees in the literature either 95% or 99% confidence intervals. However, it is possible to construct confidence intervals that correspond to other levels of statistical significance. For example, error bars around points that represent means in graphs are sometimes each one standard error wide, which corresponds roughly to $\alpha = .32$ and a 68% confidence level.

In traditional confidence intervals—those based on central test statistics (defined next)—the sample statistic is usually exactly between the lower and upper bounds. That is, the width of the interval is symmetrical around the estimator. The phrase "a confidence interval about" an estimator is sometimes used to describe a symmetrical confidence interval. However, this phrase neglects to mention the population parameter that the interval is intended to approximate. It is also the case that the estimator does not always fall at the very center of other kinds of confidence intervals, such as those based on noncentral test statistics (also defined next).

The traditional way to construct a confidence interval is by adding and subtracting from a statistic the product of its standard error and the two-tailed critical value at the α level of statistical significance in a relevant central test distribution, such as t. A *standard error* is the standard deviation of the sampling distribution of an estimator. The square of the standard error is the *conditional variance*, the variance of the sampling distribution. A *sampling distribution* is a probability distribution based on random samples all of size N. In general, standard errors vary directly with variability among population observations and inversely with sample size. The latter explains part of the law of large numbers: Distributions of statistics from larger samples are generally narrower than distributions of the same statistic from smaller samples. A *central test distribution* assumes that the null hypothesis is true. Central test distributions are used in null hypothesis significance testing (NHST) to determine the critical values of test statistics. Tables of critical values for distributions such as t, F, and χ^2 found in many introductory statistics textbooks are based on central test distributions.

Standard errors of statistics with simple sampling distributions can be estimated with formulas that have appeared in statistical textbooks for some time. By a "simple" distribution it is meant that (a) the statistic estimates only a single population parameter, and (b) both the shape and variance of its sampling distribution are constant regardless of the value of the parameter. Distributions of means and mean differences are simple as just defined, and traditional confidence intervals for them are discussed next.

Confidence Intervals for μ

The standard error in a distribution of random means is

$$\sigma_M = \sqrt{\frac{\sigma^2}{N}} \tag{2.3}$$

Because the population variance σ^2 is not generally known, this standard error is usually estimated as

$$s_M = \sqrt{\frac{s^2}{N}} = \frac{s}{\sqrt{N}} \tag{2.4}$$

This estimate is subject to sampling error because the variance s^2 is a sample statistic. The relevant test statistic for means when σ is unknown is central t, so the general form of a confidence interval for μ based on a single observed mean is

$$M \pm s_M \left[t_{2\text{-tail}, \, \alpha} \, (N - 1) \right] \tag{2.5}$$

where the term in brackets is the positive two-tailed critical value in a central t distribution with $N - 1$ degrees of freedom at the α level of statistical significance. Suppose we find in a sample of 25 cases that $M = 100.00$ and $s = 9.00$. The standard error is

$$s_M = 9.00/25^{1/2} = 1.80$$

and $t_{2\text{-tail}, .05}$ (24) = 2.064. The 95% confidence interval for μ is thus

$$100.00 \pm 1.80 \ (2.064)$$

or 100.00 ± 3.72, which defines the interval 96.28–103.72. The 99% confidence interval for μ is constructed the same way except $t_{2\text{-tail}, .01}$ (24) = 2.797:

$$100.00 \pm 1.80 \ (2.797)$$

or 100 ± 5.03, which defines the interval 94.97–105.03. The 99% confidence interval is wider than the 95% confidence interval based on the same statistic because a greater margin of error is allowed.

Let us consider now the correct interpretation of the 95% confidence interval for μ derived earlier, 96.28–103.72:

1. This interval defines a range of outcomes that should be considered equivalent to the observed result (M = 100.00) given the amount of expected sampling error at the 95% confidence level.
2. It also provides a reasonable estimate of the population mean. That is, μ could be as low as 96.28 or it could be as high as 104.72, again at the 95% confidence level.
3. Of course, there is no guarantee that μ is actually included in the confidence interval. We could construct the 95% confidence interval around the mean in another sample, but the center or endpoints of this new interval will probably be different compared with the original. This is because confidence intervals are subject to sampling error, too.
4. However, if 95% confidence intervals are constructed around the means of all random samples drawn from the same population, then 95/100 of them will include μ.

The last point gives a more precise definition of what we mean by "95% confidence level" or "95% confident" from a *frequentist* or *long-run relative-frequency* view of probability as the likelihood of an outcome over repeatable events under constant conditions except for random error. This view also assumes that probability is a property of nature that is independent of what the researcher believes. In contrast, a *subjectivist* or *subjective degree-of-belief* view defines probability as a personal belief the researcher has about nature that is independent of nature's true state. The same view also does not distinguish between repeatable and unrepeatable (unique) events (Oakes, 1986; Reichardt & Gollob, 1997). Although researchers in their daily lives probably take a subjective view of probabilities, it is the frequentist definition that generally underlies sampling theory.

A researcher is probably more interested in knowing the probability that a *specific* 95% confidence interval contains μ than in knowing that 95/100 of all such intervals do. From a frequentist view, this probability for the unique confidence interval of our example, 96.28–103.72, is either 0 or 1.0. That is, this interval either contains μ or it does not. Thus, it is generally *incorrect* from this perspective to say that the interval 96.28–103.72 has a probability of .95 of including μ. Reichardt and Gollob (1997) noted that this kind of *specific probability inference* and the related *specific confidence inference* that one is 95% confident that the interval includes μ is permitted only in a very particular circumstance, which is that every possible value of μ is considered equally likely before the study is conducted. In Bayesian estimation, which is based on a subjectivist view of probability, the same circumstance is described by the *principle of indifference*, which says that in the total absence of information about the parameter, equal probabilities are assumed for all possible values. However, rarely do we have absolutely *no* information about likely or even plausible values for the population mean. In contrast, percentages associated with Bayesian confidence intervals *are* interpreted as probabilities that the parameter lies within the interval. This is what most researchers really want to know but generally cannot get from a traditional confidence interval. The fundamentals of Bayesian estimation are considered in chapter 9.

There is a kind of compromise language for describing traditional confidence intervals that "splits the difference" between frequentist and subjectivist views of probability. Applied to our example, it goes like this: The unique interval 96.28–103.72 estimates μ, with 95% confidence. This statement may not be incorrect from a frequentist perspective because it is not quite a specific confidence inference. It also gives a nod toward the subjectivist view because it associates a degree of belief with a specific interval. Like other compromises, however, it may not please purists who hold one view of probability or the other.

The issues raised about the proper interpretation of percentages associated with unique confidence intervals foreshadow similar difficulties in interpreting probabilities (p values) from statistical tests. Part of the problem is a clash between the long-run relative-frequency view of probability generally assumed by these tests and a subjective view of probability held by perhaps most researchers who use them. Another is the gap between what researchers really want to know and what a p value from a statistical test actually tells them.

Confidence Intervals for $\mu_1 - \mu_2$

The standard error in a distribution of differences (contrasts) between pairs of means from independent samples selected from different populations is

$$\sigma_{M_1 - M_2} = \sqrt{\frac{\sigma_1^2}{n_1} + \frac{\sigma_2^2}{n_2}} \qquad (2.6)$$

where σ_1^2 and σ_2^2 are the population variances and n_1 and n_2 are the sizes of each sample (group). If we assume homogeneity of population variance (i.e., $\sigma_1^2 = \sigma_2^2$), the expression for the standard error reduces to

$$\sigma_{M_1 - M_2} = \sqrt{\sigma^2 \left(\frac{1}{n_1} + \frac{1}{n_2} \right)} \qquad (2.7)$$

where σ^2 is the common population variance. This variance is usually unknown, so the standard error is estimated by

$$s_{M_1 - M_2} = \sqrt{s_P^2 \left(\frac{1}{n_1} + \frac{1}{n_2} \right)} \qquad (2.8)$$

where s_P^2 is the pooled within-groups variance, which is the average of the two group variances weighted by the degrees of freedom. It's equation is

$$s_P^2 = \frac{SS_W}{df_W} = \frac{(n_1 - 1)s_1^2 + (n_2 - 1)s_2^2}{n_1 + n_2 - 2} \qquad (2.9)$$

where SS_W and df_W are, respectively, the pooled within-groups sum of squares and degrees of freedom. The latter can also be expressed as $df_W = df_1 + df_2 = N - 2$. Only in balanced designs can s_P^2 also be calculated as the average of the two group variances, or $(s_1^2 + s_2^2)/2$.

The general form of a confidence interval for $\mu_1 - \mu_2$ based on the difference between independent means is

$$(M_1 - M_2) \pm s_{M_1 - M_2} \left[t_{2\text{-tail}, \alpha} (N - 2) \right] \qquad (2.10)$$

where $M_1 - M_2$ is the observed mean contrast and $N - 2$ is the pooled within-groups degrees of freedom (df_W) of the positive two-tailed critical value of t at the α level of statistical significance. Suppose in a balanced two-group design where $n = 5$ we observe

$$M_1 - M_2 = 2.00, \ s_1^2 = 7.50, \ s_2^2 = 5.00$$

which implies $s_P^2 = (7.50 + 5.00)/2 = 6.25$. The standard error for the contrast is

$$s_{M_1 - M_2} = [6.25 \, (1/5 + 1/5)]^{1/2} = 1.58$$

and $t_{2\text{-tail}, .05}$ (8) = 2.306. The 95% confidence interval for the mean contrast is

$$2.00 \pm 1.58 \ (2.306) \qquad \text{or} \qquad 2.00 \pm 3.65 \qquad (2.11)$$

which defines the interval −1.65-5.65. Based on these results we can say that $\mu_1 - \mu_2$ could be as low as −1.65 or as high as 5.65, with 95% confidence. Please note that this interval includes zero as a reasonable estimate of $\mu_1 - \mu_2$. This fact is subject to misinterpretation. For example, it may be incorrectly concluded that $\mu_1 = \mu_2$ because zero falls between the lower and upper bounds of the confidence interval. However, zero is only one value within a range of estimates of $\mu_1 - \mu_2$, so in this sense it has no special status in interval estimation for this example. Besides, the confidence interval itself is subject to sampling error, so zero may not be included within the 95% confidence interval for $\mu_1 - \mu_2$ in a replication. It is the range of overlap between the two confidence intervals (if any) that would be of greater interest than whether zero is included in one interval or the other. These issues are elaborated next.

Now let us consider confidence intervals for contrasts between dependent means. Below we use the symbol M_D to refer the average *difference score* when two dependent samples are compared. A difference score is computed as $D = X_1 - X_2$ for each of the n cases in a repeated-measures design or for each of the n pairs of cases in a matched-groups design. (Difference scores are also called *gain scores* or *change scores*.) If $D = 0$, there is no difference; any other value indicates a higher score in one condition than in the other. The average of all the difference scores equals the dependent mean contrast, or $M_D = M_1 - M_2$. The standard error of M_D is

$$\sigma_{M_D} = \sqrt{\frac{\sigma_D^2}{n}} = \frac{\sigma_D}{\sqrt{n}} \qquad (2.12)$$

where the σ_D^2 and σ_D are, respectively, the population variance and standard deviation of the difference scores. The variance σ_D^2 takes account of the population correlation of the scores between the conditions, which is designated in Equation 2.13 as ρ_{12}. Assuming homogeneity of variance, the variance of the difference scores is

$$\sigma_D^2 = 2\sigma^2(1 - \rho_{12}) \qquad (2.13)$$

where σ^2 is the common population variance. When there is a stronger *subjects effect*—cases maintain their relative positions across the conditions— ρ_{12} approaches 1.00. This reduces the variance of the difference scores, which in turn reduces the standard error of the dependent mean contrast

(Equation 2.12). It is this subtraction of consistent individual differences from the standard error that makes confidence intervals based on dependent mean contrasts generally narrower than confidence intervals based on contrasts between unrelated means. It also explains the power advantage of the t test for dependent samples over the t test for independent samples, which is considered next. However, these advantages are realized only if $\rho_{12} > 0$. Otherwise, confidence intervals and statistical tests may be wider and less powerful (respectively) for dependent mean contrasts.

The population variance of the difference scores, σ_D^2, is usually unknown, but it is often estimated as

$$s_{M_D} = \frac{s_D^2}{n} = \frac{s_D}{\sqrt{n}} \qquad (2.14)$$

where s_D^2 and s_D are, respectively, the sample variance and standard deviation of the difference scores. The former is calculated as

$$s_D^2 = s_1^2 + s_2^2 - 2\ cov_{12} \qquad (2.15)$$

where cov_{12} is covariance of the observed scores across the conditions. It is the product of the cross-conditions correlation and the within-conditions standard deviations:

$$cov_{12} = r_{12}\ s_1\ s_2 \qquad (2.16)$$

As r_{12} approaches 1.00, the variance s_D^2 gets smaller, which in turn decreases the estimated standard error of the dependent mean contrast.

The general form of a confidence interval for μ_D is

$$M_D \pm s_{M_D}\ [t_{2\text{-tail},\ \alpha}\ (n-1)] \qquad (2.17)$$

Suppose for a dependent samples design we observe the following data:

$$M_1 - M_2 = 2.00,\ s_1^2 = 7.50,\ s_2^2 = 5.00,\ r_{12} = .735$$

Given the above information,

$$s_D^2 = 7.50 + 5.00 - 2\ (.735)\ (7.50^{1/2})\ (5.00^{1/2}) = 3.50$$
$$s_{M_D} = (3.50/5)^{1/2} = .837$$

The value of $t_{2\text{-tail},\ .05}\ (4)$ is 2.776, so the 95% confidence interval for μ_D is

$$2.00 \pm .837\ (2.776)\ \text{or}\ 2.00 \pm 2.32 \qquad (2.18)$$

which defines the interval $-.32–4.32$. Please note that the 95% confidence interval assuming a dependent-samples design is narrower than the 95% confidence interval based on the same means and variances for an independent-samples design, which is $-1.65–5.65$. (Compare Equations 2.11 and 2.18.) This result is expected because r_{12} is relatively high ($.735$) for the dependent-samples design (r_{12} is presumed to be zero when the samples are independent).

Confidence Intervals for Other Kinds of Statistics

Many statistics other than means have complex distributions. For example, distributions of sample proportions for a dichotomous variable are symmetrical only if the population proportion is $\pi = .50$; the same is true for the Pearson correlation r only if the population correlation is $\rho = 0$. Other statistics have complex distributions because they estimate more than one population parameter. This includes some widely used effect size indexes such as standardized mean differences, which for contrasts between independent means generally estimate $\delta = (\mu_1 - \mu_2)/\sigma$, the ratio of the population mean difference over the common population standard deviation. (Chapter 4 considers standardized mean differences in detail.)

Until recently, confidence intervals for statistics with complex distributions have been estimated with approximate methods. One such method involves *confidence interval transformation* (Steiger & Fouladi, 1997) in which the statistic is mathematically transformed into units that are normally distributed. The confidence interval is built by adding and subtracting from the transformed statistic the product of the standard error in the transformed metric and the appropriate positive two-tailed critical value of the normal deviate z. The lower and upper bounds of this interval are then transformed back into the metric of the original statistic, and the resulting interval may be asymmetrical around that statistic. The construction of confidence intervals for ρ based on the Fisher's Z transformation of r is an example of this approach, which is covered in many statistics textbooks (e.g., Glass & K. Hopkins, 1996, pp. 357–358). Other transformation-based methods for constructing confidence intervals for the population parameters estimated by effect size statistics are introduced in later chapters.

Another approximate method builds confidence intervals directly around the sample statistic and are thus symmetrical about it. The width of the interval on either side is a product of the two-tailed critical value of a central test statistic and an estimate of the *asymptotic standard error*, which estimates what the standard error of the statistic would be in a large sample (e.g., $N > 500$). However, if the researcher's sample is not large, the estimated standard error based on this approach may not be very accurate.

Another drawback to this method is that the distributions of some sample statistics, such as the multiple correlation R, are so complex that a computer is needed to derive the estimated standard error. Fortunately, there are increasing numbers of computer programs for calculating confidence intervals, some of which are mentioned later.

A more exact method for constructing confidence intervals for statistics with complex distributions is *noncentrality interval estimation* (Steiger & Fouladi, 1997). It also deals with situations that cannot be handled by approximate methods. This method is based on *noncentral test distributions* that do not assume that the null hypothesis is true. A bit of perspective is in order: Families of central distributions of t, F, and χ^2 are special cases of noncentral distributions of each test statistic just mentioned. Compared to central distributions, noncentral distributions have an additional parameter called the *noncentrality parameter*. This extra parameter basically indicates the degree of departure from the null hypothesis. For example, central t distributions are described by a single parameter, the degrees of freedom, but noncentral t distributions are described by both the degrees of freedom and a noncentrality parameter. If this parameter equals zero, the resulting distribution is the familiar and symmetrical central t distribution. As the value of the noncentrality parameter is increasingly positive, the noncentral t distributions described by it become increasingly positively skewed (e.g., Cumming & Finch, 2001, fig. 5). The same thing happens but in the opposite direction for negative values of the noncentrality parameter for t distributions.

Noncentrality interval estimation is impractical without relatively sophisticated computer programs for iterative estimation. Until just recently, such programs have not been widely available to applied researchers. A notable exception in a commercial software package for general statistical analyses is the Power Analysis module by J. Steiger in STATISTICA (StatSoft Inc., 2003), which can construct noncentral confidence intervals based on several different types of statistics (Steiger & Fouladi, 1997). This includes many of the standardized indexes of effect size introduced in later chapters. There are now also a few different stand-alone programs or scripts (macros) for noncentrality interval estimation, some available for free through the Internet. These programs or scripts are described in chapter 4, and the Web site for this book also has links to corresponding download pages.

Later chapters demonstrate the calculation of both approximate and more exact noncentral confidence intervals for standardized effect size indexes. The technique of bootstrapping, a method for statistical resampling, can also be used to construct confidence intervals. Chapter 9 reviews the rationale of bootstrapping.

LOGIC OF STATISTICAL SIGNIFICANCE TESTING

A brief history of NHST was given earlier. This section outlines the basic rationale and steps of NHST as it is often practiced today. The following review lays the groundwork for understanding limitations of NHST considered in the next chapter.

Contexts and Steps

There are two main contexts for NHST, *reject–support* (RS) and *accept–support* (AS). The former is the most common and concerns the case in which rejection of the null hypothesis supports the researcher's theory. The opposite is true in AS testing: It is the *failure* to reject the null hypothesis that supports what the researcher actually believes. Listed next are the main steps of NHST for both RS and AS testing. Each step is discussed in the sections that follow with emphasis on points that are not as well known as they should be.

1. Based on the research question, formulate the first of two statistical hypotheses, the null hypothesis H_0.
2. Formulate the second statistical hypothesis, the alternative hypothesis H_1.
3. Set the level of statistical significance α, which is the probability of a Type I error.
4. Collect the data and determine its probability p under H_0 with a statistical test. Reject H_0 if $p < \alpha$.

Null Hypotheses

The null hypothesis is a default explanation that may be rejected later given sufficient evidence. In RS testing, this default explanation is the opposite of the researcher's theory; in AS testing, the null hypothesis reflects the researcher's theory. In either RS or AS testing, the null hypothesis is usually a *point hypothesis* that specifies the numerical value of at least one population parameter. There are two different kinds of null hypotheses (J. Cohen, 1994). A *nil hypothesis* says that the value of a population parameter is zero or the difference between two or more parameters is zero. Examples of nil hypotheses are presented next:

$$H_0: \mu_D = 0 \qquad H_0: \mu_1 - \mu_2 = 0 \qquad H_0: \rho = 0$$

Nil hypotheses are usually statements of absence, whether of an effect, difference, or association. In contrast, a *non-nil hypothesis* asserts that a population parameter is not zero or that the difference between two or more parameters is not zero. It typically assumes a non-zero effect, difference, or association. Examples of non-nil hypotheses are given next:

$$H_0: \mu_D = 10.00 \qquad H_0: \mu_1 - \mu_2 = 5.00 \qquad H_0: \rho = .30$$

Nil hypotheses as default explanations are generally most appropriate when it is unknown whether effects or relations exist at all, such as in new research areas where most studies are exploratory. However, nil hypotheses are less suitable when it is known a priori that an effect is probably not zero. This is more likely in established research areas. For instance, it is known that women and men differ in certain personality characteristics (e.g., Feingold, 1994). Specification of $H_0: \mu_1 - \mu_2 = 0$ (i.e., $H_0: \mu_1 = \mu_2$) when testing gender differences in these characteristics may set the bar too low because this nil hypothesis is probably false. Accordingly, rejecting it is not an impressive scientific achievement. There are also situations where specification of a nil hypothesis is clearly indefensible. One example is using a nil hypothesis to test a reliability coefficient for statistical significance. For example, Abelson (1997a) noted that declaring a reliability coefficient to be nonzero based on such a test is the "ultimate in stupefyingly vacuous information" (p. 121). This is because what is really important to know is whether a reliability coefficient is acceptably high for a specific purpose, such as $r_{XX} > .90$ when a test is used for individual assessments that determine access to treatment resources.

Nil hypotheses are tested much more often in the social sciences than non-nil hypotheses. This is true even in established research areas where a nil hypothesis is often a "straw man" argument. There are at least three reasons for this puzzling situation: Many researchers are unaware of the possibility to specify non-nil hypotheses. Statistical software programs usually test only nil hypotheses. This means that tests of non-nil hypotheses must be computed by hand. Unfortunately, this is generally feasible only for relatively simple non-nil hypotheses, such as $H_0: \mu_1 - \mu_2 = 5.00$, which can be evaluated without difficulty with the t test.

Alternative Hypotheses

This second statistical hypothesis complements H_0. In RS testing, the alternative hypothesis H_1 represents the researcher's theory; in AS testing, it does not. Unlike the null hypothesis, the alternative hypothesis is typically a *range hypothesis* that specifies a range of values for the population parameter(s). The two kinds of alternative hypotheses are directional (one-tailed, one-sided) and nondirectional (two-tailed, two-sided). A *nondirectional alternative hypothesis* predicts any result not specified in H_0, but a *directional alternative hypothesis* specifies a range of values on only one side of the point prediction in H_0. For example, given H_0: $\mu_1 = \mu_2$, there is only one possible nondirectional alternative hypothesis, H_1: $\mu_1 \neq \mu_2$, but two possible directional alternatives, H_1: $\mu_1 > \mu_2$ or H_1: $\mu_1 < \mu_2$.

The choice between a nondirectional or directional H_1 is supposed to be made before the data are collected. If there are a priori reasons to expect a directional effect, the appropriate directional H_1 should be specified; otherwise, a nondirectional H_1 may be a safer bet. The choice between a directional or nondirectional H_1 affects the results of statistical tests as follows: It is easier to reject H_0 when a directional H_1 is specified *and* the data are in the same direction. If H_0 is actually false, there is also greater statistical power compared to a nondirectional H_1. However, if a directional H_1 is specified but the data indicate an effect in the opposite direction, then one is supposed to fail to reject H_0 even if the results are very inconsistent with it. In practice, however, these conventions are not always followed. For example, it is sometimes not possible to reject H_0 for a nondirectional H_1 but it is possible for a directional H_1. A researcher who initially specified a nondirectional H_1 may "switch" to a directional alternative hypothesis to reject the null hypothesis. It also happens that researchers "switch" from one directional H_1 to another depending on the data, again to reject H_0. Some would consider changing H_0 or H_1 based on sample results a kind of statistical "sin" that is to be avoided. Like admonitions against other kinds of sins, they are not always followed.

Level of Type I Error

Alpha (α) is the probability of making a Type I error; more specifically, it is the conditional prior probability of rejecting H_0 when it is actually true (Pollard, 1993). Alpha is a prior probability because it is specified before the data are collected, and it is a conditional probability because H_0 is assumed true. In other words,

$$\alpha = p \text{ (Reject } H_0 \mid H_0 \text{ true)} \qquad (2.19)$$

where the symbol "|" means *assuming* or *given*. Alpha can also be understood as the probability of getting a result from a random sample that leads to the incorrect decision to reject the null hypothesis. All these descriptions of α are also long-run, relative-frequency statements about the probability of a Type I error.

Conventional levels of α in the social sciences are either .05 or .01. When other levels are specified, they tend to be even lower, such as α = .001. It is rare for researchers to specify α levels higher than .05. The main reason is editorial policy: Manuscripts may be rejected for publication if

$\alpha > .05$. This policy would make more sense if the context for NHST were always RS testing where a Type I error is akin to a false positive because the evidence is incorrectly taken as supporting the researcher's theory. As noted by Steiger and Fouladi (1997), the value of α should be as low as possible from the perspective journal editors and reviewers, who may wish to guard against incorrect claims. In AS testing, however, they should worry less about Type I error and more about Type II error because false claims in this context arise from *not* rejecting H_0. Insisting on low values of α in this case may facilitate publication of erroneous claims.

It is important to realize that α sets the risk of a Type I error for a single hypothesis test. However, rarely is just one hypothesis tested. When multiple statistical tests are conducted, there is also an *experimentwise (family-wise) probability* of Type I error, designated below as α_{EW}. It is the likelihood of making one or more Type I errors across a set of tests. If each individual test is conducted at the same level of α, then

$$\alpha_{EW} = 1 - (1 - \alpha)^c \qquad (2.20)$$

where c is the number of tests, each conducted at the α level of statistical significance. In this equation, the term $(1 - \alpha)$ is the probability of *not* making a Type I error for any individual test; $(1 - \alpha)^c$ is the probability of making *no* Type I errors across all tests; and the whole expression is the likelihood of committing at least one Type I error among the tests. We need to understand a couple of things about this equation. If only one hypothesis is tested, then $\alpha_{EW} = \alpha$. If there are multiple tests, this equation is accurate only if the hypotheses or outcome variables are perfectly uncorrelated. If not, the estimated rate of experimentwise Type I error given by this equation will be too low. The result generated by the equation is the probability of one or more Type I errors, but it does not indicate how many Type I errors may have been committed (it could be 1, or 2, or 3 . . .) or on which hypothesis tests they occurred. Suppose that 20 statistical significance tests are conducted each at $\alpha = .05$ level in the same sample. The experimentwise Type I error rate is

$$\alpha_{EW} = 1 - (1 - .05)^{20} = .64$$

In other words, the risk of a making a Type I error across the whole set of 20 tests is 64%, given the assumptions just stated.

There are two basic ways to control experimentwise Type I error: Reduce the number of tests or lower α for each one. The former can be realized by honing one's questions down to the most substantively meaningful (prioritize the hypotheses). This also means that "fishing expeditions" where essentially every effect is tested are to be avoided. Another way to reduce the number of hypotheses is to use multivariate methods, which can test hypotheses across several variables at once. There is a relatively simple method to set α for individual tests called the *Bonferroni correction:* Divide a target value of α_{EW} by the number of tests, and set the corrected level of statistical significance α^* for each individual test to the value of this ratio. Suppose a researcher wishes to limit the experimentwise risk of Type I error to 10%. If a total of 20 tests are planned, then $\alpha^* = .10/20 = .005$ for each individual test. Other methods are considered in chapter 6. However, readers should know that not all methodologists believe that controlling experiment-wise Type I error is a generally desirable goal in the social sciences. This opinion stems from the apparently low general statistical power of social science research, an issue discussed later.

Like the choice between a directional and nondirectional H_1, the decision about α is supposed to be made before the data are collected. For example, if $\alpha = .01$ but the estimated probability of the data under H_0 is .03, one is supposed to fail to reject H_0. However, the temptation to increase α (or α^*) from .01 to .05 to reject H_0 may be strong in this case. Increasing α based on the data is another form of statistical sin that occurs in the real world.

Statistical Tests

The most widely used test statistics in the social sciences are probably the t, F, and χ^2 statistics, but there are many others. Although different in their applications, assumptions, and distributions, all such tests do basically the same thing: A result is summarized with a sample statistic. The difference between the statistic and the value of the corresponding population parameter(s) specified in the null hypothesis is compared against an estimate of sampling error. A computer program for general statistical analyses will convert test statistics to probabilities based on the appropriate theoretical central test distribution. These probabilities are often printed in program output under the column heading p, which is the same abbreviation used in many journal articles. One should not forget that p actually stands for the conditional probability

$$p \text{ (Data } | \text{ } H_0 \text{ true)}$$

which should be understood as the likelihood of the sample result or one even more extreme assuming the null hypothesis is true. Both p and α are derived in the same sampling distribution and are properly interpreted as long-run, relative-frequency probabilities. Unlike α, however, p is *not* the conditional prior probability of a Type I error because it is computed for a particular sample result. To differentiate the two probabilities, Gigerenzer

(1993) referred to p as the *exact level of significance*. If this exact significance level is less than the conditional prior probability of a Type I error ($p < \alpha$), then H_0 is rejected and the result is considered statistically significant at that level of α. If $\alpha = .05$ and $p = .032$, for example, then H_0 is rejected, the result is taken as statistically significant at the .05 level, and its exact level of statistical significance is .032.

It can be shown that many test statistics can be expressed as the product

$$\text{Test statistic} = f(N) \times \text{ES index} \qquad (2.21)$$

where $f(N)$ is a function of sample size for the particular test statistic and ES Index is an effect size index that expresses the degree of discrepancy between the data and H_0 in a standardized metric (R. Rosenthal, 1994). Various standardized effect size indexes are introduced in later chapters, but for now consider two implications of this equation:

1. Holding sample size constant, the absolute values of test statistics generally increase with no upper bound and their p values approach zero as the effect size increases.
2. Holding constant a non-zero effect size, increasing the sample size causes the same change in test statistics and p values.

These implications explain how it is possible for even trivial effects to be statistically significant in large samples. They also explain how even large effects may not be statistically significant in small samples. In other words, statistical significance does *not* imply that an effect is large, important, or even interesting. By the same token, one cannot conclude that the absence of statistical significance indicates a small or unimportant effect.

That p values from statistical tests (a) are both conditional and long-run, relative-frequency probabilities and (b) measure sample size as well as effect size makes them apparently difficult to correctly interpret. Evidence that p values are in fact widely misunderstood in the behavioral sciences like psychology is considered in the next chapter.

POWER

Power is the conditional prior probability of making the correct decision to reject H_0 when it is actually false, or

$$\text{Power} = p\,(\text{Reject } H_0 \mid H_0 \text{ false}) \qquad (2.22)$$

A Type II error, on the other hand, occurs when the sample result leads to the failure to reject H_0 when it is actually false. The probability of a Type II error is usually represented by β, and it is also a conditional prior probability:

$$\beta = p \text{ (Fail to reject } H_0 \mid H_0 \text{ false)} \qquad (2.23)$$

Because power and β are complementary, or

$$\text{Power} + \beta = 1.00 \qquad (2.24)$$

whatever increases power decreases the probability of a Type II error and vice versa. Summarized next are factors that affect the power of statistical tests:

1. The lower the level of α, the lower is power. Thus, reducing the chance of a Type I error increases the likelihood of a Type II error. However, there are other ways to increase power besides increasing α.
2. Power is greater in larger samples. This fact is demonstrated below for the test statistics t, F, and χ^2.
3. Power is greater when H_1 is directional and the population effect is in the same direction. If the two disagree, however, power is essentially zero.
4. Study design: (a) Correlated designs are generally more powerful than independent-samples designs. Blocking designs and covariate analyses may also increase power. (b) Balanced designs are generally more powerful than unbalanced designs. (c) Tests for effects of fixed factors are usually more powerful than tests for effects of random factors.
5. Power declines as the reliability of the scores in a particular sample is lower. With lower score reliability comes higher error variance, which makes it more difficult to detect a real effect.
6. Parametric tests such as t and F are generally more powerful than nonparametric tests. See Siegel and Castellan (1988) for information about nonparametric tests.
7. In general, the larger an effect in the population for a given design, the easier it is to detect in samples. However, the magnitude of the real effect that can theoretically be observed is somewhat under the control of the researcher. For example, a longer, more intense intervention may potentially have a larger effect than a shorter, less intense intervention.

A power analysis gives the probability of rejecting H_0. There are two kinds. An *a priori power analysis* is conducted before the data are collected. It involves (a) specification of the study's planned characteristics, such as the level of α and the sample size; and (b) estimation of the expected magnitude of the population effect. The latter may be based on theory, results of previous empirical studies, or an educated guess. If the researcher is uncertain about the population effect size, power can be calculated for a range of estimates. A variation is to specify a desired level of power and then estimate the minimum sample size needed to obtain it. A *post hoc power analysis* is conducted after the data are collected. The observed effect size is treated as the population effect size, and the probability of rejecting the null hypothesis given the study's characteristics is estimated. However, a post hoc analysis that shows low power is more like an autopsy than a diagnostic procedure. That is, it is better to think about power before it is too late.

In the past, researchers conducted power analyses by consulting special tables presented in sources such as J. Cohen (1988). Now there are several computer programs for power analysis on personal computers. Some of these programs, such as the Power Analysis module of STATISTICA, use noncentral test distributions, which are generally necessary for correct power estimates. Power analysis programs assume the user knows something about the effect size indexes described in later chapters.

Estimated power levels no higher than .50 are problematic. If power is only .50, the probability of rejecting H_0 when it is false is no greater than guessing the outcome of a coin toss. In fact, tossing a coin instead of actually conducting a study would be just as likely to give the correct decision and would save time and money, too (F. Schmidt & Hunter, 1997). Unfortunately, the results of several reviews indicate that the typical power of social science research may be no greater than about .50 (e.g., Sedlmeier & Gigerenzer, 1989). When power estimates are broken down by whether estimated effect sizes are small, medium, or large—specific definitions of these adjectives are given in chapter 4—their values are about .20, .50, and .80, respectively. Power for the study of large effects, .80, is certainly better than for the others listed but still results in a Type II error rate of 20%. Increasing sample sizes would address the problem of low power, but the number of additional cases necessary to reach even a power level of .80 when studying effects of small or medium magnitude may be so great as to be practically impossible (F. Schmidt, 1996). This is a critical limitation of NHST in the social sciences.

The concept of power does not stand by itself without NHST. As statistical tests play a smaller role in our analyses, the relevance of power will also decline. If statistical tests are not used at all, the whole idea of power is meaningless. Besides, it is a stronger scientific result to observe the same effect at $p < .10$ across two different smaller samples than to find $p < .05$ in one larger sample.

OVERVIEW OF SPECIFIC STATISTICAL TESTS

Reviewed next are essential characteristics of three widely used test statistics in the behavioral sciences, the t and F statistics for means and the χ^2 statistic for two-way contingency tables. The F statistic is part of a family of techniques known as the analysis of variance (ANOVA), but note that the F statistic is not synonymous with ANOVA. That is, we can conduct an ANOVA without computing the F statistic, but not vice versa. It is reviewed only for designs with a single fixed factor, but its basic logic generalizes to other kinds of designs with continuous outcome measures (chapters 6 and 7). The t statistic is discussed only for designs with two conditions, such as treatment versus control. It is important for readers to know that the t, F, and χ^2 statistics are not reviewed for their own sakes. This is because they are subject to the general drawbacks of all NHST methods that are considered in the next chapter. These shortcomings are so serious that it is recommended that the continued use of statistical tests as the primary inference tool in the behavioral sciences is not acceptable. However, familiarity with the sample descriptive statistics that contribute to the t, F, and χ^2 statistics gives one a head start toward understanding effect size estimation. It is also possible in many cases to compute effect size indexes from these test statistics. Please also note that the sampling distributions of the t, F, and χ^2 tests described are, respectively, the central t, central F, and central χ^2 distributions in which the null hypothesis is assumed to be true. In later chapters readers will learn more about noncentral t and noncentral F distributions in which the null hypothesis is assumed to be false. These distributions are required for calculating exact confidence intervals based on certain kinds of standardized indexes of effect size.

t TESTS FOR MEANS

The t tests reviewed compare means from either two independent or dependent samples. Both are actually special cases of the F test for means. Specifically, $t^2 = F$ when both statistics are computed for the same mean contrast for a nil hypothesis. The statistical assumptions of the t tests for independent versus dependent samples are the same as those of the corresponding F tests and are discussed later.

The general form of the t statistic for a contrast between independent means is

$$t\,(N-2) = \frac{(M_1 - M_2) - (\mu_1 - \mu_2)}{s_{M_1 - M_2}} \qquad (2.25)$$

where $N - 2$ is the pooled within-groups degrees of freedom (df_W), $M_1 - M_2$ and $s_{M_1 - M_2}$ are, respectively, the observed mean contrast and its standard error (Equation 2.8), and $\mu_1 - \mu_2$ is the population mean difference specified in the null hypothesis. If the latter is predicted to be zero, a nil hypothesis is tested; otherwise a non-nil hypothesis is tested.

The t statistic for a dependent mean contrast has the same overall form:

$$t\,(n - 1) = \frac{M_D - \mu_D}{s_{M_D}} \qquad (2.26)$$

where the degrees of freedom equal the group size (n) minus 1, M_D and s_{M_D} are, respectively, the observed average difference score and its standard error (Equation 2.14), and μ_D is the population average difference score specified in the null hypothesis. For a nil hypothesis, $\mu_D = 0$, and this term drops out of the equation.

Assuming a nil hypothesis, both forms of the t statistic defined earlier express a mean contrast as the proportion of its standard error. If $t = 1.50$, for example, the first mean is 1½ standard errors higher than the second, but note that the sign of t is arbitrary because it depends on the direction of subtraction between the two means. It is important to realize that the standard error metric of the t test is affected by sample size, which is demonstrated now.

This is explained in Tables 2.1 and 2.2, described next. Table 2.1 presents the means and variances of two groups where $M_1 - M_2 = 2.00$. Table 2.2 reports the results of the independent samples t test for the data in Table 2.1 at three different group sizes, $n = 5$, 15, and 30, for a nondirectional H_1. (Readers are encouraged to reproduce these results.) Please note in Table 2.2 that the value of the pooled within-groups variance for these data, $s_P^2 = 6.25$, is unaffected by group size. This is not true for the standard error of $M_1 - M_2$, which, as expected, gets smaller as n increases. This causes the value of t to go up and its probability to go down for the larger group sizes. Consequently, the t statistic for $n = 5$ does not indicate a statistically significant contrast at the .05 level, but it does for the two larger group sizes. Results for the latter indicate less expected sampling error, but not a

TABLE 2.1
Means and Variances for Two Independent Samples

	Group	
	1	2
M	13.00	11.00
s^2	7.50	5.00

TABLE 2.2
Results of the Independent Samples t Test for the Data in Table 2.1 at Three Different Group Sizes

Statistic	Group size (n)		
	5	15	30
$s_{M_1 - M_2}$	1.58	.913	.645
t	1.26	2.19	3.10
df	8	28	58
p	.243	.037	.003
$t_{2\text{-tail}, .05}$	2.306	2.048	2.002
95% CI for $\mu_1 - \mu_2$	−1.64–5.64	.13–3.87	.71–3.29

Note. For all analyses, $M_1 - M_2 = 2.00$ and $s_P^2 = 6.25$. CI = confidence interval.

different or more substantial mean contrast. This reduction in sampling error is also evident in the 95% confidence intervals about the observed mean difference: Their widths decrease as n gets larger.

The standard error metric of the t test is also affected by whether the means are independent or dependent. This is demonstrated next. Table 2.3 presents raw scores and descriptive statistics for a small data set where the observed mean difference is 2.00. Reported in Table 2.4 are the results of two different t tests and 95% confidence intervals for the data in Table 2.3. The first analysis assumes $n = 5$ cases in each of two unrelated samples, but second analysis assumes $n = 5$ pairs of scores across two dependent samples. Only the second analysis takes account of the positive cross-conditions correlation for these data, $r_{12} = .735$. Observe in Table 2.4 the narrower 95% confidence interval, the higher value of t, and its lower p value in the dependent samples analysis relative to the independent samples analysis of the same data.

TABLE 2.3
Raw Scores and Descriptive Statistics for Two Samples

	Condition	
	1	2
	9	8
	12	12
	13	11
	15	10
	16	14
M	13.00	11.00
s^2	7.50	5.00

Note. In a dependent-samples analysis, $r_{12} = .735$ and $= s_D^2 = 3.50$.

TABLE 2.4
Results of the Independent Samples *t* Test and the Dependent Samples
t Test for the Data in Table 2.3

Analysis	Standard error	95% CI for $\mu_1 - \mu_2$	*t*	*df*
Independent samples	1.58	−1.64–5.64	1.26[a]	8
Dependent samples	.837	.32–4.32	2.38[b]	4

Note. CI = confidence interval. For both analyses, $M_1 - M_2 = 2.00$.
[a]$p = .243$.　　[b]$p = .076$.

The results reported in Tables 2.2 and 2.4 show a special correspondence between 95% confidence intervals based on mean contrasts and results of the *t* test conducted with the same data at the .05 level for a nil hypothesis and a nondirectional alternative hypothesis: The confidence interval includes zero if H_0 is not rejected, but it does not include zero if H_0 is rejected. This relation is not surprising because the same basic information that goes into a confidence interval goes into a statistical test. However, much of this information is hidden if all that is reported is a test statistic and its *p* value. A mathematically sophisticated reader may be able to construct a confidence interval from the test statistic by solving for the standard error, but simply reporting the confidence interval makes this information accessible to all.

An important point should be made: Thompson (2002b) and others noted that it is erroneous to equate confidence intervals and statistical tests because of the special correspondence between them, mentioned previously. This is because the most informative use of confidence intervals compares them across different studies, not whether a particular interval includes zero. This most informative use concerns replication, something that results of statistical tests in a single study cannot address. The same author also makes the point that statistical tests cannot be conducted without a null hypothesis, but no hypothesis is required for a confidence interval. These ideas are elaborated in the next chapter.

F TESTS FOR MEANS

The *t* statistic compares only two means. Such contrasts are *focused comparisons*, and they address specific questions, such as whether treatment is superior to control. All focused comparisons are single-*df*, directional effects. The *F* statistic can also analyze focused comparisons—recall that $t^2 = F$ for a mean contrast. The *F* statistic, but not *t*, can also be used in *omnibus comparisons*, which simultaneously compare at least three means for equality. Suppose that factor A has $a = 3$ levels. The omnibus effect of

A has two degrees of freedom ($df_A = 2$), and the overall F test of this effect evaluates the following nil and nondirectional alternative hypotheses:

$$H_0: \mu_1 = \mu_2 = \mu_3 \quad \text{and} \quad H_1: \mu_1 \neq \mu_2 \neq \mu_3 \text{ (i.e., not } H_0)$$

Rejecting H_0 in favor of H_1 for the previous example says only that the differences among the observed means M_1, M_2, and M_3 are unlikely assuming equal population means. This result alone is often not very informative. That is, a researcher may be more interested in a series of focused comparisons, such as the contrast of the first level of A with the second (e.g., $H_0: \mu_1 = \mu_2$, $H_1: \mu_1 > \mu_2$), which break down the omnibus effect into specific directional effects. Accordingly, it is common practice to either follow an omnibus comparison with focused comparisons or forego the omnibus comparison and analyze only focused comparisons.

The logic of F as a test statistic for the omnibus comparison in a design with a single fixed factor A with two or more levels is explained next. There are separate sections about omnibus F statistics for designs with independent samples and for designs with dependent samples. The presentations for correlated designs are more technical. However, readers interested in methods for independent samples can skip the sections about correlated designs without difficulty.

Independent Samples F Test

The general form of the F statistic for the omnibus effect in a single-factor design with independent samples is

$$F\,(df_A, df_W) = \frac{MS_A}{MS_W} \tag{2.27}$$

where df_A and df_W are, respectively, the degrees of freedom for the numerator and denominator of F. The former equals the number of levels of factor A minus one, or $df_A = (a - 1)$, and the latter is the total within-groups degrees of freedom, or

$$df_W = \sum_{i=1}^{a} df_i = \sum_{i=1}^{a} (n_i - 1) = N - a \tag{2.28}$$

The numerator of F is the between-conditions (groups) mean square. Its equation is

$$MS_A = \frac{SS_A}{df_A} = \frac{\sum_{i=1}^{a} n_i\,(M_i - M_T)^2}{a - 1} \tag{2.29}$$

where SS_A is the between-conditions sum of squares, n_i and M_i are, respectively, the size and mean of the ith condition, and M_T is the mean for the total data set. The latter is the *grand mean*, the average of all N scores. The value of M_T can also be computed as the weighted average of the condition means or only in a balanced design as the arithmetic average of the condition means. Please note in this equation that group size contributes only to the numerator of the between-conditions variance, SS_A. The implication of this fact is demonstrated next.

The numerator of F, MS_A, reflects group size and sources of variability that give rise to unequal group means, such as a systematic effect of factor A or sampling error. It is the *error term* (denominator) of F, the pooled within-conditions mean square MS_W, that measures only unexplained variance. This is because cases within the same condition are treated alike, such as when patients in a treatment group are all given the same dosage of the same drug. Because drug is a constant for these patients, it cannot account for individual differences among them. The equation for the error term is

$$MS_W = \frac{SS_W}{df_W} = \frac{\sum_{i=1}^{a} df_i \, (s_i^2)}{\sum_{i=1}^{a} df_i} \tag{2.30}$$

where df_i and s_i^2 are, respectively, the degrees of freedom (i.e., $n_i - 1$) and variance of the ith group. When there are only two groups, $MS_W = s_P^2$ (Equation 2.9), and only in a balanced design can MS_W also be computed as the arithmetic average of the individual within-groups variances. Please note in this equation that group size contributes to both the numerator and denominator of MS_W, which effectively cancels out its effect on the error term of F.

The total sums of squares, SS_T, reflects the amount of variability in the total data set. It is the sum of squared deviations of the individual scores from the grand mean; it also equals $SS_A + SS_W$. We will see in later chapters that SS_T is important for effect size estimation with descriptive measures of association in essentially any comparative study where ANOVA is used.

Presented in Table 2.5 are the means and variances of three independent samples, and reported in Table 2.6 are results of the one-way F test for these data at three different group sizes, n = 5, 15, and 30. Observe that across all three ANOVA source tables in Table 2.6, the value of the error term is constant, MS_W = 5.50. The dependence of MS_A and F on group size is obvious: Both increase along with the group size, which also progressively lowers the probability values for F from p = .429 for n = 5 to p = .006 for n = 30. This change in p values occurs even though the group means and variances are constant across all analyses.

TABLE 2.5
Means and Variances for Three Independent Samples

	Group		
	1	2	3
M	13.00	11.00	12.00
s^2	7.50	5.00	4.00

TABLE 2.6
Results of the Independent Samples F Test at Three Different Group Sizes for the Data in Table 2.5

Source	SS	df	MS	F
		$n = 5$		
Between (A)	10.00	2	5.00	.91[a]
Within (error)	66.00	12	5.50	
Total	76.00	14		
		$n = 15$		
Between (A)	30.00	2	15.00	2.73[b]
Within (error)	231.00	42	5.50	
Total	261.00	44		
		$n = 30$		
Between (A)	60.00	2	30.00	5.45[c]
Within (error)	478.50	87	5.50	
Total	538.50	89		

[a]$p = .429$.   [b]$p = .077$.   [c]$p = .006$.

Weighted- Versus Unweighted-Means Analysis

The standard F statistic described earlier is used in a *weighted-means analysis*. This is because the squared deviation of each condition mean from the grand mean is weighted by group size when MS_A, the numerator of F, is computed (Equation 2.29). If the design is unbalanced, the means from the bigger groups get a larger weight. This is not a problem if unequal study group sizes reflect unequal population group sizes. An *unweighted-means analysis* may be preferred if unequal group sizes are a result more of sampling artifacts. All means are given the same weight in this method. This is accomplished by (a) computing the grand mean as the arithmetic average instead of the weighted average of the group means and (b) substituting an average group size for the actual group sizes in the equation for MS_A. This average group size is the harmonic mean:

$$n_h = \frac{a}{\displaystyle\sum_{i=1}^{a} 1/n_i} \qquad (2.31)$$

where n_i is the actual size of the ith group. Note that a weighted-means analysis and an unweighted-means analysis generate the same value of F in a balanced design.

Assumptions of the Independent Samples F Test

It is stated in many introductory statistics textbooks that the assumptions of the F test in designs with independent samples and fixed factors include independence of the observations, normal population distributions, and equal population variances. The latter is the assumption of *homogeneity of variance*, and it is necessary whenever error terms include variances averaged across different conditions (e.g., Equation 2.30). However, there are related requirements that may not be explicitly stated in introductory textbooks. These include the requirements that all levels of each fixed factor are included in the experiment and that treatments are additive and have no affect on the shapes or variances of population treatment distributions (Winer, Brown, & Michels, 1991). If a treatment is studied that is expected to affect both the average level and variability of cases, the latter requirement may be violated. Altogether these requirements are more restrictive than many researchers realize.

The p values from the F test are computed under these assumptions. If these assumptions are violated, then the p values of these tests—and decisions based on them, namely whether to reject H_0—may not be accurate. If observed p values wind up being too low because of violation of assumptions, there is a *positive bias* because H_0 is rejected more often than it should. In the RS context for statistical tests, this implies that the researcher's hypothesis is supported more often than it should be. It can also happen that observed p values can be too high because of violation of assumptions, which may reduce power.

There is a relatively large literature about the consequences of violating the assumptions of statistical tests in general and the F test in particular in fixed-effects ANOVA. It is beyond the scope of this section to review this literature in detail, so only an overview is presented; readers are referred to Winer et al. (1991, pp. 100–110) and a review article by Glass, Peckham, and Sanders (1972) for more information. The independence assumption is critical because nonindependence can seriously affect both p values and power regardless of whether the group sizes are equal or unequal. This requirement should generally be seen as an essential property of the research design. It was believed that the normality assumption is generally unimportant in that it can be violated with relative impunity with little effect on p values or power. It was also believed that the F test is relatively insensitive to variance heterogeneity. However, recent work by Wilcox (1987, 1998) and others indicate that (a) even relatively small departures from normality can sometimes distort the results of the standard t or F tests; (b) there can be serious positive bias in these tests when the ratio of the largest over the smallest within-groups variance is 9 or greater; and (c) the degree of inaccuracy in p values may be greater when the group sizes are small and unequal or when heterogeneity is associated with one outlier group than when it is spread across all the groups (Keppel, 1991). There are versions of both the t and F tests for independent samples that do not assume normality or homogeneity of variance (e.g., Winer et al., 1991, pp. 66–69; Wilcox, 1987), but they are not used nearly as often as the standard t and F tests based on these assumptions.

Reviewed in the next chapter is evidence that the assumptions of t, F, and other statistical tests seem to be infrequently met or evaluated in applied behavioral research. This is another serious shortcoming of the use of statistical tests in the behavioral sciences.

Dependent Samples F Test

The between-conditions variance, MS_A, and the pooled within-conditions variance, MS_W, are computed the same way regardless of whether the samples are independent or dependent (Equations 2.29–2.30). However, the latter no longer reflects just unexplained variance when the samples are dependent, so it is not the error term for the omnibus F statistic in a correlated design. This is because of the subjects effect, which in a one-way design is manifested in positive covariances between every pair of conditions. When the independent variable has three or more levels, the average covariance across all pairs of conditions, M_{cov}, estimates the subjects effect for the whole design. Removing this effect from the pooled within-conditions variance (literally, $MS_W - M_{cov}$) gives the error term for F in a one-way design with dependent samples. This error term reflects inconsistent performance across the conditions. This inconsistency may be a result of random variation or to a nonadditive effect, which means that the independent variable does not have the same relative impact on all cases. In other words, there is some characteristic of participants that moderates the effect of factor A, either amplifying or diminishing it. For example, a drug may be more effective for older patients than younger patients. This moderator effect is also known as a *person × treatment interaction*.

In an *additive model*, which assumes no true person × treatment interaction, the error term of the dependent samples F statistic is presumed to reflect only random error. In some sources, this error term is designated as MS_{res}, where the subscript refers to residual variance. However, an additive model is probably unrealistic for many within-subjects factors in the behavioral sciences. A *nonadditive model* assumes a true person × treatment interaction, and the error term in this model may be called $MS_{A \times S}$, where the subscript reflects this assumption. This notation is used later. Unfortunately, it is not possible to separately estimate variability because of random error versus a true person × treatment interaction when each case is measured once in each condition, which is typical in one-way within-subjects designs. This implies that $MS_{res} = MS_{A \times S}$ in the same data set, so the distinction between them is more conceptual than practical. Cases in which the assumption of additive versus nonadditive models makes a difference in effect size estimation are considered in chapter 6.

We can now define the general form of the omnibus F test for single-factor designs with dependent samples assuming a nonadditive model:

$$F\ (df_A,\ df_{A \times S}) = \frac{MS_A}{MS_{A \times S}} \tag{2.32}$$

where $df_{A \times S} = (a - 1)\ (n - 1)$ and $MS_{A \times S} = MS_W - M_{cov}$. The latter can also be expressed as

$$MS_{A \times S} = \frac{SS_{A \times S}}{df_{A \times S}} = \frac{SS_W - SS_S}{df_W - df_S} \tag{2.33}$$

where SS_S is the sum of squares for the subjects effect with $df_S = n - 1$ degrees of freedom. Equation 2.33 shows the removal of the subjects effect from the pooled within-conditions variability in a correlated design, which is the same basic subtraction that generates the error term of the dependent samples t statistic (Equation 2.15). Equation 2.33 also shows the decomposition of the total within-conditions sums of squares into two parts, one because of the subjects effect and the other associated with the error term, or $SS_W = SS_S + SS_{A \times S}$.

The F test for dependent samples has the same potential power advantage over the F test for independent samples as the t test for dependent samples has over its independent samples counterpart. This is demonstrated with the data for three samples presented in Table 2.7. The results of two different F tests conducted with these data are reported in Table 2.8. The first analysis assumes $n = 5$ cases in each of three independent samples, and the second analysis assumes $n = 5$ triads of scores across three dependent samples. Only the second analysis takes account of the positive correlations between each pair of conditions, which range from .730 to .839 (Table 2.7).

TABLE 2.7
Raw Scores and Descriptive Statistics for Three Samples

	Condition		
	1	2	3
	9	8	10
	12	12	11
	13	11	13
	15	10	11
	16	14	15
M	13.00	11.00	12.00
s^2	7.50	5.00	4.00

Note. In a dependent samples analysis, $r_{12} = .735$, $r_{13} = .730$, and $r_{23} = .839$.

Observe the higher F and lower p values for the dependent samples analysis even though the group means and variances are constant.

Assumptions of the Dependent Samples F Test

The same assumptions of the independent samples F test—independence, normality, and homogeneity of variance—apply to the dependent samples F test. However, there are additional assumptions that concern the correlations between multiple measures obtained from the same cases (or sets of matched cases). When a within-subjects factor has at least three levels, these assumptions are relatively complicated and quite difficult to meet in practice. An additional requirement is that of *sphericity* or *circularity*, which assumes that the population variances of the difference scores between every pair of conditions are equal. This assumption is critical

TABLE 2.8
Results of the Independent Samples *F* Test and the Dependent Samples
F Test for the Data in Table 2.7

Source	SS	df	MS	F
	Independent samples analysis			
Between (A)	10.00	2	5.00	.91[a]
Within (error)	66.00	12	5.50	
Total	76.00	14		
	Dependent samples analysis			
Between (A)	10.00	2	5.00	3.53[b]
Within	66.00	12	5.50	
Subjects (S)	54.67	4	13.67	
A × S (error)	11.33	8	1.42	
Total	76.00	14		

[a]$p = .429$.   [b]$p = .080$.

because even relatively minor violations of this assumption may lead to rejecting H_0 too often (i.e., resulting in a positive bias). There are statistical tests intended to detect departure from sphericity, but they have been criticized for restrictive assumptions of their own, such as normality. Some methodologists suggest that the sphericity requirement may not be tenable in most behavioral studies and that researchers should direct their efforts to controlling bias (Keppel, 1991). There are basically five options for dealing with the sphericity assumption that are briefly summarized next; see H. Keselman, Algina, and Kowalchuk (2001), Max and Onghena (1999), or Winer et al. (1991, pp. 239–273) for more information:

1. Assume maximal violation of sphericity, compute F in the usual way, but compare it against a higher critical value. This critical F has only 1 and $n - 1$ degrees of freedom; the standard critical F for comparing a dependent means has $a - 1$ and $(a - 1)$ $(n - 1)$ degrees of freedom. This method has been called the *Geisser–Greenhouse conservative test* or the *Geisser–Greenhouse correction*.
2. Estimate the degree of departure from sphericity with a statistic called estimated epsilon, $\hat{\varepsilon}$. This statistic ranges from $1/(a - 1)$, which indicates maximal departure to 1.00, which in turn indicates no violation of sphericity. The degrees of freedom for the critical value for F are then taken as $\hat{\varepsilon}$ $(a - 1)$ and $\hat{\varepsilon}$ $(a - 1)(n - 1)$, which makes the test more conservative for <1.00. There are somewhat different forms of $\hat{\varepsilon}$ that may be called the Box correction, the Geisser–Greenhouse epsilon, or the Huynh–Feldt epsilon.
3. Conduct focused comparisons between pairs of condition means instead of the omnibus comparison This implies that each contrast has its own specialized error term (i.e., it is not $MS_{A \times S}$ for the whole design). Because these unique error terms are based on data from only two conditions, the sphericity requirement does not apply.
4. Analyze data from all levels of the factor with multivariate analysis of variance (MANOVA), which also does not assume sphericity. In this approach, difference scores between adjacent levels of factor A are analyzed as multiple, correlated outcome variables (e.g., Stevens, 1992, chap. 13).
5. Use the statistical resampling method of bootstrapping to generate an empirical F test for repeated measures data. (Bootstrapping as an alternative to traditional statistical tests is discussed in chapter 9, this volume). In a recent Monte Carlo analysis, Berkovits, Hancock, and Nevitt (2000) found that

this method is relatively robust against violation of the sphericity assumption.

All of these options are concerned in large part with the estimation of accurate p values in correlated designs. Considering the limitations of p values outlined in the next chapter, perhaps an even better choice is to move away from traditional statistical tests to model-fitting techniques suitable for repeated-measures data, such as structural equation modeling or hierarchical linear modeling, among others. This point is elaborated later.

Analysis of Variance as Multiple Regression

All forms of ANOVA are nothing more than special cases of multiple regression (MR), which itself is just an extension of bivariate regression that analyzes one or more predictors of a continuous dependent variable. These predictors can be either continuous or categorical variables. Categorical predictors are represented in regression equations with special codes that each correspond to a single df contrast (i.e., a focused comparison) between the levels of that predictor. It is also possible in MR to estimate interaction effects between continuous or categorical predictors. In theory, one needs only a software program for MR to conduct any kind of ANOVA. The advantage of doing so is that the output of regression programs usually includes correlations, partial correlations, or standardized regression coefficients (beta weights), all of which are standardized measures of effect size. In contrast, software programs for ANOVA may print only source tables, and the F and p values in these tables measure both effect size and sample size (e.g., Table 2.6). The disadvantage of using MR programs instead of ANOVA programs is that the coding required for some kinds of designs, especially ones with repeated-measures factors, can become complicated. In contrast, ANOVA programs are typically easier to use because no special coding of the factors is required by the user. Fortunately, there are some straightforward ways to extract information about effect size from ANOVA source tables that are demonstrated in later chapters.

Entire books are written about the relation between ANOVA and MR (e.g., Keppel & Zedeck, 1989), so it is not possible to deal with this issue in substantive detail. However, readers should be aware of this alternative to using ANOVA to analyze means and estimate effect size.

χ^2 TEST OF ASSOCIATION

Whether there is a statistical relation between two categorical variables is the question addressed by the χ^2 test of association. A two-way contingency

TABLE 2.9
Results of the Chi-Square Test of Association for the Same Proportions
at Different Group Sizes

Group	n	Observed Frequencies Recovered	Observed Frequencies Not recovered	Recovery rate	χ^2 (1)
		Outcome			
		$n = 40$			
Treatment	40	24	16	.60	3.20[a]
Control	40	16	24	.40	
Total	80	40	40		
		$n = 80$			
Treatment	80	48	32	.60	6.40[b]
Control	80	32	48	.40	
Total	160	80	80		

[a]$p = .074$.   [b]$p = .011$.

table summarizes the data analyzed by this test. Presented in the top half part of Table 2.9 is a 2 × 2 cross-tabulation that shows the frequencies of treatment and control cases ($n = 40$ each) that either recovered or did not recover. A total of 24 cases in the treatment group recovered, or 60%. Among control cases, 16 cases recovered, or 40%. The recovery rate among treated cases is thus 20% higher than among untreated cases.

The χ^2 test of association for two-way contingency tables takes the form

$$\chi^2 (r - 1, c - 1) = \sum_{i=1}^{r} \sum_{j=1}^{c} \frac{(f_{o_{ij}} - f_{e_{ij}})^2}{f_{e_{ij}}} \qquad (2.34)$$

where the degrees of freedom are the product of the number of rows (r) minus one and the number of columns (c) minus one, $f_{o_{ij}}$ is the observed frequency for the cell in the ith row and jth column, and $f_{e_{ij}}$ is the expected frequency for the same cell under the nil hypothesis that the two variables are unrelated. There is a quick way to derive by hand the value of f_e for any cell: Divide the product of the row and column totals for that cell by the total number of cases, N. It is that simple. The statistical assumptions of the χ^2 test of association include independence of the observations, classification of each observation into one and only one category (i.e., contingency table cell), and a sample size large enough so that the minimum expected value across the cells is about 5 for tables with more than a single degree of freedom or about 10 for tables with a single degree of freedom.

For the 2 × 2 cross-tabulation in the top half of Table 2.9, the expected frequency for each cell is $f_e = (40 \times 40)/80 = 20$. This shows a pattern where outcome is unrelated to treatment status because the expected recovery rate is the same for both groups, 50% (20/40). After application of this equation, the results are χ^2 (1) = 3.20, p = .074, so the nil hypothesis that group membership and recovery status are unrelated is not rejected at the .05 level. The effect of increasing the group size but keeping all else constant on the χ^2 test is demonstrated in the bottom part of Table 2.9. Reported there are results of the χ^2 test for the same proportions but a larger group size, n = 80. The null hypothesis is now rejected at the .05 level—χ^2 (1) = 6.40, p = .011—even though the improvement in recovery rate for treated versus control cases is unchanged, 20%.

Other common applications of the χ^2 test not described include a goodness-of-fit test for categorical variables and a test for correlated proportions, among others. All tests just mentioned are also sensitive to sample size.

STATISTICAL TESTS AND REPLICATION

Statistical tests provide a framework for making a dichotomous decision—reject or fail to reject H_0—about sample results in the face of uncertainty. This uncertainty is sampling error, which is estimated in some way by essentially all statistical tests. Of course, any decision based on a statistical test may not be correct (e.g., a Type I or Type II error). In any science, though, it is replication that is the ultimate arbiter: No matter how intriguing a result from a single study, it must be replicated before it can be taken seriously. Replication also is the ultimate way to deal with the problem of sampling error. Indeed, statistical tests are unnecessary with sufficient replication.

There is a much stronger tradition of replication in the natural sciences than in the social sciences. It is also true that statistical tests are infrequently used in the natural sciences. Whether this association is causal is a matter of debate. Some authors argue that the widespread use of statistical tests in the social sciences works against the development of a stronger appreciation for replication (e.g., Kmetz, 2000; F. Schmidt & Hunter, 1997). There are probably other factors that contribute to the difference in emphasis on replication across the social and natural sciences (Kupfersmid, 1988), but the possibility that statistical tests is one of them warrants careful consideration. Replication and meta-analysis as a method for research synthesis are considered in chapter 8.

CONCLUSION

Outlined in this chapter is a basic vocabulary for comparative studies and the logic of interval estimation for statistics with simple distributions, such as means, versus those with complex distributions, such as some effect size indexes. Confidence intervals for the former are constructed with central test statistics, but the latter may require noncentral test statistics. Special software tools are also typically needed for noncentral confidence intervals. A confidence interval based on a statistic sets a reasonable lower and upper bounds for the corresponding population parameter, but there is no guarantee that the value of the parameter is included in a particular confidence interval. The essential logic of statistical tests in general and characteristics of the t and F tests for means and the χ^2 test for two-way contingency tables in particular was also reviewed. Any statistical test measures both effect size and sample size. This is why neither the values of test statistics or their associated probabilities say much useful about effect size. Additional limitations of statistical tests are considered in the next chapter.

RECOMMENDED READINGS

Cumming, G., & Finch, S. (2001). A primer on the understanding, use, and calculation of confidence intervals that are based on central and noncentral distributions. *Educational and Psychological Measurement, 61,* 532–574.

Reichardt, C. S., & Gollob, H. F. (1997). When confidence intervals should be used instead of statistical tests, and vice versa. In L. L. Harlow, S. A. Mulaik, & J. H. Steiger (Eds.), *What if there were no significance tests?* (pp. 37–64). Mahwah, NJ: Erlbaum.

Smithson, M. J. (2000). *Statistics with confidence: An introduction for psychologists.* Thousand Oaks, CA: Sage.

3

WHAT'S WRONG WITH STATISTICAL TESTS— AND WHERE WE GO FROM HERE

Statistics is a subject of amazingly many uses and surprisingly few effective practitioners.

— B. Efron and R. Tabshirani (1993, p. xiv)

This chapter considers problems with null hypothesis significance testing (NHST). The literature in this area is quite large. D. Anderson, Burnham, and W. Thompson (2000) recently found more than 300 articles in different disciplines about the indiscriminate use of NHST, and W. Thompson (2001) lists more than 400 references about this topic. As a consequence, it is possible to cite only a few representative works. General reviews of the controversy about NHST in the social sciences include Borenstein (1998), Nickerson (2000), and Nix and Barnette (1998). Examples of works more critical of NHST include J. Cohen (1994); Gigerenzer (1998a, 1998b); Gliner, Morgan, Leech, and Harmon (2001); and Kruegar (2001), and examples of works that defend NHST include Abelson (1997a, 1997b); Chow (1998a, 1998b); Harris (1997c); and Mulaik, Raju, and Harshman (1997).

After review of the debate about NHST, I argue that the criticisms have sufficient merit to support the minimization or elimination of NHST

The author wishes to thank Richard S. Herrington, as well as the anonymous reviewers, for suggestions in this chapter.

61

in the behavioral sciences. I offer specific suggestions along these lines. Some concern alternatives that may replace or supplement NHST and thus are directed at researchers. Others concern editorial policies or educational curricula. Few of the recommendations given are original in that many have been made over the years by various authors. However, as a set they deal with issues often considered in separate works. For simplicity, the context for NHST assumed is reject–support (RS) instead of accept–support (AS). The RS context is more common, and many of the arguments can be reframed for the AS context. Exercises for this chapter can be found on this book's Web site.

NHST OUTCOMES ARE INTERPRETED
AS SOMETHING THEY ARE NOT

People are by nature good at pattern recognition. We find evidence for this in almost every aspect of human life, whether it is the apparently innate preference of infants for visual stimuli that resemble a human face or the use of language by adults to construct a social reality. There are probably deep evolutionary roots of our ability to find meaning in the world around us. This ability is also at the core of some personality theories. For instance, Rollo May (1975) wrote,

> Creative people . . . do not run away from non-being, but by encountering and wrestling with it, force it to produce being. They knock on silence for answering music; they pursue meaninglessness until they force it to mean. (p. 93)

Our pattern recognition ability is so well-developed that sometimes we see *too much* meaning in otherwise random events. Sagan (1996) described several examples, including one that involved an early satellite photo of a hill in a place called Cydonia on Mars that resembles a human face. Some people took this formation as evidence for a vanished civilization. Later satellite images of the same hill showed pretty clearly that it was carved by natural forces such as wind erosion, but the tendency to see something recognizable in randomness is strong. By virtue of their training or personal dispositions, scientists may be extraordinarily good at pattern recognition, which also makes them subject to the potential error of seeing too much meaning in certain events. This seems to be true about NHST, because many common fallacies about it involve exaggerating what can be inferred from statistical tests. These incorrect inferences may be a source of cognitive misdirection that hinders progress in behavioral research.

Misinterpretations of p Values

Next we consider common misunderstandings about the probabilities generated by statistical tests, p values. Let us first review their correct interpretation. Recall that statistical tests measure the discrepancy between a sample statistic and the value of the population parameter specified in the null hypothesis, H_0, taking account of sampling error. The empirical test statistic is converted to a probability within the appropriate central test distribution. This probability is the conditional probability of the statistic assuming H_0 is true (see chap. 2, this volume). Other correct interpretations for the specific case $p < .05$ include the following:

1. The odds are less than 1 to 19 of getting a result from a random sample even more extreme than the observed one when H_0 is true.
2. Less than 5% of test statistics are further away from the mean of the sampling distribution under H_0 than the one for the observed result.
3. Assuming H_0 is true and the study is repeated many times, less than 5% of these results will be even more inconsistent with H_0 than the observed result.

That is about it. Other correct definitions may be just variations of those listed. The range of correct interpretations of p values is thus actually quite narrow. Let us refer to any correct definition as $p\,(D\,|\,H_0)$, which emphasizes probabilities from statistical tests as conditional probabilities of the data (D) given the null hypothesis.

Presented next are common misinterpretations for the case $p < .05$. Some of them arise from forgetting that p values are conditional probabilities or reversing the two events represented by p values, D and H_0. Reasons why each is incorrect are also given below:

Fallacy Number 1

A p value is the probability that the result is a result of sampling error; thus, $p < .05$ says that there is less than a 5% likelihood that the result happened by chance. This false belief is the *odds-against-chance fantasy* (Carver, 1978). It is wrong because p values are computed under the assumption that sampling error is what causes sample statistics to depart from the null hypothesis. That is, the likelihood of sampling error is *already* taken to be 1.00 when a statistical test is conducted. It is thus illogical to view p values as measuring the probability of sampling error. This fantasy together with others listed later may explain the related fallacy that statistical tests sort results into two categories, those a result of chance (H_0 is not rejected) and others a result of "real" effects (H_0 is rejected). Unfortunately, statistical tests applied in individual studies cannot make this distinction. This is because any decision based on NHST outcomes may be wrong (i.e., a Type I or Type II error).

Fallacy Number 2

A p value is the probability that the null hypothesis is true given the data; thus, $p < .05$ implies $p(H_0|D) < .05$. This is the *inverse probability error* (J. Cohen, 1994) or the *Bayesian Id's wishful thinking error* (Gigerenzer, 1993), and it stems from forgetting that p values are conditional probabilities of the data, or $p(D|H_0)$, and *not* of the null hypothesis, or $p(H_0|D)$. The latter is the posterior probability of the null hypothesis in light of the data, and it is probably what researchers would really like to know. A simplified form of Bayes's theorem shows us that $p(D|H_0)$ from a statistical test and the posterior probability of the null hypothesis are in fact related:

$$p(H_0|D) = \frac{p(H_0)\, p(D|H_0)}{p(D)} \tag{3.1}$$

In Equation 3.1, $p(H_0)$ is the prior probability that the null hypothesis is true before the data are collected, and $p(D)$ is the prior probability of the data irrespective of the truth of the null hypothesis. That is, given the p value from a statistical test along with estimates of $p(H_0)$ and $p(D)$, we could derive with this equation $p(H_0|D)$, the posterior probability of the null hypothesis. Unfortunately, those who use traditional statistical tests do not usually think about prior probabilities. If pressed to specify these values, they may venture a guess, but it may be viewed as subjective. In contrast, a Bayesian approach specifically estimates the posterior probability of the hypothesis, not just the conditional probability of the data under that hypothesis. There are also ways to estimate prior probabilities that are not wholly subjective. Chapter 9 considers the Bayesian approach to hypothesis testing.

Fallacy Number 3

If the null hypothesis is rejected, p is the probability that this decision is wrong; thus, if $p < .05$, there is less than a 5% chance that the decision to reject the null hypothesis is a Type I error. This fallacy is another kind of inverse probability error that Pollard (1993) described as confusing the conditional prior probability of a Type I error, or

$$\alpha = p(\text{reject } H_0|H_0)$$

with the conditional posterior probability of a Type I error given that the null hypothesis was rejected, or:

$$p\ (H_0\ |\ \text{reject}\ H_0)$$

Pollard uses Bayes's theorem to show it is not generally possible to estimate $p\ (H_0\ |\ \text{reject}\ H_0)$ from α. On a more intuitive level, the decision to reject the null hypothesis in an individual study is either correct or incorrect, so no probability is associated with it. Only with sufficient replication could we discern whether a specific decision to reject H_0 was correct.

Fallacy Number 4

The complement of p, $1 - p$, is the probability that the alternative hypothesis is true given the data, or $p\ (H_1\ |\ D)$. Thus, $p < .05$ says that the likelihood that H_1 is true is greater than 95%. This erroneous idea is the *validity fallacy* (Mulaik et al., 1997) or the *valid research hypothesis fantasy* (Carver, 1978). The complement of p is a probability, but it is just the likelihood of getting a result even *less* extreme under H_0 than the one actually found. Accordingly, complements of p have nothing directly to do with the posterior probability of H_1.

Fallacy Number 5

The complement of p is the probability that a result will replicate under constant conditions; thus, $p < .05$ says that the chance of replication exceeds 95%. This is the *replicability* or *repeatability fallacy* (Carver, 1978). Another variation for $p < .05$ is that a replication has a 95% probability of yielding a statistically significant result, presumably in the same direction as in the original study. If this fallacy were true, knowing the probability of finding the same result in future replications would be very useful. Alas, a p value is just the probability of a particular result under a specific hypothesis. As noted by Carver, replication is a matter of experimental design and whether an effect actually exists in the population. It is thus an empirical question for future studies and not one directly addressed by statistical tests in a single study.

Readers should note, however, that there *is* a sense in which p values concern replication. Greenwald, Gonzalez, Harris, and Guthrie (1996) made the point that p values in an original study are *monotonically* related to the statistical power of replications. A monotonic relation is typically ordinal or nonlinear; thus, there is not a uniform correspondence between p values and the probabilities of null hypothesis rejections in replications. Specifically, without special graphs like ones presented by Greenwald et al., one cannot directly convert a p value to the likelihood of repeating a null hypothesis rejection. This is a subtle point. It is probably best to keep in mind that p values have little to do with replication in the usual scientific sense.

Mistaken Conclusions After Making a Decision About the Null Hypothesis

There are also many false conclusions that may be reached after deciding to reject or fail to reject H_0 based on p values. Most require little explanation about why they are wrong:

Fallacy Number 1

A p value is a numerical index of the magnitude of an effect; thus, low p values indicate large effects. This misconception could be called the *magnitude fallacy*. Smaller p values indicate lower conditional probabilities of the data, given the required assumption that the null hypothesis exactly describes the population (J. Cohen, 1994), but that is about all that can be said without other kinds of analyses such as effect size estimation. This is because statistical tests and their p values measure sample size *and* effect size (e.g., Table 2.2), so an effect of trivial magnitude needs only a large enough sample to be statistically significant. If the sample size is actually large, low p values just confirm a large sample, which is a tautology (B. Thompson, 1992). Now, results that are truly of large magnitude may also have low p values—it is just that one cannot tell much by looking at p values alone.

Fallacy Number 2

Rejection of the null hypothesis confirms the alternative hypothesis and the research hypothesis behind it. This *meaningfulness fallacy* actually reflects two conceptual errors. First, the decision to reject H_0 in a single study does not imply that H_1 is "proven." Second, even if the *statistical* hypothesis H_1 is correct, it does not mean that the *substantive* hypothesis behind it is also correct. For example, Arbuthnot (1710) studied the birth records for London for 82 consecutive years (1629–1710). More boys than girls were born every single year during this time. For example, in 1629 there were 5,218 registered births of boys compared with 4,683 births of girls. Based on all these data, Arbuthnot rejected the hypothesis that equal proportions of babies are boys versus girls. In modern terms, he rejected the non-nil hypothesis H_0: $\pi = .50$, where π is the population proportion of boys in favor of the directional alternative hypothesis H_1: $\pi > .50$. However, Arbuthnot's substantive hypothesis was that because of divine providence, more boys are born to compensate for higher numbers of male deaths in wars, accidents, and the like so that, in the end, "every Male may have a Female of the same Country and suitable Age" (1710, p. 188). Arbuthnot was correct about the *statistical* hypothesis H_1, but his substantive hypothesis, although colorful, does not correspond to the actual underlying cause of unequal numbers of newborn boys versus girls: Sperm with Y chromosomes swim faster than those with X chromosomes and arrive in greater numbers to fertilize the egg.

The distinction between statistical and substantive hypotheses is crucial. They differ not only in their levels of abstraction (statistical: lowest; scientific: highest), but also have different implications following rejection of H_0. If H_0 and H_1 reflect only statistical hypotheses, there is little to do after rejecting H_0 except replication. However, if H_1 stands for a scientific hypothesis, the work just begins after H_0 is rejected. Part of the work involves pitting the research hypothesis against other substantive hypotheses also compatible with the statistical hypothesis H_1. If these other hypotheses cannot be ruled out, the researcher's confidence in the original hypothesis must be tempered. It may also be necessary to conduct additional studies that attempt to falsify equivalent models. This is the strategy of *strong inference* (Platt, 1964).

Fallacy Number 3

Failure to reject a nil hypothesis means that the population effect size is zero. This is not a valid inference for a few reasons. One is the basic tenet of science that absence of evidence is not evidence of absence. Also, the decision to fail to reject a nil hypothesis may be a Type II error. For example, there may be a real effect, but the study lacked sufficient power to detect it. Given the relatively low overall power of behavioral research, this is probably not an infrequent event. Poor research design or use of flawed measures can also lead to Type II errors.

Fallacy Number 4

Failure to reject the nil hypothesis H_0: $\mu_1 = \mu_2$ means that the two populations are equivalent. Suppose that an established treatment known to be effective is compared with a new treatment that costs less. It is *incorrect* to conclude that the two treatments are equivalent if the nil hypothesis H_0: $\mu_1 = \mu_2$ is not rejected. The inference of equivalence would be just as incorrect if this example concerned reliability coefficients or proportions in two groups that were not statistically different (Abelson, 1997a; B. Thompson, 2003). To rephrase the tenet cited earlier, the absence of evidence for differences is not evidence for equivalence. Proper methods for equivalence testing are described later.

Fallacy Number 5

Rejecting the null hypothesis confirms the quality of the experimental design. Poor study design can create artifactual effects that lead to incorrect rejection of H_0. Also, plain old sampling error can lead to Type I errors even in well-controlled studies.

Fallacy Number 6

If the null hypothesis is not rejected, the study is a failure. This misconception is the mirror image of the preceding one. Although improper methods or low power can cause Type II errors, failure to reject H_0 can also be the product of good science. For example, some claims based on initial studies are incorrect, which means that replication will lead to negative results. Readers may recall an announcement a few years ago by researchers who claimed to have produced cold fusion (a low energy nuclear reaction) with a relatively simple laboratory apparatus. Other scientists were unable to replicate the phenomenon, and the eventual conclusion was that the claim was premature (Taubes, 1993).

Fallacy Number 7

Rejection of H_0 means that the underlying causal mechanism is identified. This misinterpretation is related to the ones discussed to this point. It should be obvious by now that a single H_0 rejection does not prove a presumed causal effect represented by the statistical hypothesis H_1.

Fallacy Number 8

The failure to replicate is the failure to make the same decision about H_0 across studies. P. Dixon and O'Reilly (1999) refer to this idea as the *reification fallacy*. Under this sophism, a result is considered not replicated if H_0 is rejected in the first study but not in the second study. However, this view ignores sample size, effect size, and the direction of the effect across the two studies. Suppose a group mean difference is found in an initial study and a nil hypothesis is rejected. The exact same group mean difference is found in a replication study, but H_0 is not rejected because of a smaller sample size. We actually have positive evidence for replication even though different decisions about H_0 were made across the two studies.

Widespread Nature of Misinterpretations

There is evidence that many of the false beliefs just described are common even among professional researchers and educators. For instance, Oakes (1986) asked 70 academic psychologists to state their usually adopted

TABLE 3.1
Usually Adopted Interpretations of $p < .01$ by 70 Academic Psychologists

Statement	f	%
1. The null hypothesis is absolutely disproved.	1	1.4
2. The probability of the null hypothesis has been found.	32	45.7
3. The experimental hypothesis is absolutely proved.	2	2.9
4. The probability of the experimental hypothesis can be deduced.	30	42.9
5. The probability that the decision taken is wrong is known.	48	68.6
6. A replication has a .99 probability of being significant.	24	34.3
7. The probability of the data given the null hypothesis is known.	8	11.3

Note. From *Statistical Inference* (p. 81), by M. Oakes, 1986, New York: Wiley. Copyright 1986 by John Wiley and Sons. Reprinted with permission.

interpretations of $p < .01$. The respondents could offer more than one interpretation. Of the seven statements listed in Table 3.1, only the last is correct, but just 8 of 70 participants (11%) reported it. Almost 50% endorsed statements 2 and 4 in the table that p values indicate the conditional probability of H_0 (inverse probability error) or H_1 (valid research hypothesis fallacy), respectively. The majority of the respondents said in error that p values are posterior probabilities of Type I error, and about one third said that the complements of p values indicate the likelihood of replication (repeatability fallacy).

Lest one think that Oakes's results are specific to an unrepresentative group of NHST-challenged academic psychologists, results of other surveys of professionals or near-professionals in the social sciences indicate similar, apparently widespread misunderstandings (e.g., Mittag & B. Thompson, 2000; Nelson, R. Rosenthal, & Rosnow, 1986). Tversky and Kahneman (1971) described a kind of cognitive distortion among psychologists they called the *belief in the law of small numbers.* This belief holds that (a) even small samples are typically representative of their respective populations, and (b) statistically significant results are likely to be found in replication samples half the size of the original. The belief in the law of small numbers is probably just as widespread in other social science disciplines as in psychology.

One also need not look very hard in published sources to find errors similar to those in Table 3.1. J. Cohen (1994) listed several distinguished authors who have made such mistakes in print, including himself. This book probably contains similar kinds of errors. Dar, Serlin, and Omer (1994) noted that several prominent psychotherapy researchers who published in some of the best peer-reviewed journals in this area made similar mistakes over a period of three decades. At first glance, this situation seems puzzling. After all, many academicians and researchers have spent hundreds of hours studying or teaching NHST in statistics courses at both the undergraduate and graduate levels. Why does this rather large investment of educational resources and effort not have more apparent success?

Two factors warrant comment. The first is that NHST is not the most transparent of inference systems. Pollard and others noted that it is difficult to explain the logic of NHST and dispel confusion about it. Some of the language of NHST is very specific and unnatural. For example, the word *significant* implies in natural language that something is important, noteworthy, or meaningful, but not in NHST. There may also be inherent contradictions in the hybrid of the Fisher and Neyman-Pearson models on which contemporary NHST is based (P. Dixon & O'Reilly, 1999; Gigerenzer, 1993). Another problem is a general human weakness in reasoning with conditional probabilities, especially ones best viewed from a relative frequency perspective (e.g., J. Anderson, 1998).

NHST DOES NOT TELL US WHAT WE REALLY WANT TO KNOW

Many of the fallacies about NHST outcomes reviewed concern things that researchers really want to know, including the probability that H_0 or H_1 is true, the likelihood of replication, and the chance that the decision taken to reject H_0 is wrong, all given the data. Using R to stand for replication, this wish list could be summarized as:

$$p(H_0|D), \ p(H_1|D), \ p(R|D), \text{ and } p(H_0|\text{Reject } H_0)$$

Unfortunately, statistical tests tells us only $p(D|H_0)$. As noted by J. Cohen (1994), however, there is no statistical technique applied in individual studies that can fulfill this wish list. (A Bayesian approach to hypothesis testing is an exception; see chap. 9, this volume.) However, there is a method that *can* tell us what we really want to know, but it is not a statistical technique; rather, it is replication, which is not only the best way to deal with sampling error, but replication is also a gold standard in science (see chap. 2, this volume). This idea is elaborated next and again in chapter 8.

NIL HYPOTHESES ARE USUALLY FALSE

Nil hypotheses are the most common type tested in the social sciences. However, it is very unlikely that the value of *any* population parameter is exactly zero, especially if zero implies the complete absence of an effect, association, or difference (e.g., Kirk, 1996). For example, the population correlation (ρ) between any two variables we would care to name is probably not zero. It is more realistic to assume nonzero population associations or differences (see chap. 2, this volume). Meehl (1990) referred to these nonzero effects as a "crud factor" because, at some level, everything is related to everything else; Lykken's (1968) term *ambient correlational noise* means basically the same thing. Although exact values of the crud factor are unknown, correlations may depart even further from zero for variables assessed with the same measurement method. Correlations that result in common method variance may be as high as .20 to .30 in absolute value.

If nil hypotheses are rarely true, rejecting them requires only sufficiently large samples. Accordingly, (a) the effective rate of Type I error in many studies may be essentially zero, and (b) the only kind of decision error is Type II. Given that power is only about .50 on average, the typical probability of a Type II error is also about .50. F. Schmidt (1992, 1996) made the related point that methods to control experimentwise Type I error, such as the Bonferroni correction, may reduce power to levels even lower than .50. It should be said that, as point hypotheses, non-nil hypotheses are no more likely to be true than nil hypotheses. Suppose that a non-nil hypothesis is H_0: ρ = .30. The true value of the population correlation may be just as unlikely to be exactly .30 as zero. However, non-nil hypotheses offer a more realistic standard against which to evaluate sample results, when it is practical to actually test them.

Perhaps most p values reported in the research literature are associated with null hypotheses that are not plausible. For example, D. Anderson et al. (2000) reviewed the null hypotheses tested in several hundred empirical studies published from 1978 to 1998 in two prominent environmental sciences journals. They found many biologically implausible null hypotheses that specified things such as equal survival probabilities for juvenile and adult members of a species or that growth rates did not differ across species, among other assumptions known to be false before the data were collected. I am unaware of a similar survey of null hypotheses in the social sciences, but it would be surprising if the results would be appreciably different.

SAMPLING DISTRIBUTIONS OF TEST STATISTICS ASSUME RANDOM SAMPLING

Lunneborg (2001) described this issue as a mismatch between statistical analysis and design. The p values for test statistics are estimated in sampling distributions that assume random sampling from known populations. These are the same distributions in which standard errors for traditional confidence intervals are estimated. Random sampling is a crucial part of the *population inference model*, which concerns the external validity of sample results. However, most samples in the social sciences are not randomly selected—

they are samples of convenience. In experimental studies, it is the *randomization model*, which involves the random assignment of locally available cases to different conditions, that is much more common than the population inference model. Reichardt and Gollob (1999) suggested that results of standard statistical tests yield standard errors that are too conservative (too large) when randomized cases are from convenience samples. They described a modified t test that assumes the population size equals total number of cases, $N = n_1 + n_2$. Lunneborg (2001) described the use of bootstrapping to construct empirical sampling distributions for randomization studies based on convenience samples. Bootstrapping is described in chapter 9.

Bakan (1966) argued that the ideal application of NHST is manufacturing, not the social sciences. Essentially any manufacturing process is susceptible to random error. If this error becomes too great, such as when pistons are made too big relative to the cylinders in car engines, products fail. In this context, the null hypothesis represents a product specification that is reasonable to assume is true, samples can be randomly selected, and exact deviations of sample statistics from the specification can be accurately measured. It may also be possible in this context to precisely estimate the costs of certain decision errors. All of these conditions rarely hold in behavioral research. As the saying goes, one needs the right tool for the right job. Perhaps NHST is just the wrong tool in many behavioral studies.

STATISTICAL ASSUMPTIONS OF NHST METHODS ARE INFREQUENTLY VERIFIED

Statistical tests usually make certain distributional assumptions. Some are more critical than others, such as the sphericity requirement of the dependent samples F test. If critical assumptions are violated, p values may be wrong. Unfortunately, it seems that too many researchers do not provide evidence about whether distributional assumptions are met. H. Keselman et al. (1998) reviewed more than 400 analyses in studies published from 1994 to 1995 in major education research journals, and they found relatively few articles that verified assumptions of statistical tests. Max and Onghena (1999) found a similar neglect of statistical issues across 116 articles in speech, language, and hearing research journals. These surveys reflect an apparently substantial gap between NHST as described in the statistical literature and its use in practice. Results of more quantitative reviews also suggest that there may be relatively few instances in practice when widely used methods such as the standard F test give accurate results because of violations of assumptions (e.g., Lix, J. Keselman, & H. Keselman, 1996).

NHST BIASES THE RESEARCH LITERATURE

There is a sense that journal editors are not interested in publishing studies without H_0 rejections. This perception is supported by (a) comments by past editors of respected journals about favoring studies with H_0 rejections (e.g., Melton, 1962); (b) survey results that show that behavioral researchers are unlikely to submit studies without H_0 rejections for publication (e.g., Greenwald, 1975); and (c) the more causal observation that the large majority of published studies contain H_0 rejections. The apparent bias for studies with statistically significant results presents the difficulties enumerated and discussed next:

1. *The actual rate of Type I error in published studies may be much higher than indicated by* α. Suppose that a treatment is no more effective than control (the nil hypothesis is true) and 100 different studies of the treatment are each conducted at α = .05. Of the 100 t tests of the treatment versus control mean contrasts, a total of five are expected to be statistically significant. Suppose these five studies are published, but authors of the other 95 decide not to submit their studies or do so but without success. The actual rate of Type I error among the five published studies is 100%, not 5%. Also, the only studies that got it right—the 95 where H_0 was not rejected—were never published. Clark (1976) made a similar point: Because researchers find it difficult to get their failures to replicate published, Type I errors, once made, are difficult to correct.

2. *The reluctance to submit or publish studies with no statistically significant results leads to a "file drawer problem."* This term is from R. Rosenthal (1979), and it refers to studies not submitted for publication or presented in another forum, such as conferences. It is thought that many file drawer studies contain no H_0 rejections. If an effect is actually zero, results of such studies are more scientifically valid than published studies that reject nil hypotheses.

3. *Published studies overestimate population effect sizes.* Without large samples to study small- or medium-sized effects, it may be difficult to get statistically significant results because of low power. When H_0 is rejected, it tends to happen in samples where the observed effect size is larger than the population effect size. If only studies with H_0 rejections are published, the magnitude of the population effect size winds up being overestimated. An example illustrates this point. Table 3.2

TABLE 3.2
Results of Six Hypothetical Replications

Study	$M_1 - M_2$	s_1^2	s_2^2	$t\,(38)$	Reject nil hypothesis?	95% CI
1	2.50	17.50	16.50	1.91	No	−.53–6.53
2	4.00	16.00	18.00	3.07	Yes	1.36–6.64
3	2.50	14.00	17.25	2.00	No	−.03–5.03
4	4.50	13.00	16.00	3.74	Yes	2.06–6.94
5	5.00	12.50	16.50	4.15	Yes	.56–7.44
6	2.50	15.00	17.00	1.98	No	−.06–5.06
Average:	3.58				Range of overlap:	2.06–5.03

Note. For all replications, $n = 20$, $\alpha = .05$, and H_1 is nondirectional. CI = confidence interval.

summarizes the results of six different hypothetical studies where two of the same conditions are compared on the same outcome variable. Note that results of the independent samples t test leads to rejection of a nil hypothesis in three studies (50%), but not in the rest. More informative than the number of H_0 rejections is the average value of $M_1 - M_2$ across all six studies, 3.58. This result may be a better estimate of $\mu_1 - \mu_2$ than the mean difference in any individual study. Now suppose that results from the three studies with H_0 rejections in the table (studies 2, 4, and 5) are the only ones published. The average value of $M_1 - M_2$ for these three studies is 4.22, which is greater than the average based on all six studies.

NHST MAKES THE RESEARCH LITERATURE DIFFICULT TO INTERPRET

If there is a real effect but power is only .50, about half the studies will show positive results (H_0 rejected) and the rest negative results (H_0 not rejected). If somehow all studies are published, the box score of positive and negative results will be roughly equal. From this perspective, it would appear that the research literature is inconclusive (e.g., Table 3.2). Because power is generally about .50 in the social sciences, it is not surprising that only about half of the studies in some areas yield positive results (F. Schmidt, 1996). This is especially true in "soft" behavioral research where theories are neither convincingly supported or discredited but simply fade away as researchers lose interest (Meehl, 1990). Part of the problem comes from interpreting the failure to reject a nil hypothesis as implying a zero population effect size. Such misinterpretation may also lead to the discarding of treatments that produce real benefits.

There may be other negative consequences of using NHST outcomes to sort studies by whether their results are statistically significant. I have heard many psychology students say, "Research never proves anything." These same students have probably recognized that "the three most commonly seen terms in the [soft social science] literature are 'tentative,' 'preliminary,' and 'suggest.' As a default, 'more research is needed' " (Kmetz, 2000, p. 60). It is not only a few students who are skeptical of the value of research. Clinical psychology practitioners surveyed by Beutler, R. Williams, Wakefield, and Entwistle (1995) indicated that the clinical research literature was not relevant for their work. Similar concerns about research relevance have been expressed in education (D. W. Miller, 1999). These unenthusiastic views of research are the antithesis of the attitudes that academic programs try to foster.

NHST DISCOURAGES REPLICATION

Although I am unaware of data that supports this speculation, a survey would probably find just as many behavioral researchers as their natural science colleagues who would endorse replication as a critical activity. Nevertheless, there is a sense that replication is given short shrift in the social sciences compared to the natural sciences. There is also evidence that supports this concern. Kmetz (1998) used an electronic database to survey about 13,000 articles in the area of organizational science and about 28,000 works in economics. The rates of studies specifically described as replications in each area were .32% and .18%, respectively. Comparably low rates of nominal replications have also been observed in psychology and education journals (e.g., Shaver & Norton, 1980).

The extensive use of NHST in the social sciences and resulting cognitive misdirection may be part of the problem. For example, if one believes that $p < .01$ implies that the result is likely to be repeated more than 99 times out of 100, why bother to replicate? A related cognitive error is the belief that statistically significant findings should be replicated, but not ones for which H_0 was not rejected (F. Schmidt & Hunter, 1997). That NHST makes research literatures look inconclusive when power is low may also work against sustained interest in research topics.

Perhaps replication in the behavioral sciences would be more highly valued if confidence intervals were reported more often. Then readers of empirical articles would be able to see the low precision with which many studies are conducted. That is, the widths of confidence intervals for behavioral data are often, to quote J. Cohen (1994, p. 1002), "so embarrassingly large!" Relatively wide confidence intervals indicate that the study contains only limited information, a fact that is concealed when only results of statistical tests are reported (F. Schmidt & Hunter, 1997). This reality is acknowledged by the aspect of meta-analytic thinking that does not overemphasize outcomes of statistical tests in individual studies (see chap. 1, this volume).

NHST OVERLY AUTOMATES THE REASONING PROCESS

Social science researchers and students alike seem to universally understand the importance of precise operationalization. The method of NHST offers many of the same apparent advantages in the realm of inference: It is a detailed, step-by-step procedure that spells out the ground rules for hypothesis testing (see chap. 2, this volume). It is also a public method in that its basic rules and areas for researcher discretion are known to all. One of the appeals of NHST is that it automates much of the decision-making process. It may also address a collective need in the social sciences to appear as objective as the natural sciences. However, some critics claim that too much of our decision making has been so automated. Some of the potential costs of letting statistical tests do our thinking for us are summarized next.

1. *Use of NHST encourages dichotomous thinking.* The ultimate outcome of a statistical test is dichotomous: H_0 is either rejected or not rejected. This property may encourage dichotomous thinking in its users, and nowhere is this more evident than for p values. If $\alpha = .05$, for instance, some researchers see a result where $p = .06$ as qualitatively different than one where $p = .04$. These two results lead to different decisions about H_0, but their p values describe essentially the same likelihood of the data (Rosnow & R. Rosenthal, 1989). More direct evidence of dichotomous thinking was described by Nelson et al. (1986), who asked researchers to rate their confidence in results as a function of p values. They found a relatively sharp decline in rated confidence when p values were just above .05 and another decline when p values were just above .10. These changes in confidence are out of proportion to changes in continuous p values.

   That NHST encourages dichotomous thinking may also contribute to the peculiar practice to describe results where

p is just above the level of α as "trends" or "approaching significance." These findings are also typically interpreted along with statistically significant ones. However, results with p values just lower than α, such as $p = .04$ when $\alpha = .05$, are almost never described as "approaching nonsignificance" and subsequently discounted. There is a related tendency to attribute the failure to reject H_0 to poor experimental design rather than to the invalidity of the substantive hypothesis behind H_1 (Cartwright, 1973).

2. *Use of NHST diverts attention away from the data and the measurement process.* If researchers become too preoccupied with H_0 rejections, they may lose sight of other, more important aspects of their data, such as whether the variables are properly defined and measured. There is a related misconception that reliability is an attribute of tests rather than of the scores for a particular population of examinees (B. Thompson, 2003). This misconception may discourage researchers from reporting the reliabilities of their own data. Interpretation of effect size estimates also requires an assessment of the reliability of the scores (Wilkinson & the Task Force on Statistical Inference [TFSI], 1999).

3. *The large investment of time to learn NHST limits exposure to other methods.* There is a large body of statistical methods other than NHST that can deal with a wide range of hypotheses and data, but social science students generally hear little about them, even in graduate school. The almost exclusive devotion of formal training in statistics to NHST leaves little time for learning about alternatives. Those who become professional researchers must typically learn about these methods on their own or in workshops.

4. *The method of NHST may facilitate research about fad topics that clutter the literature but have little scientific value.* Meehl's (1990) observations on soft psychology research topics with short shelf lives were mentioned earlier. The automatic nature of NHST has been blamed by some authors as a contributing factor: With very little thought about a broader theoretical rationale, one can collect data from a sample of convenience and apply statistical tests. Even if the numbers are random, some of the results are expected to be statistically significant. The objective appearance and mechanical application of NHST may lend an air of credibility to studies with otherwise weak conceptual foundations.

NHST IS NOT AS OBJECTIVE AS IT SEEMS

The level of α and the forms of H_0 (nil versus non-nil) and the alternative hypothesis (directional versus nondirectional) should be specified before the data are collected. This does not always happen in practice. Under a strict view, this is paramount to cheating. Even under a less demanding standard, the ability to change the rules to enhance the outcome makes the whole process seem more subjective than objective. Selective reporting of results, such as only those where H_0 was rejected, presents a similar problem.

MANY NHST METHODS ARE MORE CONCERNED WITH GROUPS THAN INDIVIDUALS

Statistical tests that analyze means, such as t and F, are concerned with group statistics. They provide little information about individuals within these groups. Indeed, within-groups variances contribute to the error terms of both t and F. However, there are times when it is crucial to understand the nature of individual differences within groups. For instance, it can happen that the group mean difference is statistically significant, but there is substantial overlap of the two frequency distributions. This suggests that the difference at the group level does not trickle down to the case level. Some methods of effect size estimation introduced in chapter 4 analyze differences at the case level.

NHST AND SCHOOLS OF PROBABILITY

In the fields of mathematics, statistics, and philosophy of science, there are several different schools of thought about probabilities, including classical, frequentist, and subjective, among others. There are also deep and long-standing divisions between these schools about the exact meaning of probabilities and their proper interpretation. These debates are complex and highly nuanced, and whole books have been written on the subject (e.g., Hogben, 1957). For these reasons, these debates cannot be summarized in this section. However, readers should know that NHST is associated with only some of these schools of thought about probability; specifically, ones that view probabilities as relative frequencies of repeatable events that can be empirically observed or approximated with theoretical sampling distributions. The method of NHST also uses little previous knowledge other than to assume that H_0 is true. But in no way does NHST represent a consensual view of probability either within or outside the social sciences.

CONTINUED USE OF NHST IS A RESULT OF INERTIA

Several critics have described the continued use of NHST as an empty, ritualized practice, one carried out with little reflection. Education in social science statistics that fails to inform about alternatives may encourage the belief that there is no other way to test hypotheses (F. Schmidt & Hunter, 1997). This belief is unfounded. It is also worth noting that some of the most influential work in psychology, including that of Piaget, Pavlov, and Skinner, was conducted without rejecting null hypotheses (Gigerenzer, 1993). The natural sciences have thrived despite relatively little use of statistical tests.

Others note the general difficulty of changing established methods in science. A familiar, well-entrenched method is like a paradigm, and changing paradigms is not quick or easy (Kuhn, 1996). Such change sometimes awaits the passing of an older generation of scholars and its replacement with younger colleagues who are not as set in their ways. Recall that the adoption of NHST as the standard for hypothesis testing in psychology took about 20 years (see chap. 1, this volume).

IS THERE ANYTHING RIGHT WITH NHST?

The litany of criticisms of NHST reviewed in this chapter raise the question of whether there is anything right about NHST. However, NHST is not without its defenders. Some positive aspects of NHST are enumerated and discussed next.

1. *If NHST does nothing else, it addresses sampling error.* Sampling error is one of the core problems of behavioral research. For all the limitations of *p* values, they are at least derived taking account of sampling error. Accordingly, some behavioral researchers see NHST as addressing an important need and thus may be less like passive followers of tradition than supposed by critics. Any proposed alternative to NHST must deal with the problem of sampling error lest it be seen as irrelevant to the needs of these researchers. Critics of NHST rightly point out that confidence intervals convey more information about sampling error than test statistics and *p* values. They also suggest that excessive preoccupation with statistical tests is one reason why confidence intervals are not reported more often. However, confidence intervals are subject to some of the same kinds of inference errors as NHST. Abelson (1997a) made this point in a lighthearted way by describing the "law

of diffusion of idiocy," which says that every foolish practice of NHST will beget a corresponding practice with confidence intervals. However, just because a confidence interval can be interpreted in some ways like a statistical test does not mean that it must be.

Confidence intervals are not a magical alternative to NHST. However, interval estimation in individual studies and replication together offer a much more scientifically credible way to address sampling error than the use of statistical tests in individual studies. Consider again the data in Table 3.2 for six hypothetical replications. A 95% confidence interval about the observed mean contrast is reported for each replication. Each interval estimates sampling error, but itself is also subject to sampling error. The range of overlap among the six confidence intervals is 2.06 to 5.03. This information is more useful than knowing that a nil hypothesis was rejected in 3/6 studies. F. Schmidt (1996) and others have noted that even if our initial expectations regarding parameters are very wrong, we will eventually discover our error by plotting the related confidence intervals across studies.

2. *Misinterpretations of NHST are not the fault of the method.* Defenders of NHST generally acknowledge widespread misinterpretations. They also note that such misunderstandings are the responsibility of those who use it (Krantz, 1999). Critics may counter that any method with so much apparent potential to be misconstrued by so many intelligent and highly educated users must ultimately assume some of the blame.

3. *More careful use of technical terms may avoid unwarranted connotations.* An area of suggested reform concerns the language used to report the results of statistical tests (e.g., D. Robinson & Levin, 1997). For example, some have suggested that the term *significant* should always be qualified by the word *statistically*—which may prompt readers to distinguish between statistical significance and substantive significance (B. Thompson, 1996)—and that exact p values should be reported instead of just whether they are less than or greater than α, such as:

$$t\,(20) = 2.40, \, p = .026$$

instead of

$$t\,(20) = 2.40, \, p < .05$$

The latter recommendation has some problems, however. The possibility that p values are incorrect in many behavioral studies was mentioned earlier, so their reporting to three- or four-decimal accuracy may give a false impression. In large samples, p values are often very low, such as .000012, and reporting such small probabilities may actually encourage misinterpretation. It must also be said that these kinds of suggestions have been made many times over the past 50 years with little apparent impact. Critics would probably feel little conviction that any of the modifications just described would ameliorate the limitations of NHST for most applications in the social sciences. For them, the following expression may be pertinent: You can put candles in a cow pie, but that does not make it a birthday cake.

4. *Some research questions require a dichotomous answer.* The final outcome of NHST is the decision to reject or fail to reject H_0. There are times when the question that motivates the research is also dichotomous, including, for instance, should this intervention program be implemented? Is this drug more effective than placebo? The method of NHST addresses whether observed effects or relations stand out above sampling error, but it is not as useful for estimating the magnitudes of these effects (Chow, 1996). There are also times when theories predict directions of effects but not their specific magnitudes. One reading instruction method may be believed to be more effective than another by some unknown amount, for example. The testing of theories that predict directions but not amounts is also probably more typical in the social sciences than in the natural sciences. However, it is always useful to measure the magnitude of an effect. Indeed, if we cannot think about magnitudes, then we may never get to theories that predict magnitudes instead of just directions. Estimating the average size of an effect with meta-analysis instead of counting the numbers of H_0 rejections is also a better way to synthesize results across a set of studies (chap. 8, this volume).

5. *Nil hypotheses are sometimes appropriate.* The criticism that nil hypotheses are typically false was discussed earlier. As noted by Frick (1995), D. Robinson and Wainer (2002), and others, there are cases when the assumption of a zero effect is justified. For example, there may be no reason in a complex study to predict an effect when just one independent variable is manipulated.

6. *The method of NHST is a gateway to statistical decision (utility) theory.* In this approach—well known in fields such as engineering and environmental studies—probabilities of Type I and Type II errors are weighted by estimated costs of each kind of mistake. The net anticipated gains and losses are then evaluated to make rational decisions about alternative actions in the face of uncertainty. In contrast to NHST, the probability of a Type I error is not arbitrarily set to either .05 or .01 in statistical decision theory. The latter method may be able to detect long-term negative consequences of an intervention even while statistical tests are unable to reject the nil hypothesis of no short-term effect (Johnson, 1999). Statistical decision theory is a very powerful method if it is possible to estimate the costs of different decisions in dollars, life expectancy, or some other quantitative, objective metric. This is not usually possible in behavioral research.

VARIATIONS ON NHST

This section identifies some specialized methods that are modifications of the basic NHST model. These methods may avoid some of the problems of traditional statistical tests and can be very useful in the right situation. It is possible to give only brief descriptions, but interested readers can look to the works cited next for more information.

Range Null Hypotheses and Good-Enough Belts

As mentioned, any point null hypothesis is probably false. Serlin (1993) described the specification of H_0 as a range hypothesis that indicates the values of the population parameter considered equivalent and uninteresting. The alternative hypothesis is still a range hypothesis, but it specifies a minimum result based on substantive considerations that is necessary for additional analysis. These ranges for H_0 and H_1 are called *good-enough belts*, which implies that one hypothesis or the other is considered supported within predefined margins. The specification of range null hypotheses in the social sciences is relatively rare—a notable exception is the evaluation of model fit in structural equation modeling (e.g., Kaplan, 2000, chap. 6)—and there is some question whether this approach would make any practical difference (Cortina & Dunlap, 1997).

Equivalence Testing

Equivalence testing is better known in pharmacological research and the environmental and biological sciences. It deals with the problem of establishing equivalence between two groups or conditions. For example, a researcher may wish to determine whether a generic drug can be substituted for a more expensive drug. In traditional NHST, the failure to reject H_0: $\mu_1 = \mu_2$ is not evidence that the drugs are equivalent. In one form of equivalence testing, a single point null hypothesis is replaced by two range subhypotheses. Each subhypothesis expresses a range of $\mu_1 - \mu_2$ values that corresponds to substantive mean differences. For example, the pair of subhypotheses

$$H_0: \begin{cases} H_{0_1}: (\mu_1 - \mu_2) < -10.00 \\ H_{0_2}: (\mu_1 - \mu_2) > 10.00 \end{cases}$$

says that the population means cannot be considered equivalent if the absolute value of their difference is greater than 10.00. The complementary interval for this example is the equivalence hypothesis

$$-10.00 \leq (\mu_1 - \mu_2) \leq 10.00$$

which is a good-enough belt for the equivalence hypothesis. Standard statistical tests are used to contrast the observed mean difference against each of these one-sided null hypotheses for a directional alternative hypothesis. Only if *both* range subhypotheses are rejected at the same level of α can the compound null hypothesis of nonequivalence be rejected. The same decision can also be reached on the basis of a confidence interval around the observed mean difference. In the approach just outlined, Type I error is the probability of declaring two populations or conditions to be equivalent when in truth they are not. In a drug study, this risk is the patient's (consumer's) risk. McBride (1999) showed that if Type I error risk is to be the producer's instead of the patient's, the null hypothesis appropriate for this example would be

$$H_0: -10.00 \leq (\mu_1 - \mu_2) \leq 10.00$$

and it would be rejected if either the lower end of a one-sided confidence interval about the observed mean difference is greater than 10.00 or the upper end of a one-sided confidence interval is less than -10.00. Rogers, K. Howard, and Vessey (1993) introduced equivalence testing to social scientists, and P. M. Dixon (1998) described its application in risk assessment.

Inferential Confidence Intervals

Tryon (2001) proposed an integrated approach to testing means for statistical difference, equivalence, or indeterminancy (neither statistically different or equivalent). It is based on *inferential confidence intervals*, which are modified confidence intervals constructed around individual means. The width of an inferential confidence interval is the product of the standard error of the mean (Equation 2.4) and a two-tailed critical t value reduced by a correction factor that equals the ratio of the standard error of the mean difference (Equation 2.8) over the sum of the individual standard errors. Because values of this correction factor range from about .70 to 1.00, widths of inferential confidence intervals are generally narrower than those of standard confidence intervals about the same means.

A statistical difference between two means occurs in this approach when their inferential confidence intervals do not overlap. The probability associated with this statistical difference is the same as that from the standard t test for a nil hypothesis and a nondirectional alternative hypothesis. In other words, this method does not lead to a different conclusion than standard NHST, at least in difference testing. Statistical equivalence is concluded when the *maximum probable difference* between two means is less than an amount considered inconsequential as per an equivalence hypothesis. The maximum probable difference is the difference between the highest upper bound and the lowest lower bound of two inferential confidence intervals. For example, if the 10.00 to 14.00 and 12.00 to 18.00 are the inferential confidence intervals based on two different means, the maximum probable difference is $18.00 - 10.00 = 8.00$. If this difference lies within the range set by the equivalence hypothesis, statistical equivalence is inferred. A contrast neither statistically different or equivalent is indeterminant, and it is not evidence for or against any hypothesis. Tryon claimed that this method is less susceptible to misinterpretation because (a) the null hypothesis is implicit instead of explicit, (b) the model covers tests for both differences and equivalence, and (c) the availability of a third outcome—statistical indeterminancy—may reduce the interpretation of marginally nonsignificant differences as "trends." It remains to be seen whether this approach will have a positive impact.

Three-Valued Logic

Kaiser (1960) may have been one of the first social science authors to suggest substituting *three-valued logic* for the standard two-valued (dichotomous) logic of NHST. Briefly, three-valued logic allows split-tailed alternative hypotheses that permit statistically significant evidence against a substantive hypothesis if the direction of the observed effect is not as predicted. This is basically a simultaneous test of two directional alternative hypotheses, one for and the other against the research hypothesis. The third kind of test is for a standard nondirectional alternative hypothesis. Harris (1997b) provides a very clear, contemporary description of three-valued logic, but notes that it has not been used much.

WHAT DO WE DO NOW? BUILDING A BETTER FUTURE

After considering criticisms of statistical tests, we can choose one of the following courses of action:

1. Do nothing; that is, continue using statistical tests just as we have for the past 50 years.
2. Stop using statistical tests entirely. Stop teaching them in university courses. Effectively ban their use by refusing to publish studies in which they are used. Although this option sounds hypothetical or even radical, some highly respected researchers have called for such a ban (e.g., Hunter, 1997; F. Schmidt, 1996).
3. Chart a course between the two extremes listed, one that calls for varying degrees of use of statistical tests—from none to somewhat more pivotal, depending on the research context, but with strict requirements for their use.

The first option is not acceptable because there are negative implications for the advancement of behavioral research that rule out doing nothing. A ban on statistical tests in psychology journals does not seem imminent in the short term, but the fact that some journals require the reporting of effect sizes is an effective ban on the use of statistical tests by themselves (see chap. 1, this volume). The first two options are thus excluded.

Outlined next are recommendations based on the third option. They are intended as a constructive framework for change. It is assumed that reasonable people could disagree with some of the specifics put forward. Indeed, a lack of consensus has characterized the whole debate about NHST, so no single set of recommendations will satisfy everyone. Even if the reader does not endorse all the points outlined, he or she may at least learn new ways of looking at the controversy about statistical tests or, even better, data, which is the ultimate goal of this book.

The main theme of the recommendations can be summarized like this: The method of NHST may have helped us in psychology and related behavioral sciences through a difficult adolescence during which we struggled to differentiate ourselves from the humanities while at the same time we strived to become more like our primary role model, the natural sciences. However, just as few adults wear the same style of clothes, listen to the same types of music, or have the same values they did as teenagers, behavioral research needs to leave its adolescence behind and grow into new ways of doing things. Arrested development is the only alternative.

Recommendations

Specific suggestions are listed and then discussed afterward:

1. Only in very exploratory research where it is unknown whether effects exist may a primary role for NHST be appropriate.
2. If statistical tests are used, (a) information about power must be reported, and (b) the null hypothesis must be plausible.
3. In any kind of behavioral research, it is not acceptable anymore to describe results solely in terms of NHST outcomes.
4. Drop the word "significant" from our data analysis vocabulary. Use it only in its everyday sense to describe something actually noteworthy or important.
5. It is the researcher's responsibility to report and interpret, whenever possible, effect size estimates and confidence intervals for primary results. This does *not* mean to report effect sizes only for H_0 rejections.
6. It is also the researcher's responsibility to demonstrate the substantive (theoretical, clinical, or practical) significance of the results. Statistical tests are inadequate for this purpose.
7. Replication is the best way to deal with sampling error.
8. Education in statistical methods needs to be reformed, too. The role of NHST should be greatly deemphasized so that more time can be spent showing students how to determine whether a result has substantive significance and how to replicate it.
9. Researchers need more help from their statistical software to compute effect sizes and confidence intervals.

A Primary Role for NHST May Be Suitable Only in Very Exploratory Research

The ability of NHST to address the dichotomous question of whether relations are greater than expected levels of sampling error may be useful in some new research areas. Considering the many limitations of NHST discussed, the period of this usefulness should be brief. Given evidence that an effect exists, the next steps should involve estimation of its magnitude and evaluation of its substantive significance, both of which are beyond the range of what NHST can tell us. More advanced study of the effect may require model-fitting techniques, such as structural equation modeling (e.g., Kline, 1998), hierarchical linear modeling (e.g., Raudenbush & Bryk, 2002), or latent class analysis (e.g., Hagenaars & McCutcheon, 2002), among other techniques that test models instead of just individual hypotheses. It should be the hallmark of a maturing research area that NHST is not the primary inference tool.

Report Power for Any Use of Statistical Tests, and Test Only Plausible Null Hypotheses

The level of power reported should be a priori power, not observed power (see chap. 2, this volume; also Wilkinson & TFSI, 1999). It is especially important to report power if most of the results are negative—that is, there were few H_0 rejections. This is because readers of an empirical study should be able to tell whether the power of the study is so low (e.g., $< .50$) that negative results are expected. Knowing that H_0 was rejected is useful only if that hypothesis is plausible. Also, one minus power is the probability of a Type II error, which can only occur if H_0 is not rejected when there is a real effect. We probably see so few examples of reporting power in the research literature when the results are mainly negative because of bias toward only publishing studies with H_0 rejections. In a less biased literature, however, information about power would be more relevant. Low p values that exaggerate the relative infrequency of the results are expected under implausible null hypotheses. If it is feasible to test only a nil hypotheses but a nil hypothesis is implausible, interpretation of the results of statistical tests should be accordingly modified.

It Is Not Acceptable to Describe Results Only on the Basis of NHST Outcomes

All of the shortcomings of NHST considered provide the rationale for this recommendation. For journal editors and reviewers, NHST outcomes should also not be the primary consideration for deciding whether to accept or reject submissions for publication.

Stop Using the Word "Significant" in Connection With NHST

In hindsight, the choice of the word "significant" to describe the event $p < \alpha$ was very poor. Although statisticians understand that significant in NHST does *not* imply a large or important effect, the use of this word may foster false beliefs among nonstatisticians. Accordingly, we in the behavioral sciences should "give" this word back to the general public and use it only as does everyone else—to denote importance, meaningfulness, or substantialness. Use of just the word "statistical" when H_0 is rejected should suffice. For instance, rejection of the hypothesis H_0: $\rho = 0$ could be described as evidence for a statistical association or correlation between the variables, and rejection of the hypothesis H_0: $\mu_1 = \mu_2$ could be described as evidence for a statistical mean difference (Tryon, 2001). Calling an effect statistical implies that it was observed, but not also noteworthy. Of course, statistical effects may also be meaningful effects, but this is a not a question for NHST. The simple phrasing just suggested also seems preferable to the expression "statistically reliable" to describe H_0 rejections. This is because one connotation of reliable is repeatable, but p values say nothing directly about the chances of replication. At the very least, if the word significant is used in an oral or written interpretation of the results, it should *always* be preceded by the qualifier "statistical" (B. Thompson, 1996).

Whenever Possible, Researchers Should Be Obliged to Report and Interpret Effect Sizes and Confidence Intervals

That increasing numbers of journals require effect size estimates supports this recommendation (see chap. 1, this volume). Reporting confidence intervals for effect size estimates is even better: Not only does the width of the confidence interval directly indicate the amount of sampling error associated with an observed effect size, it also estimates a range of effect sizes in the population that may have given rise to the observed result. However, it is recognized that it is not always possible to compute effect sizes in certain kinds of complex designs or construct confidence intervals based on some types of statistics. However, effect size can be estimated and confidence intervals can be reported in most behavioral studies.

Researchers Should Also Be Obliged to Demonstrate the Substantive Significance of Their Results

Null hypothesis rejections do not imply substantive significance. Thus, researchers need other frames of reference to explain to their audiences why the results are interesting or important. A quick example illustrates this idea. In a hypothetical study titled "Smiling and Touching Behaviors of Adolescents in Fast Food Restaurants," effects were statistically significant, but might not be deemed substantively important to many of us, especially if we are not adolescents, or do not frequent fast food restaurants. It is not easy to demonstrate substantive significance, and certainly much more difficult than using p values as the coin of the social scientific realm. Estimation of effect size gives a starting point for determining substantive significance; so does consulting meta-analytic works in the area (if they exist). It is even better for researchers to use their domain knowledge to inform the use of the methods just mentioned (Kirk, 1996). These ideas are elaborated in the next chapter.

Replication Is the Best Way to Deal With Sampling Error

The rationale for this recommendation is also obvious. It would make a very strong statement if journals or granting agencies required replication. This would increase the demands on the researcher and result in fewer published studies. The quality of what would be published might improve, however. A requirement for replication would also filter out some of the fad social science research topics that bloom for a short time but then quickly disappear. Such a requirement could be relaxed for original results with the potential for a large impact in their field, but the need to replicate studies with unexpected or surprising results is even greater (D. Robinson & Levin, 1997).

Education in Statistical Methods Should Be Much Less NHST-Centric and More Concerned With Replication and Determining Substantive Significance

The method of NHST is often presented as the pinnacle in many introductory statistics courses. This situation is reinforced by the virtually monolithic, NHST-based presentation in many undergraduate-level statistics textbooks. Graduate courses often do little more than inform students about additional NHST methods and strategies for their use (Aiken et al., 1990). The situation is little better in undergraduate psychology programs, which emphasize traditional approaches to analysis (i.e., statistical tests) and have not generally kept pace with changes in the field (Frederich, Buday, & Kerr, 2000). It is also true that many statistics textbooks still do not emphasize methods beyond traditional statistical tests, such as effect size (e.g., R. Capraro & M. Capraro, 2002).

Some topics already taught in introductory courses should be given more prominence. Many effect size indexes are nothing more than correlations, proportions of standard deviations, or percentages of scores that fall at certain points. These are all basic kinds of statistics covered in many introductory courses. However, their potential application outside classical descriptive or inferential statistics is often unexplained. For example, students usually learn about the t test for comparing independent means. These same students often do not know about the point-biserial correlation, r_{pb}. In a two-sample design, r_{pb} is the correlation between a dichotomous independent variable (group membership) and a quantitative dependent variable. It is easily derived from the t test and is just a special case of the Pearson correlation r.

Less emphasis on NHST may also encourage students to choose simpler methods of data analysis (e.g., Wilkinson et al., 1999). Doing so may help them appreciate that NHST is *not* necessary to detect meaningful or noteworthy effects, which should be obvious to visual inspection of relatively simple kinds of statistics or graphical displays (J. Cohen, 1994). The description of results at a level closer to the data may also help students develop better communication skills. This is important for students who later take up careers where they must explain the implications of their results to policy makers (McCartney & R. Rosenthal, 2000).

We also need better integration between courses in research methods and statistics. In many undergraduate programs, these subjects are taught in separate courses, and there may be little connection between the two. The consequence is that students learn about data analysis methods without getting a good sense of their potential applications. This may be an apt time to rethink the partition of the teaching of research skills into separate statistics and methods courses.

Statistical Software Should Be Better at Computing Effect Sizes and Confidence Intervals

Most general statistical software programs are still very NHST-centric. That more of them now optionally print at least some kinds of effect size indexes is encouraging. Considering these discussions, however, perhaps results of statistical tests should be the optional output. Literally dozens of effect size indexes are available (e.g., Kirk, 1996), and at least some of the more widely used indexes should be available in computer program output for every analytical choice. It should also be the case that for a given analytical choice, several different effect sizes are options. Many contemporary general statistical programs also optionally print confidence intervals for population means or regression coefficients, but they should also give confidence intervals for population effect sizes. It was mentioned that special computational methods required for exact confidence intervals for effect sizes have only recently become more widely available, but one hopes that these algorithms will soon be incorporated into general statistical packages.

CONCLUSION

Statistical tests have been like a collective Rorschach inkblot test for the social sciences: What we see in them has had more to do with wish fulfillment than what is really there. This collective magical thinking has impeded the development of psychology (and related areas) as a cumulative science. There is also a mismatch between the characteristics of many behavioral studies and what is required for results of statistical tests to be accurate. That is, if we routinely specified plausible null hypotheses, studied random samples, checked distributional assumptions, estimated power, and understood the correct meaning of p values, there would be no problem with statistical tests as our primary inference tool. *None* of these conditions are generally true in the behavioral sciences. I offered several suggestions in this chapter, all of which involve a much smaller role—including none whatsoever—for traditional statistical tests. Some of these suggestions include the computation of effect sizes and confidence intervals for all effects of interest, not just ones in which a null hypothesis is rejected, and evaluation of the substantive significance of results, not just their statistical significance. Replication is the most important reform of all.

RECOMMENDED READINGS

Cohen, J. (1994). The earth is round ($p < .05$). *American Psychologist, 49*, 997–1003.

Nickerson, R. S. (2000). Null hypothesis significance testing: A review of an old and continuing controversy. *Psychological Methods, 5*, 241–301.

Schmidt, F. L., & Hunter, J. E. (1997). Eight common but false objections to the discontinuation of significance testing in the analysis of research data. In L. L. Harlow, S. A. Mulaik, & J. H. Steiger (Eds.), *What if there were no significance tests?* (pp. 37–64). Mahwah, NJ: Erlbaum.

II
EFFECT SIZE ESTIMATION IN COMPARATIVE STUDIES

4

PARAMETRIC EFFECT SIZE INDEXES

Statistical significance is the least interesting thing about the results. You should describe the results in terms of measures of magnitude—not just, does a treatment affect people, but how much does it affect them.
—Gene V. Glass (quoted in Hunt, 1997, pp. 29–30)

This chapter introduces effect size estimation in comparative studies with continuous outcome variables. It also reviews conceptual issues and potential limitations of effect size estimation in general. Research designs considered in this chapter compare only two independent or dependent samples. Readers more interested in methods for independent samples can skip the sections about dependent samples without difficulty. Supplemental readings about effect size estimation in two-group multivariate designs plus exercises with answers for this chapter are available on the Web site for this book.

CONTEXTS FOR EFFECT SIZE ESTIMATION

There are five main contexts for effect size estimation. The first is when units of the outcome variable are arbitrary rather than meaningful. Examples of meaningful scales include salaries in dollars, athletic performance in seconds, and survival time in years. The substantive (theoretical, clinical, or practical) significance of group differences on variables with meaningful scales is usually more apparent than when the scale is arbitrary. An example of an arbitrary scale is the total score on a checklist of true–false items. Because item responses can be coded using any two different numbers, the total score is arbitrary. Even standard scores for such measures are

95

arbitrary because one score metric can be substituted for another. Standard-ized effect size statistics can be computed to interpret group differences when the scale of the outcome variable is arbitrary.

A second context is the comparison of results across outcomes measured on different scales. Suppose that the same two conditions are compared in two different studies. The outcome variable in each study reflects the same construct, but the standard deviation is 10.00 in the first study and 100.00 in the second. The observed mean contrast—the unstandardized mean difference—is $M_1 - M_2 = 3.00$ in both studies. This result actually represents a larger effect size in the first study than in the second. This is because a mean contrast of 3.00 corresponds to about a third of a standard deviation in the first study (3.00/10.00) but to only 3% of a standard deviation in the second (3.00/100.00). The ratios just given are standardized mean differences, and they express mean contrasts in a common metric, as the proportion of a standard deviation. Standardized mean differences and other standardized effect size indexes provide a common language for comparing results measured on different scales.

A third context is a priori power analysis, which requires specification of the expected population effect size magnitude (see chap. 2, this volume). These estimates are often expressed as population versions of the effect size indexes introduced later. The fourth context is meta-analysis, which typically describes the central tendency and variability of standardized effect sizes across a set of studies. To understand power analysis or meta-analysis, one needs to know how effect size is measured. The fifth context involves statistical tests. The use of both methods together can help resolve two interpretational quandaries that can arise if statistical tests are used alone: Effects of trivial magnitude can lead to rejection of the null hypothesis when the sample size is large, and it may be difficult to reject the null hypothesis in small samples even for large effects (see chap. 2, this volume). The measurement of the magnitude of an effect apart from the influence of sample size distinguishes effect size estimation from statistical tests.

TERMS AND IDEAS ABOUT EFFECT SIZE

Terminology about effect size estimation in the literature is not consis-tent: Different names or symbols for the same effect size index are sometimes used in different sources, and the same name or symbol may be used by different authors to refer to different effect size indexes. For example, the symbol d is used in some sources (including this book) to refer to a generic sample standardized mean difference, but in other sources it refers to a population parameter or to a particular kind of sample standardized mean difference. Indeed, the very term *effect size* is used with somewhat different connotations. These inconsistencies make it difficult for newcomers.

Effect Size Versus Cause Size

Effect size refers to the magnitude of the impact of the independent variable on the dependent variable. It can also be described as the degree of association or covariation between the two. The first description is more applicable in experimental designs, and the second is more suitable for nonexperimental designs. Regardless of the design, effect size is measured on the dependent variable. *Cause size,* on the other hand, refers to the independent variable and specifically to the amount of change in it that produces a given effect on the dependent variable (Abelson, 1997a). If levels of a factor represent drug dosage, for instance, the amount of increase in dosage associated with a certain behavior change is the cause size. The idea of cause size is most relevant when the factor is experimental and its levels quantitative. It also plays a role in deciding whether an effect size that seems small is actually important.

Families of Effect Sizes

There are two broad families of effect size indexes for comparative studies with continuous outcomes, standardized mean differences, and measures of association (Maxwell & Delaney, 1990). R. Rosenthal (1994) described these same two categories as, respectively, the *d* family and the *r* family when we are referring to sample statistics, and Huberty (2002) distinguished them as, respectively, *group difference indexes* and *relationship indexes.* Both families of indexes are *metric-free effect sizes* that can be used to compare results across different studies or variables measured in different units (B. Thompson, 2002b).

The population parameter estimated by a sample standardized mean difference is

$$\delta = \frac{\mu_1 - \mu_2}{\sigma^*} \tag{4.1}$$

where the numerator is the population mean contrast and the denominator is a population standard deviation. There is more than one possible population standard deviation for a comparative study. For example, σ^* could be the standard deviation in just one of the populations (e.g., $\sigma^* = \sigma_1$) or under the homogeneity of variance assumption it could be the common population standard deviation (i.e., $\sigma^* = \sigma_1 = \sigma_2 = \sigma$).

The form of a generic sample standardized mean difference is

$$d = \frac{M_1 - M_2}{\hat{\sigma}^*} \qquad (4.2)$$

where the numerator is the observed mean contrast and the denominator—also known as the *standardizer*—is an estimator of σ^* that is not the same in all kinds of d statistics. This is because there is more than one population standard deviation that can be estimated. In other words, specific types of d statistics differ in their standardizers, and a standardizer estimates a particular population standard deviation. To understand what a specific type of d statistic measures, one needs to know which population standard deviation its standardizer approximates.

Putting aside for now the issue of how standardizers for specific kinds of d statistics are calculated, the basic interpretation of d is straightforward: If $d = .50$, for example, then M_1 is half a standard deviation higher than M_2. The sign of d is arbitrary because the direction of the subtraction between the means is arbitrary. Always indicate the meaning of its sign when reporting d; also explain how its standardizer was derived. This need arises because of the absence of universal names and symbols for d. Note that d can exceed 1.00 in absolute value. For example, $d = 4.00$ says that the mean contrast is four standard deviations large. However, it is relatively rare in behavioral studies to find mean differences so large.

Presented in the top part of Table 4.1 are the results of two hypothetical studies in which the same group contrast is measured on variables with different scales. The unstandardized mean difference is larger in the first study (75.00) than in the second (11.25), but the estimated population standard deviation is greater in the first study (100.00) than in the second (15.00). Because $d_1 = d_2 = .75$, we conclude equal effect size magnitudes in standard deviation units. Reported in the bottom part of the table are results of two other hypothetical studies with the same unstandardized mean difference, 75.00. Because the standard deviation in the third study (500.00) is greater than in the fourth (50.00), we conclude unequal effect sizes because $d_3 = .15$ and $d_4 = 1.50$. Specifically, the mean difference in the third study is one tenth the magnitude of that in the fourth study in standard deviation units.

A *measure of association* describes the amount of the covariation between the independent and dependent variables. It is expressed in an unsquared metric or a squared metric. (The metric of d is unsquared.) An unsquared measure of association is typically a sample correlation. For instance, the Pearson correlation r indicates the observed strength of the relation between two continuous variables, and the square of r (r^2) is the

TABLE 4.1

Standardized Mean Differences for Two Different Sets of Hypothetical
Group Contrasts

Study	$M_1 - M_2$	$\hat{\sigma}^*$	d
	Different mean contrasts, same effect size		
1	75.00	100.00	.75
2	11.25	15.00	.75
	Same mean contrast, different effect sizes		
3	75.00	500.00	.15
4	75.00	50.00	1.50

proportion of explained (shared) variance. The latter estimates the parameter ρ^2. A sample measure of association for a comparative study where two independent samples (e.g., treatment and control) are compared on a continuous outcome is the point-biserial correlation r_{pb}. (This coefficient is described later.) This statistic is a special case of the Pearson r, which is in turn a special case of the sample multiple correlation R. The latter can be calculated when there are two or more independent or dependent samples (see chap. 2, this volume).

In comparative studies in which the analysis of variance (ANOVA) is used, the square of R (R^2) is often called the *correlation ratio* or estimated eta-squared ($\hat{\eta}^2$). The symbol $\hat{\eta}^2$ is used below instead of R^2, but do not forget that $\hat{\eta}^2$ is just a squared sample correlation. The parameter estimated by $\hat{\eta}^2$ is η^2, the proportion of total population variance accounted for by an effect of interest when all factors are fixed. The general form of η^2 is

$$\eta^2 = \frac{\sigma^2_{effect}}{\sigma^2_{tot}} \tag{4.3}$$

where the denominator is the variance of the dependent variable computed about the population grand mean and the numerator is the variance due to the effect of interest.

Because of *capitalization on chance*, the statistic $\hat{\eta}^2$ is a positively biased estimator of η^2, which means that the expected (average) value of $\hat{\eta}^2$ is greater than that of η^2. When a sample correlation or squared correlation such as $\hat{\eta}^2$ is calculated, its value reflects all possible predictive power. In doing so, it takes advantage of variability that may be idiosyncratic in the sample. This is a greater problem when the sample size is small. There are numerous methods for comparative studies that generate corrected estimates of η^2 that are generally functions of $\hat{\eta}^2$, the number of conditions or their variances, and group size. Two bias-adjusted estimators from the ANOVA literature for designs with fixed factors are estimated omega-squared ($\hat{\omega}^2$) and estimated epsilon-squared ($\hat{\varepsilon}^2$). Please note that some sources use the symbols η^2, ω^2, and ε^2 to refer to sample statistics. This is potentially confusing because lowercase Greek letters without the hat symbol (^) usually refer to population parameters (e.g., μ, σ). It is generally true for the same data that $\hat{\eta}^2 > \hat{\varepsilon}^2 > \hat{\omega}^2$, but their values converge in large samples. Many other corrected estimates of ρ^2 are described in the regression literature. Some of these shrinkage-corrected squared multiple correlations ($\hat{R}^2$) adjust for bias not only in the present sample but also in future, hypothetical replications.

Unfortunately, different methods for adjusting squared sample correlations for bias do not all yield identical estimates of the population proportion of explained variance for the same data. There is also limited consensus about which method is best for a particular case. Bias corrections are also unnecessary in large samples. For all these reasons, adjusted estimates of η^2 or ρ^2 are not covered in great detail in this book. An exception is made for $\hat{\omega}^2$, which next to $\hat{\eta}^2$ is one of the most commonly reported measures of association in comparative studies where ANOVA is used and the factors are fixed. It is introduced in chapter 6. See Olejnik and Algina (2000) and Snyder and Lawson (1993) for more information about bias-adjusted estimates of η^2 or ρ^2.

A squared sample correlation such as $\hat{\eta}^2$ is in a squared metric, and it tells us the observed proportion of explained variance. A measure of association in a squared metric is also called a *variance-accounted-for effect size*. Unless a correlation is zero, its square is less than its original (unsquared) absolute value. For example, if $r = .20$, then $r^2 = .20^2 = .04$. Because squared correlations can make some effects look smaller than they really are in terms of their substantive significance, some methodologists prefer unsquared correlations (e.g., R. Rosenthal et al., 2000). For example, it may not seem impressive to explain only 4% of the variance, but an effect so "small" in a squared metric can actually be important. Hunter and F. Schmidt (1990) and R. Rosenthal (1994) described several examples in medicine, education, and other areas where potentially valuable findings may have been overlooked because of misinterpretation of variance-accounted-for effect sizes. Some statistical properties of measures of association are easier to understand by referring to a squared metric, however.

Kirk (1996) described a category of miscellaneous effect size indexes that include some statistics not described in this book, including the binomial effect size display and the counternull value of an effect size; see R. Rosenthal et al. (2000) for more information.

LEVELS OF ANALYSIS

The *d* and *r* families of indexes describe effect size at the group level. As a consequence, they do not directly reflect the status of individual cases, and there are times when effects at the group level do not tell the whole story. However, it is possible to evaluate group differences at the case level. This type of analysis involves comparison of the proportions of scores in different groups that fall above or below certain reference points. These proportions may be observed or predicted, and the reference points may be relative, such as the median of one group, or more absolute, such as a cutting score on an admissions test. Huberty (2002) referred to these statistics as *group overlap indexes*, and they are usually appropriate for communication with audiences who are not researchers. In contrast, one needs to know something about at least descriptive statistics to understand standardized mean differences or correlations. There is an old saying that goes, "The more you know, the more simply you should speak." Case-level analysis can help a researcher do just that for general audiences.

STANDARDIZED MEAN DIFFERENCES

This section introduces particular standardized mean differences for comparing independent or dependent means. It also deals with interval estimation for standardized mean differences.

Two Independent Samples

Two different specific kinds of sample standardized mean differences for univariate group mean contrasts are described, Hedges's *g* and Glass's Δ. For reasons given, *g* may be the most generally useful.

The population parameter estimated by *g* is $\delta = (\mu_1 - \mu_2)/\sigma$, where the denominator is the common population standard deviation; that is, it is assumed that $\sigma_1 = \sigma_2 = \sigma$. The equation for *g* is

$$g = \frac{M_1 - M_2}{s_p} \tag{4.4}$$

where the standardizer is the square root of the pooled within-groups variance, s_p^2. The latter is an unbiased estimator of σ^2 and assumes homogeneity of population variance. Its equation is

$$s_p^2 = \frac{SS_W}{df_W} = \frac{(n_1 - 1)\, s_1^2 + (n_2 - 1)\, s_2^2}{n_1 + n_2 - 2} \qquad (4.5)$$

where SS_W and df_W are, respectively, the total within-groups sums of squares and degrees of freedom, n_1 and n_2 are the group sizes, and s_1^2 and s_2^2 are the group variances.

Another way to compute g requires only the group sizes and the value of the independent samples t statistic for a nil hypothesis (see Equation 2.25):

$$g = t\sqrt{\frac{1}{n_1} + \frac{1}{n_2}} \qquad (4.6)$$

This equation is handy when working with secondary sources that do not report sufficient group descriptive statistics to use Equations 4.4 and 4.5. Solving Equation 4.6 for t represents this test statistic as the product of g, a standardized effect size index, and a function of sample size (see chap. 2, this volume). It is also possible to transform the correlation r_{pb} to g for the same data:

$$g = r_{pb}^2 \sqrt{\left(\frac{df_W}{1 - r_{pb}^2}\right)\left(\frac{1}{n_1} + \frac{1}{n_2}\right)} \qquad (4.7)$$

Hedges's g is a positively biased estimator of δ. However, the magnitude of this bias is slight unless the group size is quite small, such as $n < 20$. Hedges (1982) gave the following approximate unbiased estimator of δ:

$$\hat{\delta} = \left(1 - \frac{3}{4df_W - 1}\right)g \qquad (4.8)$$

where the expression in parentheses in Equation 4.8 is a correction factor applied to g. For $n = 10$, for example, the correction factor equals .9578, but for $n = 20$ it is .9801. For even larger group sizes, the correction factor is close to 1.0, which implies little adjustment for bias.

Before we can go further, we must deal with a notational problem about sample standardized mean differences. Many people use the term Cohen's d to refer to Hedges's g or other sample standardized mean differences. This association is probably based on J. Cohen's (1988) book about power analysis, but it is technically incorrect. This is because the symbol d in J. Cohen's book refers to δ, the population standardized mean difference, whereas the symbol d_s in the same work refers to the statistic g. To make matters even more confusing, some authors such as R. Rosenthal et al. (2000) use the term Cohen's d to refer to the sample statistic $(M_1 - M_2)/S_P$, where the denominator is the square root of SS_W/N. In contrast, the denominator of g is s_P, the square root of SS_W/df_W (see Equation 4.5). Because S_P is generally smaller than s_P for the same data, it is also true that $(M_1 - M_2)/S_P$ is generally larger than $g = (M_1 - M_2)/s_P$ in absolute value. However, values of the two statistics just mentioned are similar except in small samples, and they are asymptotically equal in large samples. For these reasons, we do not consider the statistic $(M_1 - M_2)/S_P$ in later discussions.

The parameter estimated by Glass's Δ is the ratio of the population mean contrast over the standard deviation of just one of the populations, usually that of the control condition. In this case Δ estimates $\delta = (\mu_1 - \mu_2)/\sigma_{control}$, and the equation for Δ is

$$\Delta = \frac{M_1 - M_2}{s_{control}} \tag{4.9}$$

Because the standardizer of Δ comes from only one group, homogeneity of variance is not assumed. Glass's Δ may be preferred over Hedges's g when a treatment is expected to affect both central tendency and variability. Suppose most treated cases improve, others show no change, but some get worse, perhaps because of the treatment itself. Such a pattern may increase the variability of treated cases compared to untreated cases. Glass's Δ based on the control group standard deviation describes in this case the effect of treatment only on central tendency.

Suppose that the two groups do not correspond to treatment versus control and their variances are heterogeneous, such as $s_1^2 = 400.00$ and $s_2^2 = 25.00$. Rather than pool these dissimilar group variances for g, the researcher opts for Δ. Now, which group standard deviation goes in the denominator? The choice is critical because it determines the value of Δ. For example, given $M_1 - M_2 = 5.00$, the two possible results for this example are

$$\Delta_1 = 5.00/400.00^{1/2} = .25$$

and

$$\Delta_2 = 5.00/25.00^{1/2} = 1.00$$

The statistic Δ_2 indicates a mean difference four times larger in standard deviation units than Δ_1. However, both results are equally correct if there are no conceptual grounds to choose one group standard deviation or the other as the standardizer. It would be best in this case to report both possible values of Δ, not just the one that gives the most favorable result.

When the group variances are reasonably similar, g is preferred over Δ. This is because the standardizer of g is based on more information, the

TABLE 4.2
Means and Variances for Two Independent Samples

	Condition	
	1	2
M	13.00	11.00
s^2	7.50	5.00

variances of two groups instead of just one. If the ratio of the largest over the smallest group variance exceeds, say, 4.0, then pooling them makes less sense, so Glass's Δ may be preferred in this case.

Olejnik and Algina (2000) noted that the denominators of g and Δ estimate the full range of variation for experimental factors, but perhaps not for individual-difference factors. Suppose that women and men are compared on a quantitative variable. If there is a gender effect, both the pooled within-groups variance s_P^2 and the separate group variances reflect a partial range of individual differences. The full range is estimated by the total variance $s_T^2 = SS_T/df_T$, where the numerator is the total sum of squares across both genders and the denominator is the total degrees of freedom, $N - 1$. Gender-mean contrasts standardized against s_T would be smaller in absolute value than when the standardizer is s_P for g or the standard deviation of either women or men for Δ, assuming a gender effect. Although it is not common practice to compute standardized mean differences in two-group designs as $(M_1 - M_2)/s_T$, readers should be aware of this option. However, whether denominators of d estimate partial versus full ranges of variability is a crucial problem in factorial designs (chap. 7, this volume).

Table 4.2 presents descriptive statistics for two independent samples, where $M_1 - M_2 = 2.00$ and $s_P^2 = 6.25$. Table 4.3 reports results of the t test and values of the d statistics described previously for the data in Table 4.2 at three different group sizes, $n = 5$, 15, and 30. The t test clearly shows the influence of group size. In contrast, $g = .80$ for all three analyses and is in general invariant to group size, keeping all else constant, including the relative proportion of n_1 to n_2 in unbalanced designs. The approximate unbiased estimator $\hat{\delta}$ is generally less than g, but their values converge as n increases. The two possible values of Δ for these data are $\Delta_1 = .73$ based on $s_1 = 7.50^{1/2} = 2.74$ from the first group and $\Delta_2 = .89$ based on $s_2 = 5.00^{1/2} = 2.24$ from the second group.

Two Dependent Samples

Recall from chapter 2 that the symbols μ_D and M_D are used in this book to refer, respectively, to the population-dependent mean contrast and

TABLE 4.3
Results of the *t* Test and Effect Size Indexes at Three Different Group
Sizes for the Data in Table 4.2

Statistic	Group size (n)		
	5	15	30
t test			
t	1.26	2.19	3.1
df_W	8	28	58
p	.243	.037	.003
Standardized mean differences			
g	.80	.80	.80
$\hat{\delta}$	.72	.78	.79
Δ_1	.73	.73	.73
Δ_2	.89	.89	.89
Point-biserial correlation			
r_{pb}	.41	.38	.38

Note. For all analyses, $M_1 - M_2 = 2.00$ and $s_p^2 = 6.25$, and p values are two-tailed for a nil hypothesis.

a sample estimator of μ_D. Standardized mean differences in correlated designs are also called *standardized mean changes* or *standardized mean gains*. There are two different methods to standardize an observed mean contrast in these designs. The first method does so just as one would in a design with independent samples. For example, one possibility is to calculate Hedges's *g*. This statistic in a correlated design is computed as $g = M_D/s_P$, where the denominator is the pooled within-conditions standard deviation that assumes homogeneity of variance (Equation 4.5). The parameter estimated by *g* in a correlated design is $\delta = \mu_D/\delta$, where the denominator is the common population standard deviation, just as in an independent samples design. However, the homogeneity assumption may not be tenable in a repeated-measures design when treatment is expected to appreciably change the variability among cases from pretest to posttest. A better alternative in this case is Glass's Δ, where the denominator in a correlated design is the standard deviation from the pretest condition, which estimates population variability before treatment. Please note that S. Morris (2000) referred to the statistic just described, M_D/s_1, as Becker's *g* instead of Glass's Δ.

The second method to compute a standardized mean change in a correlated design is to divide M_D by s_D, the standard deviation of the difference scores. This standard deviation takes account of the cross-conditions correlation r_{12} (Equation 2.15), but the standard deviations s_P and s_1 (or s_2) do not. (They actually assume it is zero.) If r_{12} is reasonably high and positive, it can happen that s_D is quite smaller than the other standard deviations just mentioned. This implies that the standardized mean change based on s_D can be quite larger than in absolute value than the standardized mean change based on either s_P or s_1 (or s_2) for the same contrast. The ratio M_D/s_D also estimates a different parameter compared to g and Δ. It is

$$\delta = \frac{\mu_D}{\sigma \sqrt{2(1 - \rho_{12})}} \qquad (4.10)$$

where σ and ρ_{12} are, respectively, the common population standard deviation and cross-conditions correlation. Please note in this equation that the denominator is less than σ when $\rho_{12} > .50$. In contrast, g estimates the parameter μ_D/σ in a correlated design.

A drawback to calculating standardized mean changes in correlated designs as M_D/s_D is that the scale of s_D is that of the difference scores, not the original scores. An example from Cumming and Finch (2001, pp. 569–570) illustrates this problem: A verbal ability test is administered before and after an intervention to the same people. Standard scores on the test are based on the metric where in the general population the mean is 100.00 and the standard deviation is 15.00. The observed standard deviations in the study at both occasions are also 15.00 (i.e., $s_1 = s_2 = s_P = 15.00$). The standard deviation of the difference scores across the two occasions is $s_D = 7.70$, about half that of the original scores. The observed mean change is $M_D = 4.10$ in favor of the intervention. If our natural reference for thinking about scores on the verbal ability measure is their original standard deviation, it makes most sense to report a standardized mean change as 4.10/15.00 = .27 instead of as 4.10/7.70 = .53. This is true even though the latter standardized effect size estimate is about twice as large as the former.

Glass, McGaw, and M. Smith (1981) and others suggested that the choice in correlated designs between a standardizer based on original scores versus difference scores should reflect substantive considerations in the research area. For example, a standardized mean change based on s_D may be preferred in an intrinsically repeated-measures design where the emphasis is on the measurement of change. In contrast, Cortina and Nouri (2000) argued that d should have a common meaning regardless of the design, which implies that the standardizer in correlated designs should be in the metric of the original scores. This advice seems sound for nonintrinsically repeated-measures designs where the same factor could theoretically also be studied with unrelated groups. This is the approach emphasized in this book.

With two exceptions, Equations 4.4 through 4.9 for standardized mean differences in independent samples designs can be used to calculate standardized mean changes in correlated designs. The first exception is Equation 4.6, which generates Hedges's g from the independent samples t statistic. Dunlap, Cortina, Vaslow, and Burke (1996) show that the corresponding equation in a correlated design is

$$g = t \sqrt{\frac{2s_D^2}{n(s_1^2 + s_2^2)}} \qquad (4.11)$$

where the test statistic in Equation 4.11 is the dependent samples t statistic for a nil hypothesis (see Equation 2.26). For the special case where $s_1^2 = s_2^2$, Equation 4.11 reduces to $g = t [2(1 - r_{12})/n]^{1/2}$. The second exception is Equation 4.7, which coverts r_{pb} to g, but r_{pb} is for independent samples. Other kinds of correlation effect sizes for correlated designs are discussed later.

Table 4.4 presents a small data set, where $M_1 - M_2 = 2.00$, $s_P^2 = 6.25$, and $n = 5$. If we assume that scores in each row come either from the same case or from matched cases, then $r_{12} = .735$ and $s_D^2 = 3.50$. The dependent samples t statistic for a nil hypothesis for these data is $t (4) = 2.38$. Hedges's g for these data is

$$g = 2.00/6.25^{1/2} = 2.38 \{[2 (3.50)]/[5 (7.50 + 5.00)]\}^{1/2} = .80$$

which is the same result in Table 4.3 for the independent samples analysis of the same group means and variances for $n = 5$. The standardized mean change based on s_D is $2.00/3.50^{1/2} = 1.07$, which as expected is greater than g for the same contrast.

The following sections deal with interval estimation based on standardized mean differences. The first section covers traditional confidence intervals for δ, and the second section deals with exact confidence intervals for δ. The method of bootstrapping provides an alternative way to obtain confidence intervals based on observed effect sizes (see chap. 9, this volume).

TABLE 4.4
Raw Scores and Descriptive Statistics for Two Samples

	Condition	
	1	2
	9	8
	12	12
	13	11
	15	10
	16	14
M	13.00	11.00
s^2	7.50	5.00

Note. In a dependent samples analysis, $r_{12} = .735$ and $s_D^2 = 3.50$.

Traditional Confidence Intervals for δ

Distributions of d are complex because these statistics estimate the ratio of two different parameters, the population mean contrast and a population standard deviation (Equation 4.1). Therefore, a traditional confidence interval for δ is approximate. The width of a traditional confidence for δ is the product of the appropriate two-tailed critical value of the central test statistic z (i.e., the normal deviate) and an asymptotic standard error. The latter is the estimated standard error of d in a large sample. The general form of a traditional confidence for δ is

$$d \pm s_d \ (z_{2\text{-tail}, \ \alpha}) \tag{4.12}$$

where s_d is the asymptotic standard error of d and $z_{2\text{-tail}, \ \alpha}$ is the positive two-tailed critical value of z at the α level of statistical significance. Table 4.5 lists three equations for asymptotic standard errors of Hedges's g and Glass's Δ. The first two equations in the table assume independent samples, but the third equation for g takes account of the cross-conditions correlation r_{12} when the means are dependent. Two examples of the use of these equations to construct approximate 95% confidence intervals for δ are presented next.

Suppose that $n = 30$ for each of two unrelated samples and $g = .80$ for the observed mean contrast. Using Equation 4.6, we can determine that $t \ (58) = 3.10$ for these data. We estimate the standard error of g with the first equation in Table 4.5 as:

$$s_{g_1} = [.80^2/(2 \times 58) + 60/(30 \times 30)]^{1/2} = .0722^{1/2} = .2687$$

TABLE 4.5
Asymptotic Standard Errors for Standardized Mean Differences

Statistic	Equation
	Means treated as independent
g	$\sqrt{\dfrac{g^2}{2df_W} + \dfrac{N}{n_1 n_2}}$
Δ	$\sqrt{\dfrac{\Delta^2}{2(n_2 - 1)} + \dfrac{N}{n_1 n_2}}$
	Means treated as dependent
g	$\sqrt{\dfrac{g^2}{2(n - 1)} + \dfrac{2(1 - r_{12})}{n}}$

Note. The equation for Δ assumes that s_1 is the standardizer; r_{12} = cross-conditions correlation.

The value of $z_{2\text{-tail, }.05}$ is 1.96, so the approximate 95% confidence interval for δ is

$$.80 \pm .2687 \, (1.96) \qquad \text{or} \qquad .80 \pm 53$$

which defines the interval .27–1.33. Thus, the data are just as consistent with a population effect size as low as $\delta = .27$ as they are with a population effect size as high as $\delta = 1.33$, with 95% confidence. This wide range of imprecision is mainly a result of the relatively small sample size ($N = 60$).

Now let us assume the same group size ($n = 30$) and observed effect size ($g = .80$) but for a correlated design where the cross-conditions correlation is $r_{12} = .75$. We estimate the standard error of g taking account of r_{12} with the last equation in Table 4.5 as:

$$s_{g_2} = \{.80^2/[2(30-1)] + 2(1-.75)/30\}^{1/2} = .0277^{1/2} = .1664$$

As expected, the estimated standard error for $g = .80$ is lower in the correlated design (.1664) than in the design with independent samples (.2687) because of the relatively high value of r_{12} in the former. This also means that the approximate 95% interval for δ in the correlated design:

$$.80 \pm .1664 \, (1.96) \qquad \text{or} \qquad .80 \pm .33$$

which defines the interval .47–1.13, is narrower than the corresponding interval in the independent samples design (.27–1.33) for the same value of g. However, because the group size is not large in this example ($n = 30$), the asymptotic standard errors on which these intervals are based may not be very accurate.

Exact Confidence Intervals for δ

Methods to construct exact confidence intervals for δ when the estimator of effect size is Hedges's g are outlined next, but note that a computer program is needed. Exact confidence intervals for δ are based on noncentral t distributions. Recall that the standard t tests for means are based on central t distributions with a single parameter (df) in which the null hypothesis is assumed to be true. Also recall that a noncentral t distribution has two parameters, df and the noncentrality parameter. This latter quantity is designated as ncp, although it is actually a population parameter.[1] It indicates

---

[1] A real notational problem must be mentioned. The symbol δ is used in this book and many other non-mathematical works to refer to the population standardized mean difference. The same symbol is also used in the mathematical literature for the noncentrality parameter for t and other noncentral test distributions (e.g., Steiger & Fouladi, 1997). For this reason, Cumming and Finch (2001) used the symbol Δ instead of δ to refer to the noncentrality parameter, but the former is used in this book and related works to refer to Glass's standardized mean difference.

the degree to which the null hypothesis is false. If the null hypothesis is true, then $ncp = 0$ and the resulting distribution is a symmetrical central t distribution with the same df. As the null hypothesis becomes increasingly false, ncp departs further from zero. Noncentral t distributions where $ncp > 0$ are positively skewed, and noncentral t distributions where $ncp < 0$ are negatively skewed (see chap. 2, this volume).

Assuming an independent samples design, the value of ncp for noncentral t is related to the population effect size $\delta = (\mu_1 - \mu_2)/\sigma$ and the group sizes as follows:

$$ncp = \delta \sqrt{\frac{n_1 n_2}{n_1 + n_2}} \qquad (4.13)$$

When the null hypothesis is true, $\delta = 0$ and $ncp = 0$; otherwise, $\delta \neq 0$ and ncp has the same sign as δ. Equation 4.13 can be rearranged to express the population effect size as a function of the noncentrality parameter and group size:

$$\delta = ncp \sqrt{\frac{n_1 + n_2}{n_1 n_2}} \qquad (4.14)$$

Steiger and Fouladi (1997) showed that if we can obtain a confidence interval for ncp, then we can also obtain a confidence interval for δ using the confidence interval transformation principle (see chap. 2, this volume). In theory, we first construct a $100 (1 - \alpha)\%$ confidence interval for ncp based on the data. The lower and upper bounds of this interval are in ncp units. Next we convert the lower and upper bounds of the interval for ncp using Equation 4.14 to δ units. The resulting interval is the $100 (1 - \alpha)\%$ confidence interval for δ.

In practice, though, it is not straightforward to construct a confidence interval for ncp, at least not without a computer program. The lower bound of a $100 (1 - \alpha)\%$ confidence interval for ncp, ncp_L, is the value of the noncentrality parameter for the noncentral t distribution in which the observed t statistic (i.e., from the independent samples t test) falls at the $100 (1 - \alpha/2)$th percentile. The upper bound, ncp_U, is the value of the noncentrality parameter for the noncentral t distribution in which the observed t falls at the $100 (\alpha/2)$th percentile. If $\alpha = .05$, for example, then the observed t falls at the 97.5th percentile in the noncentral t distribution where the noncentrality parameter equals ncp_L. The same observed t also falls at the 2.5th percentile in the noncentral t distribution where the noncentrality parameter equals ncp_U. However, we need to find which *partic-*

ular noncentral *t* distributions are most consistent with the data, and it is this problem that can be solved with the right computer program. The use of three different programs to do so is demonstrated next.

Suppose that $n = 30$ for each of two unrelated samples, $g = .80$ and $t (58) = 3.10$. (These are the same data for the first example in the previous section.) J. Steiger's Power Analysis module of STATISTICA (StatSoft Inc., 2003) has a distribution calculator for noncentral t, F, and χ^2 distributions. It is easy to use because of a relatively simple graphical user interface. To get the lower bound of the 95% confidence interval for *ncp* for this example, just enter observed $t = 3.10$, $df = 58$, and cumulative probability = .975 in the appropriate boxes under the parameters heading, click the "delta" radio button under the "compute" heading to specify estimation of the noncentrality parameter, and then click the compute button to the far right. (Delta refers to the noncentrality parameter in this program.) The number 1.04844 will then appear in the box for delta. In other words, the observed statistic 3.10 falls at the 97.5th percentile in the noncentral t distribution, where $df = 58$ and the noncentrality parameter equals 1.04844. The latter is also the lower bound of the 95% confidence interval—that is, $ncp_L = 1.04844$. To get the upper bound of the 95% confidence interval for *ncp*, repeat the previous steps, except enter .025 in the cumulative probability box under the parameters heading. After clicking on the compute button, the number 5.12684 will appear in the delta box. This result says that the observed statistic 3.10 falls at the 2.5th percentile in the noncentral t distribution where $df = 58$ and the noncentrality parameter is 5.12684. The latter is also the upper bound of the 95% confidence interval— that is, $ncp_U = 5.12684$.

The 95% confidence interval for *ncp* for this example is thus 1.04844– 5.12684. Equation 4.14 shows us that multiplying each of these endpoints by the following quantity

$$[(30 + 30)/(30 \times 30)]^{1/2} = .25820$$

converts them to δ units. The resulting interval, .27071–1.32374—or .27– 1.32 at two-decimal accuracy—is the exact 95% confidence interval for δ. Thus, the observed effect size of $g = .80$ is just as consistent with a population effect size as low as $\delta = .27$ as it is with one as high as $\delta = 1.32$, with 95% confidence. This rather wide range of imprecision is a result of the relatively small sample size ($N = 60$). The traditional 95% confidence for δ calculated in the previous section for the same data is .47–1.13. The approximate interval is narrower, but it assumes a large sample.

A second computer tool that is handy for constructing confidence intervals for δ is the SAS noncentrality function TNONCT in the

SAS/STAT program (SAS Institute, 2000). This function returns the value of the noncentrality parameter given the observed t, its df, and a specified percentile in a noncentral t distribution. Some programming in SAS syntax is required, but it is not too difficult for a two-group design. The top part of Table 4.6 presents the SAS syntax for calculation of the lower and upper bounds of exact 95% confidence intervals for ncp and δ using the data from the earlier example. The bottom part of Table 4.6 reports the output from SAS/STAT after running the program listed in the top part of the table. The exact 95% confidence interval for δ calculated by SAS/STAT for the example data, .27071–1.32374, is the same result we calculated earlier using a different computer tool. The SAS syntax in Table 4.6 can be reused by substituting the values in boldface with the appropriate values from a new sample.

Two other computer tools do all the work for you—that is, they directly calculate endpoints of exact confidence intervals in δ units. These programs include the STATISTICA Power Analysis module, which can also calculate noncentral confidence intervals for several different kinds of population

TABLE 4.6
SAS Syntax to Compute an Exact 95% Confidence Interval for δ in Designs With Two Independent Samples and Output

Syntax

```
data noncentral_ci_for_delta;
  /* two-group design */
  /* data */
t=3.10;
df=58;
n1=30;
n2=30;
  /* lower, upper bounds for ncp */
ncp_lower=tnonct(t,df,.975);
ncp_upper=tnonct(t,df,.025);
  /* lower, upper bounds for delta */
delta_lower=ncp_lower*sqrt((n1+n2)/(n1*n2));
delta_upper=ncp_upper*sqrt((n1+n2)/(n1*n2));
output;
run;
proc print;
run;
```

Output

Obs	t	df	n1	n2	ncp_lower	ncp_upper	delta_lower	delta_upper
1	3.1	58	30	30	1.04844	5.12684	0.27071	1.32374

effects sizes, including for δ in one- and two-sample designs. Another program that calculates exact confidence intervals for δ in the same designs is Exploratory Software for Confidence Intervals (ESCI; Cumming, 2002),[2] which runs under Microsoft Excel. The ESCI program is also structured as a tool for teaching concepts about noncentral test statistics, confidence intervals, and meta-analytic thinking. Both programs just mentioned assume that the observed effect size is Hedges's g when there are two unrelated samples. In a correlated design, both programs calculate exact confidence intervals for δ only when the mean contrast is standardized against s_D, the standard deviation of the difference scores. Cumming and Finch (2001) noted that distributions of dependent-mean contrasts standardized against either s_P, the pooled within-groups standard deviation, or against the standard deviation of one of the individual groups are complex and follow neither central nor noncentral t distributions. An approximate confidence interval is needed in this case (see the previous section).

Limitations

Possible limitations of d statistics considered next apply to all designs considered in this book, not just two-sample designs. Heterogeneity of within-conditions variances across studies can limit the value of d as a standardized effect size index. Suppose that $M_1 - M_2 = 5.00$ in two different studies with the same outcome variable. The pooled within-conditions variance in the first study is 625.00 but is only 6.25 in the second. As a consequence, Hedges's g for these two studies reflects the difference in their variances:

$$g_1 = 5.00/625.00^{1/2} = .20$$

and

$$g_2 = 5.00/6.25^{1/2} = 2.00$$

These results indicate a mean difference tenfold standard deviations greater in the second study than in the first, even though both statistics refer to the same mean contrast. In this case, the unstandardized result $M_1 - M_2 = 5.00$ is a better statistic to compare across the two studies than d. This suggestion is also consistent with a preference for unstandardized statistics when comparing results of regression analyses across samples with appreciably unequal variances.

---

[2] A trial version can be downloaded from http://www.latrobe.edu.au/psy/esci/index.html

The relative insensitivity of d statistics to sample size is a potential shortcoming. Suppose that Hedges's $g = 2.00$. According to interpretive conventions discussed later, a group mean difference of this magnitude *may* indicate a "large" difference. However, if we then learn that $n = 5$, we should not get too excited about this result until it is replicated, among other considerations. Other limitations of effect size indexes in general are considered later.

MEASURES OF ASSOCIATION

The r family effect size indexes discussed next assume a fixed factor. In a squared metric they all estimate η^2 with positive bias. Later chapters introduce bias-adjusted measures of association and special indexes for random factors.

Two Independent Samples

The observed strength of the relation between a dichotomous factor and a continuous outcome is measured by the point-biserial correlation, r_{pb}. It can be derived using the standard equation for the Pearson correlation r if group membership is coded as 0 or 1 or any two different numbers. However, it may be more convenient to use one of the methods described next.

A conceptual equation is

$$r_{pb} = \left(\frac{M_1 - M_2}{\sqrt{SS_T/N}}\right) \sqrt{pq} \qquad (4.15)$$

where $(SS_T/N)^{1/2}$ is the standard deviation of the total dataset computed with the sample size in the denominator and p and q are the proportions of cases in each group ($p + q = 1.0$). Note that the expression in Equation 4.15 in parentheses is actually a d statistic, where the standardizer estimates the full range of variability on the outcome variable. It is the multiplication of this d statistic by the standard deviation of the dichotomous factor, $(p\,q)^{1/2}$, that transforms the whole expression to correlation units. The sign of r_{pb} is arbitrary because the direction of the subtraction between the two means is arbitrary. Always indicate the meaning of the sign of r_{pb}.

It may be handier to compute r_{pb} from the independent samples t statistic for a nil hypothesis:

$$r_{pb} = \frac{t}{\sqrt{t^2 + df_W}} \qquad (4.16)$$

The absolute value of r_{pb} can also be derived from the independent samples F test of the mean contrast:

$$|r_{pb}| = \sqrt{\frac{F}{F + df_W}} = \sqrt{\frac{SS_A}{SS_T}} = \hat{\eta} \qquad (4.17)$$

Equation 4.17 shows r_{pb} as a special case of $\hat{\eta}$, which is the square root of the ratio of the between-groups sums of squares, SS_A, over the total sum of squares. (Equation 4.17 also shows that $r_{pb}^2 = \hat{\eta}^2$ in a two-group design.) Unlike r_{pb}, however, $\hat{\eta}$ is an unsigned correlation, so it is insensitive to the direction of the mean difference. It is also possible to convert Hedges's g to r_{pb}:

$$r_{pb} = \frac{g}{\sqrt{g^2 + df_W \, (1/n_1 + 1/n_2)}} \qquad (4.18)$$

Equation 4.18 is useful when a secondary source reports g in a two-sample design but a correlation effect size is desired.

The population parameter estimated by r_{pb}^2 is η^2, which for a design with a single fixed factor A and $a \geq 2$ independent samples takes the form

$$\eta^2 = \frac{\sigma_\mu^2}{\sigma_{tot}^2} = \frac{\sigma_\mu^2}{\sigma_\mu^2 + \sigma_\varepsilon^2} \qquad (4.19)$$

where the numerator is the variance of the population means $\mu_1, \mu_2, ..., \mu_a$ around the grand mean μ, and the denominator is the total variance of all scores around μ. The difference $\sigma_{tot}^2 - \sigma_\mu^2$ equals σ_ε^2, the variance of the scores taken about their respective population means (the within-population variance); it is also the error variance. The parameter η^2 is thus the proportion of total variability that is accounted for by population means. The terms that make up η^2 are *population variance components*, and the whole ratio $\eta^2 = \sigma_\mu^2/\sigma_{tot}^2$ is estimated with positive bias by $\hat{\eta}^2 = SS_A/SS_T$. We will see in later chapters that there are other estimators of the proportion of total explained variance besides $\hat{\eta}^2$ that are adjusted for bias (e.g., $\hat{\omega}^2$) or suitable for designs with random factors.

In some sources it is said that the maximum absolute value of r_{pb} is about .80. However, this is true only if groups were formed by dichotomizing a continuous independent variable (Hunter & Schmidt, 1990). This practice is generally not a good idea—MacCallum, Zhang, Preacher, and Rucker (2002) showed that dichotomizing continuous predictors may lead to inaccurate estimates of their true relation with outcome. However, similar problems can arise when continuous predictors are categorized to form more than just two levels. Quantitative predictors are better analyzed with regression than ANOVA (see chap. 2, this volume). If groups are formed by random assignment or by a characteristic of the cases, absolute values of r_{pb} can approach 1.00.

The correlation r_{pb} is affected by the proportion of cases in one group or the other, p and q. It tends to be highest in balanced designs. As the design becomes more unbalanced, holding all else constant, r_{pb} approaches zero. Suppose that $M_1 - M_2 = 5.00$ and $(SS_T/N)^{1/2} = 10.00$ in each of two different studies. The first study has equal group sizes, or $p_1 = q_1 = .50$. The second study has 90% of its cases in the first group and 10% in the second group, or $p_2 = .90$ and $q_2 = .10$. Using Equation 4.15, we get

$$r_{pb_1} = (5.00/10.00) \, (.50 \times .50)^{1/2} = .50 \, (.50) = .25$$
$$r_{pb_2} = (5.00/10.00) \, (.90 \times .10)^{1/2} = .50 \, (.30) = .15$$

The values of these two point-biserial correlations are different even though the mean contrast and total standard deviation are the same. Thus, r_{pb} may not be directly comparable across studies with dissimilar relative group sizes.

Look back to Table 4.3. The lower part of this table reports the values of r_{pb} for the means and variances in Table 4.2 at three different group sizes, $n = 5, 15,$ and 30. For the smallest group size, $r_{pb} = .41$, but for the larger group sizes, $r_{pb} = .38$. This pattern illustrates a characteristic of r_{pb} and other sample correlations that approach their maximum absolute values in very small samples. In the extreme case where the size of each group is $n = 1$ and the two scores are not equal, $r_{pb} = \pm 1.00$. This happens out of mathematical necessity and is not real evidence for a perfect association. Taking the value of r_{pb} in Table 4.3 for the larger group sizes as the most reasonable, we can say that the correlation between group membership and outcome is .38 and that the former explains about $.38^2 = .144$, or 14.4% of the total observed variance.

Two Dependent Samples

The correlation r_{pb} is for designs with two independent samples. When the samples are dependent, we can instead calculate the correlation coefficient of which r_{pb} is a special case, $\hat{\eta}$. It is derived the same way in correlated designs as in designs with independent samples, $\hat{\eta} = (SS_A/SS_T)^{1/2}$. However, there is concern that $\hat{\eta}$ may not be directly comparable when the same factor is studied in two different designs, one with dependent samples and the other with independent samples (Keppel, 1991). This is because the composition of SS_T is different in the two designs. In an independent samples analysis it is true that

$$SS_T = SS_A + SS_W \qquad (4.20)$$

where SS_W is the sums of squares for the error term of the independent samples F test. In a dependent samples analysis, however, it is the case that

$$SS_T = SS_A + SS_S + SS_{A \times S} \qquad (4.21)$$

where $SS_{A \times S}$ is the sum of squares for the error term of the dependent samples F test assuming a nonadditive model and SS_S is the sum of squares for the subjects effect (see chap. 2, this volume). Comparing Equations 4.20 and 4.21, we can see that SS_T reflects only one systematic effect (A) when the means are independent, but two (A, S) when the means are dependent.

There is a partial correlation effect size for within-subjects designs with a single fixed factor that removes the subjects effect from the total variance. It is

$$\text{partial } \hat{\eta} = \sqrt{\frac{SS_A}{SS_A + SS_{A \times S}}} \qquad (4.22)$$

where the denominator under the radical in Equation 4.22 represents only one systematic effect (A). This denominator can also be expressed as

$$SS_A + SS_{A \times S} = SS_T - SS_S \qquad (4.23)$$

which more clearly shows the removal of the subjects effect from total variance. The parameter estimated by partial $\hat{\eta}^2$ in a single-factor within-subjects design is

$$\text{partial } \eta^2 = \frac{\sigma_\mu^2}{\sigma_\mu^2 + \sigma_\varepsilon^2} \qquad (4.24)$$

where the denominator in Equation 4.24 reflects one source of systematic variance (the population A effect) and error variance. (Compare Equations 4.19 and 4.24.) If the two samples are independent, however, the parameters η^2 and partial η^2 are identical and $\hat{\eta}^2 = $ partial $\hat{\eta}^2$ for the same data.

If the subjects effect in a correlated design is relatively large, then partial $\hat{\eta}$ can be substantially greater than $\hat{\eta}$ for the same contrast. This is not contradictory because the two statistics estimate the correlation between the factor and outcome relative to two different variances, total observed variance ($\hat{\eta}$) versus an adjusted total variance (partial $\hat{\eta}$). These different reference points may pose no real interpretive dilemma in an intrinsically repeated-measures design. Otherwise, it may be $\hat{\eta}$ in a nonintrinsically repeated-measured design that is actually more directly comparable with r_{pb} from a between-subjects design with the same factor and dependent variable.

Please refer back to the small data set in Table 4.4, where $n = 5$, $M_1 - M_2 = 2.00$, and $r_{12} = .735$ in a dependent samples analysis. It is left as an exercise for the reader to conduct the dependent samples ANOVA for these data to confirm the following results:

$$SS_A = 10.00, \ SS_W = 50.00, \ SS_S = 43.00, \ SS_{A \times S} = 7.00, \ \text{and} \ SS_T = 60.00$$

From the information given previously, we compute

$$\hat{\eta} = (10.00/60.00)^{1/2} = .41$$

which says that the correlation between factor A and outcome is .41 and that about $.41^2 = .168$, or 16.8% of the total variance is explained. We also compute from the above sums of squares

$$\text{partial} = \hat{\eta} \ [10.00/(10.00 + 7.00)]^{1/2} = .77$$

which says that the correlation between the factor and outcome is .77 after removing the subjects effect and that about $.77^2 = .593$, or 59.3% of the residual variance is explained. The results for $\hat{\eta}$ and partial $\hat{\eta}$ are so different for these data because most of the within-condition variation is a result of the subjects effect ($SS_W = 50.00$, $SS_S = 43.00$).

Confidence Intervals

There are approximate methods to construct a traditional confidence interval for ρ when the correlation effect size is the Pearson r for two continuous variables. The method that is probably the most widely known is based on the confidence interval transformation principle. It builds confidence intervals around the Fisher's Z transformation of r. Pearson correlations transformed to Fisher Z units tend to be normally distributed. The endpoints of a confidence interval around the Z transformation of r are then converted back to correlation units, and the resulting interval is the approximate confidence interval for ρ. This method is demonstrated in many statistics textbooks (e.g., Glass & K. Hopkins, 1996, pp. 357–358). Another approximate method by Hunter and F. Schmidt (1990) builds an approximate confidence interval for ρ directly in correlation units.

The problem with these approximate methods is that they may not be accurate when the correlation effect size is r_{pb} instead of r. This may be especially true in unbalanced designs. There are more accurate methods described by Fidler and B. Thompson (2001), Smithson (2001), and Steiger and Fouladi (1992) that construct noncentral confidence intervals for η^2 in designs with independent samples and fixed factors when the observed effect size is $\hat{\eta}^2$ (of which r_{pb}^2 is a special case). These intervals are based on noncentral F distributions, which have three parameters in designs with a single fixed factor A and independent samples, df_A, df_W, and the noncentrality parameter. The interpretation of the noncentrality parameter for noncentral F distributions is similar to that for noncentral t distributions. The general method for obtaining an exact confidence interval for η^2 is also similar to that for obtaining an exact confidence interval for δ. First, the confidence interval for the noncentrality parameter of F that is best supported by the data is obtained using a specialized computer program. Assuming the 95% level of confidence, the lower bound of this interval, ncp_L, is the noncentrality parameter of the noncentral F distribution in which the observed F for the contrast falls at the 97.5th percentile. The upper bound, ncp_U, is the noncentrality parameter of the noncentral F distribution in which observed F falls at the 2.5th percentile. The endpoints of the interval ncp_L–ncp_U are then converted to η^2 units. Specifically, the lower bound of the 95% confidence interval for η^2 equals the ratio $ncp_L/(ncp_L + N)$, and the upper bound equals the ratio $ncp_U/(ncp_U + N)$. An example follows.

We will use the same basic data as for the corresponding examples in previous sections. For two unrelated samples in a balanced design, $n = 30$, Hedges's $g = .80$, and $t (58) = 3.10$. Using Equation 4.18 to convert g for these data to a correlation effect size, we get $r_{pb} = \hat{\eta} = .379$, and $\hat{\eta}^2 = .142$. Thus, a group mean difference .80 standard deviations in magnitude corresponds to a variance-accounted-for effect size of about 14.2%. The F (1, 58) statistic for the mean contrast is 9.60, the square of the t statistic. The distribution calculator for noncentral F in the Power Analysis module of STATISTICA was used to obtain the upper and lower bounds of the 95% confidence interval for the noncentrality parameter. The observed F statistic for this example falls at the 97.5th percentile in the noncentral F distribution with the corresponding degrees of freedom and where the noncentrality parameter is 1.09473, and it falls at the 2.5th percentile in the noncentral F distribution where the noncentrality parameter is 26.26713. Thus, the 95% confidence interval for the noncentrality parameter is 1.09473–26.26713. The endpoints of this interval are converted to η^2 units as follows:

$$1.09473/(1.09473 + 60) = .01792$$
$$26.26713/(26.26713 + 60) = .30449$$

The 95% confidence interval for η^2 for this example is .01792–.30449, or .018–.304 at three-decimal accuracy. Therefore, the observed effect size of $\hat{\eta}^2 = .142$ is just as consistent with a population variance-accounted-for

TABLE 4.7
SAS Syntax to Compute an Exact 95% Confidence Interval for η^2 in Designs With Independent Samples and a Single Fixed Factor and Output

Syntax

```
data noncentral_ci_for_eta_squared;
  /* one-way between-subjects design */
  /* data */
F=9.61;
df1=1;
df2=58;
  /* lower, upper bounds for ncp */
ncp_lower=fnonct(F,df1,df2,.975);
ncp_upper=fnonct(F,df1,df2,.025);
  /* lower, upper bounds for rho-squared */
rho_sq_lower=ncp_lower/(ncp_lower+df1+df2+1);
rho_sq_upper=ncp_upper/(ncp_upper+df1+df2+1);
output;
run;
proc print;
run;
```

Output

Obs	F	df1	df2	ncp_ lower	ncp_ upper	rho_sq_ lower	rho_sq_ upper
1	9.61	1	58	1.09794	26.2844	0.017970	0.30463

effect size as low as 1.8% as it is with a population variance-accounted-for effect size as high as 30.4%. The range of imprecision is quite wide because of the relatively small sample size ($N = 60$).

Other computer tools for obtaining noncentral confidence intervals in two-group designs with fixed factors are briefly mentioned. The top part of Table 4.7 presents the SAS syntax that uses the noncentral F function FCONCT to calculate the 95% confidence interval for η^2 with the data from the previous example. The bottom part of the table lists the output from SAS/STAT, which agrees with the results described earlier. The syntax in Table 4.7 can be re-used by substituting the values in boldface with the corresponding values from a new sample. This syntax is also good for calculating confidence intervals for η^2 based on the omnibus effect or for partial η^2 in designs with three or more independent samples and a single fixed factor (chap. 6, this volume).

Noncentral confidence intervals for ρ^2 based on squared-sample multiple correlations (R^2) are calculated by the Power Analysis module of STATISTICA and by the freely available program R2 by Steiger and Fouladi (1992).[3] Both programs anticipate a general regression analysis where a

---

[3] http://www.interchg.ubc.ca/steiger/homepage.htm

continuous criterion is regressed on a set of predictors that are continuous or categorical. However, both programs can also compute confidence intervals for η^2 in comparative studies where the samples are independent. All that is needed is a little modification to program input. Just enter the value of $\hat{\eta}^2$ in dialogs that request the value of R^2, and count each degree of freedom for the effect as a predictor in dialogs that request the number of predictor variables. Suppose that $\hat{\eta}^2 = .20$ in a two-group design. The number of predictor variables is 1 because the group contrast is a single-*df* effect. Smithson (2001)[4] described a freely available script (macro) for computing confidence intervals for η^2 in comparative studies with independent samples and fixed factors that runs under version 10 or higher of SPSS (SPSS, 1999).

There is a paucity of computer tools that calculate confidence intervals for η^2 or partial η^2 in correlated designs. This is mainly because the distributions of effect sizes in such designs tend to be quite complex and may follow neither central nor noncentral test distributions. Although this situation will probably change in the future, for now it is not practically possible to obtain exact confidence intervals based on variance-accounted-for effect sizes in some designs with dependent samples.

Limitations

These remarks concern measures of association in general, not just those for two-sample designs such as r_{pb}. Some potential limitations were mentioned earlier: Correlations can be affected by sample variances and whether the samples are independent versus dependent, the design is balanced versus unbalanced, or the factors are fixed versus random. They also tend to increase in absolute value as more levels of the independent variable are added to the design, such as when four dosages of a drug are studied instead of just two. Thus, values of measures of association are to some extent under the control of the researcher. Study artifacts that may distort sample correlations include attrition of cases, range restriction, categorization of continuous variables, and measurement error (Hunter & F. Schmidt, 1994). The latter means that use of measures with poor psychometric characteristics may result in artificially low observed correlations. Baugh (2002) gave a succinct description of ways to correct correlation effect sizes for measurement error, and B. Thompson (2002a) gave similar information for *d*.

Some researchers see standardized mean differences as potentially less problematic than measures of association. It is true that *d* statistics may depend less on the particular study design, at least when their standardizers are computed the same way across different designs. To be fair, *d* statistics

---

[4]http://www.anu.edu.au/psychology/staff/mike/CIstuff/CI.html

have their own potential problems, and study artifacts like measurement error can distort d, too. Measures of association also have some advantages over d in multifactor designs (chap. 7, this volume). Additional limitations of standardized effect size indexes in general are considered later.

CASE-LEVEL ANALYSES OF GROUP DIFFERENCES

Standardized mean differences and measures of association describe effect size at the group level. The methods outlined next describe effects at the case level with either observed or predicted proportions of scores from two different groups that fall above or below certain reference points. A total of four different case-level analyses are reviewed. The first is based on observed proportions of scores that fall within areas of overlap versus nonoverlap between two frequency distributions, and the second concerns relative observed proportions of scores that fall within the tails (extremes) of the combined frequency distribution. The third analysis generates proportions of scores predicted to fall at various points given the observed mean difference and within-groups variances, and the fourth is based on estimated error rates in the statistical classification of individual cases.

Measures of Overlap

Figure 4.1 presents three pairs of frequency distributions that each illustrate one of J. Cohen's (1988) measures of overlap, U_1, U_2, and U_3. All three distribution pairs in the figure show a higher mean in the second group than in the first, normal distributions, and equal group sizes and variances. The shaded regions in Figure 4.1(a) depict areas where the two distributions do *not* overlap, and U_1 is the proportion of scores across both groups within these areas. The difference $1 - U_1$ is thus the proportion of scores within the area of overlap. If the group mean contrast is zero, then $U_1 = 0$. A mean difference so large that no scores overlap is indicated by $U_1 = 1.00$, so the range of U_1 is 0–1.00. Figure 4.1(b) illustrates U_2, the proportion of scores in the lower group exceeded by the same proportion in the upper group. If the mean difference is zero, $U_2 = .50$ because the two frequency distributions are identical; if $U_2 = 1.00$, all scores in the lower group are exceeded by all scores in the upper group (i.e., $U_1 = 1.00$). The range of U_2 is thus .50–1.00. Figure 4.1(c) represents U_3, the proportion of scores in the lower group exceeded by the typical score in the upper group, usually the median. The U_3 statistic has the same range as U_2, .50–1.00. If $U_3 = .50$, the two distributions are identical; if $U_3 = 1.00$, the means are so different that the typical score in the upper group exceeds all scores in the lower group.

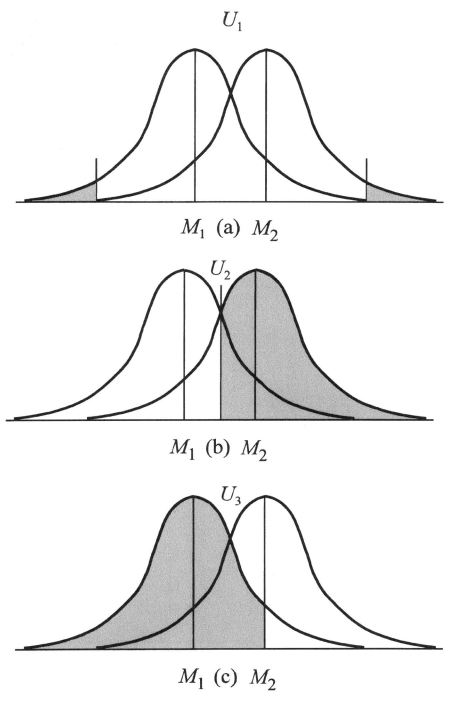

Figure 4.1. J. Cohen's (1988) measures of distribution overlap, U_1, U_2, and U_3.

In actual data sets, U_1, U_2, and U_3 are derived by inspecting frequency distributions. For U_1, count the total number of scores from one group outside the range of the other group and divide this number by N. For U_3, locate the typical score of the upper group in the frequency distribution of the lower group and find the proportion of scores below this point. Computing U_2 is not so straightforward: Unless both frequency distributions have the same shape, interpolation is needed to find the points in both distributions where the proportion of scores in the upper group exceeds the same proportion in the lower group. This can be tedious if done by hand. There is also a potential problem with U_1: If the range of the outcome variable is limited, the proportion of nonoverlapping scores may be zero even if the mean difference is substantial.

It is also possible in graphical displays about group means to give information about overlap at the case level. Wilkinson and the Task Force on Statistical Inference (1999) give a simple example reproduced in Figure 4.2. Panel A shows means for two hypothetical groups in a format often used to show the results of a t test. Panel B adds to the line graphic 95% confidence intervals shown as vertical bars above and below each mean. It also shows individual scores as circles. This representation shows the degree of overlap of the two groups at the case level. There are other graphical techniques for showing both group- and case-level information, including box plots, and stem-and-leaf displays, among other techniques of exploratory data analysis (e.g., Tukey, 1977).

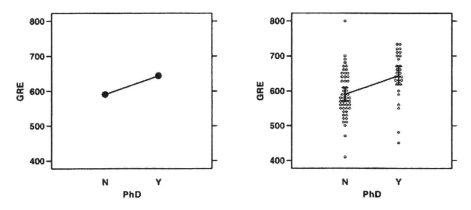

Figure 4.2. A graphical display of group means only (A) versus one that shows means, confidence intervals, and scores for individual cases (B). From "Statistical Methods in Psychology Journals: Guidelines and Explanations," by L. Wilkinson and the Task Force on Statistical Inference, 1999, *American Psychologist, 54,* p. 602. Copyright 1999 by the American Psychological Association. Reprinted with permission.

Tail Ratios

There are two kinds of tail ratios. A *right-tail ratio* (RTR) is the relative proportion of scores from two different groups that fall in the upper extreme of the combined frequency distribution. Likewise, a *left-tail ratio* (LTR) is the relative proportion of scores that fall in the lower extreme of the combined distribution. Because left- and right-tail ratios are computed with the largest portion in their numerators, their values are ≥ 1.0. For example, RTR = 2.00 says that cases from one group are twice as likely to have scores in the right tail of the combined distribution than cases in the other group. Tail ratios have no upper bound, but the higher their value, the more the two distributions differ in the extremes.

Tail ratios are usually computed based on cutting points relative to the mean and standard deviation of the total data set. This mean is the grand mean, M_T, and the total standard deviation is $s_T = (SS_T / df_T)^{1/2}$. Figure 4.3 illustrates a RTR for two normal distributions with the same variance but where $M_2 > M_1$. The cutting point in the figure is $M_T + s_T$, one standard deviation above the grand mean. The symbol p_1 stands for the proportion of scores in the lower distribution that exceed the cutting point, and p_2 is the proportion of scores in the upper distribution above the same point. The RTR for the figure is $p_2/p_1 \geq 1.0$. Right-tail ratios can be calculated relative to other cutting points, such as $M_T + 2 s_T$, or two standard deviations above the grand mean. Left-tail ratios are defined according to cutting points below the grand mean. Although a left-tail ratio is not illustrated in the figure, it would estimate the relative overrepresentation of scores from the lower group in the left-tail of the combined distribution. For symmetrical distributions with equal variances, left- and right-tail ratios are equal for cutting points the same relative distance from the grand mean.

Maccoby and Jacklin (1974) reported the following descriptive statistics for samples of young women (n_W = 3,139) and young men (n_M = 3,028) on a test of verbal ability, respectively:

$$M_W = 103.00, \ s_W^2 = 219.00 \quad \text{and} \quad M_M = 100.00, \ s_M^2 = 202.00$$

The mean of the total data set is

$$M_T = [3{,}139 \ (103.00) + 3{,}028 \ (100.00)] \ /6{,}167 = 101.5270$$

Four-decimal accuracy for the total mean and right-tail ratios is used in computations that follow to avoid excessive rounding error. The total sum of squares is computed as the total of the between-groups sums of squares and the within-groups sums of squares (see Equations 2.29–2.30):

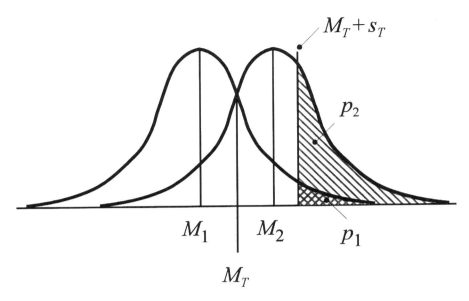

Figure 4.3. The right tail ratio p_2/p_1 relative to a cutting point one standard deviation above the grand mean.

$$SS_T = 3{,}139\ (103.00 - 101.5270)^2 + 3{,}028\ (100.00 - 101.5270)^2$$
$$+ 3{,}138\ (219.00) + 3{,}027\ (202.00)$$
$$= 13{,}871.25 + 1{,}298{,}676.00 = 1{,}312{,}547.25$$

The total standard deviation is

$$s_T = (1{,}312{,}547.25/6{,}166)^{1/2} = 14.59$$

so the cutting point one standard deviation above the mean of the combined distribution is

$$M_T + s_T = 101.53 + 14.59 = 116.12$$

The z equivalents of a score of 116.12 in the separate distributions for young women and young men are, respectively:

$$z_W = (116.12 - 103.00)/219.00^{1/2} = .89$$

and

$$z_M = (116.12 - 100.00)/202.00^{1/2} = 1.13$$

Assuming normal distributions, the proportion of scores to the right of z = .89 for the young women is .1867. A lower proportion of scores are higher than $z = 1.13$ for the young men, .1292. Given these proportions, the right-tail ratio for this example is

$$RTR = .1867/.1292 = 1.45$$

Thus, young women are about 1½ times more likely than young men to have verbal test scores more than one standard deviation above the grand mean; see Feingold (1995) for additional examples. The method described may not give accurate results if the distributions are not reasonably normal. One should instead analyze the frequency distributions of each group to find the exact proportions of scores beyond the cutting point.

Common Language Effect Size

McGraw and Wong's (1992) common language effect size (CL) is the predicted probability that a random score from the upper group exceeds a random score from the lower group. If two frequency distributions are identical, $CL = .50$, which says that it is just as likely that a random score from the upper group exceeds one from the lower group as the opposite. As the two frequency distributions become more distinct, the value of CL increases up to its theoretical maximum of 1.00, which says that any score from the upper group exceeds all scores from the lower group. The range of CL is thus .50–1.00. Derivation of CL is based on theoretical distributions of differences between pairs of random scores from the two groups. This implies that one needs neither the group frequency distributions nor access to the raw data to compute CL.

Suppose that $M_2 > M_1$ for two unrelated groups. The expected average difference between pairs of random scores from the two groups equals the lower mean subtracted from the upper mean, $M_2 - M_1$, and the variance of the differences is the sum of the within-groups variances, $s_1^2 + s_2^2$. If both distributions are normal, the theoretical differences are normally distributed, too. Within this theoretical distribution, one finds the z equivalent of a difference score of zero, which is

$$z_{CL} = \frac{0 - (M_2 - M_1)}{\sqrt{s_1^2 + s_2^2}} \qquad (4.25)$$

Differences between pairs of random scores above the point marked by z_{CL} are all positive, which implies $X_2 > X_1$. Thus, the total proportion of observations to the right of z_{CL} in a normal curve is the probability that a random score from the upper group exceeds one from the lower group.

Let us calculate z_{CL} for the data from Maccoby and Jacklin (1974) described earlier, where $M_W = 103.00$, $s_W^2 = 219.00$, $M_M = 100.00$, and $s_M^2 = 202.00$:

$$z_{CL} = -(103.00 - 100.00)/(219.00 + 202.00)^{1/2} = -3.00/421.00^{1/2} = -.15$$

The proportion of scores to the right of $z = -.15$ in a normal curve is .5596, so CL = .56. Thus, in any random pairing of young people of different gender, the probability that the woman has the higher verbal ability score is .56. See McGraw and Wong (1992) for additional examples.

McGraw and Wong (1992) studied the effects of skew, kurtosis, and heterogeneity of variance on the accuracy of CL values generated by the computational method described earlier. Given moderate skew or kurtosis and within-groups variances that differed by a factor of up to 4.0, they found that the absolute error in CL was generally less than .10. Of course, even more extreme departures from normality or homogeneity of variance may lead to even greater error.

Error Rates in Classification Analysis

Hess, Olejnik, and Huberty (2001) described the application of two different statistical methods that estimate the degree of group overlap through classification analysis. These methods for two-group univariate comparisons are univariate discriminant function analysis (DFA)—also known as predictive discriminant analysis or just discriminant analysis—and logistic regression (LR). Both methods can be extended to compare more than two groups across more than one variable (i.e., they are multivariate methods). It is beyond the scope of this section to describe these methods in detail, but the assumptions of DFA are generally more strict. These include normal distributions and homogeneity of population variances and covariances. See Silva and Stam (1995) and Wright (1995) for more information about DFA and LR.

In both univariate DFA and LR, group membership is considered the criterion and the continuous variable the predictor, which is opposite of their usual status in techniques such as ANOVA. Both methods also optionally include a classification phase in which conditional probabilities of group membership are estimated for every case. These predicted probabilities are based in part on the degree of overlap between the group frequency distributions. Suppose that a particular case is estimated to be more similar to cases in its own group than to those in the other group. The observed and predicted group memberships for this particular case are the same, so the classification is correct. Two groups are perfectly distinct at the case level if the percentage of correct classification across all cases—the *hit rate*—is 100%. Perfect classification also means an error rate of zero. As distribution overlap increases, there will be more and more cases where the observed and predicted group memberships disagree. Maximum overlap between two groups is indicated by a hit rate that is no higher than that expected by chance (random classification).

Huberty and Lowman (2000) described the case-level statistic I that measures *improvement over chance classification*. Its general form is

$$I = \frac{(1 - H_e) - (1 - H_o)}{1 - H_e} = \frac{H_o - H_e}{1 - H_e} \qquad (4.26)$$

where H_o and $1 - H_o$ are, respectively, the observed cross-group hit rate and error rates, and H_e and $1 - H_e$ are, respectively, the corresponding rates expected by chance. That is, I estimates the proportionate reduction in the error rate compared to that of random classification. One definition of H_e given by Huberty and Lowman is the *proportional chance criterion*, which says that the chance hit rate equals the sum of the products of the prior probabilities of the group and their sizes divided by the total number of cases across all groups. *Prior probabilities* are the expected relative sizes of the populations from which the samples were drawn. They are expressed as proportions and sum to 1.0 across the groups. For a two-group design:

$$H_e = \frac{pr_1 n_1 + pr_2 n_2}{N} \qquad (4.27)$$

where pr_1 and pr_2 are the prior probabilities of the two groups. For example, given $pr_1 = .50$, $n_1 = 100$, $pr_2 = .50$, and $n_2 = 75$ and assuming random classification, the expected chance hit rate is

$$H_e = [.50\ (100) + .50\ (75)]/175 = 87.50/175 = .50$$

and the expected chance error rate is also .50. If the observed cross-group classification hit rate is .60, then

$$I = (.60 - .50)/.50 = .20$$

which says that the observed error rate of .40 is 20% less than that expected by random classification. Huberty and Lowman suggested that $I \leq .10$ may indicate a "low" (smaller) effect, whereas $I \geq .35$ may indicate a "high" (larger) effect, both at the case level. Some cautions about guidelines for interpreting qualitative effect size magnitudes are discussed momentarily.

RELATION OF GROUP-LEVEL EFFECT SIZE
TO CASE-LEVEL PROPORTIONS

Under the assumptions of normality, homogeneity of variance, and large and equal group sizes, the case-level proportions described earlier are functions of effect size magnitude at the group level. The first column in Table 4.8 shows selected values of d in the range 0–4.00. (Because Hedges's g and Glass's Δ are asymptotically equal under these assumptions, no distinction is made between them.) Listed in the remaining columns of the table are values of r_{pb} and case-level proportions that correspond to d in each row under the conditions stated earlier. Reading each row of the table gives a case-level perspective on a group mean difference of a particular magnitude. For example, if $d = .50$, the expected value of r_{pb} is .24 (6% explained variance). For the same effect size, we expect at the case level that:

1. About one third of all scores are *not* in the area of overlap between the two frequency distributions ($U_1 = .33$).
2. The upper 60% of the scores in the group with the highest mean exceeds the same proportion in the other group ($U_2 = .60$).
3. The typical score in the upper group is higher than about 70% of the scores in the lower group ($U_3 = .69$).
4. A random score from the upper group will exceed a random score from the other group about 64% of the time (CL = .64).
5. A score from the upper group is a little more than twice as likely to fall more than one standard deviation above the grand mean than a score from the lower group (RTR = 2.17).

However, the relations summarized in Table 4.8 hold only under the assumptions of normality, homogeneity of variance, and a balanced design with large samples. Otherwise it can happen that the group statistics d or r_{pb} tell a different story than case-level proportions. Consider the situation illustrated in Figure 4.4 for two symmetrical distributions. The distributions have the same central tendency, so $d = r_{pb} = 0$. However, the tail ratios are not also generally 1.00. Because the first distribution is more variable than the second, scores from it are overrepresented in both extremes of the combined distribution. If the researcher wants only to compare the central tendencies, this disagreement between the tail ratios and the group statistics d and r_{pb} may not matter. In a selection context where a cutting point is based on the combined distribution, the tail ratios would be of critical interest.

TABLE 4.8
Relation of Selected Values of the Standardized Mean Difference to the
Point-Biserial Correlation and Case-Level Proportions

Group level		Case level				
d	r_{pb}	U_1	U_2	U_3	CL	RTR
0	0	0	.500	.500	.500	1.00
.10	.05	.007	.520	.540	.528	1.16
.20	.10	.148	.540	.579	.556	1.36
.30	.15	.213	.560	.618	.584	1.58
.40	.20	.274	.579	.655	.611	1.85
.50	.24	.330	.599	.691	.638	2.17
.60	.29	.382	.618	.726	.664	2.55
.70	.33	.430	.637	.758	.690	3.01
.80	.37	.474	.655	.788	.714	3.57
.90	.41	.516	.674	.816	.738	4.25
1.00	.45	.554	.691	.841	.760	5.08
1.25	.53	.638	.734	.894	.812	8.14
1.50	.60	.707	.773	.933	.856	13.56
1.75	.66	.764	.809	.960	.892	23.60
2.00	.71	.811	.841	.977	.921	43.04
2.50	.78	.882	.894	.994	.961	—[b]
3.00	.83	.928	.933	.999	.983	—[b]
3.50	.87	.958	.960	—[a]	.993	—[b]
4.00	.89	.977	.977	—[a]	.998	—[b]

Note. CL = common language effect size; RTR = right tail ratio for a cutting point one standard deviation above the grand mean.
[a] > .999.   [b] > 99.99.

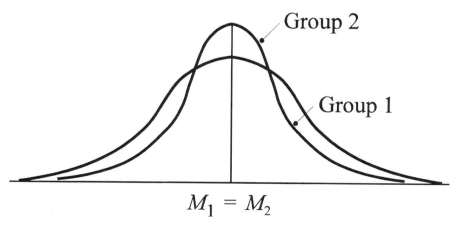

Figure 4.4. Two distributions with the same central tendency but different variances.

INTERPRETIVE GUIDELINES FOR EFFECT SIZE MAGNITUDE AND CAUTIONS

This section provides guidelines for interpreting effect size indexes and also some possible shortcomings of these guidelines. I also consider how to avoid fooling yourself in effect size estimation.

Questions

When researchers first learn about effect size indexes such as d or r_{pb}, some of the questions they ask are, What is a large effect? A small effect? A *substantive* (important) effect? J. Cohen (1988) devised what are probably the best known guidelines for describing qualitative effect size magnitudes that seem to answer the first two questions. The descriptor *medium* in these guidelines corresponds to a subjective average effect size magnitude in the behavioral science literature. The other two descriptors are intended for situations where neither theory nor previous empirical findings differentiate between small versus large effects. These guidelines are also fraught with the potential problems noted by J. Cohen and mentioned later. Table 4.9 presents J. Cohen's interpretive guidelines for absolute values of d and r_{pb} assuming normality, homogeneity of variance, and large and equal group sizes. To summarize,

1. A small-sized mean contrast corresponds to $d = .20$ or $r_{pb} = .10$ (1% explained variance);
2. A medium-sized difference corresponds to $d = .50$ or $r_{pb} = .25$ (6% explained variance); and
3. A large-sized difference corresponds to $d = .80$ or $r_{pb} = .40$ (16% explained variance).

For the sake of comparison, J. Cohen's interpretive guidelines for the Pearson correlation r are also shown in Table 4.9.

Cautions

Cautions about the interpretive guidelines in Table 4.9 are summarized next:

1. These guidelines are not empirically based. This is why J. Cohen encouraged researchers to look first to the empirical literatures in their areas before using them.
2. The descriptors small, medium, and large are not intended to be applied rigidly. For example, it would be silly to refer to $d = .49$ in one study as a small-sized effect but to $d = .51$ in

TABLE 4.9
J. Cohen's Interpretive Guidelines for Standardized Mean Differences and Correlations

Qualitative description	Statistic		
	d	r_{pb}	r
Small	.20	.10	.10
Medium	.50	.25	.30
Large	.80	.40	.50

another study as a medium-sized effect. Rigid thinking about effect-size magnitudes should be avoided.

3. If the group sizes are unequal or the distributions have different shapes, the relation between d and r_{pb} assumed in Table 4.9 may not hold. For example, it is possible to find $d = .50$ and $r_{pb} = .10$ for the same mean contrast. The former corresponds to a medium-sized effect under J. Cohen's guidelines, but the latter corresponds to a small-sized effect. However, both statistics describe the same result.

4. The definitions do not apply across all behavioral research areas. This is because what may be considered a large effect in one area may be modest in another.

5. The definitions in Table 4.9 may be more suitable for nonexperimental studies than experimental studies. Typical effect size magnitudes may be greater in experimental studies because of lower error variance.

6. In more mature research areas, meta-analytic studies offer the most convenient and systematic way to operationally define smaller versus larger effect sizes (chap. 8, this volume). If no meta-analytic studies are available, the researcher may be able to compute effects sizes indexes for published studies. Only in new areas with few published studies may there be little choice other than to use generic interpretive guidelines.

7. The real benefit from reporting standardized effect sizes comes not from comparing them against arbitrary guidelines but instead from comparing effect sizes directly with those reported in previous studies (B. Thompson, 2002b; Wilkinson & TFSI, 1999). This is part of meta-analytic thinking.

What Is a Substantive Effect?

The third question about effect size magnitude listed at the beginning of this section—what is a substantive result?—is probably the toughest.

This is because demonstration of an effect's significance, whether theoretical, practical or clinical, calls for more discipline-specific expertise than the estimation of its magnitude (Kirk, 1996). For example, an effect that could be described as large according to the guidelines in Table 4.9 may not also have substantive significance. For example, the average gender difference in height is about two standard deviations in magnitude ($d = 2.00$). Is this large difference also a substantive one? The answer clearly depends on the research context. In terms of general psychological adjustment, the large gender difference in height is probably irrelevant. In the context of automobile safety, however, the gender difference in height may be critical. Remember a problem with the front air bags in automobiles manufactured before the late 1990s: Their deployment force could injure or kill a small-stature driver or passenger, which presents a greater risk to women. In cars with "intelligent" air bag systems that vary deployment force according to driver weight, a large gender difference in height is less important.

By the same logic, effects gauged to be small according to Table 4.9 are not necessarily unimportant. Prentice and D. T. Miller (1992) described contexts for when small effects may be noteworthy. These include situations where minimal manipulation of the independent variable results in some change in the outcome variable—that is, a small cause size nevertheless produces an observable effect size—or an effect is found for an outcome variable that is theoretically unlikely to be influenced by the factor. It can also happen that effect sizes in early stage research are larger than in later research. This may occur as researchers shift their attention from determining whether an effect exists to study of more subtle mechanisms of the effect at boundary conditions (Fern & Monroe, 1996). Recall the concern that variance-accounted-for effect sizes (measures of association in a squared metric) can make some effects look smaller than they really are in terms of real importance. It is not uncommon for some health-related effects, such as that of taking aspirin daily to reduce the risk of a cardiac condition, to explain only about 2% of the total variance. Some important and beneficial public health policies have been made on the basis of such "weak" effects (Gage, 1978).

In general, effect size magnitudes that are "unimportant" may be ones that fall within the margins of measurement error. Even this general definition does not always hold, however. For example, the difference in vote totals for the two major candidates in the 2000 presidential election in the United States was within the margin of error for vote counting in certain key precincts, but these small differences determined the outcome. In contrast, effect sizes magnitudes that are important should not only stand out from measurement error, they must also have theoretical, practical, or clinical implications given the research context. Unfortunately, just as there is no absolute standard for discriminating between small versus large effects, there is also none for determining whether a particular effect size is important applicable across different research areas. Part of the challenge of a new research area is to develop benchmarks for theoretical or practical significance. An awareness of typical effect size magnitudes in one's research area helps as does an appreciation of the need to examine effects at both the group and case levels.

The idea of clinical significance needs some elaboration. There is a specific set of methods for evaluating clinical significance. As the name suggests, the term *clinical significance* refers to whether an intervention makes a meaningful difference in an applied setting. A related idea is whether, after treatment, a typical afflicted case is indistinguishable from a typical nonafflicted case (P. Kendall & Grove, 1988). Clinical significance can be evaluated at both the group and case levels. There are specific statistical conventions for describing clinical significance at the group level. They involve *criterion contrasts* between two groups that represent a familiar difference on an outcome variable of interest, such as patients with the same illness who have the most severe symptoms versus those with the least severe symptoms or patients who require inpatient treatment versus outpatient treatment (Lipsey & Wilson, 2000). A variation is a *normative contrast* where a clinical group is compared with a nonclinical (normal) group. The magnitude of the difference between the two criterion groups is measured with a standardized mean difference. The numerator of this *criterion contrast effect size* is typically computed by subtracting the mean in the lowest functioning group from the mean in the highest functioning group.

The criterion contrast effect size can be used as a benchmark against which to compare observed effect sizes for a treatment. Suppose that the criterion groups are patients with the same illness who have the least versus most severe symptoms, and the criterion contrast effect size is $d = .80$ before any treatment is given. Some treatment for the illness is evaluated, and the magnitude of the effect of treatment relative to control is $d = .40$. The observed effect size for treatment is one half the magnitude of the criterion contrast effect size, or $.40/.80 = .50$. That is, the treatment effect is equivalent to closing half the gap between the most severe and least severe patients. Please note that a treatment can have clinical significance but not statistical significance or vice versa. See Ogles, M. Lambert, and Masters (1996) for more information about the evaluation of clinical significance.

Kirk (1996) noted that the evaluation of practical significance is ultimately a qualitative judgment. This judgment should be based on the researcher's knowledge of the area, but it will also reflect the researcher's personal values and societal concerns. This is not unscientific because the evaluation of all findings in science involves some degree of subjectivity. It is better to be open about this fact, however, than to base such decisions solely on "objective" statistical tests, which are unsuited to evaluate practical significance. See B. Thompson (2002a) for additional discussion of these issues.

HOW TO FOOL YOURSELF WITH EFFECT SIZE ESTIMATION

Some ways to mislead yourself with effect size estimation were mentioned earlier but are summarized altogether in this section. There are probably other paths to folly, but one hopes the major ones are included below; see Fern and Monroe (1996) and Lenth (2001) for more information:

1. Measure effect size magnitude only at the group level (ignore the case level).
2. Apply generic definitions of effect size magnitude without first looking to the empirical literature in one's area.
3. Believe that an effect size judged as large according to generic interpretive conventions must be an important result and that a small effect is unimportant.
4. Ignore the critical question of how theoretical or practical significance should be gauged in one's research area.
5. Conduct effect size estimation only for results that are statistically significant.
6. Believe that effect size estimation somehow lessens the need for replication.
7. Report values of effect size indexes only as point estimates; that is, forget that effect size indexes are subject to sampling error, too.
8. Forget that effect size for fixed factors is specific to the particular levels selected for study. Also forget that effect size is in part a function of the design of the study.
9. Forget that standardized effect sizes encapsulate other quantities or characteristics, including the unstandardized effect size, error variance, and experimental design. These are all crucial aspects in the planning of the study and must not be overlooked.
10. As a journal editor or reviewer, substitute effect size magnitude for statistical significance as a criterion for whether a work is published.

SOFTWARE FOR EFFECT SIZE ESTIMATION

Many effect size indexes can be computed with a hand calculator given a few descriptive statistics. This is fortunate because software programs for general statistical analyses are still not as helpful as they should be for effect size estimation. There is also a small but growing number of specialized programs designed as tools for effect size estimation. Some of these programs were mentioned earlier, including the Power Analysis module of STATIS-TICA, ESCI, R2, and the Smithson (2001) scripts for SPSS. Another software tool described in more detail in chapter 6 is PSY by Bird, Hadzi-Pavlovic, and Isaac (2000), a freely available program that calculates approximate confidence intervals based on unstandardized or standardized contrasts in factorial designs with continuous outcome variables.[5] Other programs that compute effect sizes are intended for researchers who conduct meta-analyses. These programs often feature the capabilities to estimate, record, document, and organize effect size indexes computed for large numbers of studies. An example of a recent program of this type is Effect Size (ES) by Shadish, Robinson, and Lu (1999).[6] The ES program accepts many different forms of input data and computes for all a common effect size index, d. However, the ES program does not calculate confidence intervals for δ.

RESEARCH EXAMPLES

Examples of effect size estimation at both the group and case levels in three actual empirical studies are presented next. The first two examples concern the comparison of independent groups and the third concerns a repeated-measures design.

Demographic and Referral Status Effects on Teacher Ratings

Data for this example are from Wingenfeld, Lachar, Gruber, and Kline (1998), who collected teacher ratings on the Student Behavior Survey (SBS) within samples of regular education students ($n = 1,173$; 49% boys; 50% younger than 12 years old) and students referred to school or clinical psychologists ($n = 601$; 69% boys; 47% younger than 12 years old). The SBS has 11 primary scales, including four that assess academic strengths and seven that reflect adjustment problems. Wingenfeld et al. estimated the relative magnitudes of gender, age, and referral status effects on SBS scores within and across both samples. Because of relatively large group sizes, virtually all of the t tests had low p values. Wingenfeld et al. instead reported Hedges's g for all contrasts. Results are summarized in Table 4.10 for selected SBS scales.

Overall magnitudes of demographic effects on teacher ratings are about .20 to .30 standard deviations in absolute value. Within both samples,

---

[5] http://www.psy.unsw.edu.au/research/PSY.htm
[6] A trial version can be downloaded from http://www.assess.com/Software/ES.htm

TABLE 4.10
Standardized Mean Differences for Selected Scales on the Student
Behavior Survey by Gender, Age, and Referral Status

| Scale | Contrasts[a] | | | | |
| | Gender | | Age | | Referral status |
	Reg	Ref	Reg	Ref	
Positive adjustment					
Academic Performance	.18	.20	.26	.15	1.46
Academic Habits	.34	.42	−.04	−.06	.92
Social Skills	.32	.46	.06	.06	.73
Poor adjustment					
Health Concerns	.15	.08	−.34	.17	−.41
Social Problems	−.25	−.42	−.17	.02	−.76
Physical Aggression	−.36	−.54	−.36	−.05	−.63
Behavior Problems	−.44	−.13	−.16	.15	−.72

Note. Reg = regular education sample; Ref = referred sample. From "Development of the Teacher–Informant Student Behavior Survey," by S. A. Wingenfeld, D. Lachar, C. P. Gruber, and R. B. Kline, 1998, *Journal of Psychoeducational Assessment, 16,* p. 236. Copyright 1998 by The Psychoeducational Corporation. Reprinted with permission.
[a]Directions of subtraction are $M_{Girls} - M_{Boys}$; $M_{\geq 12\ yrs} - M_{<12\ yrs}$; and $M_{Reg} - M_{Ref}$.

girls have generally higher means than boys on scales that reflect positive classroom adjustment (e.g., $g = .18$ for the Academic Performance scale in the regular education sample) and lower averages on scales that indicate behavior problems (e.g., $g = -.42$ for the Social Problems scale in the referred sample). These results are expected. The magnitudes of age effects tend to be even smaller than those of gender and less consistent. Referral status effects are generally about .70 to .80 standard deviations in magnitude and thus greater than demographic effects. Regular education students have higher means on scales that reflect positive adjustment (e.g., $g = 1.49$ for the Academic Performance scale) and lower averages on scales that measure poor adjustment (e.g., $g = -.72$ for the Behavior Problems scale). Overall, SBS scales are more sensitive to students' referral status than to their demographic characteristics. The practical significance of the group-level differences just described are considered in the test's manual (Lachar, Wingenfeld, Kline, & Gruber, 2000).

Gender Differences in Basic Math Skills

The data set for this example can be downloaded from this book's Web site. At the beginning of an undergraduate course in introductory statistics, I administered to a total of 667 students (M age = 23.3 years, s = 6.6 years; 77% women, 23% men) a 17-item test of basic math skills. Their scores had no bearing on subsequent course grades. The left side of Table

4.11 presents descriptive statistics by gender for the number of items correct. The right side lists effect size indexes and case-level proportions for the gender contrast. The men performed somewhat better (M = 11.49, or 67.6% correct) than the women (M = 10.37, or 61.0% correct). The mean difference is .36 standard deviations in magnitude, and the exact 95% confidence interval for δ is .18–.55. The observed gender difference measured by g is just as consistent with a population effect size as low as two-tenths of a standard deviation in magnitude as it is with a population effect size as high as about half a standard deviation in magnitude, with 95% confidence. The correlation between gender and test scores is .15, and the proportion of total explained variance is .02 with the exact 95% confidence interval for η^2 of .01–.05. The observed effect size measured by $\hat{\eta}^2$ is thus just as consistent with a population percentage of explained variance as low as 1% as it is with a population percentage of explained variance as high as 5%, with 95% confidence. These effect size magnitudes at the group level are consistent with other findings of gender differences in quantitative skills (e.g., Hyde, Fennema, & Lamon, 1990).

The case-level proportions in Table 4.11 except CL and I were computed from the frequency distributions presented in Table 4.12 by gender. (Readers should verify these results using interpolation.) The median score for men of 11.98 exceeds about 70% of all scores for women (U_3 = .69), and in about 60% of random pairings of men and women, the man is expected to have the higher score (CL = .60). Men are also about ⅓ times more likely than women to have a score more than one standard deviation above the grand mean (RTR = 1.35). Results of a univariate DFA where the math skills test is the predictor indicate an overall correct classification rate of 54.7%. A total of 103/153 men (67.3%) were correctly classified, but only 262/514 women (51.0%) were so classified. Assuming equal prior probabilities of men and women, the proportionate reduction in the error rate compared to chance classification is $I = (.547 - .50)/.50 = .094$, or 9.4%.

TABLE 4.11

Descriptive Statistics and Effect Size Indexes for the Gender Contrast on a Test of Basic Math Skills

| | | | | | | Effect size | | | | |
| | | | | | | Group level | | Case level | | |
Group	n	M	s^2	Mdn	t (665)	g	r_{pb}	U_3	CL	RTR	I
Men	153	11.49	8.57	11.98	3.95[a]	.36[b]	.15[c]	.69	.60	1.35	.094
Women	514	10.37	10.21	10.43							

Note. CL = common language effect size; RTR = right tail ratio for the cutting point 13.80, which is one standard deviation above the mean of the combined distribution; I = improvement over chance classification.
[a]$p < .001$.   [b]Exact 95% confidence interval for δ is .18–.55.   [c]Exact confidence interval for η^2 is .01–.05.

TABLE 4.12
Frequency Distributions of Math Test Scores for Men and Women

	Men		Women	
Score	f	%	f	%
17	2	100.0	6	100.0
16	6	98.7	20	98.8
15	16	94.6	31	94.9
14	14	84.3	38	88.9
13	32	75.2	39	81.5
12	32	60.8	50	73.9
11	11	39.9	68	73.9
10	15	32.7	65	51.0
9	11	22.9	57	38.3
8	5	15.7	47	27.2
7	5	12.4	32	18.1
6	9	9.2	26	11.9
5	3	3.3	12	6.8
4	2	1.3	15	4.5
3	0	0	4	1.6
2	0	0	2	.8
1	0	0	1	.4
0	0	0	1	.2

Note. Percentages are cumulative.

This result corresponds to a low effect size ($I \leq .10$) at the case level in Huberty and Lowman's (2000) guidelines.

What is the practical significance of the somewhat stronger basic math skills of the men in this sample? Perhaps the best way to address this question is to look at course outcome at the end of the semester. A satisfactory outcome was defined as a final letter grade of C or better, but earning a grade of D (marginal pass), F (failed), or dropping out was considered unsatisfactory. Proportions of men and women with these two different outcomes are

	Satisfactory	Unsatisfactory
Men	.797	.203
Women	.757	.243

We see that men had a 4% advantage over women in the rate of satisfactory outcomes. This association between gender and dichotomous course outcome is not a statistical one: $\chi^2 (1) = 1.08, p = .299$. However, the lack of statistical significance would be irrelevant if replication bears out a relative male advantage of roughly the same magnitude. Another question is whether a relative male advantage in introductory statistics (if any) is actually a result of stronger basic math skills than women. That is, competing explanations such as greater interest in the subject must be considered.

Effect of Caffeine on 2000-Meter Rowing Performance

Bruce et al. (2000) evaluated in a repeated-measures design the effect of a moderate dose of caffeine—the equivalent of about 2 to 4 cups of coffee—on the 2000 meter (m) rowing performance times in seconds (s) of eight competitive male rowers. The rowers were actually tested under three different conditions: placebo and two different doses of caffeine, 6 and 9 $mg \cdot kg^{-1}$. Because the effects of both doses of caffeine on rowing times were similar, Bruce et al. averaged data from the two caffeine conditions and compared these results with those from the placebo condition. These data, provided by C. R. Bruce (personal communication, August 22, 2001), are summarized in the upper left side of Table 4.13. The rowers completed the distance an average of 4.38s faster in the caffeine condition than in the placebo condition. Because four seconds could make a big difference in finish order for competitive 2000-m rowers, this finding is practically significant, irrespective of the statistical significance.

Because the outcome variable for this example is measured in a meaningful scale (time), there is little need for metric-free effect size indexes. For pedagogical value, however, we consider both kinds of standardized mean changes for this correlated design. The reduction in rowing time from the placebo to the caffeine condition is one third of a standard deviation in the metric of the original performance times (Hedges's g = .33). This result ignores the substantial subjects effect apparent in the cross-conditions correlation of r_{12} = .95. The ratio of the mean change over the standard deviation of the differences in rowing times across the conditions takes account of this correlation and equals .90, almost three times as large as g for the same effect. The exact 95% confidence interval for δ based on the observed standardized mean change of .90 is .05–1.71. That is, the observed standardized effect size is just as consistent with a population effect size as

TABLE 4.13
Performance Times in Seconds to Row 2000 Meters Under Placebo and Caffeine Conditions

					Effect Size	
Condition	M	s^2	M_D	t (7)	g	M_D/s_D
Placebo	415.39	211.12	4.38	2.55[a]	.33	.90[b]
Caffeine	411.01	146.47				

Note. r_{12} = .95, s_D^2 = 23.63.
[a]p = .038.   [b]Exact 95% confidence interval for δ is .05–1.71.

low as $\delta = .05$ as it with a population effect size as high as $\delta = 1.71$, with 95% confidence. This range of imprecision is so wide because of the very small sample size ($n = 8$). Of the two sample standardized mean changes reported, only g would be directly comparable to d from a study where the effect of caffeine versus placebo is tested with unrelated groups.

CONCLUSION

This chapter introduced basic principles of effect size estimation and two families of effect size indexes for continuous outcomes: standardized mean differences and measures of association. Denominators of standardized mean differences for contrasts between independent means, such as Hedges's g and Glass's Δ, are standard deviations in the metric of the original scores. It was recommended that the denominators of standardized mean changes in nonintrinsically repeated-measures designs be similarly scaled. Descriptive measures of association considered in this chapter are all forms of the correlation $\hat{\eta}$, the square root of the sums of squares for the contrast over the total sums of squares. When the two samples are dependent, it is also possible to compute partial $\hat{\eta}$, the correlation between the factor and outcome controlling for the subjects effect. Case-level analyses of proportions of scores from one group versus another group that fall above or below certain reference points can illuminate practical implications of difference at the group level. Although estimating the magnitude of an effect is part of determining its substantive significance, the two are not synonymous. The next chapter introduces effect size indexes for categorical outcomes.

RECOMMENDED READINGS

Fern, E. F., & Monroe, K. B. (1996). Effect-size estimates: Issues and problems. *Journal of Consumer Research, 23,* 89–105.

Huberty, C. J. (2002). A history of effect size indices. *Educational and Psychological Measurement, 62,* 227–240.

Steiger, J. H., & Fouladi, R. T. (1997). Noncentrality interval estimation and the evaluation of statistical models. In L. L. Harlow, S. A. Mulaik, & J. H. Steiger (Eds.), *What if there were no significance tests?* (pp. 221–257). Mahwah, NJ: Erlbaum.

5

NONPARAMETRIC EFFECT SIZE INDEXES

The whole of science is nothing more than a refinement of everyday thinking.

—Albert Einstein (1973, p. 283)

Some outcomes are categorical instead of continuous. The levels of a categorical outcome are mutually exclusive, and each case is classified into just one level. Nonparametric effect size indexes for categorical outcomes that are widely used in areas such as medicine, epidemiology, and genetics are introduced in this chapter. They are also frequently analyzed in meta-analysis. Note that some of these indexes can also be estimated in techniques such as log-linear analysis or logistic regression (W. Rodgers, 1995; Wright, 1995). Doing so bases nonparametric effect size indexes on an underlying statistical model. In contrast, the same indexes computed with the methods described later should be considered descriptive statistics. Exercises with answers for this chapter are available on this book's Web site.

CATEGORICAL OUTCOMES

The simplest categorical outcomes are binary variables (dichotomies) with only two levels, such as relapsed or not relapsed. When two groups are compared on a dichotomy, the data are frequencies that are represented in a 2×2 contingency table, also known as a *fourfold table*. Categorical variables can also have more than two levels, such as *agree*, *disagree*, and *uncertain*. The size of the contingency table is larger than 2×2 if two groups are contrasted across more than two outcome categories. Only some effect size indexes for 2×2 tables can be extended to larger tables. These same statistics can also be used when three or more groups are compared on a categorical outcome.

The levels of a categorical variable are either unordered or ordered. *Unordered categories* do not imply a rank order. Examples of unordered categories include those for ethnicity or marital status. *Ordered categories*— also called *multilevel ordinal categories*—imply a rank order. The Likert-type response format *strongly agree, agree, disagree,* or *strongly disagree* is an example of ordered categories. There are specialized methods for ordered categories (Darlington, 1996), but they are not as well developed or known as for unordered categories. As a consequence, they are not discussed in detail. One alternative is to rescale ordered categories to interval data and then apply methods for parametric variables. Another approach collapses multi-level categories into two clinically meaningful, mutually exclusive outcomes. Estimation of effect size magnitude is then conducted with methods for fourfold tables.

Another framework that analyzes data from fourfold tables is the sensitivity, specificity, and predictive value model. Although better known in medicine as a way to evaluate the accuracy of screening tests for disease, this approach can be fruitfully applied to psychological tests that screen for problems such as depression or learning disabilities (e.g., Glaros & Kline, 1988; Kennedy, Willis, & Faust, 1997). Because screening tests are not usually as accurate as more individualized and costly diagnostic methods, not all persons with a positive screening test result really have the disorder the test is intended to detect. Likewise, not everyone with a negative test result is actually free of the disorder. The 2×2 table analyzed is the cross-tabulation of screening test results (positive–negative) and true status (disorder–no disorder), and "effect sizes" concern the estimated accuracies of positive and negative test results.

EFFECT SIZE INDEXES FOR 2×2 TABLES

Various effect size indexes for fourfold tables are introduced next. I also discuss how to construct confidence intervals for the population parameters estimated by these indexes.

Parameters

A total of four parameters that reflect the degree of relative risk for an undesirable outcome across different populations are introduced next. These same parameters can also be defined when neither level of outcome dichotomy corresponds to something undesirable, such as agree–disagree. The idea of "risk" is just replaced by that of comparing relative proportions for the two different outcomes. See Fleiss (1994) and Haddock, Rindskopf, and Shadish (1998) for more detailed presentations.

Suppose in a comparative study that treatment and control groups are to be compared on the dichotomy relapsed–not relapsed. The proportion of cases that relapse in the treatment population is π_T, and $1 - \pi_T$ is the proportion that do not relapse. The corresponding proportions in the control population are, respectively, π_C and $1 - \pi_C$. The simple difference between the two probabilities, $\pi_C - \pi_T$, is the population *risk difference,* also called the *proportion difference.* So defined, $\pi_C - \pi_T = .10$ indicates a relapse rate 10% higher in the control population than in the treatment population. Likewise, $\pi_C - \pi_T = -.20$ indicates a higher relapse rate in the treatment population by 20%.

The population *risk ratio*—also called the *rate ratio*—is the ratio of the proportions for the undesirable outcome, in this case relapse. It is defined as π_C/π_T. If this ratio equals 1.30, for example, the risk for relapse is 1.3 times higher in the control population than in the treatment population. Likewise, if the risk ratio is .80, the relapse risk among treated cases is only 80% as great as that among control cases. The risk ratio thus compares the proportionate difference in relapse risk across the two populations.

The population *odds ratio* is designated below as ω, but note that the symbol "ω^2" refers to a different parameter for a continuous outcome (see chap. 4, this volume). The parameter ω is the ratio of the within-populations odds for the undesirable outcome. The odds for relapse in the control population equals $\Omega_C = \pi_C/(1 - \pi_C)$, the corresponding odds in the treatment population equals $\Omega_T = \pi_T/(1 - \pi_T)$, and the odds ratio equals $\omega = \Omega_C/\Omega_T$. Suppose that $\pi_C = .60$ and $\pi_T = .40$. The odds for relapse in the control population are $\Omega_C = .60/.40 = 1.50$; that is, the chances of relapsing are 1½ times greater than not relapsing. The odds for relapse in the treatment population are $\Omega_T = .40/.60 = .67$; that is, the chances of relapsing are two thirds that of not relapsing. The odds ratio is $\omega = \Omega_C/\Omega_T = 1.50/.67 = 2.25$, which means that the odds for relapse are 2¼ times higher in the control population than in the treatment population.

The population Pearson correlation between the treatment–control and relapsed–not relapsed dichotomies is the φ coefficient, which equals:

$$\varphi = \frac{\pi_{CR}\,\pi_{TNR} - \pi_{CNR}\,\pi_{TR}}{\sqrt{\pi_{C\bullet}\,\pi_{T\bullet}\,\pi_{\bullet R}\,\pi_{\bullet NR}}} \tag{5.1}$$

The subscripts C, T, R, and NR mean control, treatment, relapsed, and not relapsed. The proportions in the numerator represent the four possible outcomes and thus sum to 1.0. For example, π_{CR} is the probability of being in the control population and relapsing, and π_{TNR} is the probability of being in the treatment population and not relapsing. The subscript "·" indicates a total (marginal) proportion. For example, $\pi_{C\cdot}$ and $\pi_{T\cdot}$ are, respectively, the relative proportions of cases in the control and treatment populations, and they sum to 1.0. Likewise, $\pi_{\cdot R}$ and $\pi_{\cdot NR}$ are, respectively, the relative proportions of cases across both populations that relapsed or did not relapse, and they also sum to 1.0.

Statistics and Evaluation

Table 5.1 presents a 2×2 table for the contrast of treatment and control groups on the dichotomy relapsed–not relapsed. The letters in the table stand for observed frequencies in each cell. For example, the size of the control group is $n_C = A + B$, where A and B, respectively, stand for the number of untreated cases that relapsed or did not relapse. The size of the treatment group is $n_T = C + D$, where C and D stand for the number of treated cases that relapsed or did not relapse, respectively. The total sample size is thus $N = A + B + C + D$.

Table 5.2 presents definitions of sample estimators of the parameters described in the previous section. These definitions are expressed in terms of the observed cell frequencies represented in Table 5.1. The population proportions of cases that relapsed are estimated by the observed proportions p_C and p_T, respectively. The sample risk difference (RD) is computed as $RD = p_C - p_T$, and it estimates the population risk difference. The statistic RD is easy to interpret, but it has a significant limitation: Its range depends on the values of π_C and π_T. Specifically, the range of RD is greater when both π_C and π_T are closer to .50 than when they are closer to 0 or 1.0. The implication is that values of RD may not be comparable across different studies where the associated values of π_C and π_T are quite different.

The sample risk ratio (RR) indicates the difference in the observed proportionate risk for relapse across the control and treatment groups. It is defined in Table 5.2 as $RR = p_C / p_T$. If $RR > 1.0$, relapse risk is higher among the untreated cases, and $RR < 1.0$ indicates higher risk among treated cases. The statistic RR is also easy to interpret, but it has some drawbacks too. Only the finite interval 0–1.0 indicates lower risk in the group represented in

TABLE 5.1
A Fourfold Table for an Observed Group Contrast on a Dichotomy

Group	Relapsed	Not relapsed
Control	*A*	*B*
Treatment	*C*	*D*

Note. The letters *A–D* represent observed cell frequencies.

TABLE 5.2
Definitions of Effect Size Statistics for 2 × 2 Contingency Tables

Parameter	Statistic	Equation
Proportions of undesirable outcome		
π_C	p_C	$A/(A + B)$
π_T	p_T	$C/(C + D)$
Comparative risk		
$\pi_C - \pi_T$	RD	$p_C - p_T$
π_C/π_T	RR	$p_C/p_T = \dfrac{A/(A + B)}{C/(C + D)}$
$\omega = \Omega_C/\Omega_T$	OR	$\dfrac{o_C}{o_T} = \dfrac{p_C/(1 - p_C)}{p_T/(1 - p_T)} = \dfrac{A/B}{C/D} = AD/BC$
Measure of association		
φ	$\hat{\varphi}$	$\dfrac{AD - BC}{\sqrt{(A + B)(C + D)(A + C)(B + D)}} = \sqrt{\chi^2(1)/N}$

Note. RD = risk difference; RR = risk ratio; OD = odds ratio. The letters A–D represent observed cell frequencies in Table 5.1. If A, B, C, or D = 0 in the computation of OR, add .5 to all cells.

the numerator, but the interval from 1.0 to infinity is theoretically available for describing higher risk in the other group. The range of possible values of RR thus vary according to its denominator. Suppose that p_T is .40 in one sample but .60 in another sample. The theoretical range of RR = p_C/p_T in the first sample is 0–2.50, but in the second sample it is 0–1.67. This characteristic limits the value of RR as a standardized index for comparing results across different samples. This problem can be addressed by analyzing logarithm transformations of RR and then converting the results back to RR units with antilog transformations. This point is elaborated momentarily.

The sample odds ratio (OR) is the ratio of the within-groups odds. It is defined in Table 5.2 as the ratio of the odds for relapse in the control group, $o_C = p_C (1 - p_C)$, over the odds in the treatment group, $o_T = p_T (1 - p_T)$. In fourfold tables where all margin totals are equal, the odds ratio equals the squared risk ratio, or OR = RR^2. The statistic OR shares with RR the limitation that the finite interval 0–1.0 indicates lower risk in the group represented in the numerator, but the interval from 1.0 to infinity describes higher risk for other group. Analyzing logarithm transformations of OR and then taking antilogarithms of the results can deal with this limitation, just as for RR.

A convenient property of OR is that it can be converted to a kind of standardized mean difference for a fourfold table known as a *logit d*. A *logit* is the natural log (base $e \cong 2.7183$) of OR, ln (OR). The logistic distribution is approximately normal with a standard deviation that equals $pi/3^{1/2}$, which is about 1.8138. The ratio of ln (OR) over $pi/3^{1/2}$ is a logit d that is directly comparable to a standardized mean difference for a contrast of the same two groups on a continuous outcome. Shadish, Robinson, and Lu (1999) showed that the logit d can also be expressed in basically the same form as a standardized mean difference:

$$\text{logit } d = \frac{\ln(OR)}{pi/\sqrt{3}} = \frac{\ln(o_C) - \ln(o_T)}{pi/\sqrt{3}} \qquad (5.2)$$

where o_C and o_T are, respectively, the relapse odds in the control and treatment groups. Suppose that $p_C = .60$ and $p_T = .20$, which implies $o_C = 1.50$, $o_T = .25$, and $OR = 6.00$. The logit d for the group contrast equals:

$$\text{logit } d = \ln (6.00)/1.8138 = [\ln (1.50) - \ln (.25)]/1.8138 = .9878$$

Thus, the finding that the odds for relapse are six times higher among untreated cases corresponds to a treatment effect size magnitude of about a full standard deviation in logistic units. The Effect Size (ES) program by Shadish et al. (1999) automatically calculates logit d for dichotomous outcomes. There are other ways to adjust for dichotomization of the outcome variable, including arcsine and probit transformations—see Lipsey and Wilson (2000, pp. 52–58) for more information.

The sample odds ratio may be the least intuitive index of comparative risk indexes reviewed, but it probably has the best overall statistical properties, especially in epidemiological studies of risk factors for disease. This is because OR can be estimated in prospective studies, in studies that randomly sample from exposed and unexposed populations, and in retrospective studies where groups are first formed based on the presence or absence of a disease before their exposure to a supposed risk factor is determined (Fleiss, 1994). Other indexes may not be valid in retrospective studies, such as RR, or in studies without random sampling, such as $\hat{\varphi}$, which is described next.

The estimator of the population Pearson correlation between two dichotomies, φ, is the sample correlation $\hat{\varphi}$. It can be calculated using the standard equation for the Pearson correlation r if the levels of both dichotomies are coded as 0 or 1. It may be more convenient to calculate $\hat{\varphi}$ directly from the cell frequencies and margin frequencies using the equation in Table 5.2. The theoretical range of $\hat{\varphi}$ derived this way is -1.00 to $+1.00$, but the sign of $\hat{\varphi}$ is arbitrary because it is determined by the particular arrangement of the cells. For this reason, some researchers report absolute values of $\hat{\varphi}$. However, keep in mind that effects in 2×2 tables are directional. For example, either treated or untreated cases will have a higher relapse rate (if there is a difference). The absolute value of $\hat{\varphi}$ also equals the square root of $\chi^2(1)/N$, the ratio of the chi-square statistic with a single degree of freedom for the fourfold table over the sample size. The relation just described can be algebraically manipulated to express the contingency table chi-square statistic as a function of sample size and standardized effect size measure by $\hat{\varphi}$ (see Table 2.9). The square of $\hat{\varphi}$, $\hat{\varphi}^2$, equals the proportion of variance in the dichotomous outcome explained by group membership. In fourfold tables where the row and column marginal totals are all equal (which implies equal group sizes), the absolute values of the risk difference and the phi coefficient are identical (RD = $\hat{\varphi}$).

The correlation $\hat{\varphi}$ can reach its maximum absolute value of 1.00 only if the marginal proportions for rows and columns in a fourfold table are equal. For example, given a balanced design, the theoretical maximum absolute value of $\hat{\varphi}$ is 1.00 only if the marginal proportions for the outcome dichotomy are also .50. As the row and column marginal proportions diverge, the maximum absolute value of $\hat{\varphi}$ approaches zero. This implies that the value of $\hat{\varphi}$ will change if the cell frequencies in any row or column are multiplied by an arbitrary constant. Because of this characteristic, Darlington (1996) described $\hat{\varphi}$ as a *margin-bound* measure of association; the point-biserial correlation r_{pb} for continuous outcomes is also margin bound because of the influence of relative group size (see chap. 4, this volume). The effect of marginal proportions on $\hat{\varphi}$ also suggests that it may not be an appropriate effect size index when sampling is not random (Fleiss, 1994). The correlation $\hat{\varphi}$ also treats the two dichotomous variables symmetrically—that is, its value is the same if the fourfold table is "flipped" so that the rows become columns and vice versa. There are other measures of association that differentiate between predictor and criterion variables, and thus treat the rows and columns asymmetrically; see Darlington (1996) for more information.

Interval Estimation

Sample estimators of population proportions tend to have complex distributions, and most methods of interval estimation for them are approximate and based on central test statistics. Table 5.3 presents equations for the estimated (asymptotic) standard errors in large samples for each of the statistics described except the correlation $\hat{\varphi}$. The equation for the asymptotic standard error of $\hat{\varphi}$ is quite complicated; interested readers can find it in Fleiss (1994, p. 249). The width of a 100 $(1 - \alpha)$% confidence interval based on any of the statistics listed in Table 5.3 is the product of its asymptotic standard error and $z_{2\text{-tail}, \alpha}$, the positive two-tailed critical value of z in a normal curve at the α level of statistical significance. Some examples follow.

Suppose the following results are from a study of the relapse rates among treated and untreated cases: $n_C = n_T = 100$, $p_C = .60$, and $p_T = .40$. The sample risk difference is RD = .20 in favor of the treatment group.

TABLE 5.3
Asymptotic Standard Errors for Sample Proportions

Statistic	Standard error
Proportions of undesirable outcome	
p_C	$\sqrt{\dfrac{p_C(1 - p_C)}{n_C}}$
p_T	$\sqrt{\dfrac{p_T(1 - p_T)}{n_T}}$
Comparative risk	
RD	$\sqrt{\dfrac{p_C(1 - p_C)}{n_C} + \dfrac{p_T(1 - p_T)}{n_T}}$
ln (RR)	$\sqrt{\dfrac{1 - p_C}{n_C\, p_C} + \dfrac{1 - p_T}{n_T\, p_T}}$
ln (OR)	$\sqrt{\dfrac{1}{n_C\, p_C\,(1 - p_C)} + \dfrac{1}{n_T\, p_T\,(1 - p_T)}}$

Note. RD = risk difference, RR = risk ratio, and OR = odds ratio, and ln = natural log.

Using the third equation in Table 5.3, the asymptotic standard error of RD is estimated as follows:

$$s_{RD} = \{[.60\,(1 - .60)]/100 + [.40\,(1 - .40)]/100\}^{1/2} = .0693$$

The value of $z_{2\text{-tail},\,.05}$ equals 1.96, so the 95% confidence for $\pi_C - \pi_T$ is

$$.20 \pm .0693\,(1.96) \qquad \text{or} \qquad .20 \pm .14$$

which defines the interval .06–.34. Thus, RD = .20 is just as consistent with a population risk difference as low as .06 as it is with a difference as high as .34, with 95% confidence.

For the data reported earlier, RR = .60/.40 = 1.50 and OR = (.60/ .40)/(.40/.60) = 2.25, both of which indicate higher risk for relapse in the control group. Distributions of RR and OR are not generally normal, but natural log transformations of both are approximately normal. Consequently, the method of confidence interval transformation (see chap. 2, this volume) can be used to construct approximate confidence intervals based on ln (RR) or ln (OR). The lower and upper bounds of these intervals in logarithm units are then converted back to their original metric by taking their antilogs. Because the method is the same for both indexes, it is demonstrated below only for OR. The log transformation of the observed odds ratio is ln (2.25) = .8109. The estimated standard error of the log-transformed odds ratio calculated using the fifth equation in Table 5.3 equals

$$s_{\ln (OR)} = \{1/[100 \times .60\,(1 - .60)] + 1/[100 \times .40\,(1 - .40)]\}^{1/2} = .2887$$

The approximate 95% confidence interval for $\ln(\omega)$, the log population odds ratio, is

$$.8109 \pm .2887\,(1.96) \qquad \text{or} \qquad .8109 \pm .5659$$

which defines the interval .2450–1.3768 in log units. To convert the lower and upper bounds of this interval back to the original metric, we take their antilogs:

$$\ln^{-1}(.2450) = e^{.2450} = 1.2776 \qquad \text{and} \qquad \ln^{-1}(1.3768) = e^{1.3768} = 3.9622$$

The approximate 95% confidence interval for ω is thus 1.28–3.96 at two-decimal accuracy. We can say that the observed result OR = 2.25 is just as consistent with a population odds ratio as low as $\omega = 1.28$ as it is with a population odds ratio as high as $\omega = 3.96$, with 95% confidence.

EFFECT SIZE ESTIMATION FOR LARGER TWO-WAY TABLES

If the categorical outcome variable has more than two levels or there are more than two groups, the contingency table is larger than 2×2. Measures of relative risk (RD, RR, OR) can be computed for such a table only if it is reduced to a 2×2 table by collapsing or excluding rows or columns. What is probably the best known measure of association for contingency tables with more than two rows or columns is Cramér's V, an extension of the $\hat{\phi}$ coefficient. Its equation is

$$V = \sqrt{\frac{\chi^2(r - 1,\, c - 1)}{\min\,(r - 1,\, c - 1) \times N}} \tag{5.3}$$

where the numerator under the radical is the chi-square statistic with degrees of freedom equal to the product of the number of rows (r) minus one and the number of columns (c) minus one. The denominator under the radical is the product of the sample size and smallest dimension of the table minus one. For example, if the table is 3×4 in size, then min $(3 - 1, 4 - 1) = 2$. For a 2×2 table, the equation for Cramér's V reduces to that for $\hat{\phi}$. For larger tables, however, V is not technically a correlation coefficient, although its range is 0–1.00. Thus, one cannot generally interpret the square of V as a proportion of explained variance. Because Cramér's V is a generalization of $\hat{\varphi}$, it is a margin-bound, symmetrical measure of association subject to the same general limitations as $\hat{\varphi}$. See Darlington (1996) for descriptions of other measures of association for two-way contingency tables.

SENSITIVITY, SPECIFICITY, AND PREDICTIVE VALUE

Suppose for some disorder there is a "gold standard" diagnostic method that is individualized and relatively expensive, such as a series of laboratory or psychological tests. There is also a screening test for the disorder that is not as accurate as the gold standard, but it costs less. For example, it may be possible to administer the screening test to groups instead of just to individuals. Screening tests are often continuous measures, such as the blood concentration of a particular substance or the number of items endorsed on a questionnaire. Such measures also typically have a cutting point that differentiates between a positive (clinical) result that predicts the presence of the disorder versus a negative (normal) result that predicts its absence. Distributions on screening tests of groups with the disorder and without the disorder tend to overlap. This situation is illustrated in Figure 5.1 in which the group with the disorder has a higher mean than the group without the disorder. Also depicted in the figure is a cutting point that differentiates positive and negative screening test results. Note that some of the cases with the disorder have negative test results; likewise, some of the cases without the disorder have positive test results. The two sets of scores just described represent potential diagnostic errors.

The fourfold table in the top part of Table 5.4 represents the relation between screening test results (positive–negative) and actual status as determined by a gold standard diagnostic method (disorder–no disorder). The letters in the table stand for observed cell frequencies. For example, the letter A represents the number of cases with the disorder who obtain a positive screening test result, and D represents the number of cases without the disorder who obtain negative results. Both cells just described correspond to correct predictions on the screening test. The other two cells in the table, B and C, respectively, represent the numbers of false positive and false negative screening test results.

Defined in the bottom part of Table 5.4 are sensitivity, specificity, predictive value, and base rate, all computed with cell frequencies represented in the top part of the table. *Sensitivity* is the proportion of screening results from cases with the disorder that are correct, $A/(A + C)$. If sensitivity is .80, then 80% of test results in this group are valid positives and the rest, 20%, are false negatives. *Specificity* is the proportion of results from cases

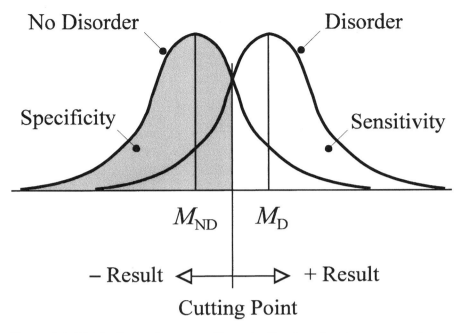

Figure 5.1. Distributions of groups with and without a disorder on a continuous screening test.

without the disorder that are correct, $D/(B + D)$. If specificity is .70, then 70% of the results in this group are valid negatives and the rest, 30%, are false positives. The ideal screening test is 100% sensitive and 100% specific. Given overlap of distributions such as that illustrated in Figure 5.1, this ideal is not attainable. Sensitivity and specificity are determined by the

TABLE 5.4
Definitions of Sensitivity, Specificity, Predictive Value, and Base Rate

Screening test result	Prediction	True status	
		Disorder	No disorder
+	Disorder	A	B
−	No disorder	C	D

Statistic	Definition
Sensitivity	$A/(A + C)$
Specificity	$D/(B + D)$
Predictive value	
Positive (+PV)	$A/(A + B)$
Negative (−PV)	$D/(C + D)$
Base rate	$(A + C)/(A + B + C + D)$

Note. The letters *A–D* represent observed cell frequencies.

TABLE 5.5
Positive and Negative Predictive Values at Two Different Base Rates for a
Screening Test 80% Sensitive and 70% Specific

Screening test result	True status			Predictive value	
	Disorder	No disorder	Total	+PV	−PV
Base rate = .10					
+	80	270	350	.23	.97
−	20	630	650		
Total	100	900	1,000		
Base rate = .75					
+	600	75	675	.89	.54
−	150	175	325		
Total	750	250	1,000		

cutting point on the screening test. Accordingly, the relative costs of either kind of diagnostic error, false negative or false positive, may be considered in setting the cutting point.

Sensitivity and specificity affect *predictive value,* the proportion of screening test results that are correct, and in this sense it reflects the confidence that diagnosticians can place in screening test results. There are two kinds of predictive value: positive and negative. *Positive predictive value* (+PV) is the proportion of all positive results that are correct—that is, obtained by cases with the disorder, or $A/(A + B)$ in Table 5.4. *Negative predictive value* (−PV) is the proportion of negative test results that are correct, that belong to people without the disorder, or $D/(C + D)$ in the table. In general, +PV and −PV are higher as sensitivity and specificity increase.

Predictive value is also influenced by another very important factor, the *base rate* (BR), the proportion of all individuals with the disorder, or $BR = (A + C)/N$ in Table 5.4. The effect of base rate on predictive value is demonstrated in Table 5.5. Two different fourfold tables are presented there for hypothetical populations of 1,000 cases and a screening test where sensitivity is .80 and specificity is .70. For the first fourfold table, BR = .10 because 100/1,000 cases have the disorder, and 80% of them (80) have a correct test result (positive). A total of 90% of the cases do not have the disorder (900), and 70% of them (630) have a correct test result (negative). However, of all positive test results, only 80/350 = 23% are correct, so +PV = .23. In contrast, the large majority of all negative results are correct, or 630/650 = 97%, so −PV = .97. Given these predictive values, we can say that the screening test is quite accurate in ruling out the disorder, but not in detecting its presence.

If the base rate is not 10%, both predictive values change. This is shown in the second 2 × 2 cross-tabulation in Table 5.5 for the same screening test but for a base rate of 75%. (The base rates of certain parasitic diseases in some parts of the world are this high.) Of all 675 cases with positive test results, a total of 600 belong to cases with the disorder, so +PV = 600/675 = .89. Likewise, of all 325 negative results, a total of 175 are from cases without the disorder, so −PV = 175/325 = .54. Now more confidence is warranted in positive screening test results than negative results, which is just the opposite of the situation for a 10% base rate. In general, +PV decreases and −PV increases as the base rate approaches zero. This means that screening tests tend to be more useful for ruling out the presence of relatively rare disorders than in correctly predicting their presence. Just the opposite is generally true for more common disorders: As the base rate increases, +PV increases and −PV decreases; that is, the test is now more useful for detecting the disorder than ruling it out.

The effect of base rate on predictive value is striking but often overlooked, even by experienced diagnosticians (e.g., Medin & Edelson, 1988). The most common misunderstanding seems to involve confusing sensitivity and specificity, which are invariant to base rate, with +PV and −PV, which are not. This implies that diagnosticians often fail to adjust their estimates of screening test accuracy for changes in base rates.

RESEARCH EXAMPLES

The three research examples presented next demonstrate effect size estimation with dichotomous outcomes. The last example concerns the evaluation of the predictive value of a cutting score for predicting the presence of attentional or learning problems.

Smoking and the Risk of Coronary Heart Disease

The data for this example are from Glass and K. Hopkins (1996), who matched 120 employees with coronary heart disease with 120 employees in the same company without the disease. All workers were then classified into one of four smoking categories: nonsmoking, less than one pack per day, one pack per day, and more than one pack per day. These categories are ordered, but they are analyzed later with methods for unordered categories. This study is also retrospective because cases were identified based on the presence or absence of an illness before assessing their level of exposure to a putative risk factor, smoking. Because the study is retrospective, the odds ratio is probably the most appropriate effect size index. However, the other nonparametric indexes discussed earlier are calculated for pedagogical value.

TABLE 5.6
Contingency Table for Level of Smoking and Coronary Heart Disease

| | | Coronary heart disease | |
Group	n	Yes	No
Smoking (packs/day)			
< 1	42	19	23
1	64	39	25
> 1	31	20	11
Nonsmoking	103	42	61

Note. From *Statistical Methods in Education and Psychology* (3rd ed., p. 335), by G. Glass and K. Hopkins, 1996, Boston: Allyn and Bacon. Copyright 1996 by Pearson Education. Adapted with permission.

Table 5.6 presents the 4×2 cross-tabulation of smoking category and illness status. The chi-square statistic is $\chi^2(3) = 9.56$, and Cramér's V = $(9.56/240)^{1/2} = .20$, which describes the overall magnitude of association between these two variables. To estimate the relative risk for coronary heart disease, the three smoking categories in Table 5.6 were collapsed into a single category. The resulting fourfold table is presented in the left side of Table 5.7. The right side reports values of nonparametric effect size indexes and corresponding approximate 95% confidence intervals. (Readers should reproduce these results.)

A total of 78 of 137 smokers have coronary heart disease, so the risk for this group is $p_S = 78/137 = .57$. Among the 103 nonsmokers, a total of 42 have the disease, so $p_N = 42/103 = .41$. The observed risk difference is RD = $.57 - .41 = .16$, so smokers have a 16% greater risk for heart disease than nonsmokers. The approximate 95% confidence interval for the population risk difference is .03–.29, so RD = .16 is just as consistent with a population risk difference as low as .03 as it is with a population risk

TABLE 5.7
Fourfold Table for Smokers Versus Nonsmokers for Presence Versus
Absence of Coronary Heart Disease for the Data in Table 5.6

| | | Coronary heart disease | | Effect size | | | | | |
Group	n	Yes	No	p_S	p_N	RD	RR	OR	$\hat{\varphi}$
Smoking	137	78	59	.57	.41	.16[a]	1.39[b]	1.92[c]	.16
Nonsmoking	103	42	61						

Note. S = smoking, N = nonsmoking, RD = risk difference, RR = risk ratio, OR = odds ratio, $\chi^2(1) = 6.14$, $p = .013$.
[a]Approximate 95% confidence interval for $\pi_S - \pi_N$ is .03–.29.
[b]Approximate 95% confidence interval for π_S/π_N is 1.06–1.84.
[c]Approximate 95% confidence interval for ω is 1.14–3.22.

difference as high as .29, with 95% confidence. The risk ratio is RR = .57/.41 = 1.39, which says that the rate of disease is about 1.4 times higher among smokers. The approximate 95% confidence interval for the population risk ratio is 1.06–1.84, so RR = 1.39 is just as consistent with a true risk ratio as low as 1.06 as it is with a true risk ratio as high as 1.84, with 95% confidence. The observed odds ratio is

$$OR = .57 \ (1 - .57)/.41 \ (1 - .41) = 1.92$$

so the odds of heart disease are almost twice as high among smokers as nonsmokers. The approximate 95% confidence interval for the population odds ratio is 1.14–3.22. Thus, OR = 1.92 supports a population odds ratio as low as 1.14 just as well as it does a population odds ratio as high as 3.22 with 95% confidence. All three confidence intervals just reported indicate a fairly wide margin of imprecision. This is mainly a result of the relatively small sizes of the groups. The correlation between smoking status and heart disease status is $\hat{\varphi} = .16$, so the former explains about 2.5% of the variance in the latter. This is a fairly typically variance-accounted-for effect size magnitude in this area and should not be discounted as "unimportant" (see chap. 4, this volume).

Driving Outcomes of Youth With Attentional Difficulties

In a prospective study, Woodward, Fergusson, and Horwood (2000) estimated the relation between attentional problems in adolescence and later driving records. At age 13 years, a birth cohort of 941 adolescents were classified into one of five ordered categories based on the extent of parent or teacher reports of attentional problems. Youth with the lowest level of rated problems had scores in the bottom 50% of the sample, and those with highest level had scores in the upper 5%. The driving records of the study participants were assessed when they were 18 to 21 years of age. Of the 11 outcomes analyzed by Woodward et al., results for only three of the categorical driving outcomes are summarized in Table 5.8. In general, greater attentional problems at age 13 years are associated with worse driving records later. Values of Cramér's V for the three 5 × 2 cross-tabulations implied by the percentages in Table 5.8 range from .10 for injury-related accidents to .23 for driving without a license. These coefficients may not seem high, but they are associated with potentially serious or even fatal outcomes.

The four upper categories of attentional problems in Table 5.8 were collapsed into a single higher attentional problem category ($n_H = 466$) and compared with the low attention problem category ($n_L = 475$) across the three dichotomous outcomes. Table 5.9 reports the values of comparative risk measures and the correlation $\hat{\varphi}$ for all outcomes. The values of the risk

TABLE 5.8
Driving Outcomes by Level of Attentional Difficulties

Driving outcome at age 21 years	Attentional Difficulties at Age 13 Years					$\chi^2(4)$	Cramér's V
	1 (low) (1–50)[a]	2 (51–75)	3 (76–90)	4 (91–95)	5 (high) (96–100)		
n	475	185	188	47	46		
Injury-related accident (%)	3.6	4.3	6.4	10.6	10.9	9.45[b]	.10
Arrested for drinking and driving (%)	2.9	5.9	8.5	6.4	13.0	14.82[c]	.13
Driving without license (%)	8.2	10.3	23.4	27.7	32.6	50.21[d]	.23

Note. From "Driving Outcomes of Young People With Attentional Difficulties in Adolescence," by L. J. Woodward, D. M. Fergusson, and L. J. Horwood, 2000, *Journal of the American Academy of Child and Adolescent Psychiatry, 39*, p. 630. Copyright 2000 by Lippincott Williams & Wilkins. Adapted with permission.
[a]The numbers in parentheses are percentile ranges.
[b]$p = .051.$ [c]$p = .005.$ [d]$p < .001.$

difference, RD, and $\hat{\varphi}$ are all negative, which means that young adults rated as having low attentional problems in adolescence are at less risk for problematic driver outcomes than age cohorts rated as having higher attentional problems. For the same reason, values of the risk ratio, RR, and the odds ratio, OR, are all less than 1.00. Overall, drivers with histories of attentional problems in adolescence are about twice as likely to be involved in risky driving behavior.

Predictive Values of a Cognitive Test Profile in Detecting Learning or Attentional Problems

Many children referred by their teachers to school psychologists are administered the Wechsler Intelligence Scale for Children–Third Edition (WISC–III; Wechsler, 1991). Scores from its 13 tasks contribute to four factor-based indexes, including Verbal Comprehension, Freedom From Distractibility, Processing Speed, and Perceptual Organization. Because the Verbal Comprehension factor reflects language skills and factual knowledge, scores on it may be depressed for children with learning problems. The four tasks that make up the Freedom From Distractibility factor and the Processing Speed factor are identified with the acronym SCAD (Symbol Search, Coding, Arithmetic, Digit span). All SCAD tasks involve short-term memory, so a limited attention span may result in lower scores. The four tasks that contribute to the Perceptual Organization factor involve visual–spatial reasoning, so scores on this factor may be less affected by learning or attentional problems.

TABLE 5.9
Effect Size Statistics for Driving Outcomes by Lower Versus Higher Levels of Attentional Difficulties for the Data in Table 5.8

Outcome at age 21 years	Attentional difficulties at age 13 years		$\chi^2(1)$	Effect size			
	Lower	Higher		$\hat{\phi}$	RD	RR	OR
n	475	466					
Injury-related accident (%)	3.6	6.4	4.05[a]	−.07	−.03	.56	.58
Arrested for drinking and driving (%)	2.9	7.7	10.41[b]	−.11	−.05	.38	.40
Driving without license (%)	8.2	19.5	25.30[b]	−.16	−.11	.42	.48

Note. RD = risk difference; RR = risk ratio; and OR = odds ratio.
[a]*p* = .044.   [b]*p* < .001.

Suppose that the difference score PO − SCAD is computed for an individual child where PO is the total score across the four visual-spatial tasks of the Perceptual Organization factor and SCAD is the total score across the four short-term memory tasks listed earlier. Based on evidence that children with learning or attentional deficits are more likely to obtain positive PO − SCAD scores than normal children, the predictive value of this difference score as a diagnostic indicator is estimated next.

Table 5.10 reports estimated sensitivity and specificity values for the entire range of positive PO − SCAD differences, 1–18. The sensitivity values are proportions of children diagnosed with learning or attentional deficits who obtained PO − SCAD scores greater than or equal to the value indicated for each row (Prifitiera & Dersh, 1993). The specificity values are proportions of children in the normative sample of the WISC–III who obtained difference scores less than or equal to the value indicated in each row (Kaufman, 1994). For example, PO − SCAD ≥ 9 is a statistical difference at the .05 level for an individual profile. About 54% of children with learning–attentional problems obtain PO − SCAD scores of 9 or higher, but only about (1 − .84) = .26, or 26% of children in the normative sample obtain a difference score so high. A score of 12 is required for a statistical difference at the .01 level for an individual profile. About 37% of children with learning–attentional problems have PO − SCAD scores so high, but this is true for only about 1 − .91 = .09, or 9% of normative sample children. Because practitioners may not interpret a difference between two scores for the same profile unless it is statistical, only PO − SCAD values ≥ 9 and ≥ 12 are considered.

The predictive value of PO − SCAD ≥ 9 as a diagnostic indicator of learning–attentional problems is analyzed in Table 5.11 for a hypothetical

TABLE 5.10

Estimated Sensitivity and Specificity Values for Differences Between
Scores on Visual–Spatial and Short-Term Memory Tasks for Normal
and Attentional-Learning Problem Children

Value of (PO–SCAD)	Sensitivity[a]	Specificity[b]
18	.17	.98
17	.21	.97
16	.23	.96
15	.26	.96
14	.29	.94
13	.33	.93
12[c]	.37	.91
11	.43	.89
10	.49	.86
9[d]	.54	.84
8	.58	.81
7	.63	.77
6	.65	.74
5	.68	.70
4	.74	.66
3	.80	.61
2	.82	.56
1	.84	.52

Note. PO = sum of the tasks for the Perceptual Organization factor and SCAD = sum of the tasks for Free-dom from Distractibility factor and Processing Speed factor of the Wechsler Intelligence Scale for Chil-dren–Third Edition (WISC–III; Wechsler, 1991).
[a]Sensitivity values were computed based on data from 164 children classified as either learning-disabled or as having attention deficit hyperactivity disorder and reported in "Base Rates of WISC–III Diagnostic Subtest Patterns Among Normal, Learning-Disabled, and ADHD Samples," by A. Prifitiera and J. Dersh, 1993. In B. A. Bracken and R. S. McCallum (Eds.), *Journal of Psychoeducational Assessment Monograph Series, Advances in Psychological Assessment: Wechsler Intelligence Scale for Children–Third Edition*, p. 39. Copyright 1993 by the Psychoeducational Corporation. Adapted with permission.
[b]Specificity values were computed based on data from 2,158 children in the WISC–III normative sample and reported in *Intelligent Testing With the WISC–III*, by A. S. Kaufman, 1994, New York: Wiley, p. 220. Copyright 1994 by John Wiley and Sons. Adapted with permission.
[c]$p < .05$ for an individual profile.
[d]$p < .01$ for an individual profile.

population of 1,000 children at two different base rates, 10% and 25%. Only the 10% base rate is realistic, but comparing predictive values for the two different base rates is instructive. For a 10% base rate, assuming sensitiv-ity is .54 and specificity is .84 for PO – SCAD ≥ 9 (Table 5.10), the positive predictive value is +PV = .27. Thus, the prediction of learning–attentional problems given a difference between a child's PO and SCAD scores of 9 or higher will be correct only about a quarter of the time. The negative predictive value is –PV = .94, which means that the prediction that a child does *not* have a learning–attentional problem given a difference score less than 9 will be correct in the large majority of cases. Considering the relatively low base rate (10%), a low +PV and a much higher –PV is not surprising. It is only for the unrealistically high base rate of 25% for learning–attentional

TABLE 5.11

Estimated Predictive Values for a Difference Between Scores on
Visual–Spatial and Short-Term Memory Tasks of Nine Points at
Two Different Base Rates

Result (PO–SCAD)	Prediction	True status			Predictive value	
		Learning-attentional problem	No problem	Total	+PV	–PV
		Base rate = .10				
≥ 9	Learning-attention problem	54	144	198	.27	.94
< 9	No problem	46	756	802		
	Total	100	900	1,000		
		Base rate = .25				
≥ 9	Learning-attention problem	135	120	255	.53	.84
< 9	No problem	115	630	745		
	Total	250	750	1,000		

Note. Sensitivity = .54 and specificity = .84 for (PO–SCAD) ≥ 9; see Table 5.10. PO = sum of the tasks for the perceptual organization factor and SCAD = sum of the tasks for freedom from distractibility factor and processing speed factor of the Wechsler Intelligence Scale for Children–Third Edition (Wechsler, 1991).

problems that the +PV of PO – SCAD ≥ 9 just exceeds 50%. The derivation of predictive values for PO – SCAD ≥ 12 is left to readers as an exercise, but values for a 10% base rate are +PV = .31 and –PV = .93. Thus, requiring a greater positive difference between PO and SCAD does not appreciably increase +PV for a realistic base rate.

Of course, the diagnosis of learning or attentional problems is not made on the basis of a single difference score. However, there have been dozens—if not hundreds—of difference scores such as PO – SCAD described in the cognitive test literature as having potential value for detecting cognitive, learning, or even psychiatric problems. Very few have been analyzed from the perspective of sensitive, specificity, and predictive value. This is unfortunate because this framework requires diagnosticians to consider the effect of base rates on predictive value.

CONCLUSION

This chapter introduced effect size indexes for comparing groups across categorical outcomes. Some of these indexes measure relative risk across two different groups for a less desirable outcome versus a more desirable outcome, such as recovered–not recovered. These data are summarized in a fourfold table. The comparative risk index with the best overall psychometric properties is the odds ratio, the ratio of the within-groups odds for a particular outcome. The correlation $\hat{\varphi}$ for fourfold tables is more problematic. This is because $\hat{\varphi}$ is affected by the marginal proportions for group membership and the dichotomous outcome. The sensitivity, specificity, and predictive value framework was also introduced. This approach takes explicit account of the effect of population base rates on the accuracy of decisions based on a screening test for the presence or absence of a disorder or condition. In general, screening tests are not very useful for detecting the presence of a rare condition, but they may be quite accurate in ruling it out. The opposite tends to be true when the base rate is closer to 1.0 than 0. The next chapter considers effect size estimation in comparative studies with three or more conditions and continuous outcomes.

RECOMMENDED READINGS

Fleiss, J. L. (1994). Measures of effect size for categorical data. In H. Cooper & L. V. Hedges (Eds.), *The handbook of research synthesis* (pp. 245–260). New York: Russell Sage Foundation.

Griner, P. F., Mayewski, R. J., Mushlin, A. I., & Greenlan, P. (1981). Selection interpretation of diagnostic tests and procedures: Principles and applications. *Annals of Internal Medicine, 94,* 557–592.

Kennedy, M. L., Willis, W. G., & Faust, D. (1997). The base-rate fallacy in school psychology. *Journal of Psychoeducational Assessment, 15,* 292–307.

6

EFFECT SIZE ESTIMATION
IN ONE-WAY DESIGNS

It's all very well in practice,
but it will never work in theory.
—Anonymous management maxim (Larman, 2002, p. 127)

This chapter discusses estimation of effect size magnitude in one-way designs with at least three conditions and continuous outcome variables. Greater emphasis is placed on focused comparisons (contrasts) with a single degree of freedom (df) than on the omnibus comparison of all the means where $df \geq 2$. This is because the latter are often uninformative (see chap. 2, this volume). A large omnibus effect can also be misleading if it is a result of a single discrepant mean that is not of substantive interest. The next two sections address contrast specification and effect size estimation with standardized mean differences for fixed factors. Later sections review measures of association for fixed or random factors and special issues for effect size estimation in covariate analyses. A supplemental reading on this book's Web site reviews effect size estimation in multivariate one-way designs with independent samples. Exercises with answers for this chapter are also available on the Web site.

CONTRAST SPECIFICATION AND TESTS

This section describes the basic rationale of contrast specification. It can be skipped by readers who are already familiar with this topic; otherwise it needs close study. A design with a single fixed factor is assumed. Because the levels of a random factor are selected by a chance-based method to enhance generalizability, analysis of the omnibus effect is usually more appropriate than contrast analyses that compare just two levels at a time.

Specification

A contrast is a directional effect that corresponds to a particular facet of the omnibus effect. Contrasts are often represented in the statistical literature with the symbols ψ or $\hat{\psi}$. The former is a parameter that represents a weighted sum of population means:

$$\psi = \sum_{i=1}^{a} c_i \mu_i \qquad (6.1)$$

where $(c_1, c_2, \ldots, c_a)$ is the set of *contrast weights* or *coefficients* that specifies the comparison. Application of the same weights to sample means estimates ψ:

$$\hat{\psi} = \sum_{i=1}^{a} c_i M_i \qquad (6.2)$$

The weights that specify a contrast must respect certain rules: They must sum to zero ($\Sigma c_i = 0$), and the weights for at least two different means should not equal zero. Means assigned a weight of zero are excluded from the contrast, and means with positive weights are compared with means given negative weights. Suppose factor A has $a = 3$ levels. The weights $(1, 0, -1)$ meet all the requirements stated earlier and specify the contrast

$$\hat{\psi}_1 = (1)\, M_1 + (0)\, M_2 + (-1)\, M_3 = M_1 - M_3$$

which is the *pairwise comparison* of M_1 with M_3 excluding M_2. The weights $(-1, 0, 1)$ just change the sign of ψ_1. In general, the sign of a contrast is arbitrary. By the same logic, the sets of weights

$$(\tfrac{1}{2}, 0, -\tfrac{1}{2}),\ (5, 0, -5),\ \text{and}\ (1.7, 0, -1.7)$$

among innumerable others with the same pattern of coefficients all specify the same pairwise comparison as the set $(1, 0, -1)$. The scale of $\hat{\psi}_1$ will change depending on which of the sets of weights is applied to the means. This does not affect statistical tests or measures of association for contrasts because their equations correct for the scale of the weights.

However, the scaling of contrast weights is critical if a comparison should be interpreted as the difference between the averages of two subsets of means. If so, the weights should make up what Keppel (1991) called a *standard set* and satisfy what Bird (2002) called *mean difference scaling*. The sum of the absolute values of the coefficients in a standard set is two ($\Sigma|c_i| =$ 2.0). This implies for a pairwise comparison that one weight must be +1, another must be −1, and the rest are all zero. For example, the coefficients (1, 0, −1) are a standard set for the comparison of M_1 with M_3, but the set (½, 0, −½) is not.

At least three means contribute to a *complex comparison*. An example of a complex comparison is when a control condition is compared with the average of two treatment conditions. A complex comparison is still a single-*df* effect because only two means are compared, at least one of which is averaged over two or more conditions. A standard set of weights for a complex comparison is specified as follows: The coefficients for one subset of conditions to be averaged together each equals +1 divided by the number of conditions in that subset; the coefficients for the other subset of conditions to be averaged over all equal −1 divided by the number of conditions in that subset; and weights for any excluded condition are zero. For example, the set of coefficients (½, −1, ½) is a standard set for the contrast

$$\hat{\psi}_2 = (½) M_1 + (−1) M_2 + (½) M_3 = (M_1 + M_3)/2 − M_2$$

which compares M_2 with the average of M_1 and M_3. However, the weights (1, −2, 1) are not a standard set for the same comparison because the sum of their absolute value is 4.0, not 2.0.

Two contrasts are *orthogonal* if they each reflect an independent aspect of the omnibus effect; that is, the result in one comparison says nothing about what may be found in the other. In a balanced one-way design, two contrasts are orthogonal if the sum of the products of their corresponding weights is zero, or:

$$\sum_{i=1}^{a} c_{1_i} c_{2_i} = 0 \qquad (6.3)$$

In an unbalanced design, two contrasts are orthogonal if

$$\sum_{i=1}^{a} \frac{c_{1_i} c_{2_i}}{n_i} = 0 \qquad (6.4)$$

where n_i is the number of cases in the *i*th condition. A pair of contrasts is *nonorthogonal* (correlated) if their weights do not satisfy Equation 6.3 in a

TABLE 6.1
Examples of Orthogonal and Correlated Mean Difference Contrasts

Contrast	Weights			Sum
	c_1	c_2	c_3	
Orthogonal pair				
$\hat{\psi}_1$	1	0	−1	0
$\hat{\psi}_2$	½	−1	½	0
Cross-product	.5	0	−.5	0
Correlated pair				
$\hat{\psi}_2$	½	−1	½	0
$\hat{\psi}_3$	1	−1	0	0
Cross-product	.5	1	0	1.5

balanced design or Equation 6.4 in an unbalanced design. Correlated contrasts describe overlapping facets of the omnibus effect.

Table 6.1 presents the standard sets of weights for two different pairs of contrasts in a balanced one-way design. The first pair is orthogonal because the sum of the cross-products of their weights is zero. Intuitively, these contrasts are unrelated because the two means compared in $\hat{\psi}_1$, M_1 and M_3, are combined in $\hat{\psi}_2$ and contrasted against a third mean, M_2. The second pair of contrasts in Table 6.1 is not orthogonal because the sum of the cross-products of their weights is 1.5, not 0. Contrasts $\hat{\psi}_2$ and $\hat{\psi}_3$ are correlated because M_2 is one the of the two means compared in both.

If every pair in a set of contrasts is orthogonal, the entire set is orthogonal. The maximum number of orthogonal comparisons is limited by the degrees of freedom of the omnibus effect, $df_A = a - 1$. The overall A effect can theoretically be broken down into $a - 1$ independent directional effects. Expressed in terms of sums of squares, this is

$$SS_A = \sum_{i=1}^{a-1} SS_{\hat{\psi}_i} \qquad (6.5)$$

where SS_A and $SS_{\hat{\psi}_i}$ are, respectively, the sum of squares for the omnibus effect and the ith contrast in a set of $a - 1$ orthogonal comparisons. The same idea can also be expressed in terms of variance-accounted-for effect sizes:

$$\hat{\eta}_A^2 = \sum_{i=1}^{a-1} \hat{\eta}_{\hat{\psi}_i}^2 \qquad (6.6)$$

where $\hat{\eta}_A^2$ and $\hat{\eta}_{\hat{\psi}_i}^2$ are, respectively, the observed correlation ratios for the omnibus effect and the ith contrast in a set of all possible orthogonal contrasts. All the terms mentioned are defined later.

There is generally more than one set of orthogonal comparisons that could be specified for the same one-way design. For example, contrasts $\hat{\psi}_1$ and $\hat{\psi}_2$ in Table 6.1 defined by the weights (1, 0, −1) and (½, −1, ½), respectively, make up an orthogonal set for a factor with three levels. A different pair of orthogonal contrasts is specified by the weights (1, −1, 0) and (½, ½, −1). In general, any set of a −1 orthogonal contrasts satisfies Equations 6.5 and 6.6. Statisticians like orthogonal contrasts because of their statistical independence. However, it is better to specify a set of nonorthogonal comparisons that addresses substantive questions than a set of orthogonal comparisons that does not. See B. Thompson (1994) for more information about orthogonal versus nonorthogonal contrasts.

If the levels of factor A are equally spaced along a quantitative scale, such as the drug dosages 3, 6, and 9 mg · kg⁻¹, special contrasts called *trends* or *polynomials* can be specified. A trend describes a particular shape of the relation between a continuous factor and outcome. There are as many possible trend components as there are degrees of freedom for the omnibus effect. For example, if a continuous factor has three equally spaced levels, there are only two possible trends, linear and quadratic. If there are four levels, an additional polynomial, a cubic trend, may be present. However, it is rare in behavioral research to observe nonlinear trends beyond a quadratic effect.

There are standard weights for polynomials. Some statistical software programs that analyze trends automatically generate these weights. Tables of standard polynomial weights are also available in several statistics textbooks (e.g., Winer, Brown, & Michels, 1991, p. 982). For example, the set of standard weights for a pure linear trend for a factor with three equally spaced levels is (−1, 0, 1). The weight of zero in this set can be understood as the prediction that M_2 is halfway between M_1 and M_3. The set of standard weights for a pure quadratic trend is (1, −2, 1), and it predicts that $M_1 = M_3$ and that M_2 differs from both. More than one trend component may be present in the data. For example, learning curves often have both linear and quadratic components. Trends in balanced designs are always orthogonal and thus are called *orthogonal polynomials*. Please note that except for linear trends in one-way designs with two or three samples, the sum of the absolute values of the weights that define trends is not 2.0; that is, they are not standard sets. This is not a problem because trends are not generally mean difference contrasts in the sense discussed earlier. Also, the effect size magnitude of trends are usually estimated with measures of association, not standardized mean differences.

Statistical Tests

The test statistic for a contrast is $t_{\hat{\psi}}$ or $F_{\hat{\psi}}$. When a nil hypothesis is tested for the same contrast, $t_{\hat{\psi}}^2 = F_{\hat{\psi}}$, but $t_{\hat{\psi}}$ preserves the sign of the contrast and can test non-nil hypotheses, too. When the samples are independent, one can compute a standardized mean difference or a correlation effect size from either $t_{\hat{\psi}}$ or $F_{\hat{\psi}}$ for a nil hypothesis. This makes these test statistics useful even if a nil hypothesis is probably false.

The form of the t statistic for a contrast between independent means in either a balanced or unbalanced one-way design is $t_{\hat{\psi}}(df_W) = (\hat{\psi} - \psi_0)/s_{\hat{\psi}}$, where df_W is the total within-conditions degrees of freedom $N - a$, ψ_0 is value of the contrast specified in the null hypothesis, and $s_{\hat{\psi}}$ is the standard error of the contrast. The latter is

$$s_{\hat{\psi}} = \sqrt{MS_W \left(\sum_{i=1}^{a} \frac{c_i^2}{n_i} \right)} \qquad (6.7)$$

where MS_W is the pooled within-conditions variance (see also Equation 2.30).

The form of the F statistic for a contrast between independent means is $F_{\hat{\psi}}(1, df_W) = SS_{\hat{\psi}}/MS_W$ where the numerator equals

$$SS_{\hat{\psi}} = \frac{\hat{\psi}^2}{\sum_{i=1}^{a} \frac{c_i^2}{n_i}} \qquad (6.8)$$

The statistical assumptions of the t and F tests for contrasts between independent means are described in chapter 2.

The situation is more complicated when the samples are dependent. The omnibus error term—which may be designated $MS_{A \times S}$ for a nonadditive model or MS_{res} for an additive model—assumes sphericity, which may be unlikely in many behavioral studies (see chap. 2, this volume). Error terms of $t_{\hat{\psi}}$ or $F_{\hat{\psi}}$ printed by statistical software programs that analyze data from correlated designs may be based on scores from just the two conditions involved in the contrast (e.g., Keppel, 1991, pp. 356–361). These tests are actually forms of the dependent samples t test, which does not require sphericity because only two conditions are compared. The form of this t statistic for a contrast in a correlated design is $t_{\hat{\psi}}(n - 1) = (\hat{\psi} - \psi_0)/s_{\hat{\psi}}$, where the standard error in the denominator is

$$s_{\hat{\psi}} = \sqrt{\frac{s_{D_{\hat{\psi}}}^2}{n}} \qquad (6.9)$$

In Equation 6.9, $s^2_{D_{\hat\psi}}$ is the variance of the contrast difference scores and n is the group size. A difference score $D_{\hat\psi}$ can be computed for each contrast and for every case in a repeated-measures design or set of matched cases in a matched-groups design. Each difference score is a linear combination of the original scores across the levels of the factor weighted by the contrast coefficients. Suppose in a one-way design with three levels of a repeated-measures factor A that the coefficients for $\hat\psi_2$ are ($\frac{1}{2}$ −1, $\frac{1}{2}$). The scores across the levels of A for a particular case are 17, 20, and 25. The difference score for this case on this contrast equals

$$D_{\hat\psi_2} = (\tfrac{1}{2})\ 17 - (1)\ 20 + (\tfrac{1}{2})\ 25 = 1$$

Difference scores for the other cases on the same contrast are computed the same way, and their average for the whole sample equals $\hat\psi_2$.

The variance $s^2_{D_{\hat\psi}}$ takes account of the cross-conditions correlation for that contrast (e.g., Equation 2.15). In general, this variance decreases as the correlations increase. If the cross-conditions correlations are reasonably positive, the contrast standard error may be smaller than that which may be found for the same contrast in a between-subjects design with the same factor and outcome variable.

Control of Type I Error

With the caveats given next, it is useful to know something about methods to control experimentwise Type I error across multiple comparisons. Methods for *planned comparisons* assume a relatively small number of a priori contrasts, but methods for *unplanned comparisons* anticipate a larger number of post hoc tests, such as all possible pairwise contrasts. A partial list of methods is presented in Table 6.2 in ascending order by degree of protection against experimentwise Type I error and in descending order by power. These methods generally use $t_{\hat\psi}$ or $F_{\hat\psi}$ as test statistics but compare them against critical values higher than those from standard tables (i.e., it is more difficult to reject H_0). For example, the adjusted level of statistical significance for an individual comparison (α^*) in the Dunn–Bonferroni methods equals α_{EW}/k, where the numerator is the rate of experimentwise rate of Type I (see chap. 2, this volume) and k is the number of contrasts. If $\alpha_{EW} = .05$ and $k = 10$, the level of statistical significance for each individual contrast is $\alpha^* = .05/10 = .005$ in the Dunn–Bonferroni method. In unprotected tests of the same 10 contrasts, the level of α would be .05 for each contrast. The methods listed in the table are also associated with the construction of simultaneous confidence intervals for ψ (defined later).

TABLE 6.2
Partial List of Methods That Control Experimentwise Type I Error for Multiple Comparisons

Method	Nature of protection against experimentwise type I error
Planned comparisons	
Unprotected	None; uses standard critical values for t_ψ and F_ψ
Dunnett	Across pairwise comparisons of a single control group with each of $a - 1$ treatment groups
Bechhofer–Dunnett	Across a maximum of $a - 1$ orthogonal a priori contrasts
Dunn–Bonferroni	Across a priori contrasts that are either orthogonal or nonorthogonal
Unplanned comparisons	
Newman-Keuls,[a] Tukey HSD[b]	Across all pairwise comparisons
Scheffé	Across all pairwise and complex comparisons

[a]Also called Student–Newman–Keuls.
[b]HSD = honestly significant difference; also called Tukey A.

See Winer et al. (1991, pp. 140–197) for more information about methods to control for Type I error across multiple comparisons in single-factor designs.

It was mentioned earlier that there is not a clear consensus that control of experimentwise Type I error is desirable if the power of the unprotected tests is already low (see chap. 3, this volume). There is also little need to worry about experimentwise Type I error if a relatively small number of contrasts is specified. Wilkinson and the Task Force on Statistical Inference (1999) noted that the tactic of testing all pairwise comparisons following rejection of H_0 in the test of the omnibus effect is typically *wrong*. Not only does this approach make the individual comparisons unnecessarily conservative when a classical post hoc method such as the Newman–Keuls procedure is used, but it is rare that all such contrasts are interesting. The cost for reducing Type I error across all comparisons is reduced power for the specific tests the researcher really cares about.

Confidence Intervals for ψ

Distributions of sample contrasts are simple, and correct confidence intervals for ψ can be constructed with central test statistics. The general form of an individual $100(1 - \alpha)\%$ confidence interval for ψ is

$$\hat{\psi} \pm s_{\hat{\psi}} \left[t_{\hat{\psi} 2\text{-tail}, \, \alpha} \, (df_{\text{error}}) \right] \tag{6.10}$$

The standard error of the contrast, $s_{\hat{\psi}}$, is defined by Equation 6.7 when the samples are independent and by Equation 6.9 when they are dependent. The term in brackets is the positive two-tailed critical value of t at the α level of statistical significance with degrees of freedom equal to those of the corresponding analysis of variance (ANOVA) error term for the same contrast. It is also possible to construct *simultaneous confidence intervals*—also known as *joint confidence intervals*—based on more than one observed contrast. The width of a simultaneous confidence interval for ψ is typically wider than that of the individual confidence interval for ψ based on the same contrast. This is because simultaneous confidence intervals take account of multiple comparisons—that is, they control for experimentwise Type I error. For example, the level of α^* for a simultaneous confidence interval in the Dunn–Bonferroni method equals α_{EW}/k where k is the number of contrasts. If $\alpha_{EW} = .05$ and $k = 10$, the level of statistical significance for the critical t statistic in Equation 6.10 is $\alpha^* = .05/10 = .005$. The resulting simultaneous 99.5% confidence interval based on $t_{\hat{\psi}_{2\text{-tail}, .005}}$ will be wider than the corresponding 95% individual confidence interval based on $t_{\hat{\psi}_{2\text{-tail}, .05}}$ for the same comparison. See Bird (2002) for more information about simultaneous confidence intervals for ψ.

STANDARDIZED CONTRASTS

Contrast weights that are standard sets are assumed next. A standardized mean difference for a contrast is *standardized contrast*. The parameter estimated by a sample standardized contrast is $\delta_{\psi} = \psi/\sigma^*$, where the numerator is the unstandardized population contrast and the denominator is a population standard deviation. Recall that there is more than one population standard deviation for a comparative study. For example, σ^* could be the standard deviation in just one of the populations or, under the homogeneity of variance assumption, it ocould be the common population standard deviation across all conditions. The form of a generic standardized contrast is $d_{\hat{\psi}} = \hat{\psi}/\hat{\sigma}^*$, where the numerator is the observed contrast and the denominator—the standardizer—is an estimator of σ^* that is not the same in all kinds of $d_{\hat{\psi}}$ statistics.

Independent Samples

Three basic ways to estimate σ^* in one-way designs with independent samples are listed next. Olejnik and Algina (2000) described another method for individual difference factors (see chap. 4, this volume), but it is not used as often. The first two options are based on methods for two-group designs, so they may be better for pairwise comparisons than complex comparisons. The third method is good for either kind of comparison:

1. Select the standard deviation of only one group, usually the control group when treatment is expected to affect both central tendency and variability. This makes $d_{\hat{\psi}}$ analogous to Glass's Δ. This method may also be preferred if the within-groups variances are heterogenous, but it may be necessary to report more than one value of $d_{\hat{\psi}}$ for the same contrast.
2. Estimate σ^* as the square root of the pooled within-groups variance for only the two groups being compared (i.e., s_P; Equation 2.9). This makes $d_{\hat{\psi}}$ analogous to Hedges's g. However, this method ignores the variances in all the other groups. Another possible drawback is that the standardizer of $d_{\hat{\psi}}$ could be different for each contrast.
3. Standardize $\hat{\psi}$ against the square root of the pooled within-groups variance for all a groups in the design, MS_W. Now $d_{\hat{\psi}}$ for different contrasts will all be based on the same estimator of σ^*, which in this case is the common population standard deviation σ. An implication of this choice is that the standardizer $(MS_W)^{1/2}$ assumes homogeneity of variance across all conditions.

Given reasonably similar within-groups variances, the third method may be the best choice. It generates a standardized contrast that is an extension of Hedges's g for designs with three or more groups. For this reason it is referred to as $g_{\hat{\psi}}$.

The value of $g_{\hat{\psi}} = \hat{\psi}/(MS_W)^{1/2}$ can also be computed from $t_{\hat{\psi}}$ for a nil hypothesis (Equation 6.7), the contrast weights, and the group sizes as follows:

$$g_{\hat{\psi}} = t_{\hat{\psi}} \sqrt{\sum_{i=1}^{a} \frac{c_i^2}{n_i}} \tag{6.11}$$

If the design is balanced, Equation 6.11 reduces to $g_{\hat{\psi}} = t_{\hat{\psi}}(2/n)^{1/2}$ for a pairwise contrast. Please note that $g_{\hat{\psi}}$ takes the sign of $t_{\hat{\psi}}$. If the square root of $F_{\hat{\psi}}$ is substituted for $t_{\hat{\psi}}$ in this equation, $g_{\hat{\psi}}$ will be positive regardless of the direction of the mean contrast.

Table 6.3 presents a small data set for a balanced design where $n = 5$. Table 6.4 reports the results of an independent samples ANOVA of the omnibus effect and two orthogonal contrasts defined by the weights $(1, 0, -1)$ and $(\frac{1}{2}, -1, \frac{1}{2})$ where

$\hat{\psi}_1 = M_1 - M_3 = 13.00 - 12.00 = 1.00$
$\hat{\psi}_2 = (M_1 + M_3)/2 - M_2 = (13.00 + 12.00)/2 - 11.00 = 1.50$

TABLE 6.3
Raw Scores and Descriptive Statistics for Three Samples

	Condition		
	1	2	3
	9	8	10
	12	12	11
	13	11	13
	15	10	11
	16	14	15
M	13.00	11.00	12.00
s^2	7.50	5.00	4.00

Note. In a dependent samples analysis, $r_{12} = .735$; $r_{13} = .730$; and $r_{23} = .839$.

Please note in Table 6.4 that

$$SS_A = SS_{\hat{\psi}_1} + SS_{\hat{\psi}_2} = 2.50 + 7.50 = 10.00$$

which is just as predicted by Equation 6.5. The values of $g_{\hat{\psi}}$ for the two contrasts are

$$g_{\hat{\psi}_1} = 1.00/5.50^{1/2} = .45^{1/2} \, (2/5)^{1/2} = .43$$
$$g_{\hat{\psi}_2} = 1.50/5.50^{1/2} = 1.36^{1/2} \, [.5^2/5 + (-1^2)/5 + .5^2/5]^{1/2} = .64$$

Based on these results, we can say that the difference between M_1 and M_3 is .43 standard deviations large. The size of this effect is somewhat smaller than that of the contrast between the average of these two means and M_2, which is .64 standard deviations in magnitude.

TABLE 6.4
Independent Samples Analysis of the Data in Table 6.3

Source	SS	df	MS	F	Effect size		
					$g_{\hat{\psi}}$	$\hat{\eta}^2$	Partial $\hat{\eta}^2$
Between (A)	10.00	2	5.00	.91[a]	—	.13	—
$\hat{\psi}_1 = 1.00$	2.50	1	2.50	.45[b]	.43	.03	.04
$\hat{\psi}_2 = 1.50$	7.50	1	7.50	1.36[c]	.64	.10	.10
Within (error)	66.00	12	5.50				
Total	76.00	14					

Note. The contrast weights for $\hat{\psi}_1$ are (1, 0, −1) and for $\hat{\psi}_2$ are (½, −1, ½).
[a]$p = .429$.   [b]$p = .509$.   [c]$p = .332$.

Dependent Samples

There are three basic ways to calculate a standardized mean change in a one-way design with dependent samples. They differ only in the choice of the standardizer:

1. With one exception, use any of the methods described in the previous section for contrasts between unrelated means. These methods estimate population standard deviation in the metric of the original scores, but they ignore the cross-conditions correlations in a correlated design. The exception is Equation 6.11, which generates $g_{\hat{\psi}}$ but requires an independent samples test statistic.

2. Standardize the dependent mean change against the standard deviation of the contrast difference scores, $s_{D_{\hat{\psi}}}$. This option takes account of the cross-conditions correlation, but it does not describe change in the metric of the original scores. The ratio $\hat{\psi}/s_{D_{\hat{\psi}}}$ estimates the parameter $\psi/\sigma_{D_{\psi}}$, where the denominator is the population standard deviation of the contrast difference scores (see Equation 2.13). The ratio $\hat{\psi}/s_{D_{\hat{\psi}}}$ may not be directly comparable with $d_{\hat{\psi}}$ from an independent samples design with the same factor and outcome variable.

3. Standardize the contrast against the square root of the error term of $F_{\hat{\psi}}$. This error term for a dependent contrast is a residual variance after removing the subjects effect and either the omnibus effect or the contrast from total variance. However, the metric of this residual mean square is not generally that of either the original scores or the contrast difference scores, so it may not provide a meaningful reference point. This option is *not* recommended.

Table 6.5 reports the results of a dependent-samples analysis of the data in Table 6.3 for the omnibus effect and the same two contrasts analyzed in Table 6.4. Note that the error terms, F ratios, and p values are all different across Tables 6.4 and 6.5. However, the values of $g_{\hat{\psi}_1}$ and $g_{\hat{\psi}_2}$ are the same across both analyses—.43 and .64, respectively. This is because $g_{\hat{\psi}}$ is calculated the same way regardless of the design. The value of the ratio $\hat{\psi}/s_{D_{\hat{\psi}}}$ for each contrast is also reported in Table 6.5. These values are, respectively, .53 and 1.18, and they are each greater than the corresponding value of $g_{\hat{\psi}}$ for the same contrasts. This is expected given the relatively high cross-conditions correlations for these data, .730–.839 (see Table 6.3).

TABLE 6.5

Source	SS	df	MS	F	$g_{\hat{\psi}}$	$\hat{\psi}/s_{D_{\hat{\psi}}}$	$\hat{\eta}^2$	Partial $\hat{\eta}^2$
Between (A)	10.00	2	5.00	3.53[a]	—	—	.13	.47
$\hat{\psi}_1 = 1.00$	2.50	1	2.50	1.76[b]	.43	.53	.03	.18
$\hat{\psi}_2 = 3.00$	7.50	1	7.50	5.28[c]	.64	1.18	.10	.40
Within	66.00	12	5.50					
Subjects (S)	54.67	4	13.67					
$A \times S$ (error)	11.33	8	1.42					
Total	76.00	14						

Note. The contrast weights for $\hat{\psi}_1$ are (1, 0, −1) and for $\hat{\psi}_2$ are (½, −1, ½). The variances of the contrast difference scores for the data in Table 6.3 are $s^2_{D_{\psi 1}} = 3.500$ and $s^2_{D_{\psi 2}} = 1.625$.
[a]$p = .080$. [b]$p = .221$. [c]$p = .051$.

Approximate Confidence Intervals for δ_{ψ}

Distributions of sample contrasts are simple, but this is not true for standardized contrasts. When the samples are independent and the observed effect size is $g_{\hat{\psi}}$, an approximate confidence interval for δ_{ψ} can be obtained by dividing the endpoints of the corresponding confidence interval for ψ (Equation 6.10) by the square root of MS_W, the pooled within-groups variance. The general form of the resulting interval is

$$g_{\hat{\psi}} \pm s_{g_{\hat{\psi}}} [t_{\hat{\psi}_{2\text{-tail}, \alpha}} (df_W)] \qquad (6.12)$$

where the approximate standard error of $g_{\hat{\psi}}$ equals

$$s_{g_{\hat{\psi}}} = \sqrt{\sum_{i=1}^{a} \frac{c_i^2}{n_i}} \qquad (6.13)$$

Bird recommends the same method when the samples are dependent and the observed effect size is $g_{\hat{\psi}}$. This method standardizes the bounds of the confidence interval for ψ with a standard deviation in the metric of the original scores, just as when the samples are independent. The resulting interval also takes account of the cross-conditions correlations for the contrast because the standard error of $\hat{\psi}$ does so in a correlated design (Equation 6.9). Another alternative is to standardize the bounds of the confidence interval for ψ on the basis of the standard deviation of the contrast difference scores, s_{D_ψ}. The endpoints of the resulting standardized interval are symmetrical around $\hat{\psi}/s_{D_\psi}$, the standardized contrast that expresses change in difference score units. A drawback to this approach is that the confidence interval for δ_ψ in a correlated design will not be directly comparable with the corresponding interval in a design with the same factor and outcome measure but where the samples are independent.

Refer back to Table 6.4 and look over the results of the independent samples analysis of the data in Table 6.3. The standard errors of $\hat{\psi}_1 = 1.00$ and $\hat{\psi}_2 = 1.50$ are

$$s_{\hat{\psi}_1} = \{5.50\,[1^2/5 + 0^2/5 + (-1)^2/5]\}^{1/2} = 1.48$$
$$s_{\hat{\psi}_2} = \{5.50\,[.5^2/5 + (-1)^2/5 + .5^2/5]\}^{1/2} = 1.29$$

Given $t_{\hat{\psi}2\text{-tail},\,.05}\,(12) = 2.179$, the individual 95% confidence intervals for ψ based on $\hat{\psi}_1$ and $\hat{\psi}_2$ are, respectively,

$1.00 \pm 1.48\,(2.179)$ or 1.00 ± 3.23 with the endpoints -2.23 and 4.32
$1.50 \pm 1.29\,(2.179)$ or 1.50 ± 2.80 with the endpoints -1.30 and 4.30

If we divide the endpoints of these intervals by the square root of $MS_W = 5.50$, we obtain the approximate 95% confidence intervals for δ_ψ. The lower and upper bounds of the standardized interval based on $g_{\hat{\psi}_1} = .43$ are, respectively, $-.95$ and 1.80, and the corresponding bounds of the interval based on $g_{\hat{\psi}_2} = .64$ are, respectively, $-.55$ and 1.83. The range of imprecision is so wide because of the small group size ($n = 5$).

Now look at the results of the dependent samples analysis in Table 6.5 for the same data. The variances of the contrast difference scores are $s_{D_{\psi_1}}^2 = 3.500$ and $s_{D_{\psi_2}}^2 = 1.625$. The standard errors of $\hat{\psi}_1 = 1.00$ and $\hat{\psi}_2 = 1.50$ are

$$s_{\hat{\psi}_1} = (3.500/5)^{1/2} = .837 \qquad \text{and} \qquad s_{\hat{\psi}_2} = (1.625/5)^{1/2} = .570$$

Given $t_{\hat{\psi}2\text{-tail},\,.05}\,(4) = 2.776$, the individual 95% confidence intervals for ψ based on $\hat{\psi}_1$ and $\hat{\psi}_2$ are, respectively,

$1.00 \pm .837\,(2.776)$ or 1.00 ± 3.323 with the endpoints -1.323 and 3.323
$1.50 \pm .570\,(2.776)$ or 1.50 ± 1.583 with the endpoints $-.083$ and 3.083

Dividing the endpoints of these intervals for ψ by the square root of $MS_W = 5.50$ gives the endpoints of individual approximate 95% confidence intervals for δ_ψ. The lower and upper bounds of the resulting interval for δ_ψ based on $g_{\hat{\psi}_1} = .43$ are, respectively, $-.564$ and 1.417, and the corresponding bounds of the resulting interval for δ_ψ based on $g_{\hat{\psi}_2} = .64$ are, respectively, $-.035$ and 1.315. As expected, each of the 95% confidence intervals for ψ or δ_ψ in the dependent samples analysis is narrower than the corresponding interval in the independent samples analysis of the same data.

The freely available computer program PSY by Bird, Hadzi-Pavlovic, and Isaac (2000) automatically constructs individual or simultaneous confidence intervals for ψ or approximate confidence intervals for δ_ψ when the observed effect size is $g_{\hat{\psi}}$ in designs with one or more between-subjects or within-subjects factors.[1] This program standardizes contrasts based on the square root of MS_W in all the designs it analyzes. It accepts only whole-number contrast coefficients, but it can automatically rescale them as mean difference contrast coefficients.

Exact Confidence Intervals for δ_ψ

The rationale to construct an exact individual confidence interval for $\delta_\psi = \psi/\sigma$ in a design with three or more independent samples when $g_{\hat{\psi}}$ is the observed effect size is similar to that in a two-group design. Briefly, the population standardized contrast δ_ψ is related to the noncentrality parameter (*ncp*) of noncentral t as follows:

$$\delta_\psi = ncp \sqrt{\sum_{i=1}^{a} \frac{c_i^2}{n_i}} \qquad (6.14)$$

If we can find a confidence interval for *ncp*, then we can find one for δ_ψ. The lower bound of a $100 (1 - \alpha)$% confidence interval for *ncp*, ncp_L, is the noncentrality parameter of the noncentral t distribution in which the observed $t_{\hat{\psi}}$ falls at the $100 (1 - \alpha/2)$th percentile. The upper bound, ncp_U, equals the noncentrality parameter of the noncentral t distribution in which the observed $t_{\hat{\psi}}$ falls at the $100 (\alpha/2)$th percentile. To find which particular noncentral t distributions correspond to ncp_L and ncp_U, we can use basically the same computer tools described in chapter 4. Once we have the interval ncp_L–ncp_U, we then use Equation 6.14 to convert the endpoints to values in δ_ψ units. An example follows.

Refer back to Table 6.4, which reports the results of an independent samples analysis of the data in Table 6.3. The first contrast analyzed is defined by the weights $(1, 0, -1)$. The standardized contrast is $g_{\hat{\psi}_1} = .43$ and the test statistic is $F_{\hat{\psi}_1} (1, 12) = .45$. The square root of the latter is

---

[1] http://www.psy.unsw.edu.au/research/PSY.htm

$t_{\hat{\psi}_1}(12) = .674$. The noncentral t distribution calculator of the Power Analysis module of STATISTICA (StatSoft Inc., 2003) was used to find the lower and upper bounds of the individual 95% confidence interval for ncp for this contrast. The observed $t_{\hat{\psi}_1}$ of .674 falls at the 97.5th percentile in the noncentral t distribution where the noncentrality parameter equals -1.31766. The same observed $t_{\hat{\psi}_1}$ falls at the 2.5th percentile in the noncentral t distribution where the noncentrality parameter equals 2.63840. The 95% confidence interval for ncp is thus -1.31766–2.63840. Using Equation 6.14, the endpoints of this interval are transformed to δ_ψ units by multiplying them by the following quantity:

$$[1^2/5 + 0^2/5 + (-1)^2/5]^{1/2} = .63246$$

The resulting interval, $-.83336$ to 1.66867, which is $-.83$ to 1.67 at two-decimal accuracy, is the exact 95% confidence interval for δ_ψ. Thus, the observed effect size of $g_{\hat{\psi}_1} = .43$ is just as consistent with a population effect size as low as $\delta_\psi = -.83$ as it is with a population effect size as high as $\delta_\psi = 1.67$, with 95% confidence. This wide range of imprecision is a result of the small group size ($n = 5$).

The top of Table 6.6 presents a SAS syntax that calculates the lower and upper bounds of the individual 95% confidence intervals for ncp and δ_ψ for the previous example. The lower part of the table reports the output from SAS/STAT (SAS Institute Inc., 2000) after running the code in the top part of the table. These lower and upper bounds of the 95% confidence intervals computed by SAS/STAT are the same as those as derived earlier for the same data but using a different computer tool. The syntax in Table 6.6 can be reused for any contrast in a three-group design by substituting the values in boldface with those from a new sample. The same syntax can be extended for use in designs with four or more groups by making appropriate modifications (e.g., give values for n4 and c4 when there are four groups, and include these variables in subsequent equations in the proper places).

Another computer tool for obtaining exact individual confidence intervals for δ_ψ in designs with fixed factors is the Exploratory Software for Confidence Intervals (ESCI) program by Cumming (2002). When the samples are independent, ESCI standardizes each contrast based on pooled within-groups standard deviation from only the conditions compared in the contrast. When the samples are dependent, ESCI standardizes the contrast based on $s_{D_{\hat{\psi}}}$, the standard deviation of the contrast difference scores. If the researcher wishes to standardize the dependent mean contrast based on the square root of MS_W instead of $s_{D_{\hat{\psi}}}$, an approximate confidence interval for δ_ψ could be calculated instead.

TABLE 6.6
SAS Syntax to Compute an Exact 95% Confidence Interval for δ_ψ in One-Way Designs With Independent Samples and Output

Syntax

```
data noncentral_ci_for_delta_psi;
  /* one-way between-subjects design */
  /* data */
t_contrast=.674; df=12;
n1=5; n2=5; n3=5;
c1=1; c2=0; c3=-1;
  /* lower, upper bound for ncp */
ncp_lower=tnonct (t_contrast, df, .975);
ncp_upper=tnonct (t_contrast, df, .025);
  /* lower, upper bounds for delta */
delta_psi_lower=ncp_lower*sqrt(c1**2/n1 + c2**2/n2 + c3**2/n3);
delta_psi_upper=ncp_upper*sqrt(c1**2/n1 + c2**2/n2 + c3**2/n3);
output;
run;
proc print;
run;
```

Output

Obs	t_contrast	df	n1	n2	n3	c1	c2	c3	ncp_lower	ncp_upper	delta_psi lower	delta_psi upper
1	0.674	12	5	5	5	1	0	-1	-1.31766	2.63840	-0.83336	1.66867

MEASURES OF ASSOCIATION

Descriptive and inferential measures of association are discussed next. Some differences among them are outlined. The descriptive measure is the squared sample correlation estimated eta-squared, $\hat{\eta}^2$. The inferential measures include estimated omega-squared, $\hat{\omega}^2$, and the sample intraclass correlation, $\hat{\rho}_I$, which is already in a squared metric. All the indexes just mentioned estimate the proportion of total variance explained by an effect, but they differ in how they do so and their underlying distributional assumptions. There are also partial forms of all three measures of association that remove variance as a result of other sources of between-conditions variability from the total variance for a comparative study. The statistics $\hat{\eta}^2$ and $\hat{\omega}^2$ assume a fixed factor, but $\hat{\rho}_I$ is for a random factor. The latter is typically calculated only for the omnibus A effect in a one-way design. The statistics $\hat{\omega}^2$ and $\hat{\rho}_I$ assume a balanced design, but $\hat{\eta}^2$ does not. Compared to $\hat{\eta}^2$, the statistic $\hat{\omega}^2$ is generally a less biased estimator of the population proportion of explained variance for a comparative study. However, values of the two estimators for the same effect converge as the sample size increases, keeping all else constant. In a large sample, there is thus no need to prefer $\hat{\omega}^2$ over $\hat{\eta}^2$. In a smaller sample, though, $\hat{\omega}^2$ may give a more realistic estimate than $\hat{\eta}^2$.

Descriptive Measures

The following discussion applies to designs with independent or dependent samples unless otherwise indicated. The statistic $\hat{\eta}^2$ can be computed for basically any effect in a comparative study with fixed factors and continuous outcome variables. Its general form is

$$\hat{\eta}^2_{\text{effect}} = \frac{SS_{\text{effect}}}{SS_T} \tag{6.15}$$

where SS_{effect} is the sum of squares for the effect and SS_T is the total sum of squares. The value of $\hat{\eta}^2_{\text{effect}}$ is the proportion of total observed variance explained by effect, and its square root is the correlation between that effect and the outcome variable. If the degrees of freedom for the effect are greater than one, this correlation is a multiple correlation (R).

The parameter estimated with positive bias is $\eta^2_{\text{effect}} = \sigma^2_{\text{effect}}/\sigma^2_{\text{tot}}$, where the numerator is the population variance due to the effect and the denominator is total population variance. The composition of σ^2_{tot} in a one-way design with independent samples is $\sigma^2_\mu + \sigma^2_\varepsilon$. The former variance component is the variability of the population means that correspond to the omnibus effect, $\mu_1, \mu_2, \ldots, \mu_a$, around the grand mean μ; the latter variance component concerns error variance (see chap. 4, this volume). When the samples are dependent, the total variance also reflects variability because of the subjects effect for both additive and nonadditive models, and for a nonadditive model only it reflects a person × treatment interaction, too. If every case is measured just once in each condition, however, it is not possible to separately estimate error variance and variability as a result of a person × treatment interaction (see chap. 2, this volume).

If $SS_{\text{effect}} = SS_A$ in Equation 6.15 and $df_A > 1$, then $\hat{\eta}_A$ is the multiple correlation between the omnibus effect of factor A and outcome. If the samples are independent, $\hat{\eta}_A$ can also be computed in a one-way design as

$$\hat{\eta}_A = \sqrt{\frac{F_A}{F_A + df_W/df_A}} \tag{6.16}$$

where F_A is the test statistic for the omnibus effect with df_A and df_W degrees of freedom (Equation 2.27).

The form of estimated-eta for a contrast is $\hat{\eta}_{\hat{\psi}} = (SS_{\hat{\psi}}/SS_T)^{1/2}$, which is the absolute value of the bivariate correlation between the contrast and outcome. Within the same data set, $\hat{\eta}_{\hat{\psi}} \leq \hat{\eta}_A$. It is also true that the sum of the $\hat{\eta}_{\hat{\psi}}^2$ values in a set of all possible orthogonal contrasts equals $\hat{\eta}_A^2$ (Equation 6.6). To preserve the sign of the contrast, one can compute the bivariate correlation $r_{\hat{\psi}}$ in a one-way design with independent samples as

$$r_{\hat{\psi}} = t_{\hat{\psi}} \sqrt{\frac{1}{F_A + df_W}} \qquad (6.17)$$

The correlation between the outcome variable and all noncontrast sources of between-conditions variability is $\hat{\eta}_{\text{non-}\hat{\psi}} = (SS_{\text{non-}\hat{\psi}}/SS_T)^{1/2}$, where $SS_{\text{non-}\hat{\psi}} = (SS_A - SS_{\hat{\psi}})$. Comparison of $\hat{\eta}_{\hat{\psi}}$ and $\eta_{\text{non-}\hat{\psi}}$ indicates the relative importance of a contrast versus all noncontrast effects analyzed together. Suppose that $SS_A = 200.00$, $df_A = 3$, $SS_{\hat{\psi}} = 5.00$, and $SS_T = 500.00$. Given these data:

$$\hat{\eta}_{\hat{\psi}} = (5.00/500.00)^{1/2} = .10$$
$$\hat{\eta}_{\text{non-}\hat{\psi}} = [(200.00 - 5.00)/500.00]^{1/2} = .62$$

In words, the predictive power of the contrast is limited compared to that of both noncontrast effects evaluated together. We can also say that at least one of the noncontrast effects must have a higher bivariate correlation with outcome than $\hat{\psi}$.

The general form of the squared correlation between an effect and outcome after removing all noneffect sources of between-conditions variation from total variance is

$$\text{partial } \hat{\eta}_{\text{effect}}^2 = \frac{SS_{\text{effect}}}{SS_{\text{effect}} + SS_{\text{error}}} \qquad (6.18)$$

where SS_{error} is the sums of squares for the effect ANOVA error term. For the omnibus effect in a one-way design with independent samples, $\hat{\eta}_A =$ partial $\hat{\eta}_A$. This is concretely true because the sums of squares for the error term of F_A is SS_W, and $SS_A + SS_W = SS_T$. Conceptually, there is no systematic effect besides the omnibus effect that can be removed from total variance. In a correlated design, however, partial $\hat{\eta}_A$ can be substantially higher than $\hat{\eta}_A$. This is because the former removes the subjects effect from total variance (see chap. 4, this volume). The parameter estimated by partial $\hat{\eta}_{\text{effect}}^2$ is partial $\eta_{\text{effect}}^2 = \sigma_{\text{effect}}^2/(\sigma_{\text{effect}}^2 + \sigma_{\varepsilon}^2)$, the proportion of partial population variance explained by the effect.

In designs with independent samples, partial $\hat{\eta}_{\hat{\psi}}$ is the absolute value of the correlation between the contrast and outcome controlling for all noncontrast effects. In a correlated design, partial $\hat{\eta}_{\hat{\psi}}$ also controls for the subjects effect. For the same contrast, partial $\hat{\eta}_{\hat{\psi}}$ can be substantially higher than $\hat{\eta}_{\hat{\psi}}$ and more similar in magnitude to $\hat{\eta}_A$ for the omnibus effect. This is especially true if neither the effect of the contrast nor all noncontrast effects are relatively small. The square of partial $\hat{\eta}_{\hat{\psi}}$ is the proportion of residual variance explained by the contrast. These proportions are not generally additive over a set of contrasts, orthogonal or not, because each proportion may refer to a different subset of the total variance. For designs with unrelated samples, the sign of the contrast is preserved by the following partial correlation:

$$\text{partial } r_{\hat{\psi}} = t_{\hat{\psi}}\sqrt{\frac{1}{t_{\hat{\psi}}^2 + df_W}} \tag{6.19}$$

Refer back to Table 6.4 and review the results of an independent samples analysis of the data in Table 6.3. Computing correlations from results in Table 6.4, we obtain

$$\hat{\eta}_A = (10.00/76.00)^{1/2} = .36$$
$$\hat{\eta}_{\hat{\psi}_1} = (2.50/76.00)^{1/2} = .18$$
$$\hat{\eta}_{\hat{\psi}_2} = (7.50/76.00)^{1/2} = .31$$

That is, the multiple correlation between factor A and the outcome variable is .36. The bivariate correlation between $\hat{\psi}_2$ (which compares with M_2 with the average of M_1 and M_3) and outcome is nearly as large, .31. The bivariate correlation for $\hat{\psi}_1$ (which compares M_1 with M_3) is .18. Because the contrasts are orthogonal,

$$\hat{\eta}_A^2 = \hat{\eta}_{\hat{\psi}_1}^2 + \hat{\eta}_{\hat{\psi}_2}^2 = .36^2 = .18^2 + .31^2 = .03 + .10 = .13$$

Thus, of the 13% total variance explained by the omnibus effect, 3% is due to $\hat{\psi}_1$ and the rest, 10%, is due to $\hat{\psi}_2$. Partial correlation effect sizes for the same contrasts are

$$\text{partial } \hat{\eta}_{\hat{\psi}_1} = [2.50/(2.50 + 66.00)]^{1/2} = .19$$
$$\text{partial } \hat{\eta}_{\hat{\psi}_2} = [7.50/(7.50 + 66.00)]^{1/2} = .32$$

which are only slightly larger than the respective values of $\hat{\eta}_{\hat{\psi}}$ for the same contrasts, .18 and .31. This happens for these data because the effect of $\hat{\psi}_1$ is relatively small compared to that of $\hat{\psi}_2$, so removing the effects of one contrast from total variance makes little difference in the correlation of the other with outcome.

Refer back to Table 6.5 to scan the results of a dependent samples analysis of the same data. The corresponding values of $\hat{\eta}$ and its square for the omnibus effect, $\hat{\psi}_1$, and $\hat{\psi}_2$ are all the same in both the independent and dependent samples analyses (see Table 6.4). However, the partial correlation between the omnibus effect and outcome in Table 6.5 is

$$\text{partial } \hat{\eta}_A = [10.00/(10.00 + 11.33)]^{1/2} = .68$$

which is substantially higher than the correlation that does not remove the subjects effect, $\hat{\eta}_A = .36$. For the same reason, partial $\hat{\eta}_{\hat{\psi}}$ is quite a bit larger than $\hat{\eta}_{\hat{\psi}}$ for the same contrast in the dependent samples analysis:

$$\hat{\eta}_{\hat{\psi}_1} = (2.50/76.00)^{1/2} = .18 \text{ and}$$
$$\text{partial } \hat{\eta}_{\hat{\psi}_1} = [2.50/(2.50 + 11.33)]^{1/2} = .43$$

$$\hat{\eta}_{\hat{\psi}_2} = (7.50/76.00)^{1/2} = .31 \text{ and}$$
$$\text{partial } \hat{\eta}_{\hat{\psi}_2} = [7.50/(7.50 + 11.33)]^{1/2} = .63$$

Inferential Measures

The parameters estimated by the inferential measures of association $\hat{\omega}^2$ and $\hat{\rho}_I$ are, respectively, ω^2 and ρ_I. To understand these parameters and their estimators, it helps to know something about ANOVA structural models. A *structural model* expresses a hypothetical score as the sum of population parameters that correspond to sources of variation. The classical ANOVA structural model in a single-factor design with independent samples and either a fixed or random factor is

$$X_{ij} = \mu + \alpha_i + \varepsilon_{ij} \tag{6.20}$$

where X_{ij} is the jth score in the ith level of the factor, μ is the population grand mean and a constant part of every score, and ε_{ij} is a random error component.[2] The term α_i represents the effect of the ith level of the factor as a deviation from the grand mean—that is, α_i equals the contrast $\alpha_i = \mu_i - \mu$. Because the sum of all deviations from the mean is zero, $\Sigma\alpha_i = 0$. If the nil hypothesis for the omnibus effect is true, all values of α_i equal 0.

The classical structural model for a design with dependent samples and either a fixed or random factor for an additive model is

$$X_{ij} = \mu + \alpha_i + \pi_j + \varepsilon_{ij} \tag{6.21}$$

---

[2] An alternative structural model, the *cell means model*, is not described here; see Kirk (1995, pp. 240–244) for more information.

where π_j represents the subjects effect. The equation for a nonadditive model is

$$X_{ij} = \mu + \alpha_i + \pi_j + \alpha\pi_{ij} + \varepsilon_{ij} \qquad (6.22)$$

where $\alpha\pi_{ij}$ represents a person × treatment interaction. However, recall that it is not possible to separately estimate variance because of random error versus a true person × treatment interaction when cases are measured just once in each condition. The implication of this statement for effect size estimation is explained later.

For a given structural model, there is a population variance component associated with each term except the constant μ. The sum of all variance components for the model equals the total population variance. For example, the total population variance for a one-way design with independent samples is

$$\sigma^2_{tot} = \sigma^2_\alpha + \sigma^2_\varepsilon \qquad (6.23)$$

where σ^2_α represents systematic variance due to factor A and σ^2_ε designates error variance. For a one-way design with dependent samples assuming an additive model, the total population variance is

$$\sigma^2_{tot} = \sigma^2_\alpha + \sigma^2_\pi + \sigma^2_\varepsilon \qquad (6.24)$$

where σ^2_π is the variance due to the subjects effect. Assuming a nonadditive model:

$$\sigma^2_{tot} = \sigma^2_\alpha + \sigma^2_\pi + \sigma^2_{\alpha\pi} + \sigma^2_\varepsilon \qquad (6.25)$$

where $\sigma^2_{\alpha\pi}$ is the variance due to a person × treatment interaction.

The form of ω^2 for an effect of a fixed factor is $\omega^2_{effect} = \sigma^2_{effect}/\sigma^2_{tot}$. If we are referring to the omnibus effect, then $\omega^2_A = \sigma^2_\alpha/\sigma^2_{tot}$; if referring to a contrast, then $\omega^2_\psi = \sigma^2_\psi/\sigma^2_{tot}$. There is also partial ω^2, which has the general form $\sigma^2_{effect}/(\sigma^2_{effect} + \sigma^2_\varepsilon)$, where the denominator reflects variance due to the effect of interest and error variance. In a one-way design with independent samples, ω^2_A = partial ω^2_A; otherwise, the value of partial ω^2 can be greater than that of ω^2 for the same effect because only the denominator of the former controls for other effects. As mentioned, the parameter ρ_I for a design with a random factor usually concerns just the omnibus effect. Its general form is $\rho_I = \sigma^2_\alpha/\sigma^2_{tot}$ which is the same as that of ω^2 for the omnibus effect of a fixed factor. However, the sample estimators of the variance components in the numerator or denominator of ρ_I versus ω^2 are different depending on the characteristics of the factor and the design. There is also partial $\rho_I = \sigma^2_\alpha/(\sigma^2_\alpha + \sigma^2_\varepsilon)$, which in a correlated design controls for the subjects effect.

Several advanced textbooks about ANOVA, such as Kirk (1995), Myers and Well (2002), and Winer et al. (1991), give equations that express expected sample mean squares as functions of population variance components. This information is useful for identifying proper ANOVA error terms for various effects. By "proper" it is meant that the expected mean square of the error term has all the variance components of the numerator except that of the effect being tested. From an effect size perspective, however, it is more interesting to rearrange these equations so that population variance components can be estimated from the observed mean squares and other information. Extensive sets of equations for variance component estimators in Dodd and Schultz (1973) and Vaughn and Corballis (1969) provide a basis for computing inferential measures of association in various kinds of designs. It is not always possible to estimate variance components without bias, and some population variance components cannot be expressed as unique functions of sample data in some designs. There are heuristic estimators that may let one get by in the latter case, however.

Readers already know that ANOVA error terms for the same effect are different in an independent samples design versus a correlated design. This is because the distributional assumptions for the two ANOVA models are different (see chap. 2, this volume). For the same reason, estimates of population variance components for the same effect are different when the factor is fixed versus random even though the observed mean squares are calculated the same way. Schuster and von Eye (2001) showed that random-effects models and repeated-measures models are actually variations of each other. This is because both allow for dependencies among the observations. In a random-effects model, observations within the same level are presumed to be more like each other than observations in different levels. This implies basically the same covariance model and assumptions that underlie a repeated-measures ANOVA.

For example, the general form of the variance component estimator for any effect in a balanced one-way design with a fixed factor is

$$\hat{\sigma}^2_{\text{effect}} = \frac{df_{\text{effect}}}{an} (\text{MS}_{\text{effect}} - \text{MS}_{\text{error}}) \tag{6.26}$$

where $\text{MS}_{\text{effect}}$ and df_{effect} are, respectively, the effect mean square and degrees of freedom, MS_{error} is the effect ANOVA error term, a is the number of levels of the factor, and n is the group size. Using Equation 6.26, the variance component estimator for the omnibus effect is

$$\hat{\sigma}^2_\alpha = \frac{a-1}{an} (\text{MS}_A - \text{MS}_{\text{error}}) \tag{6.27}$$

and for a contrast it is

$$\hat{\sigma}_{\psi}^2 = \frac{1}{an} \, (SS_{\psi} - MS_{\text{error}}) \tag{6.28}$$

However, when the factor is random, the estimator for the omnibus effect is

$$\hat{\sigma}_{\alpha}^2 = \frac{1}{an} \, (MS_A - MS_{\text{error}}) \tag{6.29}$$

Compare Equations 6.27 and 6.29. For a fixed factor, the ratio $\hat{\sigma}_{\alpha}^2/\hat{\sigma}_{\text{tot}}^2$, where $\hat{\sigma}_{\alpha}^2$ is based on Equation 6.27 equals $\hat{\omega}_A^2$, but the same ratio equals $\hat{\rho}_I$ when the factor is random and $\hat{\sigma}_{\alpha}^2$ is based on Equation 6.29. Likewise, the ratio $\hat{\sigma}_{\alpha}^2/(\hat{\sigma}_{\alpha}^2 + \hat{\sigma}_{\varepsilon}^2)$ equals partial $\hat{\omega}_A^2$ when the factor is fixed, but it equals partial $\hat{\rho}_I$ when the factor is random.

Table 6.7 presents equations for variance component estimators for one-way designs with independent samples. The equations in the top part of Table 6.7 assume a fixed factor. To calculate $\hat{\omega}_{\text{effect}}^2$ or partial $\hat{\omega}_{\text{effect}}^2$ for an effect of a fixed factor, just apply the appropriate equations from this part of the table. For example, the entire equation for $\hat{\omega}_{\text{effect}}^2 = \hat{\sigma}_{\text{effect}}^2/\hat{\sigma}_{\text{tot}}^2$ is assembled from the equations for variance component estimators in Table 6.7 as follows:

$$\begin{aligned}
\hat{\omega}_{\text{effect}}^2 &= \frac{df_{\text{effect}}/an \, (MS_{\text{effect}} - MS_W)}{(a-1)/an \, (MS_A - MS_W) + MS_W} \\
&= \frac{df_{\text{effect}} \, (MS_{\text{effect}} - MS_W)}{SS_T + MS_W}
\end{aligned} \tag{6.30}$$

This equation is actually good for any effect in a completely between-subjects design with one or more fixed factors—simply substitute the overall sample size (N) for the terms an in the right-hand side of Equation 6.30. Again working with the information in the top part of Table 6.7, the entire equation for partial $\hat{\omega}_{\text{effect}}^2 = \hat{\sigma}_{\text{effect}}^2/(\hat{\sigma}_{\text{effect}}^2 + \hat{\sigma}_{\varepsilon}^2)$ for any effect in the type of design just mentioned is

$$\begin{aligned}
\text{partial } \hat{\omega}_{\text{effect}}^2 &= \frac{df_{\text{effect}}/an \, (MS_{\text{effect}} - MS_W)}{df_{\text{effect}}/an \, (MS_{\text{effect}} - MS_W) + MS_W} \\
&= \frac{df_{\text{effect}} \, (F_{\text{effect}} - 1)}{df_{\text{effect}} \, (F_{\text{effect}} - 1) + an}
\end{aligned} \tag{6.31}$$

The equations for variance component estimators in the bottom part of Table 6.7 assume a single random factor and independent samples. These

TABLE 6.7
Equations for Variance Component Estimators in One-Way Designs With
Independent Samples

Factor	Estimator
Fixed	$\hat{\sigma}^2_{\text{effect}} = \dfrac{df_{\text{effect}}}{an}(MS_{\text{effect}} - MS_W)$
	$\hat{\sigma}^2_\alpha = \dfrac{a-1}{an}(MS_A - MS_W)$
	$\hat{\sigma}^2_\varphi = \dfrac{1}{an}(SS_\varphi - MS_W)$
	$\hat{\sigma}^2_\varepsilon = MS_W$
	$\hat{\sigma}^2_{\text{tot}} = \hat{\sigma}^2_\alpha + \hat{\sigma}^2_\varepsilon$
Random	$\hat{\sigma}^2_\alpha = \dfrac{1}{n}(MS_A - MS_W)$
	$\hat{\sigma}^2_\varepsilon = MS_W$
	$\hat{\sigma}^2_{\text{tot}} = \hat{\sigma}^2_\alpha + \hat{\sigma}^2_\varepsilon$

Note. Assumes a balanced design; a = number of levels of factor A; and n = group size.

component equations are assembled to make the entire equation of $\hat{\rho}_I = \sigma^2_\alpha/\hat{\sigma}^2_{\text{tot}}$ for the omnibus effect as follows:

$$\hat{\rho}_I = \frac{(MS_A - MS_W)/n}{(MS_A - MS_W)/n + MS_W} = \frac{MS_A - MS_W}{MS_A + (n-1)\,MS_W} \quad (6.32)$$

An example is presented next.

Suppose that the following results are observed for a balanced design with $a = 3$ groups and $n = 30$ cases in each group: $SS_A = 60.00$, $SS_W = 478.50$, and $SS_T = 538.50$. From these results we can infer that $MS_A = 30.00$, $MS_W = 5.50$, and $F\,(2, 87) = 5.45$. Assuming a fixed factor, the observed proportion of total variance explained by the omnibus effect is $\hat{\eta}^2_A = 60.00/538.50 = .111$, or 11.1%. Using the equations in the top part of Table 6.7 and Equation 6.30:

$$\hat{\omega}^2_A = \frac{2/90\,(30.00 - 5.50)}{2/90\,(30.00 - 5.50) + 5.50} = \frac{2(30.00 - 5.50)}{538.50 + 5.50} = .090$$

The bias-adjusted estimated percentage of total variance explained by the omnibus effect is thus 9.0%. As expected, this estimate is lower than that given by $\hat{\eta}_A^2$ for the same data. Assuming a random factor and using the equations in the bottom part of Table 6.7 and Equation 6.32, we calculate,

$$\hat{\rho}_I = \frac{(30.00 - 5.50)/30}{(30.00 - 5.50)/30 + 5.50} = \frac{30.00 - 5.50}{30.00 + (30 - 1)\,5.50} = .129$$

Thus, the sample intraclass correlation equals .129, so the estimate of the percentage of total variance explained by the omnibus effect of the random factor is 12.9%. This value is different from that of both $\hat{\eta}_A^2$ and $\hat{\omega}_A^2$ based on the same scores because $\hat{\rho}_I$ assumes a different underlying distributional model. See Olejnik and Algina (2000) for additional computational examples.

Tables 6.8 and 6.9 present equations for variance component estimators for one-way designs with dependent samples. These tables assume that each case is measured just once in every condition. The equations in Table 6.8 are for an additive model that assumes no person × treatment interaction. When the factor is fixed, the estimated proportion of total variance explained by an effect is $\hat{\omega}_{effect}^2 = \hat{\sigma}_{effect}^2/(\hat{\sigma}_\alpha^2 + \hat{\sigma}_\pi^2 + \hat{\sigma}_\varepsilon^2)$, and the proportion of partial variance explained by an effect is partial $\hat{\omega}_{effect}^2 = \hat{\sigma}_{effect}^2/(\hat{\sigma}_{effect}^2 + \hat{\sigma}_\varepsilon^2)$. The proportion of explained variance when the factor is random is estimated as $\hat{\rho}_I = \hat{\sigma}_\alpha^2/(\hat{\sigma}_\alpha^2 + \hat{\sigma}_\pi^2 + \hat{\sigma}_\varepsilon^2)$. All the expressions just given assume use of the appropriate equation for $\hat{\sigma}_\alpha^2$ given a factor that is fixed or random.

The equations for variance component estimators listed in Table 6.9 are for a nonadditive model that assumes a true person × treatment interaction. When the factor is fixed, it is not possible to calculate unique estimates of σ_π^2, $\sigma_{\alpha\pi}^2$, and σ_ε^2, the population variance components for the subjects effect, the person × treatment interaction and random error, respectively. Accordingly, combinations of these parameters are heuristically estimated by the equations given in the top part of Table 6.9. The total population variance winds up being estimated as

$$\hat{\sigma}_{tot}^2 = \hat{\sigma}_\alpha^2 + (\hat{\sigma}_\pi^2 + \hat{\sigma}_\varepsilon^2/a) + (\hat{\sigma}_{\alpha\pi}^2 + \hat{\sigma}_\varepsilon^2) \qquad (6.33)$$

which is actually too large by the factor $\hat{\sigma}_\varepsilon^2/a$. This implies that $\hat{\omega}_{effect}^2 = \hat{\sigma}_{effect}^2/\hat{\sigma}_{tot}^2$, where the denominator as defined by Equation 6.33 is too small by the same factor (Winer et al., 1991, p. 276). This problem also complicates calculation of an estimator of partial ω_{effect}^2 because there is no unique estimate of σ_ε^2. The statistic partial $\hat{\eta}^2$ is an alternative in this case. The bottom part of Table 6.9 presents equations for a nonadditive model in

TABLE 6.8
Equations for Variance Component Estimators in One-Way Designs With
Dependent Samples for an Additive Model

Factor	Estimator
Fixed	$\hat{\sigma}^2_{\text{effect}} = \dfrac{df_{\text{effect}}}{an} \, (MS_{\text{effect}} - MS_{\text{error}})$
	$\hat{\sigma}^2_{\alpha} = \dfrac{a-1}{an} \, (MS_A - MS_{\text{error}})$
	$\hat{\sigma}^2_{\varphi} = \dfrac{1}{an} \, (SS_{\varphi} - MS_{\text{error}})$
	$\hat{\sigma}^2_{\pi} = \dfrac{1}{a} \, (MS_S - MS_{\text{error}})$
	$\hat{\sigma}^2_{\varepsilon} = MS_{\text{error}}$
	$\hat{\sigma}^2_{\text{tot}} = \hat{\sigma}^2_{\alpha} + \hat{\sigma}^2_{\pi} + \hat{\sigma}^2_{\varepsilon}$
Random	$\hat{\sigma}^2_{\alpha} = \dfrac{1}{n} \, (MS_A - MS_{\text{error}})$
	$\hat{\sigma}^2_{\pi} = \dfrac{1}{a} \, (MS_S - MS_{\text{error}})$
	$\hat{\sigma}^2_{\varepsilon} = MS_{\text{error}}$
	$\hat{\sigma}^2_{\text{tot}} = \hat{\sigma}^2_{\alpha} + \hat{\sigma}^2_{\pi} + \hat{\sigma}^2_{\varepsilon}$

Note. Assumes a balanced design; MS_{error} = effect error term; a = number of levels of factor A; and n = group size.

which the factor is random. Observe in the table that the ANOVA error term for the effect of interest estimates variability because of both a person × treatment interaction and random error whether the factor is fixed or random.

An alternative to ANOVA-based estimation of variance components in designs with random factors is *maximum likelihood estimation.* This method typically uses an iterative algorithm to improve the estimates until certain statistical criteria are satisfied. It also requires large samples. It is beyond the scope of this section to describe maximum likelihood estimation in any detail—see Eliason (1993) for a succinct but technical overview. A problem that arises with both ANOVA and maximum likelihood methods is negative variance estimates, which is most likely to happen in small samples or when the effect size is small. A negative variance estimate is usually interpreted as though its value were zero.

TABLE 6.9
Equations for Variance Component Estimators in One-Way Designs With
Dependent Samples for a Nonadditive Model

Factor	Estimator
Fixed	$\hat{\sigma}^2_{\text{effect}} = \dfrac{df_{\text{effect}}}{an}(MS_{\text{effect}} - MS_{\text{error}})$
	$\hat{\sigma}^2_\alpha = \dfrac{a-1}{an}(MS_A - MS_{\text{error}})$
	$\hat{\sigma}^2_\varphi = \dfrac{1}{an}(SS_\varphi - MS_{\text{error}})$
	$\hat{\sigma}^2_\pi = \dfrac{\hat{\sigma}^2_\varepsilon}{a} = \dfrac{1}{a}(MS_S)$
	$\hat{\sigma}^2_{\alpha\pi} + \hat{\sigma}^2_\varepsilon = MS_{\text{error}}$
	$\hat{\sigma}^2_{\text{tot}} = \hat{\sigma}^2_\alpha + (\hat{\sigma}^2_\pi + \hat{\sigma}^2_\varepsilon/a) + (\hat{\sigma}^2_{\alpha\pi} + \hat{\sigma}^2_\varepsilon)$
Random	$\hat{\sigma}^2_\alpha = \dfrac{1}{n}(MS_A - MS_{\text{error}})$
	$\hat{\sigma}^2_\pi = \dfrac{1}{a}(MS_S - MS_{\text{error}})$
	$\hat{\sigma}^2_{\alpha\pi} + \hat{\sigma}^2_\varepsilon = MS_{\text{error}}$
	$\hat{\sigma}^2_{\text{tot}} = \hat{\sigma}^2_\alpha + \hat{\sigma}^2_\pi + \hat{\sigma}^2_{\alpha\pi} + \hat{\sigma}^2_\varepsilon$

Note. Assumes a balanced design; MS_{error} = effect error term; a = number of levels of factor A; and n = group size.

Interval Estimation

The measures of association $\hat{\eta}^2$, $\hat{\omega}^2$, and $\hat{\rho}^2_I$ all have complex distributions. Methods for obtaining approximate confidence intervals based on these statistics are not really amenable to hand computation. The same computer programs described in chapter 4 for constructing exact confidence intervals for η^2 based on noncentral test statistics in two-group designs can be used in one-way designs with independent samples and fixed factors. These include a script for SPSS by Smithson (2001), which calculates exact confidence intervals for η^2 when the omnibus effect is analyzed and for partial η^2 when any other effect such as a contrast is analyzed. The SAS syntax listed in Table 4.7 does the same thing. To reuse this syntax, just enter the appropriate value of the observed F statistic and its degrees of freedom for the effect of interest. The Power Analysis module of STATISTICA (StatSoft Inc., 2003) and the R2 program (Steiger & Foudali, 1992) can also derive exact confidence intervals for η^2.

Fidler and Thompson (2001) give a modification to Smithson's SPSS script that constructs noncentral confidence intervals for ω^2. Fidler and Thompson also demonstrate methods to construct exact confidence intervals for ρ_I in one-way designs with independent samples and random factors. These authors noted that confidence intervals based on variance-accounted-for effect sizes are typically wider (less precise) when the factor is random than when it is fixed. This is one of the costs of generalizing beyond the particular levels randomly selected for study. There is at present a paucity of computer programs that calculate exact confidence intervals based on measures of association in correlated designs, but one hopes this situation will change soon.

EFFECT SIZE ESTIMATION IN COVARIATE ANALYSES

The basic rationale of a covariate analysis was given in chapter 2. Recommendations in the statistical literature about effect size estimation in covariate analyses are not consistent. This is probably because effect size can be viewed from more than one perspective in such analyses. To understand these perspectives, one should know basic principles of the analysis of covariance (ANCOVA). These principles are outlined next for one-way designs with a single covariate, but these ideas extend to designs with more than one factor or covariate. The ANCOVA removes variability from the outcome variable that is explained by the covariate. This reduces error variance and may increase the power of statistical tests of group differences compared to ANOVA. The ANCOVA also yields group means on the outcome variable adjusted for the covariate. These adjustments reflect (a) the pooled within-groups regression of the outcome variable on the covariate, and (b) the amount of deviation of the group covariate mean from the grand mean. If this deviation is slight, there is little adjustment. Otherwise, the adjusted means can be substantially higher or lower than the corresponding unadjusted means.

In experimental designs where cases are randomly assigned to conditions, covariate group means differ from each other only by chance. As a consequence, (a) adjusted group means on the outcome variable tend to be similar to the unadjusted means, and (b) it may be only the error term that differs appreciably across ANCOVA and ANOVA results for the same data. In nonexperimental designs, however, the groups may differ systematically on the covariate. Suppose that two intact groups are compared on an outcome measure that reflects social reasoning. The groups also differ in average IQ, which covaries with social reasoning. The ANCOVA compares the groups on social reasoning controlling for IQ. Because the covariate is related to both the independent and dependent variables in this case, the

ANCOVA error term and the adjusted group means can be substantially different from their ANOVA counterparts. However, unless the IQ covariate reflects basically all sources of group differences in social reasoning ability, the adjusted group means can be incorrect, either too high or too low. If there is only one covariate, such inaccuracy is rather likely (e.g., Cronbach, Rogosa, Floden, & Price, 1977). This is why ANCOVA in nonexperimental designs is a not magical cure for group differences on confounding variables—see T. Cook and Campbell (1979, chap. 3) or Campbell and Erlebacher (1975) for excellent reviews.

In designs with independent samples, the ANCOVA has the same statistical requirements as ANOVA (see chap. 2, this volume) plus two others. The first is *homogeneity of regression*, which requires equal within-populations unstandardized coefficients for predicting the outcome variable with the covariate. The second is that the covariate is measured without error (i.e., its scores are perfectly reliable). Violation of either assumption may lead to inaccurate results. For example, an unreliable covariate in an experimental design causes loss of statistical power and in a nonexperimental design may also cause inaccurate adjustment of the means; see Kirk (1995, chap. 15) or Winer et al. (1991, chap. 10) for more information.

McWhaw and Abrami (2001) conducted a 30-minute workshop for Grade 11 students about how to find the main ideas in text. One week later, the same students were randomly assigned to one of two incentive conditions, extrinsic and intrinsic. Students in both conditions were asked to find the main ideas in the same 1,000-word passage. Those in the extrinsic condition were offered a monetary reward if they found 75% of the main ideas, but students in the intrinsic condition were merely encouraged to see the task as a challenge. The outcome variable was the number of main ideas found, and the covariate was the students' grades in school. Descriptive statistics for all variables are summarized in Table 6.10. Because the incentive factor is experimental, it is not surprising that the groups have essentially equal average grades. The correlation between the incentive factor and grades is only $r_{pb} = .03$, and the pooled within-groups correlation between grades and the reading task is .464. Observed means on the reading task indicate that the extrinsic motivation group found on average about one more main idea than the intrinsic motivation group, 3.05 versus 2.08, respectively. The means on the outcome variable for the extrinsic and intrinsic conditions controlling for grades are, respectively, 3.02 and 2.11. The adjusted means are so similar to the observed means because the factor and covariate are essentially unrelated in this study.

The top part of Table 6.11 reports the ANOVA source table for the data in Table 6.10. This analysis ignores the covariate. Key results from the ANOVA are

TABLE 6.10
Descriptive Statistics on the Outcome Variable and Covariate for Two Learning-Incentive Conditions

Variables		Incentive condition	
		Extrinsic	Intrinsic
	n	37	55
Midterm grades (covariate)			
Observed	M	75.13	74.58
	s	10.69	7.37
Number of main ideas found (outcome variable)			
Observed	M	3.05	2.08
	s	2.42	2.09
Adjusted	M'	3.02	2.11

Note. These data are from McWhaw (personal communication, September 20, 2001) and are used with permission. The pooled within-groups correlation between the covariate and the outcome variable equals .464, and the pooled within-groups unstandardized coefficient for the regression of the outcome variable on the covariate equals .1168.

$$MS_W = 4.96, \; F\,(1, 90) = 4.21, \; p = .043$$

The middle part of Table 6.11 presents the traditional ANCOVA source table for the same data. The symbol "'" designates results adjusted for the co-variate:

$$MS'_W = 3.94, \; F\,(1, 89) = 4.63, \; p = .034$$

Note that the ANCOVA error term and probability of the F test of the incentive factor are both smaller than their ANOVA counterparts. Winer et al. (1991, p. 780) showed that the ANCOVA error term is related to the ANOVA error term as follows:

$$MS'_W = MS_W \left(\frac{(1 - r_p^2)\,(N - a)}{N - a - 1} \right) \qquad (6.34)$$

where r_p^2 is the squared pooled within-groups correlation between the covariate and outcome variable. The term in parentheses corrects the ANOVA error term for the covariate. For this example,

$$MS'_W = 4.96 \; \{[(1 - .464^2)\,(92 - 2)]/(92 - 2 - 1)\} = 3.94$$

TABLE 6.11

Analysis of Variance (ANOVA) and Analysis of Covariance (ANCOVA)
Results for the Data in Table 6.10

Source	SS	df	MS	F	$\hat{\eta}^2$
		ANOVA			
Between (incentive)	20.91	1	20.91	4.21[a]	.045
Within (error)	446.77	90	4.96		
Total	467.68	91			
		Traditional ANCOVA			
Between (incentive)	18.25	1	18.25	**4.63**[b]	.049
Within (error)	350.63	89	3.94		
Total	368.88				
		ANCOVA-as-regression			

Step	Predictors	R^2	R^2 change	F change	df_1	df_2
1	Grades	.212	—	—	—	—
2	Grades, incentive	.250	.038	**4.63**[b]	1	89

[a]$p = .043.$ [b]$p = .034.$

Other results in Table 6.11 will be described later in this section.

Let us consider estimation of the magnitude of the effect of incentive condition on the number of main ideas found with a standardized mean difference. There are two different possibilities for the numerator of $d_{\hat{\psi}}$ in this analysis: the contrast of the two unadjusted means, $M_1 - M_2$, or means adjusted for the covariate, $M'_1 - M'_2$. There are also two different possibilities for the standardizer: A standard deviation in the metric of the original scores or in the metric of the adjusted scores. This makes altogether a total of four different possible forms of $d_{\hat{\psi}}$ for the same contrast. In an experimental design, there should be little difference between $M_1 - M_2$ and $M'_1 - M'_2$. Unless the highly restrictive conditions described earlier hold in a nonexperimental design, the value of $M'_1 - M'_2$ may be inaccurate, so $M_1 - M_2$ as the numerator of $d_{\hat{\psi}}$ may be the best overall choice. The most general choice for a denominator of $d_{\hat{\psi}}$ in the metric of the original scores is the square root of the ANOVA error term, MS_W. This term reflects variability due to the covariate. In contrast, the ANCOVA error term MS'_W and related adjusted variances (e.g., Avery, Cole, Hazucha, & Hartanto, 1985) hold the covariate constant.

Cortina and Nouri (2000) suggested that if the covariate varies naturally in the population to which the results should generalize, selection of $(MS_W)^{1/2}$ as the standardizer may be the best choice. This would be true even if MS'_W is substantially less than MS_W. The grades covariate for the present example varies naturally among students, so the standardized mean

194 EFFECT SIZE ESTIMATION IN ONE-WAY DESIGNS

difference for the comparison of the extrinsic and intrinsic conditions is calculated as

$$g_{\hat{\psi}} = (M_1 - M_2)/(MS_W)^{1/2} = (3.05 - 2.08)/4.96^{1/2} = .44$$

There are also different ways to derive measures of association in covariate analyses. To consider them, refer back to Table 6.11. From the ANOVA results,

$$\hat{\eta}_A^2 = SS_A/SS_T = 20.91/467.68 = .045$$

so incentive explains 4.5% of the total variance in the number of main ideas found ignoring grades. From the traditional ANCOVA results:

$$\hat{\eta}_A^{2\prime} = SS_A'/SS_T' = 18.25/368.88 = .049$$

which says that incentive explains 4.9% of the variance after the effect of grades has been removed (i.e., $\hat{\eta}_A^{2\prime}$ is already a partial correlation ratio).

The results reported in the bottom part of Table 6.11 represent a third perspective. They are from a hierarchical multiple regression in which the grades covariate is entered as a predictor of the reading task at step 1 and incentive condition is entered at step 2. At step 1, the result $R_1^2 = .212$ is just the squared Pearson correlation between grades and outcome. At step 2, the squared multiple correlation between grades and incentive condition together with outcome is $R_2^2 = .250$. From a regression perspective, a covariate and a factor are just two different predictors of the same criterion, so $R_2^2 = .250$ in this view describes the overall predictive power (25% explained variance) in a squared metric. The F ratio reported in boldface for the regression results tests against a nil hypothesis the observed increase in the overall squared multiple correlation of about .04 because of adding the incentive factor to the equation. This increase in the overall proportion of explained variance of about 4% because of incentive is another way to describe effect size magnitude in a squared metric. The regression results also explain why $\hat{\eta}_A^2$ and $\hat{\eta}_A^{2\prime}$ are so similar for these data: The effect of incentive condition is relatively small, so removing the much larger effect of grades from the total observed variance has relatively little impact. See Cortina and Nouri (2000) for more examples of effect size estimation in covariate analyses.

RESEARCH EXAMPLES

Examples of effect-size estimation in three actual one-way designs are presented next. The first two involve the comparison of independent samples and the last concerns a repeated-measures design for learning data.

Cognitive Status of Recreational Ecstasy (MDMA) Users

Ecstasy (MDMA) and related stimulant drugs (MDA, MDEA) are in a class of "recreational" drugs popular among some adolescents and young adults. Results of some animal studies indicate neurotoxic effects of high doses of ecstasy, but whether lower doses impair cognitive functioning in humans is not yet well understood. Gouzoulis-Mayfrank et al. (2000) recruited 28 ecstasy users who also smoked cannabis and compared their performance on standard neuropsychological tasks of attention, learning, and abstract thinking with that of two different control groups of similar age (M = 23 years) and educational backgrounds, cannabis-only users and nonusers of either substance. The ecstasy users agreed to abstain from the drug for at least seven days, which was confirmed by urine analysis on the day of testing.

Gouzoulis-Mayfrank et al. found numerous statistical group differences on the neuropsychological tasks but did not estimate their magnitudes. Table 6.12 presents representative results from this study for two attention tasks and three of learning or abstract thinking. Reported for each task are group descriptive statistics, results of the F test for the omnibus comparison, and the value of $g_{\hat{\psi}}$ for each pairwise contrast. All three groups performed about the same on an attention task of simple reaction time. On a more demanding selective attention task, the ecstasy users performed worse than both other groups by about .80 standard deviations. The ecstasy users also did worse than both other groups on learning tasks and on a task of abstract thinking by about .80 standard deviations. The magnitudes of the differences between the cannabis users and nonusers were generally smaller—about .10 standard deviations—except on the verbal learning task where the nonusers had an advantage of about .40 standard deviations over the cannabis users.

Gouzoulis-Mayfrank et al. discussed at length the possibility that preexisting differences in cognitive ability or neurological status may account for the finding that the ecstasy users performed generally worse than both control groups. Leaving aside this critical issue and the equally important one of whether these results will replicate, let us consider the practical significance of group differences in cognitive functioning that are about .80 standard deviations in magnitude. Assuming normal distributions and homogeneity of variance, it is expected that the typical nonecstasy user will outperform about 80% of the ecstasy users (U_3 = .79; refer back to Table 4.8). It is also expected that ecstasy users will be underrepresented by a factor of about 3½ among those young adults who are more than one standard deviation above the mean in the combined distribution for learning and abstract reasoning ability (right-tail ratio = 3.57).

TABLE 6.12
Cognitive Test Scores for Ecstasy (MDMA) Users, Cannabis Users,
and Nonusers

Task		1 ecstasy	2 cannibis	3 nonuser	F (2,81)	p	(1–2)	(1–3)	(2–3)
		User group					**g_ψ for pairwise contrasts**		
	n	28	28	28					
Attention[a]									
Simple	M	218.9	221.1	218.7	.07	.932	–.08	.01	.09
	(s)	(28.2)	(26.3)	(27.5)					
Selective		532.0	484.4	478.6	7.23	.001	.83	.93	.10
		(65.4)	(57.9)	(48.4)					
Learning and abstract thinking									
Verbal[b]		4.46	3.71	3.29	9.22	<.001	.73	1.13	.41
		(.79)	(1.15)	(1.12)					
Visual[b]		4.61	4.00	4.11	2.12	.127	.52	.42	–.09
		(.96)	(1.41)	(1.13)					
Abstract thinking[c]		25.96	29.46	29.50	7.29	.001	–.88	–.89	–.01
		(4.10)	(4.19)	(3.64)					

Note. From "Impaired Cognitive Performance in Drug Free Users of Recreational Ecstacy (MDMA)," by E. Gouzoulis-Mayfrank, J. Daumann, F. Tuchtenhagen, S. Pelz, S. Becker, H.-J. Kunert, B. Fimm, and H. Sasa, 2000, *Journal of Neurology, Neurosurgery, and Psychiatry, 68,* p. 723. Copyright 2000 by BMJ Publishing. Adapted with permission.
[a]Scores are in milliseconds; higher scores indicate worse performance.
[b]Number of learning trials; higher scores indicate worse performance.
[c]Higher scores indicate better performance.

Basic Math Skills and Outcome in Introductory Statistics

The data set for this example was introduced in chapter 4. Briefly, a test of basic math skills was administered at the beginning of the semester to 667 students in introductory statistics courses. The top half of Table 6.13 reports average math test scores by letter grade earned in the course at the end of the semester or whether students withdrew from the class. The bottom half of the table reports ANOVA results, effect sizes, and confidence intervals for the omnibus effect, the contrast of students with satisfactory versus unsatisfactory outcomes (at least a final letter grade of C versus all other outcomes, respectively), and all noncontrast effects analyzed together. The observed standardized mean difference for the contrast is $g_\psi = .50$. The exact 95% confidence interval for δ_ψ based on this result was computed in SAS/STAT using the syntax in Table 6.6 modified for the data in this example. This interval is .26–.58, so the finding that students with a satisfactory

TABLE 6.13
Math Skills Test Scores by Course Outcome Among Introductory
Statistics Students

| Statistic | Course outcome (grades) | | | | | |
| | Satisfactory | | | Unsatisfactory | | |
	A	B	C	D	F	Withdrew
n	129	211	171	78	38	40
M	12.02	10.95	10.18	9.58	9.89	9.05
SD	2.95	3.10	2.91	2.84	3.34	3.82

| Source | SS | df | MS | F | Effect Size | | |
					$g_{\hat\psi}$	$\hat\eta^2$	Partial $\hat\eta^2$
Between (outcome)	513.69	5	102.73	10.99[a]	—	.08[d]	—
$\hat\psi_{\text{sat. vs. unsat.}} = 1.54^b$	260.53	1	260.53	27.89[d]	.50[c]	.04	.04[e]
Non-$\hat\psi_{\text{sat. vs. unsat.}}$	253.16	4	63.29	6.78[a]	—	.04	.04[f]
Within (error)	6,176.35	661	9.34				
Total	6,690.04	666					

Note. The contrast weights for $\hat\psi_{\text{sat. vs. unsat.}}$ are ($\frac{1}{3}$, $\frac{1}{3}$, $\frac{1}{3}$, $-\frac{1}{3}$, $-\frac{1}{3}$, $-\frac{1}{3}$).
[a]$p < .001$.   [b]95% confidence interval (CI) for ψ is .97–2.12.
[c]Exact 95% CI for δ_ψ is .26–.58.   [d]Exact 95% CI for η^2 is .04–.11.
[e]Exact 95% CI for partial η^2 is .02–.07.   [f]Exact 95% CI for partial η^2 is .01–.07.

course outcome scored on average one half a standard deviation higher on the math skills tests than students with an unsatisfactory outcome is just as consistent with a population effect size as small as $\delta_\psi = .26$ as it is with a population effect size as large as $\delta_\psi = .58$, with 95% confidence.

The overall correlation between grades in statistics and math test scores is $\hat\eta_A = .28$, and this association explains about $.28^2 = .08$, or 8% of the total variation in the latter. The exact 95% confidence interval for η^2, computed with SAS/STAT using the syntax in Table 4.7 modified for this example, is .04–.11. This means that the observed result $\hat\eta_A^2 = .08$ is just as consistent with a population variance-accounted-for effect size as small as 4% as it is with one as large as 11%, with 95% confidence. About half of the proportion of explained total variance is a result of the contrast between students with satisfactory versus unsatisfactory outcomes in the statistics class ($\hat\eta_{\hat\psi}^2 = .04$). The rest is a result of all other noncontrast effects ($\hat\eta_{\text{non-}\hat\psi}^2 = .04$). Because the values of $SS_{\hat\psi}$ and $SS_{\text{non-}\hat\psi}$ are so similar for these data—respectively, 260.53 and 253.16—partial $\hat\eta_{\hat\psi}^2$ is essentially equal to the corresponding value of $\hat\eta_{\hat\psi}^2$ for each effect. The exact 95% confidence intervals for partial η^2 reported in Table 6.13 based on each individual effect were computed in SAS/STAT using the syntax in Table 4.7 modified for this example. Each of these confidence intervals ranges from about 2 to 7% explained variance.

TABLE 6.14
Case-Level Analysis of the Relation Between Math Skills and Outcome in Statistics

Math score (%)	n	Course outcome		χ^2 (3)	Cramér's V
		Satisfactory	Unsatisfactory		
80–100	133	117 (88.0)	16 (12.0)	30.03[a]	.21
60–79	302	230 (76.2)	72 (23.8)		
40–59	157	123 (78.3)	72 (23.8)		
0–39	75	41 (54.7)	34 (45.3)		

[a]$p < .001$.

Implications of the results described for the contrast between students with satisfactory versus unsatisfactory course outcomes were analyzed at the case level as follows: Scores on the math skills test were partitioned into four categories according to the percentage of correct items, 0–39, 40–59, 60–79, and 80–100%. This was done to find the level of performance (if any) that distinguished students at risk for having difficulties in statistics from their peers. The 4 × 2 crosstabulation presented in Table 6.14 summarizes the relation between the categorized math test variable (rows) and satisfactory versus unsatisfactory course outcome (columns). Cramér's V for this contingency table is .21. The percentages in Table 6.14 indicate the proportion of students with satisfactory versus unsatisfactory outcomes for each of the four levels of math test performance. Only about 12% of students who correctly solved at least 80% of the math test items had unsatisfactory outcomes. The risk of this negative outcome increases to the point where about half (45.3%) of the students who correctly solved fewer than 40% of the math test items had unsatisfactory outcomes.

Analysis of Learning Curve Data

Kanfer and Ackerman (1989) administered to 137 U.S. Air Force personnel a computerized air traffic controller task presented over six 10-minute trials where the outcome variable was the number of successful landings. Table 6.15 summarizes the means, standard deviations, and correlations across all trials. The latter show a typical pattern for learning data in that correlations between adjacent trials are higher than between nonadjacent trials. This pattern violates the sphericity assumption of statistical tests for comparing three or more dependent means for equality (see chap. 2, this volume). The task means over trials show both linear and quadratic trends. The following analysis estimates the relative magnitudes of these trends.

Table 6.16 reports the results of analyses of the omnibus trials effect, the linear and quadratic trends of the learning curve, and all other higher

TABLE 6.15
Descriptive Statistics for a Computerized Air Traffic Controller Task

	Trial					
	1	2	3	4	5	6
M	11.77	21.39	27.50	31.02	32.58	34.20
SD	7.60	8.44	8.95	9.21	9.49	9.62
r^a	1.00					
	.77	1.00				
	.59	.81	1.00			
	.50	.72	.89	1.00		
	.48	.69	.84	.91	1.00	
	.46	.68	.80	.88	.93	1.00

Note. n = 137. From "Models for Learning Data," by M. W. Browne and S. H. C. Du Toit, 1991. In L. M. Collins and J. L. Horn (Eds.), *Best Methods for the Analysis of Change*, p. 49, Washington, DC: American Psychological Association. Copyright 1991 by the American Psychological Association. Adapted with permission.
[a]Lower diagonal-form matrix.

order trends combined. Probability values of all test statistics are based on the Greenhouse–Geisser conservative F (1, 136) test, which assumes maximal violation of sphericity for these data. The magnitudes of all effects are estimated with $\hat{\omega}^2$, using the equations in the top part of Table 6.8 for a fixed factor and an additive model. The error variance for all effects is estimated as MS_{res} = 20.99. (Readers should try to reproduce these results.) The omnibus effect explains 43% of the total variance in the air traffic controller task. Because the linear trend itself accounts for 38% of the total variance, it is plain to see that this polynomial is the most important aspect of the omnibus effect. The quadratic trend in the learning curve explains an additional 5% of the total variance, and all other higher order trends together account for less than 1% of the total variance. The orthogonal linear and quadratic polynomials together thus accounted for virtually all of the explained variance.

In their analysis of the same learning curve data, Kanfer and Ackerman (1989) reduced the unexplained variance even more by incorporating a cognitive ability test as a predictor of learning in addition to the within-subjects trials factor. This approach is further elaborated by Browne and Du Toit (1991), who specified and tested various latent variable models of Kanfer and Ackerman's data. These models attempted to predict not only the mean level of performance over trials but also the shapes and variabilities of the learning curves of the individual participants and whether the parameters of these curves are predicted by overall cognitive ability. In this approach, the proportions of explained variance were well over 50%, which is better than the results reported in Table 6.16. In general, Browne and Du Toit's analyses are much more sophisticated than those described here from a

TABLE 6.16
Analysis of the Learing Curve Data in Table 6.15

Source	SS	df	MS	F	$\hat{\omega}^2$
Between (trials)	49,419.08	5	9,883.82	470.88[c]	.43
$\hat{\psi}_{lin} = 149.24$[a]	43,590.62	1	43,590.62	2,076.73[c]	.38
$\hat{\psi}_{quad} = -58.20$[b]	5,524.43	1	5,524.43	263.19[c]	.05
All other trends	304.04	3	101.35	4.83[d]	<.01
Within	64,807.36	816	79.42		
Subjects (S)	50,531.23	136	371.55		
Residual (error)	14,276.13	680	20.99		
Total	114,226.44	821			

Note. The contrast weights for $\hat{\psi}_{lin}$ are (−5, −3, −1, 1, 3, 5) and for $\hat{\psi}_{quad}$ are (5, −1, −4, −4, −1, 5).
[a]95% confidence interval for ψ_{lin} is 138.41 to 160.07.
[b]95% confidence interval for ψ_{quad} is −65.21 to −51.19.
[c]$p < .001$.   [d]$p = .030$.

traditional ANOVA perspective. They also highlight the potential value of a model-fitting approach for analyzing learning curve data (e.g., Collins & Sayer, 2001).

CONCLUSION

It is usually more informative to analyze contrasts than the omnibus effect in one-way designs. The most general standardized contrast is $g_{\hat{\psi}} = \hat{\psi}/(MS_W)^{1/2}$, where the denominator is the square root of the pooled within-conditions variance. Descriptive measures of association are all forms of the sample correlation $\hat{\eta}$. The coefficient partial $\hat{\eta}$ removes from total variance all sources of between-conditions influence besides that of the effect of interest. Accordingly, partial $\hat{\eta}$ may be substantially greater than $\hat{\eta}$ for the same effect. The inferential measures of association $\hat{\omega}^2$ and partial $\hat{\omega}^2$ are appropriate for balanced designs with fixed factors. Except in large samples, $\hat{\omega}^2$ are partial $\hat{\omega}^2$ may be appreciably lower than $\hat{\eta}$ or partial $\hat{\eta}$ (respectively) for the same effect. The intraclass correlation $\hat{\rho}_I$ is an appropriate variable-level effect size index for the omnibus effect in designs with random factors. The next chapter considers designs with two or more factors.

RECOMMENDED READINGS

Bird, K. D. (2002). Confidence intervals for effect sizes in analysis of variance. *Educational and Psychological Measurement, 62,* 197–226.

Maxwell, S. E., Camp, C. J., & Arvey, R. D. (1981). Measures of strength of association: A comparative examination. *Journal of Applied Psychology, 66*, 525–534.

Smithson, M. (2001). Correct confidence intervals for various regression effect sizes and parameters: The importance of noncentral distributions in computing intervals. *Educational and Psychological Measurement, 61*, 605–632.

7

EFFECT SIZE ESTIMATION IN MULTIFACTOR DESIGNS

Creation and preservation don't do well together.
—Thomas Hardy (1874/1978, p. 295)

Designs with multiple factors and continuous outcomes require special considerations for effect size estimation. This is because some methods for one-way designs may not give the best results in multifactor designs, and ignoring this problem may introduce variation across studies because of statistical artifacts rather than real differences in effect sizes (S. Morris & DeShon, 1997). The next two sections describe various kinds of multifactor designs and review the basic logic of factorial analysis of variance (ANOVA). Readers already very familiar with factorial ANOVA may skip the latter presentation, but otherwise it requires careful study. Effect size estimation with standardized mean differences and measures of association in factorial designs are considered in the third and fourth sections of this chapter. See this book's Web site for exercises with answers for this chapter.

TYPES OF MULTIFACTOR DESIGNS

Multifactor designs arise out of a few basic distinctions, including whether the factors are (a) between-subjects versus within-subjects, (b) manipulated (experimental) versus individual difference (nonexperimental) variables, and (c) whether the relation between the factors is crossed versus nested. The most common type of multifactor design is the *factorial design* where every pair of factors is *crossed*. This means that the levels of each factor are studied in all combinations with levels of other factors. Each combination is studied with an unrelated group in a *completely between-subjects factorial design*—that is, the subjects factor is *nested* under these combinations. If cases are randomly assigned to groups, the design is a *randomized groups factorial design*, and if at least one factor is an individual difference variable and the rest are manipulated variables, it is a *randomized blocks design*. A *mixed within-subjects factorial design*—also called a *split-plot* or just a *mixed design*—has both between-subjects and within-subjects factors. Note that the term *mixed-effects model* or just *mixed model* refers to ANOVA models with both fixed and random factors. In the simplest of mixed designs, two independent samples are each measured on two different occasions. The subjects factor in this design is nested under the group factor and crossed with the repeated-measures factor. If each case in a single sample is tested under every combination of two or more crossed factors, such as three learning trials under each of two different incentive conditions, the design is a *factorial repeated-measures design* or a *completely within-subjects factorial design*. That is, the subjects factor is crossed with all independent variables.

This chapter deals mainly with factorial designs. However, many of the principles of effect size estimation for factorial designs extend to the variations briefly described here. In a *replicated experiment*, there are n/r observations in each cell, where r is the number of replications of each condition. Each set of replicated observations may be collected at different times or locations compared to the original experiment. Replication is then treated in the analysis as a random factor. In a *hierarchical design*, at least one factor is nested under another. This means that different levels of the nested factor are studied at each level of the other factor. Suppose that factor A is drug versus placebo and factor B represents one of four different patient groups from separate clinics. Patients from the first two clinics are randomly assigned to receive the drug and the other two groups get the placebo. The combinations of the two factors in this design are A_1B_1, A_1B_2, A_2B_3, and A_2B_4. Nested group factors such as B in this example are typically considered random.

Other kinds of multifactor designs include *partial* or *incomplete factorial designs*. Levels of each factor in these designs may not be studied in every combination with levels of other factors, and main effects of each factor may be estimated, but not all possible interaction effects. A Latin-Squares design, which counterbalances order effects of repeated-measures factors or allows study of additional factors without an increase in the number of cells compared to the original factorial study, is perhaps the best known example of a partial factorial design. See Kirk (1995, chaps. 13–14) for more information about incomplete designs.

FACTORIAL ANALYSIS OF VARIANCE

To understand effect size estimation in factorial designs, one needs to know about factorial ANOVA. This is a broad topic, and its coverage in applied textbooks is often quite lengthy. These facts preclude a detailed review. Accordingly, the following presentation emphasizes common principles of factorial ANOVA across different designs that also inform effect size estimation. It deals first with concepts in balanced two-way designs and then extends them to designs with three or more factors or unequal cell sizes. It also encourages readers to pay more attention to the sums of squares and mean squares in a factorial ANOVA source table than to F ratios and p values. See Kirk (1995), Myers and Well (2002), or Winer, D. Brown, and Michels (1991) for more information about factorial ANOVA.

Basic Distinctions

Factorial ANOVA models are also generated by a few basic distinctions, including whether the factors are (a) between-subjects versus within-subjects, (b) fixed versus random, and (c) whether the cell sizes are equal or unequal. Not all of these distinctions are absolutely necessary. For example, recall that random models and repeated-measures models in ANOVA are related (see chap. 6, this volume). Schuster and von Eye (2001) showed that repeated-measures ANOVA models can be estimated with basic computer programs for factorial ANOVA without special capabilities for handling repeated observations. In general, the first two distinctions listed affect only the denominators (error terms) of F tests and their statistical assumptions. They do not influence the numerators of these tests; that is, effect sums of squares and mean squares are derived the same way regardless of whether the factor is between-subjects versus within-subjects or fixed versus random; see Frederick (1999) for more information.

A basic distinction that cannot be ignored is whether the cell sizes are equal or unequal. In balanced factorial designs in which all cell sizes are equal, the main and interaction effects (defined later) are independent. This means that they can occur in any combination, and results observed for one effect say nothing about what may be found for another. For this reason, balanced factorial designs are called *orthogonal designs*. Independence of effects in orthogonal designs simplifies their analysis. This is probably why most introductory presentations about factorial ANOVA consider only balanced designs. However, many real-world factorial designs are not balanced, especially in applied research (e.g., H. Keselman et al., 1998).

We must differentiate between unbalanced designs with proportional versus disproportional cell sizes. Consider the two 2×3 factorial designs represented in the table that follows, where the numbers are cell sizes:

	B_1	B_2	B_3
A_1	5	10	20
A_2	10	20	40

	B_1	B_2	B_3
A_1	5	20	10
A_2	10	10	50

The cell sizes in the upper left matrix are proportional because the ratios of their relative values are constant across all rows (1:2:4) and columns (1:2). The cell sizes are disproportional in the upper right matrix because their relative ratios are not constant. For example, the cell size ratio in the first row of the upper right matrix is 1:4:2, but in the second row it is 1:1:5. This distinction is crucial because factorial designs with unequal-but-proportional cell sizes can be analyzed as orthogonal designs (Keren, 1993). This is true because equal cell sizes are a special case of proportional cell sizes.

Disproportional cell sizes cause the factors to be correlated, which implies that their main effects overlap. The greater the departure from proportional cell sizes, the greater is this overlap. Accordingly, factorial designs with disproportional cell sizes are called *nonorthogonal designs*, and they require special methods that try to disentangle correlated effects. Unfortunately, there are several different methods for nonorthogonal designs, and it is not always clear which one is best for a particular study. The choice among these methods affects statistical tests and effect size estimation with measures of association. These points are elaborated later.

Factorial designs tend to have proportional cell sizes if either all or all but one of the factors are experimental. If at least two factors are nonexperimental and cases are drawn from a population where these variables are correlated, the cells sizes may be disproportional. However, this nonorthogonality may be an asset if it reflects disproportional population group sizes. It may be possible to force equal cell sizes by dropping cases from the larger cells or recruiting additional participants for the smaller cells, but the resulting *pseudo-orthogonal design* may not be representative. Note that disproportional cell sizes as a result of systematic data loss from a factorial design that started out with equal cell sizes is a different matter (see chap. 2, this volume).

Basic Sources of Variability

This section defines basic sources of variability in all factorial designs. Just as in one-way ANOVA, total variability in factorial ANOVA can be broken down into two broad components, between and within conditions (cells). In both kinds of ANOVA, the latter is estimated by the pooled within-conditions variance MS_W, the weighted average of the within-conditions variances. For example, the following equation generates MS_W in any two-way factorial design where none of the cells is empty:

$$MS_W = \frac{SS_W}{df_W} = \frac{\sum_{i=1}^{a} \sum_{j=1}^{b} df_{ij} \, (s_{ij}^2)}{\sum_{i=1}^{a} \sum_{j=1}^{b} df_{ij}} \qquad (7.1)$$

In Equation 7.1, a and b are, respectively, the number of levels of factors A and B, SS_W and df_W are, respectively, the total within-conditions sums of squares and degrees of freedom, and df_{ij} and s_{ij}^2 are, respectively, the degrees of freedom $(n_{ij} - 1)$ and variance of the cell at the ith level of A and the jth level of B.

The between-conditions variance in a one-way design, MS_A, reflects the effects of factor A, sampling error, and cell size (Equation 2.29). In a factorial design, the between-conditions variance reflects the main and interactive effects of all factors, sampling error, and cell size. For example, the between-conditions variance in a two-way design is designated below as

$$MS_{A, B, AB} = \frac{SS_{A, B, AB}}{df_{A, B, AB}} \qquad (7.2)$$

where the subscript indicates the main and interaction effects analyzed together, and the degrees of freedom equal the number of cells minus one, or $ab - 1$. It is only in balanced two-way designs that $SS_{A, B, AB}$ can be computed directly as

$$SS_{A, B, AB} = \sum_{i=1}^{a} \sum_{j=1}^{b} n \, (M_{ij} - M_T)^2 \qquad (7.3)$$

where n is the size of all cells, M_{ij} is the mean for the cell at the ith level of A and the jth level of B, and M_T is the grand mean for the whole design. It is also only in balanced two-way designs that the total between-conditions sums of squares can be broken down into unique and additive values for the individual effects:

$$SS_{A, B, AB} = SS_A + SS_B + SS_{AB} \qquad (7.4)$$

This relation can also be expressed in terms of variance-accounted-for effect sizes measured by the correlation ratio:

$$\hat{\eta}_{A, B, AB}^2 = \hat{\eta}_A^2 + \hat{\eta}_B^2 + \hat{\eta}_{AB}^2 \qquad (7.5)$$

Equations 7.4 and 7.5 define orthogonality of the main and interaction effects in two-way designs.

Effects in Balanced Two-Way Designs

The representation in Table 7.1 shows the observed cell means and variances and marginal means in a balanced 2×3 factorial design. Because the cell sizes are equal, the marginal means are just the arithmetic averages of the corresponding row or column cell means. Each marginal mean can also be computed as the average of the individual scores in the corresponding row or column. In other words, the marginal means for each factor are calculated by collapsing across the levels of the other factor. The grand mean for the whole design is the arithmetic average of all six cell means. It can also be computed as the average of the row or column marginal means or as the average of the *abn* individual scores.

Conceptual equations for sample main and interaction sums of squares in balanced two-way designs are presented in Table 7.2. A *main effect* is estimated by the difference between the observed marginal means for the same factor, and the sample sums of squares for that effect is the total of the weighted squared deviations of the associated marginal means from the grand mean. For example, if $M_{A_1} = M_{A_2}$ in Table 7.1, then the estimated main effect of A is zero and $SS_A = 0$; otherwise, $SS_A > 0$, as is the estimated main effect. Because marginal means are computed by collapsing over the levels of the other factor, main effects are single-factor effects. *Simple main effects*—also called just *simple effects*—are another kind of single-factor effect, but they correspond to cell means in the same row or column. There are as many simple effects of each factor as levels of the other factor. For example, there are two estimated simple effects of factor B represented in Table 7.1. One is the simple effect of B at A_1, and it corresponds to the three cell means in the first row, M_{11}, M_{12}, and M_{13}. If any two of these means are different, then the estimate of the simple effect of B at this level of A is not zero. The other estimated simple effect of this factor, B at A_2, corresponds to the cell means in the second row, M_{21}, M_{22}, and M_{23}. The

TABLE 7.1
General Representation of a Balanced 2 × 3 Factorial Design

	B_1	B_2	B_3	Row means
A_1	$M_{11}\ (s_{11}^2)$	$M_{12}\ (s_{12}^2)$	$M_{13}\ (s_{13}^2)$	M_{A_1}
A_2	$M_{21}\ (s_{21}^2)$	$M_{22}\ (s_{22}^2)$	$M_{23}\ (s_{23}^2)$	M_{A_2}
Column means	M_{B_1}	M_{B_2}	M_{B_3}	M_T

Note. The size of all cells is *n*.

TABLE 7.2
Equations for Main and Interaction Effect Sums of Squares in Balanced Two-Way Designs

Source	SS	df
A	$\sum_{i=1}^{a} bn \, (M_{A_i} - M_T)^2$	$a - 1$
B	$\sum_{j=1}^{b} an \, (M_{B_j} - M_T)^2$	$b - 1$
AB	$\sum_{i=1}^{a} \sum_{j=1}^{b} n \, (M_{ij} - M_{A_i} - M_{B_j} - M_T)^2$	$(a-1)(b-1)$

Note. The size of all cells is n.

estimated simple effects of factor A correspond to the pair of cell means in each of the three columns, such as M_{11} versus M_{21} for the estimated simple effect of A at B_1. Sums of squares for simple effects have the same general form as for main effects (Table 7.2) except that the former are the total of the weighted squared deviations of row or column cell means from the corresponding marginal mean, not the grand mean.

The estimated two-way interaction, AB, corresponds to the cell means (see Table 7.2). An *interaction effect* can be understood in a few different ways. It is a combined or joint effect of the factors on the outcome variable above and beyond their main effects. It also a conditional effect that, if present, says that the simple effects of each factor are different across the levels of the other factor. Interaction effects are also called *moderator effects*, and the factors involved in them are *moderator variables*. Both terms emphasize the fact that each factor's influence on the outcome variable changes across the levels of the other factor when there is interaction. Do not confuse a moderator effect with a *mediator effect*, which refers to the indirect effect of one variable on another through a third (mediator) variable. Mediator effects can be estimated in structural equation modeling and meta-analysis (chap. 8, this volume), but not in the ANOVA models discussed in this chapter; see Shrout and Bolger (2002) for more information.

Suppose we observe the following cell means in a 2×3 design:

	B_1	B_2	B_3
A_1	20.00	20.00	20.00
A_2	10.00	20.00	30.00

Note that the estimated simple effect of B at A_1 is zero, because the three cell means in the first row are equal. However, the estimated simple effect of B at A_2 is not zero, because the cell means in the second row are not equal. It is also true that the three estimated simple effects of A at B are all different. The equation for MS_{AB} in Table 7.2 estimates the overall interaction as residual variability of the cell means weighted by their sizes after the main effects have been removed.

It is true in balanced two-way designs that

$$\sum_{j=1}^{b} SS_{A \text{ at } B_j} = SS_A + SS_{AB} \tag{7.6}$$

$$\sum_{i=1}^{a} SS_{B \text{ at } A_i} = SS_B + SS_{AB} \tag{7.7}$$

In words, the total of the sum of squares for all simple effects of each factor equals the total of the sum of squares for the main effect of that factor and the interaction. Equations 7.6 and 7.7 also say that when all simple effects of a factor are analyzed, it is actually the interaction effect and the main effect of that factor that are analyzed. Given their overlap in sums of squares, it is usually not necessary to analyze both sets of simple effects, A at B and B at A. The choice between them should be made on a rational basis, depending on the perspective from which the researcher wishes to describe the interaction.

Just as in one-way ANOVA, we can distinguish in factorial ANOVA between omnibus comparisons where $df \geq 2$ and single-df focused comparisons (contrasts). We must in factorial ANOVA also distinguish between single-factor contrasts and interaction contrasts. A *single-factor contrast* involves the levels of just one factor while we are controlling for the other factors. There are two kinds, *main comparisons* and *simple comparisons* (Keppel, 1991). The former compares two subsets of average marginal means, and the latter compares two subsets of average cell means. For example, the observed contrast $M_{11} - M_{12}$ in Table 7.1 is a simple comparison within the B at A_1 simple effect, but the contrast $M_{B_1} - M_{B_2}$ is a main comparison within the B main effect. Because factor A is dichotomous in this design, its main and simple effects are also contrasts. If the levels of a quantitative factor are equally spaced, trend components can be specified instead of mean difference contrasts. Single-factor comparisons in factorial designs are specified with contrast coefficients just as they are in one-way designs (see chap. 6, this volume).

An *interaction contrast* is specified by a matrix of coefficients the same size as the original design that are *doubly centered*, which means that they sum to zero in every row and column. This property makes the resulting single-df interaction effect independent of the main effects. The weights for a two-way interaction contrast can be assigned directly or taken as the product of the corresponding weights of two single-factor comparisons, one for each independent variable. If the interaction contrast should be interpreted as the difference between a pair of simple comparisons (i.e., mean difference scaling), the sum of the absolute value of the contrast coefficients must be 4.0 (Bird, 2002). This can be accomplished by selecting coefficients for the comparison on each factor that are a standard set (i.e., their absolute values sum to 2.0) and taking their corresponding products. Some examples follow.

In a 2×2 design where all effects are contrasts, a set of weights that defines the interaction effect directly as a "contrast between [mean difference] contrasts" (Abelson & Prentice, 1997) is presented in the cells of the left-most matrix:

	B_1	B_2
A_1	1	-1
A_2	-1	1

	B_1	B_2
A_1	M_{11}	M_{12}
A_2	M_{21}	M_{22}

Note that the weights are doubly centered and the sum of their absolute values is 4.0. We can get the same set of weights for this interaction contrast by taking the corresponding products of the weights $(1, -1)$ for factor A and the weights $(1, -1)$ for factor B. After applying these weights to the corresponding cell means in the above right-most matrix, we get

$$\hat{\psi}_{AB} = M_{11} - M_{12} - M_{21} + M_{22} \tag{7.8}$$

Rearranging the terms shows that $\hat{\psi}_{AB}$ equals (a) the difference between the two simple effects of A at each level of B and (b) the difference between the two simple effects of B at each level of A:

$$\begin{aligned}
\hat{\psi}_{AB} &= \hat{\psi}_{A \text{ at } B_1} - \hat{\psi}_{A \text{ at } B_2} = (M_{11} - M_{21}) - (M_{12} - M_{22}) \\
&= \hat{\psi}_{B \text{ at } A_1} - \hat{\psi}_{B \text{ at } A_2} = (M_{11} - M_{12}) - (M_{21} - M_{22})
\end{aligned} \tag{7.9}$$

In two-way designs where at least one factor has three or more levels, an interaction contrast may be formed by ignoring or collapsing across at least two levels of that factor. For example, the following coefficients define a *pairwise interaction contrast* in a 2×3 design:

	B_1	B_2	B_3
A_1	1	0	-1
A_2	-1	0	1

In the contrast specified, the simple effect of A at B_1 is compared with the simple effect of A at B_3. (It is equivalent to say that these weights specify the contrast of the simple comparison of B_1 with B_3 across the two levels of A.) The weights for the *complex interaction contrast* represented compare B_2 with the average of B_1 and B_3 across the levels of A:

	B_1	B_2	B_3
A_1	½	−1	½
A_2	−½	1	−½

It is left for the readers as an exercise on this book's Web site to show for a balanced 2×3 design that (a) the above two interaction contrasts are orthogonal, and (b) the sums of squares for the omnibus interaction can be uniquely decomposed into the sums of squares for each interaction contrast. The following equation for a balanced design will be handy for this exercise:

$$SS_{\hat{\psi}_{AB}} = \frac{n(\hat{\psi}_{AB})^2}{\left(\sum_{i=1}^{a} c_i^2 \right) \left(\sum_{j=1}^{b} c_j^2 \right)} \qquad (7.10)$$

If at least one factor is quantitative with equally spaced levels, contrast weights for an *interaction trend* may be specified. Suppose in a 2×3 design that factor A represents two different groups of patients and the levels of factor B are three equally spaced dosages of a drug. The weights for the interaction contrast presented below

	B_1	B_2	B_3
A_1	1	−2	1
A_2	−1	2	−1

compare the quadratic effect of the drug across the groups. That the sum of the absolute values of the weights is not 4.0 is not a problem because a differential trend hypothesis is tested. However, it is still necessary to adjust the scale of the resulting weighted sum of means if the effect size of the interaction trend is to be estimated with a standardized mean difference. Abelson and Prentice (1997) recommend multiplying an unstandardized interaction contrast in a two-way design by the term

$$\sqrt{\dfrac{2}{\displaystyle\sum_{i=1}^{a}\sum_{j=1}^{b}c_{ij}^{2}}} \qquad\qquad (7.11)$$

which corrects for the absolute sizes of the contrast weights before standardizing it. (How to standardize contrasts in factorial designs is discussed later.) See Abelson and Prentice (1997) for several examples of tests for differential trends.

Unlike simple effects, interaction contrasts are not confounded with the main effects in balanced designs. For this reason, researchers may prefer to analyze interaction contrasts instead of simple effects when the main effects are relatively large. It is also possible to test a priori hypotheses about specific facets of an omnibus interaction through the specification of interaction contrasts. It is not usually necessary to analyze both simple effects and interaction contrasts in the same design, so either one or the other should be chosen as a means to understand an interaction.

If the reader gets the impression that there are numerous effects that can be analyzed in two-way designs—main, simple, interaction, and contrasts for any of the aforementioned effects that are omnibus—you are correct. This is even more true in designs with three or more factors. One can easily get lost by estimating every possible effect in a factorial design. *It is thus crucial to have a plan that minimizes the number of analyses while still respecting the essential research hypotheses.* Some of the worst misuses of statistical tests are seen in factorial designs where all possible effects are tested and sorted into two categories, those found to be statistical and subsequently discussed at length versus those found to be nonstatistical and subsequently ignored. These misuses are compounded when power is ignored. This is because power can be different for all omnibus effects in a factorial design. This happens because the (a) degrees of freedom of the F statistic for different effects can be different and (b) numbers of scores that contribute to different means vary. In a balanced 2×3 design where $n = 10$, for example, the two means for the A main effect are each based on 30 scores, but the three means for the B main effect are each based on 20 scores. The power for the test of the A main effect may be different for the power of the test of the B main effect, and the power for the test of the AB effect may be different still. Estimating a priori power and effect size magnitude can help to sort substantive wheat from statistical chaff in factorial designs. It also helps to realize that as the magnitude of interaction effects become larger compared to those of the main effects, detailed analysis of the latter becomes increasingly fruitless.

Tests in Balanced Two-Way Designs

Table 7.3 presents raw scores and descriptive statistics for balanced 2×3 designs, where $n = 3$. The data in the top part of the table are arranged in a layout consistent with a completely between-subjects design, where each score comes from a different case. The same layout is also consistent with a mixed within-subjects (split-plot) design, where the three scores in each row are from the same case; that is, A is a group factor and B is a repeated-measures factor. The same data are presented in the bottom part of the table in a completely within-subjects layout, where the six scores in each row are from the same case. The following results are obtained after applying Equations 7.1 and 7.3 and those in Table 7.2 to the data in Table 7.3 in either layout:

$$SS_W = 64.00$$

$$SS_{A, B, AB} = SS_A + SS_B + SS_{AB} = 18.00 + 48.00 + 84.00 = 150.00$$

$$SS_T = 64.00 + 150.00 = 214.00$$

The results of three different factorial analyses of variance for the data in Table 7.3 assuming fixed factors are reported in Table 7.4. Results in the top of Table 7.4 are from a completely between-subjects analysis, results in the middle of the table come from a split-plot analysis, and the results in the bottom of the table are from a completely within-subjects analysis. Note that only the error terms, F ratios, and p values depend on the design. The sole error term in the completely between-subjects analysis is MS_W, and the statistical assumptions for tests with it are described in chapter 2. In the split-plot analysis, SS_W and df_W are partitioned to form two different error terms, one for between-subjects effects (A) and another for repeated-measures effects (B, AB). Tests with the former error term, designated in the table as S/A for "subjects within groups under A," assume homogeneity of variance for case average scores across the levels of the repeated-measures factor. The within-subjects error term, $B \times S/A$, assumes that both within-populations covariance matrices on the repeated-measures factor are not only spherical but equal; see Kirk (1995, chap. 12) and Winer et al. (1991, pp. 512–526) for more information. A different partition of SS_W in the completely within-subjects analysis results in sums of squares for three different error terms for repeated-measures effects, $A \times S$, $B \times S$, and $AB \times S$, and a sum of squares for the subjects effect, S.

Factorial ANOVA generates the same basic source tables when either one or both factors are considered random instead of fixed. The only difference is that main effects may not have the same error terms in a random-

TABLE 7.3
TABLE 7.3
Raw Scores and Descriptive Statistics for Balanced 2 × 3 Factorial Designs

Completely between-subjects or mixed within-subjects layout[a]

		B_1	B_2	B_3	
A_1		8 7 12	10 11 15	9 7 11	
		9.00 (7.00)[b]	12.00 (7.00)	9.00 (4.00)	10.00
A_2		3 5 7	5 5 8	10 14 15	
		5.00 (4.00)	6.00 (3.00)	13.00 (7.00)	8.00
		7.00	9.00	11.00	9.00

Completely within-subjects layout

A_1B_1	A_1B_2	A_1B_3	A_2B_1	A_2B_2	A_2B_3
8 7 12	10 11 15	9 7 11	3 5 7	5 5 8	10 14 15
9.00 (7.00)	12.00 (7.00)	9.00 (4.00)	5.00 (4.00)	6.00 (3.00)	13.00 (7.00)

[a]Assumes A is the between-subjects factor and B is the repeated measures factor.
[b]Cell mean (variance).

effects model as in a fixed-effects model. For example, the error term for the main effects in a completely between-subjects design with two random factors is MS_{AB}, not MS_W. However, MS_W is still the error term for the AB effect. Tabachnick and Fidell (2001) gave a succinct, nontechnical explanation: Because levels of both factors are randomly selected, it is possible that a special interaction occurred with these particular levels. This special interaction may confound the main effects, but the ratios

$$F_A = MS_A/MS_{AB} \quad \text{and} \quad F_B = MS_B/MS_{AB}$$

are expected to cancel out these confounds in statistical tests of the main effects. See Tabachnick and Fidell (2001, p. 665) for error terms for two-way designs of the kind analyzed in Table 7.4 when at least one factor is random. Maximum likelihood estimation as an alternative to traditional ANOVA can also be used in factorial designs with random factors (see chap. 6, this volume).

TABLE 7.4
Analysis of Variance Results for the Data in Table 7.3

Source	SS	df	MS	F	p
Completely between-subjects analysis					
Between-subjects effects					
A	18.00	1	18.00	3.38	.091
B	48.00	2	24.00	4.50	.035
AB	84.00	2	42.00	7.88	.007
Within cells (error)	64.00	12	5.33		
Mixed within-subjects analysis					
Between-subjects effects					
A	18.00	1	18.00	1.27	.323
Within-subjects effects					
B	48.00	2	24.00	26.17	<.001
AB	84.00	2	42.00	45.82	<.001
Within cells	64.00	12	5.33		
S/A (error for A)	56.67	4	14.17		
B × S/A (error for B, AB)	7.33	8	.92		
Completely within-subjects analysis					
Within-subjects effects					
A	18.00	1	18.00	5.68	.140
B	48.00	2	24.00	144.00	<.001
AB	84.00	2	42.00	25.20	.005
Within cells	64.00	12	5.33		
Subjects (S)	50.33	2	25.17		
A × S (error for A)	6.33	2	3.17		
B × S (error for B)	.67	4	.17		
AB × S (error for AB)	6.67	4	1.67		

Note. $SS_T = 214.00$ and $df_T = 17$ for all analyses.

Complete Versus Reduced Structural Models

The *complete ANOVA structural model* for a completely between-subjects two-way factorial design is

$$X_{ijk} = \mu + \alpha_i + \beta_j + \alpha\beta_{ij} + \varepsilon_{ijk} \qquad (7.12)$$

where X_{ijk} is the kth score in the cell at the ith level of factor A and the jth level of factor B; μ is the population grand mean; α_i, β_j, and $\alpha\beta_{ij}$, respectively, represent the population main and interaction effects as deviations from the grand mean; and ε_{ijk} is a random error component. This model is complete because it includes terms for all possible sources of variation; it is also the model that underlies the derivation of the sums of squares for the source table in the top part of Table 7.4. The complete structural models that underlie the other two source tables in Table 7.4 are somewhat different because either one or both independent variables are within-subjects factors, but the general idea is the same. The structural model for a factorial design also generates predicted marginal and cell means. However, these predicted means equal their observed counterparts for a complete structural model. That is, the observed marginal means estimate the population main effects and the observed cell means estimate the population interaction effect.

It is possible in some software programs for factorial ANOVA to specify a *reduced structural model* that, compared to the complete model, does not include parameters for all effects. Parameters in the complete model are typically considered for exclusion in a sequential order beginning with those for the highest order interaction. If the parameters for this interaction are retained, the complete model cannot be simplified. For example, the two-way interaction is the highest order population effect represented in Equation 7.12. If the parameters that correspond to $\alpha\beta_{ij}$ are dropped, the complete model is reduced to the *main effects model*

$$X_{ijk} = \mu + \alpha_i + \beta_j + \varepsilon_{ijk} \tag{7.13}$$

which assumes only population main effects. Two consequences arise from rejection of the complete structural model in favor of the main effects model. First, the sums of squares for the *AB* effect are pooled with those of the total within-cells variability to form a composite error term for tests of the main effects. Second, the reduced structural model generates predicted cell means that may differ from the observed cell means. It is also possible that standard errors of differences between predicted cell means may be less than those for differences between observed cell means. Accordingly, the researcher may choose to analyze the predicted cell means instead of the observed cell means. This choice also affects effect size estimation.

Briefly, there are two grounds for simplifying structural models, rational and empirical. The first is based on the researcher's domain knowledge about underlying sources of variation and the second is based on results of statistical tests. In the latter approach, parameters for nonstatistical interactions become candidates for exclusion from the model. The empirical approach is controversial because it capitalizes on sample-specific variation and also ignores effect size magnitude. The rational approach makes factorial ANOVA more like a model-fitting method than a strictly exploratory method; Lunneborg (1994) explored this theme in detail. Researchers who analyze data in comparative studies with regression computer programs are probably accustomed to testing complete versus reduced models, but those who use mainly ANOVA programs may not have the same view.

Extensions to Designs With Three or More Factors

All of the principles discussed extend to balanced factorial designs with more than two factors. For example, there are a total of seven estimated main and interaction effects in a three-way design, including three main effects (A, B, and C) each averaged over the other two factors, three two-way interactions (AB, AC, and BC) each averaged over the third factor, and the highest order interaction, ABC. A three-way interaction means that the effect of each factor on the outcome variable changes across the levels of the other two factors. It also means that the *simple interactions* of any two factors are not the same across the levels of the third factor (e.g., the AB effect changes across C_1, C_2, etc.). Omnibus ABC effects can be partitioned into three-way interaction contrasts. When expressed as a mean difference contrast, a three-way interaction contrast involves two levels from each factor. That is, a $2 \times 2 \times 2$ matrix of means is analyzed, and the sum of the absolute values of the contrast weights that specify it is 8.0. It is left as an exercise for the reader on this book's Web site to show that the three-way interaction in a $2 \times 2 \times 2$ design equals the difference between all possible pairs of simple interactions, or

$$\hat{\Psi}_{ABC} = \hat{\Psi}_{AB \ at \ C_1} - \hat{\Psi}_{AB \ at \ C_2} = \hat{\Psi}_{AC \ at \ B_1} - \hat{\Psi}_{AC \ at \ B_2}$$
$$= \hat{\Psi}_{BC \ at \ A_1} - \hat{\Psi}_{BC \ at \ A_2} \qquad (7.14)$$

See Keppel (1991, chap. 20) for examples of the specification of three-way interaction contrasts.

Just as in two-way designs, the derivation of effect sums of squares in factorial designs with three or more independent variables is the same regardless of whether the factors are between-subjects versus within-subjects or fixed versus random. However, there may be no proper ANOVA error term (see chap. 6, this volume) for some effects given certain combinations of fixed and random factors in complex designs. There are algorithms to derive by hand expected mean squares in various ANOVA designs (e.g., Kirk, 1995, pp. 402–406), and with such an algorithm it may be possible in complex designs to pool mean squares and form *quasi-F ratios* with proper error terms. Another method is *preliminary testing and pooling*, where parameters for higher order interactions with random variables may be dropped from the structural model based on results of statistical tests. The goal is to find a reduced structural model that generates expected mean squares so that all effects have proper error terms; see Winer et al. (1991, chap. 5).

Keeping track of error terms that go along with different effects in complex designs is one of the reasons why the coverage of factorial ANOVA is often quite lengthy in applied textbooks. Considering the shortcomings of statistical tests in perhaps most behavioral studies, however, it is probably best not to focus too much attention on the F test to the neglect of other, more useful information in ANOVA source tables.

Nonorthogonal Designs

If all factorial designs were balanced, there would be no need to deal with the rather difficult technical problem raised. Of particular concern in this discussion are nonorthogonal designs, unbalanced factorial designs with disproportional cell sizes. Only two-way nonorthogonal designs are discussed later, but the basic principles extend to larger nonorthogonal designs.

Nonorthogonal designs pose at least two challenges in their analysis. The first was mentioned earlier: The factors are correlated, which means that there is no single, unambiguous way to apportion either the total between-conditions sums of squares or total proportion of explained variance to the individual effects (Equations 7.4 to 7.5). The second problem concerns ambiguity in estimates for means that correspond to main effects. This happens because there are two different ways to compute marginal means in unbalanced designs: as arithmetic versus weighted averages of the corresponding row or column cell means. Consider the data in Table 7.5 for a nonorthogonal 2×2 design. The marginal mean for A_2 can be computed as the arithmetic average of the cell means in the second row or as the weighted average of the same cell means, respectively:

$$(2.00 + 5.57)/2 = 3.79 \qquad \text{versus} \qquad [2\ (2.00) + 7\ (5.57)]/9 = 4.78$$

The value to the right is the same one would find working with the nine raw scores in the second row of the 2×2 matrix in Table 7.5. There is no such ambiguity in balanced designs.

TABLE 7.5
Raw Scores and Descriptive Statistics for a Nonorthogonal 2×2
Factorial Design

	B_1	B_2	Row means
A_1	2, 3, 4 3.00 (1.00)[a]	1, 3 2.00 (2.00)	2.50/2.60[b]
A_2	1, 3 2.00 (2.00)	4, 5, 5, 6, 6, 6 5.57 (.95)	3.79/4.78
Column means	2.50/2.60	3.79/4.78	3.14/4.00

[a]Cell mean (variance).
[b]Arithmetic/weighted averages of the corresponding cell means.

There are many methods for analyzing data from nonorthogonal designs (e.g., Keren, 1993; Rencher, 1998), too many to describe. Also, statisticians do not agree about optimal methods for different situations, so it is not possible to give definitive recommendations. Most of these methods attempt to correct effect sums of squares for overlap. Unfortunately, they give the same results only in balanced designs, and estimates from different methods tend to diverge as the cell sizes become increasingly disproportional. The choice of method affects both statistical tests and effect size estimation, especially for the main effects and lower order interactions. Contemporary software programs for ANOVA that analyze data from nonorthogonal designs typically use by default one of the methods described next. However, blindly accepting a program's default method may not always be the best choice.

An older method for analyzing data from nonorthogonal designs is unweighted means analysis (see chap. 2, this volume). It comes from the ANOVA literature and is amenable to hand computation. In this method, effect sum of squares are computed using the equations for balanced designs in Table 7.2, except that the design cell size is taken as the harmonic mean of the actual cell sizes. This average in a two-way design is

$$n_h = \frac{ab}{\displaystyle\sum_{i=1}^{a} \sum_{j=1}^{b} \frac{1}{n_{ij}}} \tag{7.15}$$

The unweighted means approach estimates marginal means as arithmetic averages of the corresponding row or column cell means. It also estimates the grand mean as the arithmetic average of the cell means. A consequence of weighting all cell means equally is that overlapping variance is not attributed to any individual effect. Thus, the unweighted means method generates adjusted sums of squares that reflect unique predictive power. A related, regression-based technique called Method 1 by Overall and Spiegel (1969) estimates effect sums of squares controlling for all other effects. These sums of squares may be labeled Type III or unique in the output of statistical software programs.

The methods just described may be best for experiments designed with equal cell sizes but where there was random data loss from a few cells. This is because cells with fewer scores by chance are not weighted less heavily in either method. In nonexperimental designs, though, disproportional cell sizes may arise because of a population correlation between the factors. If so, it may be better for the actual cell sizes to contribute to the analysis. Two other regression-based methods do just that. They also give higher priority to one or both main effects compared to the methods described earlier. Overall and Spiegel (1969) referred to these techniques as Method 2 and Method 3, and sums of squares generated by them may be labeled in computer program output as Type II or classical experimental for the former versus Type I, sequential, or hierarchical for the latter.

In Method 2, sums of squares for the main effects are adjusted for overlap only with each other, but the interaction sum of squares is corrected for both main effects. Method 3 does *not* remove shared variance from the sums of squares of one main effect (e.g., A), adjusts the sums of squares of the other main effect for overlap with the first (e.g., B adjusted for A), and then adjusts the interaction sum of squares for both main effects. It is best in Method 3 that the researcher instead of the computer chooses the main effect with the highest priority. This is because some computer programs assign a default priority based on the order of the factors in the list specified by the user. If the researcher has no a priori hypotheses about effect priority but wishes the cell sizes to influence the results, Method 2 should be preferred over Method 3.

The data from the nonorthogonal 2×2 design in Table 7.5 were analyzed with the three regression-based approaches described earlier, assuming a completely between-subjects design with fixed factors. The results are summarized in Table 7.6. Observe that the sums of squares for the total effects, interaction effect, pooled within-cells variability, and total data set are the same across all three analyses. It is the estimates for the main effects that change depending on the method. For example, neither main effect is statistical at the .05 level in Method 1, which adjusts each main effect for all other effects. The observed proportions of total variance explained by the individual main effects, $\hat{\eta}_A^2 = \hat{\eta}_B^2 = .09$, are also the lowest in this method. In contrast, both main effects are statistical at the .05 level and have greater explanatory power in Method 2 and Method 3, which gives them higher priority compared to Method 1. Please also note in Table 7.6 that only in Method 3—which analyzes the A, B, and AB effects sequentially in this order—are the sums of squares and $\hat{\eta}^2$ values additive, but not unique.

Which of the three sets of results in Table 7.6 is correct? From a purely statistical view, all are because there is no single, nonpareil way to estimate effect sums of squares in nonorthogonal designs. There may be a preference for one set of results given a solid rationale about effect priority. Without such a justification, however, there is no basis for choosing among these results.

STANDARDIZED MEAN DIFFERENCES

Designs in which all factors are fixed are assumed next. Methods for standardizing contrasts in factorial designs are not as well developed as they are for one-way designs. This is especially true for simple comparisons and interaction contrasts as opposed to main comparisons. There is also not

TABLE 7.6
Results of Three Different Regression Methods for the Data in Table 7.5

Source	SS	df	MS	F	p	$\hat{\eta}^2$
Method 1/Type III[a]						
Total effects (A, B, AB)	36.29	3	12.10	10.33	.002	.76
A adjusted for B, AB	4.48	1	4.48	3.82	.079	.09
B adjusted for A, AB	4.48	1	4.48	3.82	.079	.09
AB adjusted for A, B	14.16	1	14.16	12.09	.006	.30
Method 2/Type II						
Total effects (A, B, AB)	36.29	3	12.10	10.33	.002	.76
A adjusted for B	6.89	1	6.89	5.88	.036	.14
B adjusted for A	6.89	1	6.89	5.88	.036	.14
AB adjusted for A, B	14.16	1	14.16	12.09	.006	.30
Method 3/Type I						
Total effects (A, B, AB)	36.29	3	12.10	10.33	.002	.76
A (unadjusted)	15.24	1	15.24	13.01	.005	.32
B adjusted for A	6.89	1	6.89	5.88	.036	.14
AB adjusted for A, B	14.16	1	14.16	12.09	.006	.30

Note. For all analyses, $SS_W = 11.71$; $df_W = 10$; $MS_W = 1.17$; $SS_T = 48.00$; and $df_T = 13$.
[a]Overall and Spiegel (1969) method/sums of squares type.

complete agreement across works by Glass, McGaw, and Smith (1981); S. Morris and DeShon (1997), Cortina and Nouri (2000); and Olejnik and Algina (2000); among others, that address this issue. It is therefore not possible to describe a definitive method. However, the discussion that follows is generally consistent with the overall goal of the works just cited: how to make standardized contrasts from factorial designs comparable to those that would have occurred in nonfactorial designs. This means that (a) estimates for effects of each independent variable in a factorial design should be comparable to effect sizes for the same factor studied in a one-way design, and (b) changing the number of factors in the design should not necessarily change the effect size estimates for any one of them.

Standardized mean differences may be preferred over measures of association as effect size indexes if contrasts are the main focus of the analysis. This is probably more common in designs with only two factors. When there are three or more independent variables or the factors are random, measures of association are typically more useful. It is also generally possible to compute measures of association for several effects analyzed together. For example, $\hat{\eta}_{A, B, AB}$ is the multiple correlation between the outcome variable and the main and interactive effects of factors A and B. This statistic in a two-way design would describe the total predictive power with a single number, which is very efficient. There is no analogous capability with standardized mean differences. The two families of effect size indexes can also be used together; see Wayne, Riordan, and K. Thomas (2001) for an example.

Standardized contrasts in factorial designs have the same general form as in one-way designs, $d_{\hat{\psi}} = \hat{\psi}/\hat{\sigma}^*$, where the denominator (standardizer) estimates a population standard deviation (see chap. 4, this volume). However, it is more difficult in factorial designs to figure out which standard deviation should go in the denominator of $d_{\hat{\psi}}$. This is because what is probably the most general choice in a one-way design—the square root of MS_W, which estimates the common population standard deviation σ—may not be the best choice in a factorial design. Also, there is more in the literature about standardizing main comparisons than simple comparisons in factorial designs. This is unfortunate because main comparisons may be uninteresting when there is interaction. It is recommended that main and simple comparisons for the same factor have the same standardizer. This makes $d_{\hat{\psi}}$ for these two kinds of single-factor contrasts directly comparable.

Single-Factor Contrasts in Completely Between-Subjects Designs

The choice of the standardizer for a single-factor contrast is determined by (a) the distinction between the *factor of interest* versus the *off-factors,* and (b) whether the off-factors vary naturally in the research population. Suppose in a two-way design that two levels of factor A are compared. The factor of interest in this contrast is A, and B is the off-factor. Also suppose that the off-factor varies naturally in the population. Glass et al. (1981) referred to such off-factors as being of theoretical interest, and they are more likely to be individual difference variables than manipulated or repeated-measures variables. The square root of MS_W from the two-way ANOVA may *not* be an appropriate standardizer for comparisons between levels of the factor of interest in this case. This is because MS_W controls for the effects of both factors, including their interaction. We can see this in the following expression for a balanced two-way design:

$$MS_W = \frac{SS_W}{df_W} = \frac{SS_T - SS_A - SS_B - SS_{AB}}{df_T - df_A - df_B - df_{AB}} \qquad (7.16)$$

Because MS_W does not reflect variability due to effects of the off-factor B, its square root may *underestimate* σ. This implies that $d_{\hat{\psi}} = \hat{\psi}/(MS_W)^{1/2}$ for comparisons where A is the factor of interest may *overestimate* $\delta_{\psi} = \psi/\sigma$ in absolute value. A method to compute an adjusted standardizer that reflects the whole range of variability on the off-factor is described momentarily.

Now suppose that the off-factor B does *not* vary naturally in the population. Such factors are more likely to be manipulated or repeated-measures variables than individual difference variables. For example, the theoretical population for the study of a new treatment can be viewed as follows: It is either true that every case in the population is given the treatment or none are given the treatment. In either event there is no variability because of treatment versus no treatment (Cortina & Nouri, 2000). A repeated-measures factor is not usually considered as varying naturally because time (e.g., pretest–posttest) is not a property of cases. However, it is important *not* to assume that manipulated factors never vary naturally. Suppose the levels of a manipulated factor are different dosages of caffeine (e.g., chap. 4, this volume). Because levels of caffeine consumption vary from person to person in the general population, it could be argued that the caffeine factor varies naturally. Because off-factors that do not vary naturally are not of theoretical interest (Glass et al., 1981) for the sake of variance estimation, their effects should *not* contribute to the standardizer. This implies that the square root of MS_W from the two-way ANOVA would be a suitable denominator for $d_{\hat{\psi}}$ for contrasts on factor A when the off-factor B does not vary naturally.

Two different methods to standardize main or simple comparisons that estimate the full range of variability on an off-factor of theoretical interest are described next. Both pool the variances across all levels of the factor of interest, so also they generate $d_{\hat{\psi}}$ for single-factor comparisons that is directly comparable to $g_{\hat{\psi}}$ in one-way designs (chap. 6, this volume). They also yield the same result in balanced designs. The first is the *orthogonal sums of squares method* by Glass et al. (1981). It requires a complete two-way ANOVA source table where the sums of squares are additive. This is not a problem in balanced designs, but only some methods for nonorthogonal designs generate additive—but not unique—sums of squares (e.g., Table 7.5). Assuming that A is the factor of interest, the following term estimates the full range of variability on the off-factor B:

$$MS_{W, B, AB} = \frac{SS_W + SS_B + SS_{AB}}{df_W + df_B + df_{AB}} = \frac{SS_T - SS_A}{df_T - df_A} \qquad (7.17)$$

The subscript for the mean square indicates that variability associated with the B and AB effects is pooled with error variance. Equation 7.17 also shows that $MS_{W, B, AB}$ in a two-way design has the same form as MS_W in a one-way design, where A is the sole factor. Indeed, the two terms just mentioned are equal in balanced two-way designs, where MS_W in a one-way ANOVA is computed after collapsing the data across the levels of the off-factor B.

The *reduced cross-classification method* by Olejnik and Algina (2000) does not require a complete two-way ANOVA source table with orthogonal sums of squares. It also generates unique adjusted-variance estimates in unbalanced designs. In this method, the researcher creates with a statistical software program a reduced cross-classification of the data where the off-factor of theoretical interest is omitted. Next, a one-way ANOVA is conducted for the factor of interest, and the square root of error term in this analysis is taken as the standardizer for contrasts on that factor. In balanced designs, this standardizer equals the square root of $MS_{W, B, AB}$ computed with Equation 7.17. A variation is needed when working with a secondary source that reports only cell-descriptive statistics. The variance $MS_{W, B, AB}$ can be derived from the means and variances in the original two-way classification as follows:

$$MS_{W, B, AB} = \frac{\sum_{i=1}^{a} \sum_{j=1}^{b} \left[df_{ij} \left(s_{ij}^2 \right) + n_{ij} \left(M_{ij} - M_{A_i} \right)^2 \right]}{N - a} \qquad (7.18)$$

Equation 7.18 is not as complicated as it appears. Its numerator involves the computation of a "total" sum of squares within each level of the factor of interest A that reflects the full range of variability on the off-factor B. This is done by combining cell variances across levels of B and taking account of the simple effect of B at that level of A. These "total" sums of squares are added up across the levels of A and then divided by $N - a$, the total within-conditions degrees of freedom in the reduced cross-classification where A is the only factor. The result given by Equation 7.18 in a balanced design equals $MS_{W, B, AB}$ computed with Equation 7.17 from the two-way ANOVA source table. It also equals MS_W in the one-way ANOVA for factor A after collapsing across the levels of factor B.

The methods described for standardizing contrasts that involve one factor in the presence of an off-factor of theoretical interest can be extended easily enough to designs with three or more factors. For example, we can state the following general rule for the reduced cross-classification method:

> The standardizer for a single-factor comparison is the square root of MS_W from the cross-classification that includes the factor of interest and any off-factors that do not vary naturally in the population but excludes any off-factors that do.

Suppose in a three-way design that A is the factor of interest. Of the two off-factors, B varies naturally but C does not. According to the rule, the denominator of $d_{\hat{\psi}}$ for main or simple comparisons is the square root of the MS_W from the two-way ANOVA for the reduced cross-classification that includes factors A and C but not B. This standard deviation estimates the full range of variability on off-factor B but not off-factor C. If the design were balanced, we would get the same result by taking the square root of the following variance:

$$MS_{W, B, AB, BC, ABC} = \frac{SS_W + SS_B + SS_{AB} + SS_{BC} + SS_{ABC}}{df_W + df_B + df_{AB} + df_{BC} + df_{ABC}} \quad (7.19)$$

which pools the within-conditions variability in the three-way ANOVA with all effects that involve the off-factor B. As Cortina and Nouri (2000) noted, however, there is little statistical research that supports the general rule stated earlier for different combinations of off-factors, some of theoretical interest but others not, in complex factorial designs. One hopes that such research will be forthcoming. In the meantime, readers should explain in written summaries of their analyses exactly how they standardized main or simple comparisons.

Let us consider an example for a balanced two-way design where factor A varies naturally in the population but factor B does not. The orthogonal sums of squares method is demonstrated using the ANOVA source table in the top part of Table 7.4 for the data in Table 7.3, assuming a completely between-subjects two-way design. As an exercise readers should apply the reduced cross-classification method to the same data to show that it generates the same results. An appropriate standardizer for main or simple comparisons where A is the factor of interest and B is the off-factor is the square root of MS_W from the two-way ANOVA, which for these data is

$$MS_W = SS_W / df_W = 64.00/12 = 5.33$$

This variance controls for effects of factor B, which is fine because B is not of theoretical interest for this example. Standardized contrasts for the three simple effects of A at B are derived as follows:

$$d_{\hat\psi \, A \, at \, B_1} = (9.00 - 5.00)/5.33^{1/2} = 1.73$$
$$d_{\hat\psi \, A \, at \, B_2} = (12.00 - 6.00)/5.33^{1/2} = 2.60$$
$$d_{\hat\psi \, A \, at \, B_3} = (9.00 - 10.00)/5.33^{1/2} = -.19$$

However, a better standardizer for main or simple comparisons on factor B (for which A is the off-factor) is the square root of

$$MS_{W, A, AB} = (SS_W + SS_A + SS_{AB})/(df_W + df_A + df_{AB})$$
$$= (64.00 + 18.00 + 84.00)/(12 + 1 + 2) = 11.07$$

This pooled variance is greater than MS_W from the two-way ANOVA because it includes effects of the off-factor A. This example shows that different sets of simple comparisons in the same factorial design may have different standardizers. However, the choice of which set of simple comparisons to analyze should be based on theoretical grounds, not on whichever set would have the smallest standardizer. See Olejnik and Algina (2000) for more examples.

Some other options to standardize main or simple comparisons are briefly mentioned. A version of the reduced cross-classification method demonstrated by Cortina and Nouri (2000) pools the variances from only the two levels of the factor of interest being compared. This generates $d_{\hat{\psi}}$ in a factorial design that is directly comparable to Hedges's g in a one-way design (see chap. 6, this volume). S. Morris and DeShon (1997) described a related method that standardizes main effects for dichotomous factors in factorial designs. It assumes that all off-factors vary naturally, and it derives a correction term from F ratios and df values in the ANOVA source table that is applied to the unadjusted effect size $\hat{\psi}/(MS_W)^{1/2}$. It is also possible to standardize main or simple comparisons against the square root of the variance from only one level of the factor of interest, usually a control condition. This generates $d_{\hat{\psi}}$ in a factorial design that is analogous to Glass's Δ in a one-way design. This method may be preferred if treatments are expected to affect variability or if the within-cells variances are too heterogenous to average together.

Interaction Contrasts in Completely Between-Subjects Designs

Suppose that the within-cells variances in a factorial design are similar and all contrasts are standardized against the square root of MS_W. This would make sense in a study in which none of the factors vary naturally in the population (e.g., the design is experimental). The value of $d_{\hat{\psi}}$ for a two-way interaction contrast would in this case equal the difference between either pair of standardized simple comparisons, row-wise or column-wise. For example, we would observe the following relation in a 2×2 design where all effects are contrasts:

$$d_{\hat{\psi}_{AB}} = d_{\hat{\psi}_{A \ at \ B_1}} - d_{\hat{\psi}_{A \ at \ B_2}} = d_{\hat{\psi}_{B \ at \ A_1}} - d_{\hat{\psi}_{B \ at \ A_2}} \qquad (7.20)$$

(Compare Equations 7.9 and 7.20.) However, this relation may not hold if either factor varies naturally in the population. This is because different sets of simple comparisons can have different standardizers in this case. Because an interaction is a joint effect, however, there are no off-factors in such effects; that is, *all* independent variables involved in interaction are factors of interest.

Unfortunately, there is relatively little in the statistical literature about exactly how to standardize an interaction contrast when only some factors vary naturally. Suppose in a balanced 2×2 design that factor B varies naturally, but factor A does not. Should we standardize $\hat{\psi}_{AB}$ against the square root of MS_W from the two-way ANOVA, or against the square root of $MS_{W, B, AB}$? The former exludes the interaction effect. This seems desirable in a standardizer for $\hat{\psi}_{AB}$, but it also excludes variability due to the B main effect, which implies that we may underestimate σ. The term $MS_{W, B, AB}$ reflects variability due to the interaction effect, but standardizers for single-factor comparisons do not generally reflect variability because of the main effects of those factors. Olejnik and Algina (2000, pp. 251–253) describe a way to choose between the variances just mentioned, but it requires designating one of the independent variables as the factor of interest. This may be an arbitrary decision for an interaction effect.

It is also possible to compute $d_{\hat{\psi}}$ for a three-way interaction contrast, but it is rare to see standardized contrasts for interactions between more than two factors. If all comparisons are scaled as mean difference contrasts and have the same standardizer, we would observe the following relation in a $2 \times 2 \times 2$ design where all effects are single-df comparisons:

$$
\begin{aligned}
d_{\hat{\psi}_{ABC}} &= d_{\hat{\psi}_{AB \text{ at } C_1}} - d_{\hat{\psi}_{AB \text{ at } C_2}} = d_{\hat{\psi}_{AC \text{ at } B_1}} - d_{\hat{\psi}_{AC \text{ at } B_2}} \\
&= d_{\hat{\psi}_{AB \text{ at } C_1}} - d_{\hat{\psi}_{AB \text{ at } C_2}}
\end{aligned}
\tag{7.21}
$$

That is, the standardized three-way interaction equals the difference between the standardized simple interactions for any two factors across the levels of the third factor. (Compare Equations 7.14 and 7.21.) This relation may not hold if different sets of simple interactions have different standardizers, however.

The uncertainties mentioned should not affect researchers who analyze simple effects or simple comparisons instead of interaction contrasts as a way to understand a conditional effect. These same researchers can interpret the difference between two corresponding standardized simple comparisons at different levels of the factor of interest as a standardized interaction contrast. However, the value of this standardized contrast may not be unique if some factors vary naturally in the population. There should be little problem in experimental designs where the square root of MS_W may be an appropriate standardizer for all contrasts, and researchers who can specify a priori interaction contrasts also tend to work with experimental designs. See Abelson and Prentice (1997) for examples of the analysis of interaction contrasts in such designs.

Designs With Repeated-Measures Factors

Standardized contrasts can be computed in factorial designs where some factors are within-subjects just as they are in completely between-subjects designs—that is, with standardizers in the metric of the original scores. This is the approach recommended by Olejnik and Algina (2000) among others. It makes $d_{\hat{\psi}}$ more directly comparable across different factorial designs, but it ignores the cross-conditions correlations for contrasts on repeated-measures factors.

A common type of factorial design with repeated measures is the two-way mixed within-subjects (split-plot) design in which unrelated samples are compared across two or more measurement occasions. Given homogeneity of the within-cells variances, the square root of MS_W could be used to standardize all contrasts. This is a natural choice for simple comparisons of the groups at each measurement occasion because these contrasts are purely between-subjects effects. However, this standardizer ignores the cross-conditions correlations across the levels of the repeated-measures factor for main comparisons of the groups. The same problem arises if the square root of MS_W were used to standardize simple effects of the repeated-measures factor for each group or interaction contrasts. The benefit is that $d_{\hat{\psi}}$ for the effects just mentioned would describe change in the metric of the original scores. Please note that the difference between the standardized mean changes for any two groups is a standardized interaction contrast. For example, if the pretest-to-posttest standardized mean change is .75 for the treatment group and .10 for the control group, the standardized interaction contrast is (.75 − .10) = .65. That is, the change for the treatment group is .65 standard deviations greater than the change for the control group. If there are multiple between-subjects factors arranged in a factorial layout, standardizers in the metric of the original scores can be computed with the methods described earlier. The only difference is that the repeated-measures factor is treated as an off-factor that is not of theoretical interest. The same method can also be used if multiple within-subjects factors are arranged in a factorial layout.

Some options for computing standardizers that take account of cross-conditions correlations in two-way mixed designs are briefly described. Standardizers for group mean changes can be based on the difference scores across two levels of the repeated-measures factor. This denominator computed can be computed as $s_{D_{\hat{\psi}}}$, the standard deviation of the contrast difference scores (e.g., Equation 2.15), separately for each group, and the difference between $\hat{\psi}/s_{D_{\hat{\psi}}}$ for any two groups can be interpreted as a standardized interaction contrast in the metric of the difference scores. An alternative denominator for standardized mean changes is the square root of the weighted average of $s_{D_{\hat{\psi}}}^2$ across all the groups, assuming homogeneity of covariance. Cortina and Nouri (2000) described a related method to standardize main comparisons of groups after collapsing the data across levels of a repeated-measures factor.

Interval Estimation

At present most software programs for general statistical analyses do not compute standardized contrasts in factorial designs much less construct confidence intervals for them. The freely available program PSY (Bird, Hadzi-Pavlovic, & Isaac, 2000) is an exception. It analyzes raw data from factorial designs with one or more between-subjects factors or one or more within-subjects factors. However, the program does not distinguish among multiple between-subjects factors or multiple within-subjects factors. This means that PSY in its current form is easiest to use in single-factor designs with independent or dependent samples or in mixed factorial designs with one between-subjects factors and one within-subjects factors. The PSY program standardizes all contrasts against the square root of MS_W, and it prints approximate individual or simultaneous approximate confidence intervals for δ_ψ (see chap. 6, this volume). It also prints an ANOVA source table. This is handy for computing a different standardizer for single-factor contrasts where the off-factor(s) varies naturally in the population. See Bird (2002) for examples.

The Effect Size program (ES; Shadish, Robinson, & Lu, 1999; also see chap. 4, this volume) computes standardized mean differences for main comparisons in completely between-subjects factorial designs with up to five factors and for comparisons on the group factor in two-way split-plot designs. In completely between-subjects designs, the standardizer assumes that all the off-factors vary naturally, but in two-way mixed designs the standardizer is the square root of MS_W. The ES program analyzes different combinations of summary statistics, such as mean squares and degrees of freedom for all sources and cell means and sizes, which is necessary when working with secondary sources. However, this program does not calculate confidence intervals for δ_ψ.

The software tools for calculating exact confidence intervals for δ_ψ described earlier (chaps. 4 and 6, this volume) are generally for one-way designs. As the method of noncentrality interval estimation becomes more widely known, it is expected that these tools will be adapted for more direct use in factorial designs.

MEASURES OF ASSOCIATION

Descriptive and inferential measures of association for factorial designs with fixed or random factors are outlined next. The descriptive measures are based on sample correlations, but the inferential measures estimate population proportions of explained variance.

Descriptive Measures

The descriptive measure of association estimated eta ($\hat{\eta}$) has the same general form in factorial designs as in one-way designs: It is the square root of SS_{effect}/SS_T, where SS_{effect} and SS_T are, respectively, the sums of squares for the effect of interest and the total data set (chap 6, this volume). The term SS_{effect} may be computed in a factorial design for a focused comparison, an omnibus comparison, or several effects analyzed together, such as $SS_{A, B, AB}$ for the total effects in a two-way design. The square of estimated eta, $\hat{\eta}^2$, is the proportion of total observed variance explained by the effect. In a balanced two-way design, the term $\hat{\eta}^2_{A, B, AB}$ can be uniquely partitioned into values for $\hat{\eta}^2_A$, $\hat{\eta}^2_B$, and $\hat{\eta}^2_{AB}$ (Equation 7.5). The correlation between an effect and outcome controlling for all noneffect sources of between-conditions variability is partial $\hat{\eta}$. It is the square root of $SS_{effect}/$ $(SS_{effect} + SS_{error})$, where SS_{error} is the sums of squares for the effect ANOVA error term. It is a relatively common practice in factorial designs to report $\hat{\eta}$ (or $\hat{\eta}^2$) for the total effects and partial $\hat{\eta}$ (or its square) for individual effects. The parameters estimated by $\hat{\eta}^2$ and partial $\hat{\eta}^2$, respectively, η^2 and partial η^2, were described in chapters 4 and 6.

Inferential Measures

The inferential measures of association introduced in chapter 6 for single-factor designs can also be computed in balanced factorial designs. These include estimated omega-squared ($\hat{\omega}^2$) for effects of fixed factors and the intraclass correlation ($\hat{\rho}_I$) for effects of random factors. Both statistics just mentioned estimate the population proportion of total explained variance. Both are also ratios of variance components of the form $\hat{\sigma}^2_{effect}/\hat{\sigma}^2_{tot}$, where the numerator estimates variability because of the effect of interest and the denominator estimates total variance. The composition of total variance is related to the ANOVA structural model for a particular design. For example, the complete structural model for a completely between-subjects design is defined by Equation 7.12. The composition of the estimated total variance for this model is

$$\hat{\sigma}^2_{tot} = \hat{\sigma}^2_{\alpha} + \hat{\sigma}^2_{\beta} + \hat{\sigma}^2_{\alpha\beta} + \hat{\sigma}^2_{\varepsilon} \qquad (7.22)$$

where the terms on the right side of the equality sign are, respectively, the variance components estimators for the A, B, and AB effects and random error. The form of partial $\hat{\omega}^2$ and partial $\hat{\rho}_I$ are also the same; it is $\hat{\sigma}^2_{effect}/$ $(\hat{\sigma}^2_{effect} + \hat{\sigma}^2_{\varepsilon})$, where variance as a result of all other sources of between-conditions variability other than that as a result of the effect of interest is removed from the denominator.[1]

---

[1] In mixed-effects factorial designs, Kirk (1995) and others use the symbol $\hat{\omega}^2$ only for effects of fixed factors and the symbol $\hat{\rho}_I$ only for effects of random factors. However, other authors use the latter symbol only when all factors are random.

TABLE 7.7
Equations for Variance Components Estimators in Completely Between-
Subjects Two-Way Designs

Estimator	Both factors fixed	Both factors random	A random, B fixed
$\hat{\sigma}^2_{effect}$	$\dfrac{df_{effect}}{abn} (MS_{effect} - MS_W)$	—	—
$\hat{\sigma}^2_{\alpha}$	$\dfrac{df_A}{abn} (MS_A - MS_W)$	$\dfrac{1}{bn} (MS_A - MS_{AB})$	$\dfrac{1}{bn} (MS_A - MS_W)$
$\hat{\sigma}^2_{\beta}$	$\dfrac{df_B}{abn} (MS_B - MS_W)$	$\dfrac{1}{an} (MS_B - MS_{AB})$	$\dfrac{df_B}{abn} (MS_B - MS_{AB})$
$\hat{\sigma}^2_{\alpha\beta}$	$\dfrac{df_{AB}}{abn} (MS_{AB} - MS_W)$	$\dfrac{1}{n} (MS_{AB} - MS_W)$	$\dfrac{1}{n} (MS_{AB} - MS_W)$

Note. Assumes a balanced design; a = number of levels of factor A; b = number of levels of factor B; and n = group size. In all cases, $\hat{\sigma}^2_{\epsilon} = MS_W$ and $\hat{\sigma}^2_{tot} = \hat{\sigma}^2_{\alpha} + \hat{\sigma}^2_{\beta} + \hat{\sigma}^2_{\alpha\beta} + \hat{\sigma}^2_{\epsilon}$.

Equations for the variance components estimators that make up $\hat{\omega}^2$ and $\hat{\rho}_I$ and their partial-variance counterparts depend on the number of factors in the design and whether the factors are between-subjects versus within-subjects or fixed versus random. This is because both distinctions just mentioned affect the underlying distributional theory. For example, Table 7.7 presents ANOVA-based estimators of variance components for completely between-subjects two-way designs. An expression for $\hat{\sigma}^2_{effect}$ for a generic effect with $df \geq 1$ is given in the table only for a design in which both factors are fixed. This is because measures of association are usually computed only for omnibus effects when the corresponding factor(s) is (are) random. To derive $\hat{\omega}^2$, $\hat{\rho}_I$, or either of their partial-variance counterparts for a completely between-subjects two-way design, just compute the appropriate variance components using the equations in Table 7.7 and assemble them in the correct way (see chap. 6, this volume). The statistics $\hat{\omega}^2$ and partial $\hat{\omega}^2$ can be calculated more directly using Equations 6.30 and 6.31 in any balanced factorial design with two or more between-subjects factors.

Table 7.8 presents equations for the direct computation of $\hat{\rho}_I$ and partial $\hat{\rho}_I$ when both factors in a completely between-subjects factorial design are random. Space limitations preclude listing equations for variance components estimators for direct computing of $\hat{\omega}^2$ or $\hat{\rho}_I$ in other kinds of factorial designs; see Dodd and Schultz (1973) or Vaughn and Corballis (1969). Fortunately, software for general statistical analyses is gradually getting better at reporting $\hat{\omega}^2$ or $\hat{\rho}_I$ in the output of analyses for complex ANOVA analyses. Variance components estimation with maximum likelihood methods is an alternative to ANOVA-based estimation for designs with random factors, but large samples are typically needed (see chap. 6, this volume).

TABLE 7.8

Equations for Direct Computation of the Intraclass Correlation for Balanced Completely Between-Subjects Designs With Two Random Factors

Effect	$\hat{\rho}_I$	Partial $\hat{\rho}_I$
A	$\dfrac{a\,(MS_A - MS_{AB})}{SS_T + MS_A + MS_B - MS_{AB}}$	$\dfrac{MS_A - MS_{AB}}{MS_A + bn\,(MS_W) - MS_{AB}}$
B	$\dfrac{b\,(MS_B - MS_{AB})}{SS_T + MS_A + MS_B - MS_{AB}}$	$\dfrac{MS_B - MS_{AB}}{MS_B + an\,(MS_W) - MS_{AB}}$
AB	$\dfrac{ab\,(MS_{AB} - MS_W)}{SS_T + MS_A + MS_B - MS_{AB}}$	$\dfrac{MS_{AB} - MS_W}{MS_{AB} + (n-1)\,MS_W}$

Note. Assumes a balanced design; a = number of levels of factor A; b = number of levels of factor B; and n = group size.

Table 7.9 reports values of $\hat{\eta}^2$ and $\hat{\omega}^2$ for the data in the top part of Table 7.3 for a 2×3 completely between-subjects design, where $n = 3$ and fixed factors are assumed. These measures of association are all computed from the ANOVA source table for these data in the top part of Table 7.4. The results in Table 7.9 for the total effects—the main and interaction effects analyzed together—are proportions of total variance, but results for the individual effects are proportions of partial variance. As expected, values of $\hat{\omega}^2$ are less than those of $\hat{\eta}^2$ for the same effect. For example, the A, B, and AB effects together explain 70% of the total sample variance ($\hat{\eta}^2$), but the adjusted estimate of the population proportion of explained variance is 56% ($\hat{\omega}^2$). If we were to assume that both factors are random and then compute $\hat{\rho}_I$ for the same data, we would find that the variance component estimators $\hat{\sigma}_\alpha^2$ and $\hat{\sigma}_\beta^2$ are both negative. This happens because the mean squares for both main effects are less than the mean square for the interaction effect (see Table 7.8). Recall that negative variance component estimates are usually interpreted as though the values were zero.

TABLE 7.9

Values of Descriptive and Inferential Measures of Association for the Data in Table 7.3 for a Completely Between-Subjects Design

Effect	$\hat{\eta}^2$	$\hat{\omega}^2$
Total effects	.70	.56
A	.22	.12
B	.43	.28
AB	.57	.43

Note. Assumes both factors are fixed. Results for the total effects are proportions of total variance and for the individual effects are proportions of partial variance.

Interval Estimation

The software programs or scripts described in chapter 6 for one-way designs can also be used to construct confidence intervals based on measures of association in some kinds of factorial designs. A script for SPSS by Smithson (2001) calculates exact confidence intervals for η^2 for the total effects and exact confidence intervals for partial η^2 for all other effects in completely between-subjects factorial designs with fixed factors. Fidler and Thompson (2001) gave SPSS scripts for calculating exact confidence intervals for ω^2 or partial ω^2 in balanced, completely between-subjects factorial designs with fixed factors. The R2 program (Steiger & Fouladi, 1992) and the Power Analysis module of STATISTICA (StatSoft, 2003) can also derive exact confidence intervals for η^2 in the same kinds of designs. The latter program can also construct exact confidence intervals for the Root Mean Square Standardized Effect Size (RMSSE)—which is related to the noncentrality parameter of the F distribution—in balanced two-way designs; see Steiger and Fouladi (1997; pp. 246–248) for more information. Burdick and Graybill (1992) described algorithms for hand computation of approximate central confidence intervals for ρ_I when the factors are random.

RESEARCH EXAMPLES

Four examples of effect-size estimation in factorial designs are described in this section. Three examples concern two-way factorial designs, but another involves a design with three factors. The last example concerns a mixed design with a between-subjects factor and a repeated-measures factor.

Differential Effectiveness of Aftercare Programs for Substance Abuse

T. Brown, Seraganian, Tremblay, and Annis (2002) randomly assigned 87 men and 42 women who were just discharged from residential treatment facilities for substance abuse to one of two different 10-week, group-format aftercare programs, structured relapse prevention (SRP) and 12-step facilitation (TSF). The former stressed rehearsal of skills to avoid relapse and the latter emphasized the traditional methods of Alcoholics Anonymous. The top part of Table 7.10 for this 2×2 randomized blocks design with fixed factors reports descriptive statistics for a measure of the severity of alcohol-related problems given six months later. Higher scores indicate more problems. An apparent interaction effect is indicated by the data in Table 7.10: Women who completed the SRP program have relatively worse outcomes than women who completed the more traditional TSF program. In contrast, men had similar outcomes regardless of aftercare program type.

TABLE 7.10
Descriptive Statistics, Analysis of Variance Results, and Effect Sizes for
Severity of Alcohol-Related Problems by Gender and Aftercare
Program Type

Gender	n	Aftercare program		Row means
		TSF	SRP	
Women		10.54 (15.62)[a]	27.91 (21.50)	18.40
	42	23[b]	19	
Men		17.90 (20.12)	16.95 (21.55)	17.47
	87	48	39	
Column means		15.52	20.54	17.77

Source	SS	df	MS	F	$d_{\hat{\psi}}$
Total effects	3,181.33	3	1,060.44	2.63[c]	—
Gender	24.37	1	24.33	<1.00	.04
Program	804.28	1	804.28	2.00[d]	−.25
Gender × program	2,352.69	1	2,352.69	5.84[e]	—
Simple effects of program					
Program at women	3,137.53	1	3,137.53	7.79[f]	−.85
Program at men	19.43	1	19.43	<1.00	.05
Within conditions (error)	50,367.22	125	402.94		
Total	53,548.55	129			

Note. These data are from T. Brown (personal communication, September 20, 2001), and are used with
permission. TSF = 12-step facilitation; SRP = structured relapse prevention.
[a]Cell mean (standard deviation). [b]Cell size.
[c]$p = .053$. [d]$p = .160$. [e]$p = .017$. [f]$p = .006$.

The bottom part of Table 7.10 reports the ANOVA source table and
standardized contrasts for single-factor effects. The sums of squares are Type
I, and the rationale for their selection is as follows: Men have more problems
because of alcohol use than women, so results for the main effect of gender
(G) were not adjusted for other effects. It was less certain whether one
aftercare program (P) would be more effective than the other, so estimates
for this main effect were adjusted for gender. Standardizers for single-factor
contrasts were computed assuming that the off-factor varies naturally in the
population. This is an obvious choice when the gender is the off-factor.
Because both SRP- and TSF-type aftercare programs exist in the real world,
the aftercare program factor was considered to vary naturally, too.

Although the sums of squares for the main and interaction effects are
additive, they are not unique. Therefore, standardizers were computed with

Equation 7.18 using the means and variances in the top part of Table 7.10. For example, the standardized contrast for the main effect of gender is

$$d_{\hat{\psi}G} = (M_{G_{Women}} - M_{G_{Men}})/(MS_{W, P, GP})^{1/2}$$
$$= (18.40 - 17.47)/466.31^{1/2} = .04$$

where the denominator is the square root of the pooled mean square that reflects error variance plus effects of the off-factor P (aftercare program). This variance is computed with Equation 7.18 as follows:

$$MS_{W, P, GP} = [22 \, (15.62^2) + 18 \, (27.91^2) + 23 \, (10.54 - 18.40)^2$$
$$+ 19 \, (27.91 - 18.40)^2 + 47 \, (20.12^2) + 38 \, (21.55^2)$$
$$+ 48 \, (17.90 - 17.47)^2 + 39 \, (16.95 - 17.47)^2]/(129 - 2)$$
$$= 466.31$$

which as expected is greater than $MS_W = 402.94$ from the two-way ANOVA (Table 7.10). It is left for the reader to verify that the standardizer for the main effect of aftercare program, assuming that gender varies naturally, is the square root of $MS_{W, G, GP} = 415.27$. Thus,

$$d_{\hat{\psi}P} = (15.52 - 20.54)/415.27^{1/2} = -.25$$

The standardized contrasts reported earlier for the main effects are actually not very interesting because of the obvious interaction effect. Results of analyses of the simple effects of aftercare program for women versus men are also reported in the bottom part of Table 7.10. The standardizer for these comparisons is the same as that for the main effect of aftercare program, the square root of $MS_{W, G, GP} = 415.27$. Among the women,

$$d_{\hat{\psi}P \text{ at Women}} = (10.54 - 27.91)/415.27^{1/2} = -.85$$

which says that the average number of alcohol-related problems reported by women participants in the SRP aftercare program are almost one full standard deviation higher than those in the TSF aftercare program. However, for men,

$$d_{\hat{\psi}P \text{ at Men}} = (17.90 - 16.95)/415.27^{1/2} = .05$$

which shows a slight advantage in outcome for those men in the TSF aftercare program. The difference between the two standardized simple effects is a standardized interaction contrast, or $(-.85 - .05) = -.90$. That is, the difference in outcome between the two aftercare programs for women versus men is almost one full standard deviation in magnitude.

Interpersonal Problem-Solving Skills as a Function of Gender and Level of Self-Reported Alcohol Use

The data set for this example can be downloaded from this book's Web site. Kline and Canter (1994) administered to 499 high school students anonymous questionnaires about their quantity and frequency of alcohol use. The students also completed a measure of social skills reasoning, where higher scores are a better result. The cases were subsequently classified by gender and four different levels of self-reported alcohol use based on criteria for adolescents. The cell sizes in this 2×4 cross-classification are disproportional because relatively more young men are classified as heavy drinkers than young women. The top half of Table 7.11 reports descriptive statistics on the dependent variable by gender and drinking level. It is not surprising that mean test scores are higher overall for young women than young men and lower overall for students classified as heavy drinkers. An interaction effect is also apparent because the relative weakness in social skills reasoning is greater for male students classified as heavy drinkers compared to their same-gender peers than for female students. It is also true that the relative magnitude of gender differences in social skills reasoning is greater among students classified as heavy drinkers.

The bottom half of Table 7.11 reports Type II sums of squares for these data. Because social skills reasoning is expected to vary by both gender and drinking level, the main effects were given equal priority in the analysis. Also reported in the table are descriptive variance-accounted-for effect sizes and exact 95% confidence intervals computed with Smithson's (2001) script for SPSS. The value of $\hat{\eta}^2$ for the total effects is .32, so 32% of the total variability in social skills reasoning is explained by the main and interactive effects together. This observed result is just as consistent with a population proportion of explained variance for the total effects as low as $\eta^2 = .26$ as it is with a population proportion as high as $\eta^2 = .38$, with 95% confidence. Each correlation ratio for the individual effects reported in Table 7.11 is partial $\hat{\eta}^2$, so their values are not additive. The main effect of drinking level is the largest individual effect, explaining 25% of the variance controlling for all other effects (the exact 95% confidence interval is 19–31%). The second largest effect is gender, which explains 8% of residual variance (4–12%). Although the gender $\times$ drinking level interaction accounts for about 2% of residual variance (0–4%)—which is the smallest relative effect size magnitude—it should not be concluded that this effect is unimportant.

TABLE 7.11
Descriptive Statistics, Analysis of Variance Results, and Effect Sizes for
Interpersonal Problem-Solving Skill by Gender and Level of Self-Reported
Alcohol Use

Gender	n	Drinking level				Row means
		None	Light	Moderate	Heavy	
Young women	253	64.91(8.01)[a]	65.38 (6.84)	61.16 (7.50)	54.47 (9.03)	61.26
		46[b]	52	100	55	
Young men	246	60.56 (8.40)	59.98 (9.95)	58.38 (9.36)	45.59 (11.90)	54.96
		39	45	84	78	
Column means		62.92	62.88	59.88	49.26	58.15

Source	SS	df	MS	F	$\hat{\eta}^2$
Total effects	19,157.56	7	2,736.79	33.27[d]	.32 (.26–.38)[c]
Gender	3,278.95	1	3,278.95	39.86[d]	.08 (.04–.12)
Drinking Level	13,499.74	3	4,499.91	54.70[d]	.25 (.19–.31)
Gender × Level	720.20	3	240.07	2.92[e]	.02 (0–.04)
Within-conditions (error)	40,392.07	491	82.27		
Total	59,549.63	498			

Note. Variance-accounted-effect sizes are proportions of total variance for the total effects and proportions of partial variance for the individual effects.
[a]Cell mean (standard deviation).　[b]Cell size.　[c]Exact 95% confidence interval.
[d]p = <.001.　[e]p = .034.

Earwitness Testimony and Moderation of the Face Overshadowing Effect

S. Cook and Wilding (1997) reported that identification of the once-heard voice of a stranger in test conditions that resemble an auditory police line-up is better if the speaker's face is *not* seen at the time of exposure. They called this result the face overshadowing effect (FOE). S. Cook and Wilding (2001) evaluated whether the FOE is affected by hearing the voice more than once or by explicit instructions to attend to the voice instead of the face. A total of 216 young adults were randomly assigned to one of eight conditions in this balanced $2 \times 2 \times 2$ experimental design where the fixed factors are face (present or absent), voice repetition (once or three times), and instruction (intentional—specifically told to focus on the voice—or incidental—no specific instructions given). All participants heard two different voices, one a man's and the other a woman's, say two different sentences. One week later the participants were asked to pick each voice out of separate gender voice line-ups. The outcome variable was the number of correct identifications. Its limited range (0–2) is not ideal, a point acknowledged by S. Cook and Wilding (2001), but the experimental set up is interesting.

The top part of Table 7.12 reports descriptive statistics on the voice identification task for the eight possible experimental conditions. S. Cook and Wilding (2001) did not report a complete ANOVA source table. However, these results were estimated from the study's descriptive statistics, and they are reported in the bottom part of Table 7.12 along with values of correlation effect sizes. The correlation between the number of correct identifications and all effects (seven in total) analyzed together is $\hat{\eta} = .342$; the total proportion of explained variance is thus $.342^2 = .117$, or 11.7%. The repetition main effect is the best individual predictor (partial $\hat{\eta} = .300$). As expected, there are more correct identifications when the voice is heard

TABLE 7.12

Descriptive Statistics, Analysis of Variance Results, and Effect Sizes for Accuracy of Voice Recognition by Instruction, Repetition, and Presence Versus Absence of the Speaker's Face

Condition	Instruction	
	Incidental	Intentional
Voice once	.96 (.65)[a]	.93 (.68)
Voice three times	1.26 (.76)	1.19 (.62)
Voice once + face	.59 (.64)	.63 (.69)
Voice three times + face	1.15 (.72)	1.19 (.68)

Source	SS	df	MS	F	$\hat{\eta}$
Total effects	12.7590	7	1.8227	3.94[b]	.342
Instruction	.0014	1	.0014	<1.00	.004
Face	2.0534	1	2.0534	4.42[c]	.144
Repetition	9.5256	1	9.5256	20.52[b]	.300
Instruction × face	.1094	1	.1094	<1.00	.034
Instruction × repetition	.0054	1	.0054	<1.00	.007
Face × repetition	1.0584	1	1.0584	2.28[d]	.104
Instruction × face × repetition	.0054	1	.0054	<1.00	.007
Within cells (error)	96.5473	208	.4642		
Total	109.3063	215			

Note. Cell descriptive statistics are from "Earwitness Testimony: Effects of Exposure and Attention on the Face Overshadowing Effect," by S. Cook and J. Wilding, 2001, British Journal of Psychology, 92, p. 621. Copyright 2001 by the British Psychological Society. Reprinted with permission. Correlation effect sizes are relative to total variance for the total effects and partial variance for individual effects.
[a]Cell mean (standard deviation); $n = 27$ for all cells.
[b]$p < .001$ [c]$p = .037$.   [d]$p = .133$.

three times instread of just once. The main effect of the face–no face factor has the second highest individual correlation with outcome (partial $\hat{\eta}$ = .144), and the mean overall correct recognition score is indeed higher when the face is not present (1.09) than when the face is present (.89).

Effect size correlations for the remaining effects are close to zero except for the interaction between the face (F) and repetition (R) factor for which partial $\hat{\eta}$ = .10. Means on the outcome variable for this two-way interaction averaged over the instruction factor are

	Repeat 1×	Repeat 3×
No Face	.945	1.225
Face	.610	1.170

We can see in this matrix that the size of the FOE is greater when the voice is heard just once instead of three times. Let us estimate the magnitude of the change in this effect with a standardized contrast. The value of the unstandardized interaction contrast based on the previous cell means is

$$\hat{\psi}_{FR} = .945 - 1.225 - .610 + 1.170 = .280$$

Assuming that none of the factors vary naturally, standardizing this contrast against the square root of the ANOVA error term for the whole design, MS_W = .4642, gives us

$$d_{\hat{\psi}_{FR}} = .280/.4642^{1/2} = .41$$

Thus, the magnitude of the FOE is about .4 standard deviations larger given one repetition of the voice compared to three repetitions. Although this two-way interaction explains only about 1% of the residual variance, it may not be a trivial result, especially in a legal context. Because intentional versus incidental instruction does not appreciably moderate the two-way interaction just analyzed, S. Cook and Wilding (2001) attributed the FOE to an involuntary preference for processing face information that is not overcome on hearing an unfamiliar voice just once.

Effects of Alcohol Education on Recent Drinking Quantity at Different Times

I collected the data set for this example. A total of 131 senior high school students were randomly assigned to either a 20-hour alcohol education course (n_1 = 72) or a control course of the same duration about general health issues ($n_2 = 59$). The unequal group sizes are a result of unrestricted randomization, but there were about equal numbers of male and female students in each group. A calendar-format measure of the number of alcoholic beverages consumed over the previous two weeks was administered to all students on three different occasions, just before the beginning of the courses (pretest), one month after each course concluded (posttest), and then three months later (follow-up). The students were unaware of the schedule for testing.

The top part of Table 7.13 presents descriptive statistics on the recent drinking measure for this mixed within-subjects design with fixed factors. Although mean scores increased over time for both groups, this increase is more pronounced in the control condition. The bottom part of Table 7.13 reports Type III sums of squares for the main and interaction effects and partial correlations with the outcome variable. Unique sums of squares were selected because the unequal group sizes do not reflect unequal population group sizes. All p values for tests of within-subjects effects are based on the Greenhouse–Geisser conservative $F (1, 129)$ test, which assumes maximal violation of sphericity. The partial correlations between outcome and the effects of condition, time, and their interaction are, respectively, .17, .23, and .15.

TABLE 7.13
Descriptive Statistics, Analysis of Variance Results, and Effect Sizes for
Amount of Recent Drinking by Alcohol Education Condition and Time

| Condition | n | Time | | | Row means |
		Pretest	Posttest	Follow-up	
Control	59	3.15 (6.36)[a]	3.66 (6.80)	7.15 (7.35)	4.65
Alcohol education	72	2.73 (5.90)	2.82 (6.24)	3.56 (6.55)	3.04
Column means		2.92	3.20	5.18	3.76

Source	SS	df	MS	F	Partial $\hat{\eta}$
Between-subjects					
Condition	254.26	1	254.26	3.90[b]	.17
S/condition (error)	8,402.48	129	65.14		
Within-subjects					
Time	449.46	2	224.73	7.21[c]	.23
Condition × time	192.27	2	96.14	3.08[d]	.15
Time × S/condition (error)	8,040.96	258	31.17		
Total	17,286.89	392			

Note. The pooled within-groups correlations across measurement occasions are $r_{12} = .34$; $r_{23} = .22$; and $r_{13} = .25$.
[a]Cell mean (standard deviation).   [b]$p = .050$.   [c]$p = .008$.   [d]$p = .082$.

It is informative to repartition the condition main effect and the interaction into the three simple effects of condition. These between-subjects effects concern group differences in recent drinking at each measurement occasion. Because the within-cells variances are reasonably similar, we can standardize these contrasts against the square root of MS_W for the whole design. This variance can be computed as the weighted average of the six within-cells variances. It can also be derived from sums of squares in the source table as

$$MS_W = (SS_{S/condition} + SS_{time \times S/condition})/(df_{S/condition} + df_{time \times S/condition})$$
$$= (8{,}402.48 + 8{,}040.96)/(129 + 258) = 42.49$$

Summarized next are results for the three simple effects of condition:

Condition at pretest: $SS = 5.72$, $\hat{\psi} = .42$, $d_{\hat{\psi}} = .06$
Condition at posttest: $SS = 22.88$, $\hat{\psi} = .84$, $d_{\hat{\psi}} = .13$
Condition at follow-up: $SS = 446.53$, $\hat{\psi} = 3.59$, $d_{\hat{\psi}} = .55$

These results indicate that the control group reported higher levels of recent drinking than the alcohol education group at all three times. The size of this difference is only 6% of a standard deviation at pretest, but it increases to about half a standard deviation by the follow-up.

CONCLUSION

Methods to calculate standardized mean differences for contrasts in factorial designs are not as well-developed as for one-way designs. Standardizers for single-factor contrasts should reflect variability as a result of off-factors that vary naturally in the population, but variability as a result of effects of off-factors that do not vary naturally should be excluded. Measures of associations may be preferred in designs with three or more factors or where some factors are random. They can also evaluate the predictive power of several effects analyzed together. Descriptive correlation effect sizes are all based on the sample correlation $\hat{\eta}$, and they are computed pretty much the same way in factorial designs as in one-way designs. In balanced factorial designs, the inferential measure of association $\hat{\omega}^2$ can be derived for effects of fixed factors, and the intraclass correlation $\hat{\rho}_I$ can be computed for effects of random factors.

RECOMMENDED READINGS

Abelson, R. P., & Prentice, D. A. (1997). Contrast tests of interaction hypotheses. *Psychological Methods, 2*, 315–328.

Cortina, J. M., & Nouri, H. (2000). *Effect size for ANOVA designs*. Thousand Oaks, CA: Sage.

Olejnik, S., & Algina, J. (2000). Measures of effect size for comparative studies: Applications, interpretations, and limitations. *Contemporary Educational Psychology, 25*, 241–286.

III
ALTERNATIVES TO STATISTICAL TESTS

.

8

REPLICATION AND META-ANALYSIS

Scientists have known for centuries that a single study will not resolve a major issue. Indeed, a small sample study will not even resolve a minor issue. Thus, the foundation of science is the culmination of knowledge from the results of many studies.
—Hunter, F. Schmidt, and Jackson (1982, p. 10)

Replication is a critical scientific activity, one not given its due in the behavioral sciences. Basic kinds of replication are reviewed in the next section. The rest of this chapter considers meta-analysis as a method for research synthesis. The goal of this presentation is not to teach the reader how to conduct a meta-analysis—this is impossible in a chapter-length presentation. The aim instead is to help the reader appreciate the strengths and limitations of meta-analysis and encourage meta-analytic thinking. Developing the capacity to think meta-analytically about one's own research is important even if one never intends to conduct a formal meta-analysis (B. Thompson, 2002b). Meta-analytic thinking is also a crucial part of reform in methods of data analysis and hypothesis testing in the behavioral sciences (see chap. 1, this volume).

TERMS AND IDEAS ABOUT REPLICATION

This section introduces basic concepts about replication. It also defines different kinds or degrees of replication.

Context

Thomas S. Kuhn (1996) described science as alternating between two states. One is the steady state of *normal science*, characterized by a high level of paradigm development. A *paradigm* is a shared set of theoretical structures, methods, and definitions that supports the essential activity of normal science, *puzzle solving*, the posing and working out of problems under the paradigm. If a paradigm's empirical and theoretical structures build on one another in a way that permits results of current research to extend earlier work, it provides what Hedges (1987) called *theoretical cumulativeness*. The second state involves crises that arise when certain persistent and important problems, *anomalies*, cannot be solved under the current paradigm. These crises may lead to challenges by scholars who may be younger or have backgrounds in different fields than those who defend the current paradigm. (See Sulloway, 1997, for an interesting discussion of possible birth order effects among those who challenged or defended scientific status quos in the past.) A scientific revolution occurs when the old paradigm is replaced by a new one. The assumptions of the new paradigm may be so different that the subsequent course of the discipline is radically altered. It is normal science that concerns us, in particular its cumulative nature through replication and synthesis of results.

Replication in the Behavioral Sciences

There is a paucity of reports in the behavioral research literature specifically described as replications (see chaps. 2 and 3, this volume). The use of statistical tests as if they estimated the probability of replication and editorial bias against studies without null hypothesis (H_0) rejections may exacerbate this problem (see chap. 3, this volume). Authors of behavioral studies are undoubtedly also aware of editorial preferences for novelty, or work seen as original or unique. This partiality may discourage replication that may be seen as a rehash of old ideas (Kmetz, 2000). Hedges (1987) examined another possible factor: Behavioral research results may simply be less replicable than those in the natural sciences. That is, the level of what Hedges called *empirical cumulativeness*—the observed degree of agreement of results across different studies—may just be inherently lower for behavioral data. Hedges (1987) compared the consistency of results in physics research about the mass and lifetime of stable particles, such as neutrons or protons, with the consistency of results in the hard area of gender differences in cognitive abilities and the soft area of effects of educational programs on achievement. Surprisingly, Hedges (1987) found similar degrees of consistency in the physics and behavioral research areas just mentioned as measured by a standard index of cross-study variability in results (Q; described later). Within the limitations of this comparison outlined by Hedges (1987), these findings suggest that physical science data may not be inherently more empirically cumulative than behavioral science data.

Types of Replication

B. Thompson (1997) distinguishes between internal and external replication. *Internal replication* includes *statistical resampling* and *cross-validation* by the original researcher(s). The former combines the cases in the original data set in different ways to estimate the effect of idiosyncrasies in the sample on the results. Resampling methods are described in chapter 9, but resampling is not replication in the usual scientific sense. In cross-validation, the total sample is divided at random into a *derivation sample* and a *cross-validation sample*, and the same analyses are conducted in each one. In contrast, *external replication* is conducted by those other than the original researcher(s), and it involves new samples collected at different times or places.

There are two broad contexts for external replication. The first concerns different kinds of replications of experimental studies (Carlsmith, Ellsworth, & Aronson, 1976; Lykken, 1968). One is an *exact* or *literal replication* where all major aspects of the original study—its sampling methods, design, and outcome measures—are copied as closely as possible. True exact replications exist more in theory than practice because it may be impossible to perfectly duplicate a specific study. When a study is externally replicated, there may be variations in subjects, equipment, physical settings, or personnel across laboratories great enough to preclude exact replication. Another type is *operational replication*, where just the sampling and experimental methods of the original study are duplicated. Operational replication tests whether a result can be duplicated by a researcher who follows the basic recipe in the methods section of the original study.

In *balanced replications*, operational replications are used as control conditions. Other conditions in balanced replications may represent the manipulation of additional substantive variables to test new hypotheses. For example, a drug condition from an original study could be replicated in a new study. Additional conditions in the latter may feature the administration of the same drug at different dosages, other kinds of drugs, or a different type of treatment. The logic of balanced replication is similar to that of strong inference, which features the design of studies to rule out competing explanations (see chap. 3, this volume), and to that of *dismantling research*. The latter aims to study the elements of treatments with multiple components in smaller combinations to find the ones responsible for treatment efficacy. There are now several examples of dismantling research in the psychotherapy outcome literature (e.g., Cahill, Carrigan, & Frueh, 1999).

A final type of replication departs even further from the ideal of exact replication than operational or balanced replication. A researcher who conducts a *construct replication* avoids close imitation of the specific methods of the original study. An ideal construct replication would be carried out by telling a skilled researcher little more than the original empirical result. This researcher would then specify the design, measures, and data analysis methods deemed appropriate to test the construct validity of the original finding—that is, whether it has generality beyond the situation studied in the original work. A robust phenomenon is indicated if its effect is found despite variations in study characteristics. On the other hand, the nature of the phenomenon may actually change depending on how it is measured, the particular sample studied, or the specific experimental method used. Without a systematic cataloging of how construct replications differ from each other, however, it may be difficult to associate study characteristics with observed changes in the effect.

A second context for replication concerns psychometrics, which seems to have a stronger tradition of replication compared to other behavioral research areas. This may be in part a result of the existence of professional standards that outline benchmarks for establishing score validity (e.g., American Psychological Association, 1999) and legal requirements for the use of tests in settings such as schools. The demonstration of whether a test is construct-valid requires more than one line of evidence, which requires at least construct replication. There is also an appreciation of the need to cross-validate tests that generate scores based on mathematically weighted combinations of predictor variables. These weights—usually regression coefficients—are susceptible to capitalization on chance (e.g., Nunnally & Bernstein, 1994). It is thus necessary to determine whether their values are observed in other samples.

RESEARCH SYNTHESIS

The goals and methods of research synthesis are outlined in this section. The latter include qualitative and quantitative (i.e., meta-analysis) methods. It is argued that qualitative methods of research synthesis are inadequate.

Goals

Bodies of related research in the behavioral sciences tend to consist of construct replications instead of the other types considered earlier. As such, different studies about the same general phenomenon typically feature different experimental designs, measures, types of samples, or methods of analysis. Compared to sets of operational or balanced replications, these kinds of differences among construct replications make it more difficult to synthesize the results—that is, to get a sense of the status of a literature. Despite the problems just mentioned, the more intermediate steps of research synthesis are basically the same in all sciences: Define the research question(s), find as many pertinent studies as possible, critique their designs and methods and perhaps exclude those with serious flaws, look for bias in individual studies, and identify factors that account for cross-study variation in results. A good research synthesis can be invaluable, especially in a rapidly expanding area where researchers may not be aware of what others are doing. It thus comes as no surprise that integrative reviews are among the most widely cited articles in the research literature (Cooper & Hedges, 1994a).

Qualitative Research Reviews

The traditional method for research synthesis is the *qualitative* or *narrative literature review*. Such reviews are rational exercises in that their authors do not use quantitative methods other than vote counting to arrive at conclusions. *Vote counting*—also called the *box-score method*—involves tallying the numbers and directions of H_0 rejections versus failures to reject H_0 across a set of studies. Suppose that a qualitative literature review concerns whether a treatment is effective. The vote count is the number of studies with statistical differences between treatment and control that favor the former versus the number with none. If the box score for the former outcome is higher than for the latter, the treatment is deemed to be effective; if the score is tied, the results of the review are deemed inconclusive.

However, vote counting as just described is not a scientifically sound way to synthesize results across studies (Chalmers & Lau, 1994). This is in part because it is based on outcomes of statistical tests—p values—that are subject to all the limitations discussed in chapter 3. For example, tied box scores are expected when power is only .50, which is typical in behavioral research. A related problem of traditional literature reviews is that they are sometimes restricted to published studies. Because of a bias for results with H_0 rejections, however, results of published studies may overestimate the true magnitude of an effect, among other problems.

Meta-Analysis as a Quantitative Research Synthesis

A *primary analysis* is conducted by a researcher who conducts an original (primary) study where statistical methods are used to analyze data from individual cases. A *secondary analysis* is conducted with summary statistics reported in a primary study. Some of the research examples of effect size estimation described in earlier chapters are secondary analyses. The derivation of effect size indexes from statistics reported in primary studies is a crucial part of meta-analysis. In relation to primary and secondary analyses, meta-analysis is a kind of higher order, tertiary method where the units of analysis are published or unpublished studies. Meta-analysis is also distinguished by application of some of the same kinds of statistical methods used in primary studies to accumulate results. For example, it is common in meta-analysis to summarize the results of a comparative study where the outcome variable is continuous with a standardized mean difference (d). Doing so deals with the problem that outcome measures in different studies often have different scales, and converting all unstandardized comparisons to d allows results to be directly compared across studies. When d is computed for each comparison and typically weighted by a function of sample size, the weighted average d across all studies estimates the overall magnitude of the effect. The variance among the individual d statistics estimates the consistency of the results across all studies. The higher this variance, the less consistent the results, and vice versa.

If a set of studies is made up of exact replications, there may be little quantitative analysis to do other than estimate the central tendency and variability of the results. The former could be seen as a better estimate of the population parameter than the result in any one study, and the latter could be used to identify individual results that are outliers. Because exact replications are inherently similar, outliers may be more a result of chance than systematic differences among studies. This is less certain for operational replications, and even less so for construct replications. For the latter, observed variability in results may reflect actual changes in the effect because of differences in samples, measures, or designs across studies.

Because sets of related studies in the behavioral sciences are generally made up of construct replications, the explanation of observed variability in their results is a common goal of meta-analyses in this area. This is also an aim of a traditional literature review, but the methods of meta-analysis are not primarily subjective. This is because the meta-analyst tries to identify and measure characteristics of construct replications that give rise to variability among their results. These characteristics concern the kinds of variables listed in Table 8.1. Some of them concern attributes of samples, settings in which cases are tested, or the type of treatment administered. Other factors concern properties of the outcome measures, quality of the research design, source of funding, professional background(s) of the author(s), or date of issuance. The latter reflects the potential impact of temporal factors such as changing societal attitudes on the phenomenon of interest.

Characteristics of studies such as those listed in Table 8.1 can be categorized in a few different ways. One is low versus high inference (Hall, Tickle-Degnen, R. Rosenthal, & Mosteller, 1994). A *low-inference character-istic* is one that is readily apparent in the text or tables of a primary study, such as the measurement method. In contrast, a *high-inference characteristic* requires a judgment. The quality of the research design is an example of a

TABLE 8.1
Examples of Potential Predictors of Study Outcome Coded
in Meta-Analysis

Category	Examples
Subjects	Mean age, income, IQ, or illness length Proportion men or women, minority group, or diagnosis type Number of cases
Setting	Country or geographic region Type of clinic (e.g., inpatient or outpatient) Laboratory or naturalistic observation (e.g., home visit)
Treatment	Duration, frequency, type (e.g., medication or behavioral), dosage, or method of delivery (e.g., group or individual) Professional type, level of education, or theoretical orientation
Measures	Method of measurement (e.g., self-report or observational) Informant type (e.g., parent or teacher) Reactivity of measure (e.g., low or high) Content area (e.g., internalization or externalization)
Design quality	Internal validity: Appropriate methods for assignment to conditions (e.g., randomization), presence of appropriate control groups, safeguards against experimenter expectancies (e.g., double-blinds) External validity: Appropriate (i.e., representative) sampling methods, appropriate handling of missing data
General	Design type (e.g., experimental or nonexperimental) Study presentation forum (e.g., published or unpublished) Source of funding (e.g., public or private) Author gender or professional background Date of issuance (e.g., publication year)

high-inference characteristic because it must be inferred from the information reported in the study.

Study factors can also be described as substantive, method, or extrinsic (Lipsey, 1994). *Substantive factors* are presumed relevant for understanding an effect. They include things such as specific features of treatments, subjects, or settings believed to account for differences in study outcomes. *Method factors* concern procedural aspects about how studies are conducted, such as specific instructions given to participants. The influence of method characteristics may be seen as sources of bias or distortion that confound cross-study comparison of results. *Extrinsic factors* are outside of both substantive and method factors and include things such as author attributes, the form of publication, and source of funding. Although extrinsic factors by themselves may not be expected to directly influence study results, they may affect decisions that have a bearing on study outcome, such as the choice of measurement methods in a particular research area. Note that the classification of study characteristics as substantive, method, or extrinsic depends on the research context. For example, Eagley and Carli (1981) found that author gender predicted the degree of female conformity reported across different studies of social influence. Author gender may in this case be seen as substantive rather than extrinsic.

Substantive, method, or extrinsic factors are often conceptualized as meta-analytic predictors, and study outcome measured with the same standardized index of effect size is typically the criterion. Each individual predictor in a meta-analysis is actually a *moderator variable*, which implies interaction. This is because the criterion, study outcome, usually represents the association between the independent and dependent variables in each study. If observed variation in effect sizes across a set of studies is explained by a meta-analytic predictor, the relation between the independent and dependent variables changes across the levels of that predictor. This is interaction. For the same reason, the terms *moderator variable analysis* or *meta-regression* describe the process of estimating whether factors such as those listed in Table 8.1 account for cross-study variability in results.

Models of Explanation

Suppose that a set of studies where treatment is compared with control on a continuous outcome is disaggregated by the levels of a meta-analytic predictor. If the average effect size changes across the levels of that predictor, it explains some proportion of the variability in the results. This explanatory power could be more precisely estimated by a measure of association between the meta-analytic predictor and study effect size. If there are two meta-analytic predictors, it is possible that they covary. Suppose across a set of studies that different variations of the treatment tend to be given to patients with chronic versus acute forms of an illness. This implies a correlation between the substantive factors of treatment type and illness chronicity. The predictive power of each factor just mentioned should be estimated controlling for the other. This is especially true if substantive and method or extrinsic factors covary, such as when a particular research design is used to study a certain type of treatment. In this confounded case, one should avoid attributing differences in study outcome to the substantive factor alone.

It is also possible for meta-analytic predictors to interact, which means that they have a joint influence on observed effect sizes. Interaction also implies that to understand variability in results, the predictors must be considered together. This is a subtle point, one that requires some elaboration: Each individual predictor in meta-analysis is a moderator variable. However, the relation of one meta-analytic predictor to study outcome may depend on another predictor. For example, the effect of treatment type on observed effect sizes may depend on whether cases with acute versus chronic forms of an illnesses were studied.

A different kind of relation between meta-analytic predictors and study outcome is a *mediator effect*. Recall that mediator effects are *not* moderator (interaction) effects—they are indirect effects that involve at least one intervening variable that transmits some of the effect of a prior variable onto a subsequent variable (e.g., Shrout & Bolger, 2002), in this case study effect size. Suppose that one substantive factor is degree of early exposure to a toxic agent and another is illness chronicity. The exposure factor may affect study outcome both directly and indirectly through its effect on chronicity. Specifically, cases in samples with higher levels of early exposure may have been ill longer, which in turn affects study outcome. Illness chronicity is the mediator variable in this instance. The analysis of mediator (indirect) effects is best known as part of structural equation modeling. It is not as well known that mediator effects among substantive, method, or extrinsic factors can be estimated in meta-analysis, too. The specification of a model with mediation requires specific a priori hypotheses about patterns of direct and indirect effects. For this reason, an analysis in which mediator effects are estimated is called a *model-driven* or *explanatory meta-analysis*. This type of meta-analysis is relatively rare. Accordingly, it is not discussed in more detail, but see B. Becker and Schram (1994) for more information.

STEPS OF META-ANALYSIS

The basic steps of a meta-analysis are similar to those of a primary study. In both, these steps may be iterative because it is often necessary to return to an earlier stage for refinement when problems are discovered at later stages. These steps are enumerated first and then discussed:

1. Formulate the research question.
2. Collect the data (primary studies).
3. Evaluate the quality of the data.
4. Measure the predictors (substantive, method, or extrinsic study factors) and criterion (study outcome).
5. Analyze the data (synthesize study results).
6. Describe, interpret, and report the results.

Formulate the Research Question

Because it affects all subsequent steps, the formulation of the research question is just as crucial in a meta-analysis as in a primary analysis. The basic task is to specify hypotheses and operational definitions of constructs.

These specifications in meta-analysis should also help to distinguish between relevant and irrelevant studies. A meta-analysis obviously requires that research about the topic of interest exists, which raises the question: How many studies are necessary? A researcher can use meta-analytic methods to synthesize as few as two results, but more are typically needed. Although there is no absolute minimum number, it seems to me that at least 20 different studies would be required before a meta-analysis is really viable. This assumes that the studies are relatively homogenous and that only a small number of moderator variables are associated with study outcome. The failure to find sufficient numbers of studies indicates a knowledge gap.

Collect the Data

The goal of data collection in meta-analysis is to find every study within the scope of the research question—that is, to query the population of relevant studies. (The term *universe* instead of *population* is sometimes used in the meta-analytic literature.) Now, it may be impossible to actually find all studies in a population (more about this point shortly), and some of these studies may have defects so severe that their results must be excluded. But the question of which studies are included versus excluded is critical because it determines the outcome of the meta-analysis.

Data collection is characterized by searches in multiple sources, including published works, such as journal articles, books, or reports from public agencies, and unpublished studies. The latter includes conference presentations, papers submitted for publication but rejected, graduate student theses, and technical reports from private agencies. Studies from each source are subject to different types of bias. For instance, published studies generally have more H_0 rejections and larger effect size magnitudes than unpublished studies. They may also have most of the Type I errors. Results from unpublished studies may be prone to distortion because of design or analysis problems that otherwise may be detected in peer review. The coding of study source as an extrinsic factor permits direct evaluation of its effect on study outcome, however. M. Rosenthal (1994) discussed strategies for finding different kinds of published or unpublished research studies. In established research areas, computer searches of electronic databases may identify hundreds or even thousands of potential studies. Narrowing the search criteria is the only practical way to deal with this problem. In contrast, too few studies may be found in newer research areas. If so, the search criteria need to be broadened. Either tightening or expanding the search criteria also implies reformulation of the research question (i.e., go back to step 1).

Evaluate Data Quality

For two reasons, it is crucial to assess the high-inference characteristic of research quality. The first is to eliminate from further consideration studies so flawed that their results cannot be trusted. This helps to avoid the *garbage in, garbage out problem* in which results from bad studies are synthesized along with those from sound studies. The other reason concerns the remaining (nonexcluded) studies, which may be divided into those that are well-designed versus those with significant limitations. Results synthesized from the former group may be given greater interpretative weight than those from the latter group.

The quality of a primary study concerns its validity in three areas: conceptual, methodological, and statistical (Strube & Hartmann, 1983). *Conceptual validity* concerns whether a study actually tests what it is purported to test. The correct implementation of a treatment is an example of something that reflects conceptual validity. *Methodological validity* concerns threats to a study's internal and external validity. *Statistical validity* refers to the use of proper methods of data analysis. There are some standard systems for coding research quality in meta-analysis (e.g., Wortman, 1994).

Measure the Predictors and Criterion

This step involves the actual coding of the found studies. This task may be performed by coders, such as research assistants, who are not the primary investigators. This may prevent bias because of awareness of the research question. A statistic that summarizes the results in each study must also be selected. The most common choice is a standardized effect size index, such as d for continuous outcomes or the odds ratio for dichotomous outcomes in comparative studies. It is also possible to combine p values from statistical tests in primary studies or use formal vote counting, but these methods are subject to all the limitations of p values and convey little information about effect size. However, there are times when statistics reported in primary studies are insufficient to compute effect sizes. Bushman (1994) described the use of formal vote counting to assess publication bias.

If very different kinds of outcome measures are used across a set of studies, their results may not be directly comparable even if the same kind of standardized effect size index is computed in each study. This is an example of the *apples-and-oranges problem*. Suppose that gender differences in aggression are estimated across a set of studies. There are more than one type of aggressive behavior (e.g., verbal, physical) and more than one way to measure it (e.g., self-report, observational). An average d statistic that compares men and women computed across a diverse set of measures of aggression may not be very meaningful. This would be especially true if the magnitude of gender differences changes with the type of aggression or how it is measured (Knight, Fabes, & Higgins, 1996). One way to deal with the apples-and-oranges problem is to code the content or measurement method of the outcome variable and represent this information in the analysis as one or more method factors. The apples-and-oranges problem can arise with the meta-analytic predictors, too. This can happen if relevant study factors are not coded or categories of such factors are overly broad.

It is common in meta-analysis to weight the standardized effect size for each study by a factor that represents sample size (demonstrated later). This gives greater weight to results based on larger samples, which are less subject to sampling error. It is also possible to weight study effect sizes by other characteristics, such as the reliability of the scores or ratings of the overall research quality. Hunter and F. Schmidt (1994) described an extensive set of corrections for attenuation in correlation effect sizes for problems such as artificial dichotomization in continuous outcome variables and range restriction, but primary studies do not always report sufficient information to apply these corrections.

There is also the problem of *nonindependence* of study results. It seldom happens that each individual result comes from an independent study where a single hypothesis is tested. In some studies, the same research participants may be tested with multiple outcome measures. If these measures are intercorrelated, effect sizes across these measures are not independent. Likewise, effect sizes for the comparison of variations of a treatment against a common control group are probably not independent. Gleser and Olkin (1994) referred to the kinds of dependent studies just described as *multiple-endpoint studies* and *multiple-treatment studies*, respectively. Analyzing dependent study outcomes with methods that assume independence may yield inaccurate results. Fortunately, statistical techniques are available that handle correlated effect sizes.

Analyze the Data

Lau, Ioannidis, and Schmid (1997) outlined the following iterative phases of data analysis in meta-analysis:

1. Decide whether to combine results across studies, and define what to combine.
2. Estimate a common (average) effect.
3. Estimate the heterogeneity in results across studies, and attempt to explain it—that is, find an appropriate statistical model for the data.
4. Assess the potential for bias.

The first step in the analysis phase of a meta-analyses is often the computation of a weighted average effect size. If it can be assumed that the observed effect sizes estimate a single population effect size (more about this point later), their average takes the form

$$M_{ES} = \frac{\sum_{i=1}^{k} w_i \, ES_i}{\sum_{i=1}^{k} w_i} \quad (8.1)$$

where ES_i is the effect size index (e.g., d) for the ith result in a set of k results and w_i is the weight for that effect size. A weight for each effect size that minimizes the variance of M_{ES} is

$$w_i = \frac{1}{s_{ES_i}^2} \quad (8.2)$$

where w_i is the inverse of $s_{ES_i}^2$, the conditional variance (squared standard error) of an effect size. The conditional variance of an effect size is also called the *within-study variance*. The equation for the within-study variance depends on the particular effect size index (e.g., see Table 4.5), but it generally varies inversely with sample size. In other words, results based on bigger samples are given greater weight.

The conditional variance of the weighted average effect size M_{ES} is determined by the total number of effect sizes and their weights:

$$s_{M_{ES}}^2 = \frac{1}{\sum_{i=1}^{k} w_i} \quad (8.3)$$

The square root of Equation 8.3 is the standard error of the average weighted effect size. An approximate $100(1-\alpha)\%$ confidence interval for the population average effect size μ_{ES} has the following general form:

$$M_{ES} \pm s_{M_{ES}} \, (z_{2\text{-tail}, \, \alpha}) \quad (8.4)$$

where $z_{2\text{-tail}, \, \alpha}$ is the positive two-tailed critical value of the normal deviate z at the α level of statistical significance. If a confidence interval for μ_{ES} includes zero and $z_{2\text{-tail}, \, .05} = 1.96$, the nil hypothesis that the population effect size is zero cannot be rejected at the .05 level. This is an example of a statistical test in meta-analysis.

The weighting of study effect sizes as described assumes a fixed-effects model, also called a *conditional model*. This model assumes that (a) there is one universe of studies with a single true effect size, and (b) each study effect size departs from the true effect size only because of within-study variance (Lipsey & Wilson, 2000). Accordingly, effects sizes in a fixed-effects model are weighted only by functions of their conditional variances (Equation 8.2). Between-studies variation in effect size is viewed as systematic and a result of identifiable differences between studies such as those listed in Table 8.1. Generalizations in this model are limited to studies such as those actually found.

There is a meta-analytic statistical test that evaluates whether the variability in study effect sizes is great enough to reject the hypothesis that they estimate a common population effect size. The following homogeneity test statistic,

$$Q = \sum_{i=1}^{k} \frac{(ES_i - M_{ES})^2}{s_{ES_i}^2} = \sum_{i=1}^{k} w_i (ES_i - M_{ES})^2 \qquad (8.5)$$

equals the sum of the weighted squared differences between the study effect sizes and their weighted average. It is distributed as a chi-square statistic (χ^2) with $k - 1$ degrees of freedom, where k is the number of effect sizes. Suppose that $Q = 10.00$ for a set of 15 effect sizes. The critical value for $\chi^2 (14)$ at the .05 level is 23.69, so the null hypothesis that the 15 results share a common population effect size is not rejected at the .05 level. However, the homogeneity hypothesis would be rejected for the same number of effect sizes if $Q = 25.00$.

Rejection of the homogeneity hypothesis leaves the meta-analyst with two basic options:

1. Continue to assume a fixed-effects model but disaggregate studies by the levels of one or more meta-analytic predictors. Continue until the homogeneity hypothesis is not rejected within each category.
2. Specify a random-effects or a mixed-effects model instead of a fixed-effects model.

The second option implies selection of a different model for error. There is no single universe of studies or true effect size in a random-effects model, also called an *unconditional model*. It assumes that (a) there is a distribution of population effect sizes (i.e., a different true effect size underlies each study), and (b) between-studies variation in effect sizes is random and a result of sources that cannot be identified. A mixed-effects model assumes that between-studies variation may be a result of both systematic factors that can be identified (e.g., Table 8.1) and to random sources that cannot. Effect sizes in either model are weighted by

$$w_i^* = \hat{\sigma}_\theta^2 + w_i \qquad (8.6)$$

where w_i is the within-studies variation (Equation 8.2) and $\hat{\sigma}_\theta^2$ is an estimated population variance component for random between-studies variability. There are different ways to estimate $\hat{\sigma}_\theta^2$. One method is based on the variance of the observed effect sizes around the unweighted average effect size, and another is based on the Q statistic, among others (e.g., Shadish & Haddock, 1994). The estimation of two sources of error variance instead of just one, as in a fixed-effects model, may improve the prediction of observed effect sizes. It is also consistent with generalization of the results to studies not identical to the set of found studies.

Readers should know that there is no clear census that random-effects or mixed-effects models are clearly superior to fixed-effects models. For example, a fixed-effects model may be preferred when the found studies are relatively homogeneous, treatments are precise, or their effects are generally well-understood (T. Cook, Cooper, Corday, et al., 1992). Part of the task of the data analysis phase in a meta-analysis is to select an appropriate model for error variance. Shadish and Haddock (1994) noted that this choice is not entirely statistical or conceptual, but it should be guided by the researcher's domain knowledge.

Statistical techniques for meta-analysis include analogues of the analysis of variance (ANOVA) or multiple regression for weighted effect sizes. For example, it is possible to disaggregate studies by the levels of two crossed, categorical study factors and perform a two-way ANOVA on the weighted effect sizes. This analysis would estimate both main and interaction effects of the meta-analytic predictors. Statistical tests of these effects are based on the Q statistic, not the F ratio. All ANOVA models for effect sizes are special cases of multiple regression for effect sizes. The latter can include continuous and categorical meta-analytic predictors in the same equation and estimate interactions between them. Regression methods also allow individual predictors or blocks of predictors to be entered into or removed from the equation in an order specified by the researcher—see Hedges (1994) and Raudenbush (1994) for more information about both methods for analyzing effect sizes.

Suppose in a meta-analysis that the nil hypothesis of zero population effect size has been rejected. There are ways to estimate what is known as the *fail-safe number* of file drawer (unpublished) studies not found in the literature search with an average effect size of zero needed to fail to reject the nil hypothesis of zero population effect size. R. Rosenthal's (1979) is probably the best known method, but there are others. If the estimated number of unpublished studies is so large that it is unlikely that so many studies (e.g., 2,000) with a mean nil effect size could exist, more confidence in the original result may be warranted. Some authors have criticized the assumptions that underlie estimates of the fail-safe number of studies, however (e.g., Oakes, 1986, pp. 157–159).

As is probably obvious by now, many decisions made while analyzing effect sizes influence the final results of a meta-analysis. In a *sensitivity analysis*, the data are reanalyzed under different assumptions, and the results are compared with the original findings. If both sets of results are similar, the original meta-analytic findings are robust with regard to the manipulated assumptions. Suppose that the criteria for study inclusion are modified in a reasonable way and a somewhat different subset of all found studies is retained. If the meta-analysis is repeated with the new subset and the results are not appreciably different from those under the original criteria, the meta-analytic results are robust concerning the inclusion criteria. A related tactic evaluates the effect of excluding or including individual studies in a particular order. For example, if deleting a single study changes a statistical average weighted effect size to a nonstatistical effect size, an explanation is needed.

Describe, Interpret, and Report the Results

This stage is similar to that for a primary study, so it needs little description. R. Rosenthal (1995) offered suggestions for writing and understanding a meta-analytic article.

MINI META-ANALYSIS

Table 8.2 presents characteristics and outcomes of nine hypothetical studies that compare treatment with control. It is assumed across all studies that (a) treatment is implemented the same way to patients who have the same illness, and (b) the outcome variable reflects the same construct and is measured with the same method. Studies listed in Table 8.2 are classified into three groups by illness chronicity. That is, studies 1 to 3 were conducted with patients who have a chronic form of the illness, studies 6 to 9 involved samples with acute forms, and illness duration was intermediate among the patients in studies 4 and 5. The magnitude of the treatment effect is estimated with Hedges's g, where positive values indicate an advantage over control. Also reported in the table are approximate conditional variances and weights for each effect size assuming a fixed-effects model.

The sum of the weighted effect sizes across the nine studies in Table 8.2 is $\Sigma wg = 55.596$, and the sum of weights is $\Sigma w = 118.464$. The average weighted effect size is thus

TABLE 8.2
Characteristics and Results of Nine Hypothetical Studies of
Treatment Effectiveness

Study	Illness chronicity	Group size		Outcome			
		Treatment	Control	g	s_g^2	w	wg
1	Chronic	25	20	−.05	.0900	11.108	−.555
2	Chronic	15	25	.05	.1067	9.372	.469
3	Chronic	40	40	−.10	.0501	19.974	−1.997
4	Intermediate	20	20	.55	.1040	9.617	5.289
5	Intermediate	35	35	.65	.0602	16.598	10.788
6	Acute	30	35	.90	.0683	14.634	13.171
7	Acute	15	15	.70	.1421	7.038	4.927
8	Acute	20	20	.85	.1095	9.132	7.762
9	Acute	45	45	.75	.0476	20.991	15.743
Total						118.464	55.596

Note. The conditional variances for *g* are estimated with the first equation in Table 4.5.

$$M_g = 55.596/118.464 = .4693$$

That is, the average weighted treatment effect across the nine studies is just under .50 standard deviations in magnitude. Its standard error is the square root of the reciprocal of the sum of the weights across all studies:

$$s_{M_g} = (1/118.464)^{1/2} = .0919$$

The approximate 95% confidence interval for the population average weighted effect size is

$$.4693 \pm .0919 \ (1.96) \quad \text{or} \quad .4693 \pm .1801$$

which defines the interval .29–.65 at two-decimal accuracy. The homogeneity test statistic computed for all nine studies is

$$Q = 11.108 \ (-.05 - .4693)^2 + 9.372 \ (.05 - .4693)^2$$
$$+ \ldots + 15.743 \ (.75 - .4693)^2 = 17.79$$

which exceeds the critical value of χ^2 (8) at the .05 level, 15.51. Thus, the average observed effect size does not seem to estimate a common population effect size. Inspection of the effect sizes in the table supports this conclusion: The magnitude of the treatment effect is close to zero in studies 1 to 3 where the patients have chronic forms of the illness, but it is larger in studies 4 to 9 where patients have conditions of either acute or intermediate duration.

Table 8.3 reports the results of a one-way ANOVA conducted with the weighted effect sizes in Table 8.2. The single factor is illness chronicity, and its three levels classify the nine studies into three groups: chronic (n_1 = 3), intermediate (n_2 = 2), and acute (n_3 = 4). Total variability in a one-way ANOVA for effect sizes can be broken down into between-groups variability and within-groups variability, just as in a primary study. The between-groups variability is tested with the homogeneity test statistic Q_B. It equals the sum of weighted squared deviations of the group mean effect sizes from the grand mean effect size computed earlier, M_g = .4693. The group means are the average weighted effect sizes across the studies in each category. For example, the mean effect size and standard error for studies 1 to 3 are

$$M_{g_{Chronic}} = (-.555 + .469 - 1.997)/(11.108 + 9.372 + 19.974)$$
$$= -2.063/40.454 = -.0515$$

$$s_{M_{g_{Chronic}}} = (1/40.454)^{1/2} = .1572$$

Mean effect sizes for the other two groups of studies are computed in similar ways. Across the four studies conducted with patients with acute illness, the size of the average treatment effect is .80 standard deviations, and it is .61 standard deviations across the two studies conducted with patients with intermediate illness durations, both at two-decimal accuracy.

Using four-decimal accuracy for mean effect sizes in the computations, the between-groups homogeneity test statistic is

$$Q_B = 40.454 (-.0515 - .4693)^2 + 26.215 (.6133 - .4693)^2$$
$$+ 51.795 (.8032 - .4693)^2 = 17.29$$

where the weights for each squared deviation of group mean effect sizes from the grand mean is the total of the weights for studies in each category.

TABLE 8.3
Average Effect Sizes, Confidence Intervals, and Heterogeneity Test
Results for the Data in Table 8.2

Source	df	M_g	s_{M_G}	w	Q	P
Between groups	2	—	—	—	17.29	<.001
Within groups	6	—	—	—	.49	.998
Chronic	2	−.05 (−.36–.26)[a]	.1572	40.454	.14	.932
Intermediate	1	.61 (.23–.99)	.1953	26.215	.06	.806
Acute	3	.80 (.53–1.07)	.1389	51.795	.29	.962
Total	8	.47 (.29–.65)	.0919	118.464	17.79	.023

[a]Approximate 95% confidence interval.

This statistic tests the omnibus group effect with two degrees of freedom. The critical value of $\chi^2(2)$ at the .05 level is 5.99, so the nil hypothesis that the three population effect sizes are equal is rejected.

It is also possible to compute homogeneity test statistics within each of the three groups of studies. Each statistic tests the hypothesis that a common population effect size is estimated within each group. It is computed just as Q for the total data set, except that weighted squared deviations are taken from the group mean effect size, not the grand mean M_g, across all studies. For example, the homogeneity test statistic for the three studies conducted with samples of chronically ill patients is computed as follows:

$$Q_{\text{Chronic}} = 11.108 \ [-.05 - (-.0515)]^2 + 9.372 \ [.05 - (-.0515)]^2$$
$$+ 19.974 \ [-.10 - (-.0515)]^2 = .14$$

The critical value of $\chi^2(2)$ at the .05 level is 5.99, so the homogeneity hypothesis is not rejected; that is, the three results in this group seem to estimate the same population parameter. Within-groups homogeneity test statistics for the other two sets of studies are computed the same general way. Their values are $Q_{\text{Acute}} = .06$ and $Q_{\text{Intermed}} = .29$, so the homogeneity hypothesis is not rejected in any of the groups of studies. Thus, partitioning studies by level of the illness chronicity factor results in uniform estimates of population effect size within each group. The sum of the homogeneity test statistics for each group equals the total within-groups homogeneity test statistic, or

$$Q_W = Q_{\text{Chronic}} + Q_{\text{Acute}} + Q_{\text{Intermed}} = .14 + .06 + .29 = .49$$

which is distributed as a $\chi^2(6)$ statistic. Therefore, the homogeneity hypothesis for the total within-groups variability in effect sizes is also not rejected. The sum of the between-groups and total within-groups homogeneity test statistics equals (within slight rounding error) the test statistic computed earlier for the total data set, or

$$Q = Q_B + Q_W = 17.29 + .49 = 17.78$$

THREATS TO THE VALIDITY OF A META-ANALYSIS

Both those who promote (e.g., Hunt, 1997) or dismiss (e.g., Eysenck, 1995) meta-analysis would probably agree that it is no less subject to many of the same problems that can beset the primary studies on which it is based. Meta-analysis is also subject to additional limitations specific to the technique. Some examples were already mentioned, including the apples and oranges problem and the garbage in, garbage out problem. Other concerns raised by Cooper and Hedges (1994a) and Sohn (1995), among others, are outlined next.

Although it is useful to know average effect size magnitudes in some research area, effect size by itself says relatively little about substantive significance (see chap. 4, this volume). It is also true that explaining a relatively high proportion of the observed variance in study outcomes with a set of meta-analytic predictors does not imply that these factors are actually the ones involved in the underlying processes. It is possible that an alternative set of factors may explain just as much of the variance or that some of the measured predictors are confounded with other, unmeasured factors that are actually more important. Meta-analysis is not a substitute for primary studies. Despite their limitations, primary studies are still the basic engine of science. Indeed, a single brilliant empirical or theoretical work could be worth more than hundreds of mediocre studies synthesized in meta-analysis. There is concern about the practice of guarding against experimenter bias by having research assistants code the primary studies. The worry is about a crowding out of wisdom that may occur if what is arguably the most thought-intensive part of a meta-analysis—the careful reading of the individual studies—is left to others.

It is probably best to see meta-analysis as a means to better understanding the current state of a research area than as an end in itself or some magical substitute for critical thought. Its emphasis on replication, effect sizes, and the explicit description of study retrieval methods are certainly an improvement over narrative literature reviews. It also has the potential to address hypotheses not directly tested in primary studies. If the results of a meta-analysis help researchers conduct better primary studies, then little more could be expected.

EXAMPLES OF META-ANALYSES

The idea of applying the statistical methods of primary studies to synthesize results across studies is not new. Bangert-Drowns (1986) cited works from the 1930s in which correlations, p values from statistical tests, or average treatment effects were combined across studies in agriculture, public health, and other areas. The term *meta-analysis* is generally attributed to G. Glass (1976), who along with R. Rosenthal (1976) is widely credited with furthering contemporary forms of meta-analysis. A synthesis of results about psychotherapy outcomes by Smith and Glass (1977) is perhaps the first modern meta-analysis. Features of that analysis included the estimation of a common effect size index across all studies (d), the classification of studies by several different meta-analytic predictors (e.g., group vs. individual therapy), and the elimination of studies with gross design flaws. Hundreds of meta-analytic studies have subsequently appeared in the behavioral and medical research literatures. That meta-analysis is endorsed by many as a useful way to synthesize results is hard to deny. Indeed, it is difficult to pick up some research journals without finding at least one meta-analytic article. Examples that illustrate basic meta-analytic principles follow.

Amplitude of Event-Related Potentials
From Males at Risk for Alcoholism

Polich, Pollock, and Bloom (1994) conducted a meta-analysis about the P300 component of event-related brain potentials (ERP) as a possible biological marker of the risk for alcoholism among male adolescents and young adults. The P300 component is generated when attending to or discriminating between stimuli. It may reflect physiological processes that underlie working memory. Polich et al. found and retained a total of about 20 studies where P300 amplitudes of young men with and without positive family histories for alcoholism were compared. These studies generated a total of 30 comparisons on different types of tasks. Each result was described with a d statistic, where positive values indicate lower P300 amplitudes in the positive family history group than in the negative family history group. Figure 8.1 presents a reproduction of the figure in Polich et al. that presents all 30 effect sizes as dots. Each dot is surrounded by horizontal lines that represent approximate 95% confidence intervals. The style of the horizontal lines identifies task modality (auditory vs. visual, easy vs. hard). Note in Figure 8.1 that most d statistics (20/30) are positive, which indicates generally diminished P300 amplitudes among young men with positive family histories. Most of the confidence intervals (24/30) include zero, which says that the box-score is 24 to 6 in favor of the nil hypothesis of a zero population effect size. This outcome is not surprising considering that the average group size across all studies is only about 17 (i.e., statistical power is low). However, the average weighted d statistic across all comparisons is .33, and the 95% confidence interval based on this result, .18–.49, does *not* include zero. This demonstrates how an accumulated result can be greater than the sum of its parts.

Polich et al. disaggregated individual effect sizes by task modality and participant age (<17, ≥18 years old). For easy discrimination tasks, the average weighted effect sizes for auditory versus visual task modalities are very similar, .18 and .20 standard deviations, respectively. For difficult tasks, however, the average effect sizes for auditory versus visual modalities are .06 and .65 standard deviations, respectively. Mean effect sizes are also greater in studies with younger samples than older samples, .62 versus .16 standard deviations, respectively. Other analyses by Polich et al. indicated

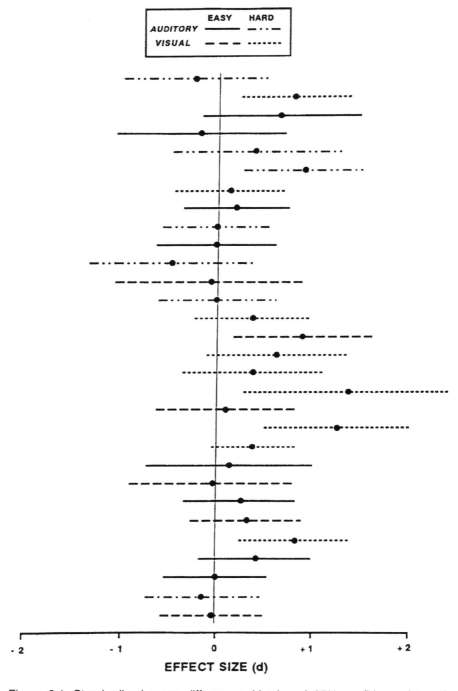

Figure 8.1. Standardized mean differences (dots) and 95% confidence intervals (horizontal lines) for 30 contrasts between young men with and without family histories for alcoholism on P300 amplitude. From "Meta-Analysis of P300 Amplitude From Males at Risk for Alcoholism," by J. Polich, V. E. Pollock, and F. E. Bloom, 1994, *Psychological Bulletin, 115*, p. 63. Copyright 1994 by the American Psychological Association. Adapted with permission.

that the source through which participants with positive family histories were recruited—whether their fathers were treated for alcoholism versus not necessarily—did not clearly predict variability in effect size magnitudes. Overall, differences in average P300 amplitudes between young men with and without family histories of alcoholism were strongest for difficult visual tasks and adolescents.

Gender Differences in Personality Characteristics

Feingold (1994) conducted four different meta-analyses to estimate the magnitudes of gender differences in personality characteristics among adults. These analyses concerned studies published in three different time periods—1958–1974, 1975–1983, and 1984–1992; and about four different traits—self-esteem, internal locus of control, anxiety, and assertiveness. Disaggregation of studies by publication date allows estimation of temporal trends in the magnitudes of gender differences in personality characteristics. Feingold found relatively little variation over time in average weighted d statistics. For example, assuming positive values indicate higher means for men than women, the range of weighted average d statistics across the three time periods is .10 to .16 for self-esteem, .12 to .20 for assertiveness, and −.31 to −.15 for anxiety. Results for internal locus of control were less consistent: Mean d statistics from studies in the earliest and latest time periods range from .07–.08, but the average gender difference in studies from the middle time period is .24 standard deviations in magnitude.

Broadly speaking, there are two possible sources of observed gender differences in personality characteristics among adults, biological (genetic, hormonal) and sociocultural (environmental). A tenet of the sociocultural model is that differential socialization of children contributes to later psychological differences between men and women. Differential socialization refers to the encouragement of certain traits or behaviors more for children of one gender than another. For example, showing interpersonal warmth may be rewarded more for girls and achievement may be cultivated more for boys. It is also possible that fathers may make greater differences between sons and daughters than do mothers. To address inconsistent results of primary studies and narrative reviews about differential socialization effects, Lytton and Romney (1991) meta-analyzed results of extant studies in the area. Their set of retained studies included 158 from North America where socialization practices for boys and girls were contrasted. Lytton and Romney partitioned these studies by parent and eight different major socialization areas, such as warmth, discipline, and gender-typed activities.

Lytton and Romney found clear evidence for a differential socialization effect in only one area, gender-typed activities. For mothers, the average weighted effect size in this area is .34 standard deviations, which indicates stronger encouragement for sons than daughters. Average effect sizes for mothers across all other major socialization areas ranged from −.07 to .07 standard deviations. For fathers, the average weighted effect size for encouragement of gender-typed activities is .49 standard deviations. In other words, fathers tend to differentiate somewhat more strongly than mothers between boys and girls in this area. Fathers also tended to emphasize somewhat more strongly than mothers' discipline and restrictiveness for boys than girls, but the magnitudes of average effects in these areas are modest, just under .20 standard deviations each. In general, these meta-analytic results do not support the view that differential socialization effects are large, pervasive, or vary strongly by mothers versus fathers.

Cross-Informant Consistency in Reports About Children's Adjustment Status

Clinical assessment of children is characterized by the collection of observations from multiple informants, including parents, teachers, mental health workers, other adult observers, and children themselves. Achenbach, McConaughy, and Howell (1987) retrieved a total of 194 studies where different combinations of informants provided a score, and cross-informant agreement was measured with Pearson correlations. The average weighted correlation for informants with similar relationships to the child were similar and ranged from .54 for pairs of mental health workers to .64 for pairs of teachers. Agreement between pairs of informants with different relationships to the child was generally lower, ranging from a mean correlation of .24 for parent–mental health worker pairs to .42 for teacher–observer pairs. And overall agreement between child self-reports and those of other informants were the lowest of all: Mean correlations ranged from .20 for child–teacher pairs to .27 for child–mental health worker pairs. Correlations were also disaggregated by child characteristics and type of behavior problems. Mean average correlations by these categories were generally similar, with two exceptions: Average agreement was somewhat higher for younger children than older children (M_r = .51, .41, respectively) and for externalizing problems than internalizing problems (M_r = .41, .32, respectively). Based on these results, Achenbach et al. argued that child assessment practices be geared toward the reality of relatively low cross-informant agreement.

CONCLUSION

Meta-analysis has become an important method for research synthesis in the behavioral sciences, so primary researchers in these areas should understand its strengths and limitations. Crucial questions about the validity of a meta-analysis concern the selection of studies, assessment of their quality and measurement of their characteristics, computation of a common measure of outcome—usually a standardized effect size index—how lack of independence in results is handled, and the underlying statistical model assumed in the analysis. Effects of decisions about the areas just mentioned on the results can be evaluated in a sensitivity analysis. The typical meta-analysis estimates an average standardized effect size and whether substantive, method, or extrinsic factors explain variability in results across studies. A good meta-analysis should summarize the status of a literature and suggest new directions for primary studies.

RECOMMENDED READINGS

Cook, T. D., Cooper, H., Corday, D. S., Hartmann, H., Hedges, L. V., Light, R. J., et al. (1992). *Meta-analysis for explanation.* New York: Russell Sage Foundation.

Hunt, M. (1997). *How science takes stock.* New York: Russell Sage Foundation.

Strube, M. J., & Hartmann, D. P. (1983). Meta-analysis: Techniques, applications, and functions. *Journal of Consulting and Clinical Psychology, 51,* 14–27.

9

RESAMPLING AND
BAYESIAN ESTIMATION

Put simply, the basic dilemma in all sciences is that of how much to oversimplify reality.

—H. M. Blalock (1964, p. 8)

The formal theory that underlies traditional statistical tests dates to the early 1900s. The title of an article by Wilcox (1998) asks the question, How many discoveries have been lost by ignoring modern statistical methods? Fortunately, there is a wealth of alternative methods, some based on contemporary statistical theory. The two methods selected for review, resampling and Bayesian estimation, are generally unfamiliar in the behavioral sciences. However, both methods are promising for the kinds of problems studied by many behavioral researchers. Both also support the evaluation of competing models. Please note that entire books are devoted to each of the techniques considered, so it is not possible in one chapter to describe them in any substantive detail. Instead, the goal of this presentation is to make the reader aware of even more alternatives to traditional statistical tests and provide references for additional study.

RESAMPLING TECHNIQUES

Techniques for *resampling*—also known as *computer-intensive methods*—are forms of internal replication (see chap. 8, this volume) that recombine the cases in a data set in different ways to estimate statistical precision, with possibly fewer assumptions about underlying population distributions

273

compared to traditional methods. The three methods described—bootstrapping, the jackknife, and randomization procedures—all work by instructing the computer to take large numbers of random samples (e.g., > 1,000) from an original data set, compute in each generated sample an estimator, and construct an empirical frequency distribution of that estimator across all generated samples. The value of the estimator in the original data set is located in this frequency distribution, and its empirical probability and standard error can be determined. The properties of the empirical frequency distribution, such as its central tendency, variability, skewness, or kurtosis, can be used to construct a confidence interval for the corresponding parameter. In contrast, traditional methods for interval estimation often rely on equations for asymptotic (large-sample) standard errors that make certain distributional assumptions, such as normality (chap. 2, this volume).

Specific Techniques

The technique of *bootstrapping*, developed by B. Efron in the late 1970s (e.g., Diaconis & Efron, 1983), is probably the best known and most flexible of the resampling methods described. The term *bootstrapping* is from the expression about lifting oneself up by one's bootstraps, which itself probably originates from a story by Rudolph Raspe (1737–1794) about the fictional Baron Munchausen, who after falling to the bottom of a lake returned himself to the surface by pulling up on his bootstraps. Perhaps the best known form of this technique is *nonparametric bootstrapping*, which makes no assumptions about the population distribution other than that the distribution of the data reflects its basic shape. It works theoretically by copying a data set onto itself an infinite number of times and drawing random samples from this pseudo-population (B. Thompson, 1993b). In practice, cases from the original data file are randomly selected with replacement to form a new sample, usually the same size as the original. Because of sampling with replacement, the same case could be selected more than once, and the composition of cases can vary across generated samples. When repeated many times by the computer, bootstrapping constructs an empirical sampling distribution. A related but older technique is the *jackknife*. This method typically excludes one case from each resampling of an original data set, which makes for a total of $N + 1$ possible analyses, including the one with all the cases. Efron and Tibshirani (1993) showed that the jackknife is a linear approximation to the generally more efficient bootstrap. As a consequence, only bootstrapping is discussed.

The bootstrap method can be implemented with just about any traditional statistical method. For example, *one-variable bootstrap methods* concern the statistical stability of estimators computed in a single sample. These methods generate *bootstrapped confidence intervals* based on statistics such as means, medians, variances, or skewness indexes in one group. *Two-variable bootstrap methods* construct confidence intervals based on statistics from two variables or groups, such as Pearson correlations or mean contrasts. If the means are independent, the computer generates pairs of bootstrapped samples, one taken from each group, and records the mean difference across the two generated samples. The frequency distribution of mean differences for all replications is then used to construct a bootstrapped confidence interval for the mean contrast. There are actually different kinds of bootstrapped confidence intervals that differ in their assumptions about the underlying distribution. *Bias-corrected bootstrapped confidence intervals* make the fewest assumptions—that is, they are based closely on the empirical sampling distribution generated from the bootstrapped samples (Lunneborg, 2000).

Parametric bootstrapping allows specific assumptions about the parameters of population distributions. Instead of sampling with replacement from an actual data set, bootstrapped samples of a specified size are drawn from a probability density function that reflects those parameters. For statistics with textbook equations for their standard errors, such as means (see chap. 2, this volume), parametric bootstrapped estimates of standard errors based on the same assumptions, such as normality, tend to be similar. Bootstrap estimation used in parametric mode can also approximate standard errors for statistics where no textbook equation is available (Efron & Tibshirani, 1993), given certain assumptions about the population distribution. These assumptions can be relaxed when bootstrapping is done in nonparametric mode. It is nonparametric bootstrapping that is seen more often in the behavioral sciences, so only this method is considered.

There are also bootstrap versions of many different types of statistical tests. Consider a bootstrap version of the independent samples t test for a data set with $n_1 = 30$ scores in the first group and $n_2 = 20$ scores in the second group: The computer randomly selects, with replacement, 50 scores from the total data set. The first 30 of these selections are assigned to the first bootstrapped sample, and the next 20 scores are assigned to the second. A t statistic is computed for the mean contrast from each pair of generated samples. After many replications, the observed value of t in the original data set is located in the empirical frequency distribution of t values from the bootstrapped samples. If the probability of the observed t is less than .05 in the empirical sampling distribution, the null hypothesis of H_0: $\mu_1 = \mu_2$ is rejected at the .05 level. The bootstrap t test just described requires the same assumptions as the standard t test for independent samples (chap. 2, this volume), and this is true even though the bootstrap mode is nonparametric. In other words, using a bootstrap version of statistical test does not free one from the distributional assumptions of the traditional version of the same test.

However, the somewhat restrictive assumptions of the independent samples t test are not necessary if the empirical sampling distribution is based on the unstandardized mean differences across all pairs of bootstrapped samples instead of the parametric t statistic. In this case, the null hypothesis is more general—Efron and Tibshirani (1993) stated it symbolically as H_0: $F = G$, where F and G are population distributions, and Sprent (1998) expressed it conceptually by arguing that there is no differential response in the measured characteristic between the populations. This null hypothesis could be false because the means or shapes of distributions F and G are different.

Related techniques of resampling include *randomization procedures*, sometimes called *rerandomization*. These techniques are related to R. Fisher's idea of a permutation test, which dates to the 1930s. This was before the advent of computers capable of actually conducting it. Contemporary randomization procedures are typically used in experimental designs with two conditions, such as randomized clinical trials. Unlike the standard t test for such designs, randomization procedures do not assume random sampling from known populations, just random assignment of cases in locally available samples to different conditions. As a consequence, there may be little concern with estimating population parameters (see chap. 3, this volume). The computer in a randomization procedure shuffles the scores in the total data set. Each shuffle may swap pairs of scores across the groups. With many iterations, this algorithm simulates the effects of chance switches of scores across the groups, and the empirical sampling distribution is based on the mean differences across all pairs of generated samples. The observed mean difference is located in this distribution, and its empirical probability is determined. If the level of statistical significance is .05 and the empirical probability of the observed mean difference is less than .05, the null hypothesis of equal population distributions is rejected. The total number of unique combinations of all the scores over two groups of even moderate size, such as 50, may be so large that it is not practical even with a computer to generate all possible combinations. As in bootstrap techniques, one may be satisfied with at least 1,000 replications, however. See Good (2000) and Lunneborg (2001) for more information.

A brief example follows. Table 9.1 presents a small data set for a two-group design where the observed mean difference is 2.00. The standard error of the mean difference estimated with the textbook formula (Equation 2.8) is

$$s_{M_1 - M_2} = \{[(7.33 + 8.00)/2]\,(1/10 + 1/10)\}^{1/2} = 1.238$$

The width of the traditional 95% confidence interval for $\mu_1 - \mu_2$ is the product of the standard error and $t_{2\text{-tail},\ .05}\,(18) = 2.101$, or

TABLE 9.1
Raw Scores and Descriptive Statistics for Two Groups

| | Group | |
	1	2
	25	24
	26	25
	31	31
	29	28
	30	26
	30	26
	31	33
	32	28
	33	30
	33	29
M	30.00	28.00
s^2	7.33	8.00

$$2.00 \pm 1.238 \, (2.101)$$

which defines the interval −.60–4.60. The bootstrap module of SimStat (Provalis Research, 1996)[1] was used to generate a bias-corrected 95% boot-strapped confidence interval for $\mu_1 - \mu_2$ with the data in Table 9.1. The empirical sampling distribution of mean differences across 5,000 pairs of bootstrapped samples is presented in Figure 9.1. The mean of this distribution is 1.993, its standard deviation is 1.195, and values of its skewness and kurtosis indexes are, respectively, −.10 and −.08. The standard deviation of 1.195 is actually the bootstrapped estimate of the standard error of the mean difference. The bias-corrected 95% bootstrapped confidence interval based on the distribution in the figure is −.40–4.25. This interval is not symmetrical about 1.993 because the empirical sampling distribution is not symmetrical. Please note that the traditional and bootstrapped estimates for this example with means are quite similar, as expected.

The observed t (18) statistic for the mean difference in Table 9.1 is 1.615, which is equivalent to F (1, 18) = 1.615^2 = 2.609. The two-tailed p value for both test statistics assuming a standard central distribution is .124. A bootstrap F test of the mean difference for the data in Table 9.1 was conducted with the freely available program Resampling Procedures (RP) by D. Howell (2001).[2] Figure 9.2 presents the empirical frequency distribution of F statistics for the mean difference across 5,000 pairs of bootstrapped samples. The empirical probability of the observed F value of

---

[1] An evaluation version can be downloaded from http://www.simstat.com/
[2] See http://www.uvm.edu/~dhowell/StatPages/Resampling/Resampling.html

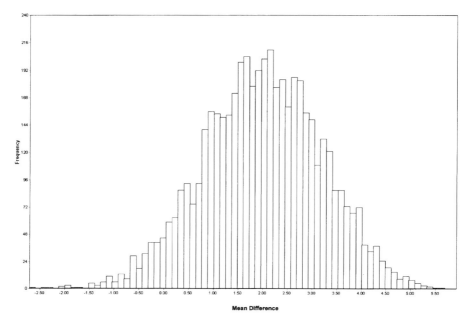

Figure 9.1. Empirical sampling distribution for mean differences in 5,000 pairs of bootstrapped samples for the data in Table 9.1.

2.609 for a nondirectional alternative hypothesis in this distribution is .148, which is somewhat higher than the p value for the traditional F test for these data. Both the traditional F test and the bootstrap F test require the same statistical assumptions for this example (see chap. 2, this volume).

Evaluation

The family of resampling techniques is versatile, and it has seen many different applications in both the social and natural sciences. That there are increasing numbers of software tools for resampling techniques also makes them more accessible to applied researchers. In addition to the programs mentioned, another includes the stand-alone program for personal computers Resampling Stats (Resampling Stats, 1999).[3] There are also add-in versions of this program that run under Microsoft Excel and MathWorks MATLAB.

The bootstrap technique seems especially well suited for interval estimation when the researcher is either unwilling or unable to make a lot of assumptions about population distributions. A potential application in this area is the estimation of confidence intervals for effect sizes, but software

---

[3] A trial version can be downloaded from http://www.resample.com/content/software/download .shtml

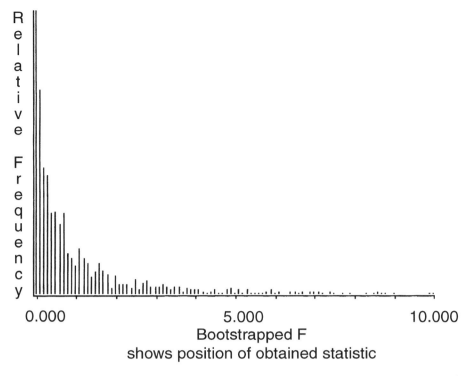

Figure 9.2. Empirical sampling distribution for the F statistic in 5,000 pairs of bootstrapped samples for the data in Table 9.1.

tools for bootstrap methods do not yet generally compute effect sizes other than correlations. I am less enthusiastic about using bootstrapping or other resampling methods to conduct statistical tests. For example, if the null hypothesis is implausible, the empirical probability of a bootstrapped test statistic may be too low, just as for traditional statistical tests. Also, both traditional and bootstrap statistical tests ignore effect size magnitude.

Some possible limitations of resampling techniques are summarized next:

1. Resampling is not a substitute for external replication (see chap. 8, this volume).
2. Resampling does not entirely free the researcher from having to make assumptions about population distributions. That assumptions can be added incrementally in some resampling methods is a positive feature, however.
3. The "population" from which bootstrap samples are drawn in nonparametric mode is merely the original data set. If this data set is small, unrepresentative, or the observations are not

independent, resampling from it will not somehow fix these problems. In fact, resampling can magnify the effects of unusual features in a data set, which can compromise external validity (J. Rodgers, 1999).

4. The accuracy of resampling estimates may be questionable for relatively small numbers of iterations, such as < 500. However, this is not generally a problem on contemporary personal computers where it may take just moments to execute thousands of iterations.

5. Results of bootstrap analyses are probably quite biased in small samples, but this is true of many traditional statistical methods, too. That is, bootstrapping does not cure small sample sizes.

BAYESIAN ESTIMATION

Traditional statistical tests estimate the probability of the data under a point null hypothesis, or $p\ (D \mid H_0)$. Also, the percentage associated with a traditional $100\ (1 - \alpha)\%$ confidence interval, such as 95%, is not generally interpretable as the chance that the interval contains the corresponding population parameter. Most researchers would rather know the probability of the hypothesis (not necessarily a point null hypothesis) in light of the data, or $p\ (H \mid D)$, and the probability that a parameter falls within a specific confidence interval (see chaps. 2 and 3, this volume). These are exactly the kinds of questions addressed in a Bayesian approach. Since the late 1950s, Bayesian methods have been widely used in many disciplines, including economics, computer science, and medicine (e.g., Gatsonis et al., 2001). Although introduced to psychology in the late 1960s by various authors (e.g., Edwards, Lindman, & Savage, 1963), Bayesian statistics never really caught on among behavioral researchers. This is unfortunate because a Bayesian approach has a lot to offer. Indeed, once some basic fundamentals are mastered, a Bayesian approach to hypothesis testing and estimation is much closer to intuitive scientific reasoning than traditional statistical tests. For example, the following principles are all supported in Bayesian analysis:

1. Not all hypotheses are equally plausible before there is evidence. And implausible hypotheses require stronger evidence to be supported. This is a basic tenet of science: Extraordinary claims require extraordinary proof. It was mentioned earlier that many nil hypotheses tested in the behavioral sciences are implausible. This results in p values from statistical tests that are too low, which exaggerates the significance of the findings (see chap. 3, this volume). In contrast, Bayesian methods take explicit account of hypothesis plausibility.

2. Not all researchers will see the same hypothesis as equally plausible before data collection. This is a basic fact of science, if not human nature. The effect of assuming different degrees of plausibility for the same hypothesis can also be explicitly estimated in a Bayesian analysis.
3. Data that are not precise will have less sway on the subsequent plausibility of a hypothesis than data that are more precise.
4. The impact of initial differences in the perceived plausibility of a hypothesis tend to become less important as results accumulate. That is, open-minded people with different initial beliefs are generally driven toward the same conclusion as new results are synthesized along with old ones. The only real long-term effect of initial differences in belief is that skeptics will require more data to reach the same level of belief as those more enthusiastic about a theory (Matthews, 2000). This is another fact of both science and everyday life.

Two factors may account for the general lack of familiarity with Bayesian methods in the behavioral sciences. One is the almost exclusive focus on traditional statistical tests in university curricula (chap. 3, this volume). Another is that Bayesian statistics are associated with a subjectivist rather than a frequentist view of probability. Recall that a subjectivist view does not distinguish between repeatable and unrepeatable (unique) events, and probabilities are considered as degrees of personal belief that may vary from person to person (see chap. 2, this volume). As outlined, it is necessary in Bayesian statistics to estimate the prior probability of some hypothesis before the data are collected, and this prior probability is a personal probability. There is a perception among those unfamiliar with Bayesian statistics that these prior probabilities are wholly subjective guesses just "plucked out of the air," perhaps to suit some whim or prejudice (Matthews, 2000). In contrast, traditional statistical tests may be seen as more objective because they are based on a frequentist view, which does not allow personal probabilities.

For a few reasons, the perceptions of Bayesian statistics described are not correct. If absolutely nothing is known about some hypothesis, the researcher has little choice other than to guess about its plausibility. However, it is rare for researchers to have absolutely no previous information, such as results of earlier studies or experience with a particular subject population, on which to base an estimate of prior probability. There are also methods from cognitive psychology for eliciting consistent prior probabilities from content experts about competing hypotheses. These methods try to avoid common difficulties that arise when people try to reason with probabilities, such as the *conjunction fallacy*, which occurs when a higher probability is estimated for two joint events than for the individual events. J. Anderson (1998, June) gave many examples, including the posing of questions for content experts in a frequency format instead of a probability format. Harsanyi (1983) and others suggested that the probability model that underlies Bayesian methods in practice is actually between a subjectivist view and a rationalist view of probability. The latter assumes there are always specific rational criteria for choosing a unique set of prior probabilities. It is also true that although traditional statistical tests appear to be objective, their use requires many subjective decisions (see chaps. 2 and 3, this volume).

It is time for psychology (and related disciplines) to reconsider its reluctance to explore Bayesian statistics. The next few sections outline the basic rationale of these statistics, consider a few potential applications, and identify other barriers to wider use of Bayesian methods in the behavioral sciences.

General Rationale

Bayesian statistics are a set of methods for the orderly expression and revision of belief as new evidence is gathered (Edwards et al., 1963). In this sense, the Bayesian approach is similar to meta-analysis in that both are methods for research synthesis, but the former specifically includes uncertainty in the analysis. Bayesian statistics are based on Bayes's theorem, which is from a posthumous publication (1763) of a letter by Rev. Thomas Bayes (1702–1761) in the *Philosophical Transactions of the Royal Society*. It is based on the mathematical fact that the joint probability of two events, D and H, is the product of the probability of the first event and the conditional probability of the second event given the first, or

$$p\,(D \wedge H) = p\,(D)\,p\,(H\,|\,D) = p\,(H)\,p\,(D\,|\,H) \qquad (9.1)$$

where the logical connective $\wedge$ designates the conjunction *and*. Solving this expression for the conditional probability $p\,(H\,|\,D)$ gives us the basic form of Bayes's theorem:

$$p\,(H\,|\,D) = \frac{p\,(H)\,p\,(D\,|\,H)}{p\,(D)} \qquad (9.2)$$

Assume now that D stands for data and H for hypothesis. The probability $p\,(H\,|\,D)$ in Equation 9.2 is the *posterior probability* of the hypothesis, given the data. This probability is a function of two *prior (marginal, unconditional) probabilities*, $p\,(H)$ and $p\,(D)$, and a conditional probability called the *likelihood*, or $p\,(D\,|\,H)$. The latter is the probability of the data under the hypothesis, and it is analogous to a p value from a traditional statistical test. The term $p(H)$ is the probability of the hypothesis before the data are collected, and the term $p(D)$ is the probability of the data irrespective of the truth of the hypothesis. In other words, this equation takes an initial belief about the hypothesis, $p(H)$, and combines it with information from the sample to generate an updated belief, $p(H|D)$. Bayes's theorem also shows us that the only way to estimate the probability of some hypothesis in light of the data is through estimation of the prior probability of each and the likelihood of the data (see chap. 3, this volume).

An example by P. Dixon and O'Reilly (1999) illustrates Bayes's theorem. Suppose we want to evaluate the probability that it will snow sometime during the day, given a below-freezing temperature in the morning. In a certain area, the chance of snow on any particular day of the year is only 10%, so $p(H) = .10$. The chance of a below-freezing morning temperature on any particular day is 20%, so $p(D) = .20$. Of all days it snowed, the chance of a below-freezing temperature in the morning is 80%, so $p(D|H) = .80$. The posterior probability is

$$p(H|D) = [.10\,(.80)]/.20 = .40$$

That is, there is a 40% chance that it will snow if it is cold in the morning.

Discrete Hypotheses

Suppose that there are k mutually exclusive and exhaustive hypotheses (H). The sum of their prior probabilities is 1.0, or

$$\sum_{i=1}^{k} p(H_i) = 1.0 \tag{9.3}$$

In this case, the prior probability of the data in Equation 9.2 can be expressed as

$$p(D) = \sum_{i=1}^{k} p(H_i)\,p(D|H_i) \tag{9.4}$$

which is the sum of the products of the prior probabilities of each of the k hypotheses and the likelihood of the data under it. An example follows.

Suppose that the distribution of scores on a continuous variable in some population is normal, the standard deviation is known ($\sigma = 12.00$), but the mean (μ) is not. There are two competing hypotheses, H_1 and H_2, that predict that μ equals 100.00 versus 110.00, respectively. Assuming no previous information, each of the two hypotheses is judged to be equally likely, or

$$p\ (\mu\ =\ 100.00)\ =\ p\ (\mu\ =\ 110.00)\ =\ .50$$

The assignment of equal prior probabilities to all competing hypotheses when there are no grounds to favor any one of them follows the *principle of indifference* (Harsanyi, 1983). Related descriptive terms include *agnostic priors* and *uninformative priors*. In contrast, *informative priors* would reflect greater confidence in one hypothesis than the other. For instance, specification of the prior probabilities

$$p\ (\mu\ =\ 100.00)\ =\ .60 \qquad p\ (\mu\ =\ 110.00)\ =\ .40$$

would reflect greater confidence in H_1 than H_2.

A sample of 16 cases is drawn from the population, and the observed mean is $M_1 = 106.00$. Because the population variance is known, the standard error of the mean is $\sigma_M = 12.00/16^{1/2} = 3.00$. The conditional probability of the sample mean under each hypothesis—the likelihoods—can be found with the standard normal density function

$$\text{ndf}\ (z)\ =\ \frac{e^{-z^2/2}}{\sqrt{2\ \text{pi}}} \tag{9.5}$$

where z is a normal deviate, e is the natural base (about 2.7183), and pi is approximately 3.1416. This function takes a z score and returns its probability, which is the height of a normal curve with a mean of zero and a standard deviation of 1.0 at that point. The z-score equivalents of the sample mean under each hypothesis are

$$z_1\ =\ (106.00\ -\ 100.00)/3.00\ =\ 2.00 \qquad \text{and}$$
$$z_2\ =\ (106.00\ -\ 110.00)/3.00\ =\ -1.33$$

and the likelihoods are

$$p\ (M_1\ =\ 106.00\ |\ \mu\ =\ 100.00)\ =\ \text{ndf}\ (2.00)/2\ =\ .0540/2\ =\ .0270$$
$$p\ (M_1\ =\ 106.00\ |\ \mu\ =\ 110.00)\ =\ \text{ndf}\ (-1.33)/2\ =\ .1640/2\ =\ .0820$$

The results of the ndf function are each divided by two because there are two hypotheses (e.g., Winkler, 1982, pp. 224–225). Given these results, the prior probability of the data is

$$p\ (M_1\ =\ 106.00)\ =\ .50\ (.0270)\ +\ .50\ (.0820)\ =\ .0545$$

and the posterior probabilities for each hypothesis are

$$p \ (\mu = 100.00 \mid M_1 = 106.00) = [.50 \ (.0270)]/.0545 = .2477$$
$$p \ (\mu = 110.00 \mid M_1 = 106.00) = [.50 \ (.0820)]/.0545 = .7523$$

Thus, our revised estimate of the probability of H_2: $\mu = 110.00$ (about .75) is higher than that for H_1: $\mu = 100.00$ (about .25), both given the data.

The posterior difference in confidence between two competing hypotheses can also be expressed as the *posterior odds*, the ratio of their posterior probabilities. Its general form is

$$\text{Posterior odds} = \frac{p \ (H_2 \mid D)}{p \ (H_1 \mid D)} = \frac{p \ (H_2)}{p \ (H_1)} \times \frac{p \ (D \mid H_2)}{p \ (D \mid H_1)} \qquad (9.6)$$

The expression to the far right shows the use of Bayes's theorem to rewrite the posterior odds as the product of the prior odds, $p \ (H_2)/p \ (H_1)$, and the *likelihood ratio*, $p \ (D \mid H_2)/p \ (D \mid H_1)$, also known as *Bayes's factor*. The latter summarizes the results of the study that allow the update of the odds of the two hypotheses from what it was before collecting the data (prior odds) to what it should be given the data (P. Dixon & O'Reilly, 1999). For the previous example,

$$\text{Posterior odds}_1 = .7523/.2477 = .50/.50 \times .0820/.0270 = 3.04$$

so the posterior odds are about 3:1 in favor of H_2: $\mu = 110.00$ over H_1: $\mu = 100.00$.

Bayes's theorem can also be applied iteratively as new data are collected. Suppose in a second sample of 16 cases it is found that $M_2 = 107.50$. The posterior probabilities from the previous analysis, .2477 for H_1 and .7523 for H_2, become the prior probabilities of the corresponding hypotheses in the new analysis. The likelihoods of the second sample mean are

$$p \ (M_2 = 107.50 \mid \mu = 100.00) = \text{ndf} \ [(107.50 - 100.00)/3.00]/2$$
$$= .0175/2 = .0088$$

$$p \ (M_2 = 107.50 \mid \mu = 110.00) = \text{ndf} \ [(107.50 - 110.00)/3.00]/2$$
$$= .2819/2 = .1410$$

the prior probability of this result is

$$p \ (M_2 = 107.50) = .2477 \ (.0088) + .7523 \ (.1410) = .1083$$

and the new posterior probabilities for the hypotheses, given both results, are

$$p \, (\mu = 100.00 \mid M_1 = 106.00, M_2 = 107.50) = [.2477 \, (.0088)]/.1083$$
$$= .0201$$

$$p \, (\mu = 110.00 \mid M_1 = 106.00, M_2 = 107.50) = [.7523 \, (.1410)]/.1083$$
$$= .9794$$

The posterior probabilities now favor H_2: $\mu = 110.00$ even more strongly over H_1: $\mu = 100.00$ compared to when only the first result was available. The new posterior odds computed as the ratio of the revised posterior probability of H_2 over that of H_1 is

$$\text{Posterior odds}_2 = .9794/.0201 = 48.73$$

Because of rounding error, the revised posterior odds computed as the product of the prior odds and the likelihood ratio is just slightly different:

$$\text{Posterior odds}_2 = .7523/.2477 \times .1410/.0088 = 48.66$$

Note that (a) the prior odds in this second analysis, which is about 3.04, equals the posterior odds in the first analysis; and (b) the likelihood ratio in the second analysis, which is about 16.02, is the factor by which the posterior odds from the first analysis is updated given the second result.

P. Dixon and O'Reilly (1999) give several examples of use of the likelihood ratio to evaluate competing statistical models, such as different analysis of variance (ANOVA) or regression models for the same data. They noted that it is possible in some cases to compute these ratios on the basis of information available in standard summaries, such as ANOVA source tables. It may also be possible to correct the likelihood ratio for model complexity. This is important because more complex models tend to fit the data better but at the cost of parsimony. P. Dixon and O'Reilly (1999) suggested that a likelihood ratio that exceeds 10:1 could be regarded as relatively strong evidence in favor of one model over another. However, this ratio was not proposed as a formal decision criterion. They also point out that the most generally correct interpretation of a likelihood ratio of 10:1 is that the data are 10 times more likely given one model versus another model. Only if (a) the prior probabilities of the two models are equal and (b) the models are of equal complexity would a likelihood ratio of 10:1 indicate that one model is 10 times more likely than another.

Continuous Random Variables

It is rare that estimation or hypothesis testing is so narrow as described in the previous example. For instance, researchers do not typically know the population standard deviation, nor do they generally evaluate competing hypotheses about discrete values of an unknown population parameter. Hypotheses are often updated as new information is gathered, too. Unknown population parameters are often conceptualized as continuous variables, such as means, proportions, or correlations. In classical statistics, an unknown continuous parameter is viewed as a constant that should be estimated with sample statistics. In Bayesian statistics, however, an unknown continuous parameter θ is seen as a random variable with its own distribution. (The symbol θ is presented in italic font to emphasize that it represents a variable, not a constant.) This distribution summarizes the current state of knowledge about θ. Its mean (expected value) is the best single guess about the true value of the parameter, and its variability reflects the amount of uncertainty. Specifically, wider distributions for θ reflect greater uncertainty and vice versa. Accordingly, the reciprocal of the variance may be taken as a measure of the precision of a distribution for θ. The precision of a sample result can also be estimated as the reciprocal of its error variance (i.e., the squared standard error), which is the same principle followed in meta-analysis (see Equation 8.2).

Prior distributions for θ are typically described by a mathematical function, $f(\theta)$. For a noninformative prior distribution, this function will specify that all possible values of θ are equally likely. A rectangular distribution is a special kind of noninformative prior distribution for a random variable with a fixed range, such as the random population proportion π with range 0–1.0. Otherwise, a noninformative prior could be just a flat distribution with infinite variance, which implies zero precision because $1/\infty = 0$. Informative prior distributions are specified by more complex functions that define a probability distribution. This distribution may be modeled after a known probability distribution, such as a normal curve for random means when the population variance is known or the sample size is not small or a central t distribution when the population variance is unknown or the sample size is small.

There are many other known probability distributions, such as the binomial distribution for proportions and the multivariate normal distribution for joint random variables such as correlations, and a Bayesian analysis is much easier if a known distribution can be selected to model the prior distribution for θ. The same family of known probability distributions— also called *conjugate distributions*—may be used in the analysis to specify the posterior distribution for θ, defined by the function $f(\theta \mid D)$, and the likelihood function for the data, defined by $f(D \mid \theta)$. If so, the parameters of each conjugate distribution are estimated in the analysis. The selection of an appropriate probability distribution is a question of statistical model fitting, and the choice can affect the results. However, the effects of selecting different distributional models can be evaluated in a sensitivity analysis in which alternative models are selected.

The mean of the posterior distribution can be seen as the new best single guess about the true value of θ. Also, the idea of a posterior probability for a discrete event or hypothesis (Equations 9.2–9.4) is replaced by a *Bayesian confidence interval*—also called a *Bayesian credible interval* or *highest density region*—for θ. The percentage associated with a Bayesian confidence interval, such as 95%, is interpreted as the probability that the true value of θ is between the lower and upper bounds of the interval. With one exception, traditional confidence intervals are *not* to be interpreted this way (see chap. 2, this volume). The exception occurs when the prior distribution is flat (uninformative), which implies that the parameters of the posterior distribution are estimated solely with the sample data. In this case, the Bayesian confidence interval is asymptotically identical in large samples to the traditional confidence interval for the unknown parameter, given the same distributional assumptions. When the prior distribution is informative, the parameters of the posterior distribution are basically a weighted combination of those from the prior distribution and those estimated in the sample. The weights reflect the precision of each source of information. In this case the Bayesian confidence interval is also generally different from the traditional confidence interval based on the same result.

Suppose the mean and variance in a normal prior distribution for a random population mean are, respectively, μ_0 and σ_0^2. The precision of this distribution is $prc_0 = 1/\sigma_0^2$. The shape of the posterior distribution will be normal, too, if (a) the distribution of scores in the population is normal and (b) the sample size is not small, such as $N > 50$, in which case at least approximate normality may hold (G. Howard, Maxwell, & Fleming, 2000). The latter also permits reasonable estimation of the population standard deviation among cases with the sample standard deviation s. The observed mean and error variance in a sample are, respectively, M and $s_M^2 = s^2/N$, and the precision of the sample mean is $prc_s = 1/s_M^2$. Given the assumptions stated earlier, the mean in the posterior distribution, μ_1, is the weighted combination of the mean in the prior distribution and the observed mean:

$$\mu_1 = \left(\frac{prc_0}{prc_0 + prc_s}\right)\mu_0 + \left(\frac{prc_s}{prc_0 + prc_s}\right)M \tag{9.7}$$

The variance of the posterior distribution, σ_1^2, is estimated as

$$\sigma_1^2 = \frac{1}{prc_0 + prc_s} \tag{9.8}$$

Note that the relative contribution of new knowledge, the observed mean M, depends on its precision, prc_s, and the precision of all prior knowledge taken together, which is reflected by prc_0.

An example demonstrates the iterative estimation of the posterior distribution for a random population mean as new data are collected. The distributional characteristics stated earlier are assumed. Suppose that the researcher has no basis whatsoever to make a prior prediction about the value of μ, so a flat prior distribution with infinite variance is specified as the prior distribution. A sample of 100 cases is selected, and the results are

$$M_1 = 106.00, \; s_1 = 25.00, \; s_{M_1} = 2.50$$

The traditional 95% confidence interval for the population mean computed with $z_{2\text{-tail}, .05} = 1.96$ instead of $t_{2\text{-tail}, .05}(99) = 1.98$ is

$$106.00 \pm 2.50 \, (1.96), \; \text{or} \; 106.00 \pm 4.90$$

which defines the interval 101.10–110.90. The precision of the observed mean is the reciprocal of the error variance, or $prc_{s_1} = 1/2.50^2 = .16$. However, because the precision of the prior distribution is $prc_0 = 0$, the mean and standard deviation of the posterior distribution given the sample results, $\mu_1 = 106.00$ and $\sigma_1 = 2.50$, respectively, equal the observed mean and standard error, respectively. The Bayesian 95% confidence interval for the random population mean μ calculated in the posterior distribution is

$$106.00 \pm 2.50 \, (1.96) \qquad \text{or} \qquad 106.00 \pm 4.90$$

which defines exactly the same interval, 101.10–110.90, as the traditional 95% confidence interval calculated earlier. Based on the data, we can say that the probability is .95 that the interval 101.10–110.90 includes the true value of μ.

All of the information just described is summarized in the first row of Table 9.2. The remaining rows in the table give the characteristics of the prior and posterior distributions and results in three subsequent samples, each based on 100 cases. For each new result, the posterior distribution from the previous study is taken as the prior distribution for that result. For example, the posterior distribution given just the results of the first sample with the characteristics

TABLE 9.2
Means and Standard Deviations of Prior Distributions and Posterior Distributions Given Data From Four Different Studies

Study	Prior distribution		Data			Posterior distribution		
	μ	σ	M	s	s_M	Traditional 95% CI	μ	σ	Bayesian 95% CI
1	—	∞	106.00	25.00	2.50	101.10–110.90	106.00	2.50	101.10–110.90
2	106.00	2.50	107.50	30.00	3.00	101.62–113.38	106.61	1.92	102.85–110.37
3	106.61	1.92	112.00	28.00	2.80	106.51–117.49	108.33	1.58	105.32–111.43
4	108.33	1.58	109.00	25.00	2.50	104.10–113.90	108.52	1.34	105.89–109.86

Note. CI = confidence interval. The sample size for all studies is $N = 100$.

$$\mu_1 = 106.00, \ \sigma_1 = 2.50, \ \text{and} \ prc_1 = 1/2.50^2 = .16$$

becomes the prior distribution for the results in the second sample, which are

$$M_2 = 107.50, \ s_2 = 30.00, \ s_{M_2} = 3.00, \ prc_{s_2} = 1/3.00^2 = .11$$

The mean and standard deviation in the posterior distribution given the results in the first and second samples are

$$\mu_2 = [.16/(.16 + .11)] \ 106.00 + [.11/(.16 + .11)] \ 107.50 = 106.61$$

$$\sigma_2 = [1/(.16 + .11)]^{1/2} = 1.92$$

In other words, our best single guess for the true population mean has shifted slightly from 106.00 to 106.61 after the second result, and the standard deviation in the posterior distribution is reduced from 2.50 before collecting the second sample to 1.92 after collecting the second sample. Our new Bayesian 95% confidence interval is 102.85–110.37, which is slightly narrower than the previous Bayesian 95% confidence interval, 101.10–110.90. The last two rows in Table 9.2 show changes in the prior and posterior distributions as results from two additional samples are synthesized. Please observe in the table that the widths of the posterior distributions get gradually narrower, which indicates decreasing uncertainty with increasing information.

Meta-analysis and Bayesian analysis are both methods for research synthesis, and it is worthwhile to briefly summarize their relative strengths. Both methods accumulate evidence about a population parameter of interest and generate confidence intervals for that parameter. Both methods also allow sensitivity analysis of the consequences of making different kinds of decisions that may affect the results. In Bayesian statistics, the basic question of a sensitivity analysis is whether the posterior results change appreciably when other reasonable probability models are specified in place of the original model (Gelman, Carlin, Stern, & Rubin, 1995). If the same basic posterior results are generated under alternative models, more confidence is warranted in the robustness of the analysis. Because meta-analysis is based on traditional statistical methods, it tests basically the same kinds of hypotheses that are evaluated in primary studies with traditional statistical tests. This limits the kinds of questions that can be addressed in meta-analysis. For example, a standard meta-analysis cannot answer the question: What is the probability that treatment has a beneficial effect? It could be determined whether zero is included in the confidence interval based on the average effect size across a set of studies, but this would not address the question just posed. In contrast, there is no special problem dealing with this kind question in Bayesian statistics. A Bayesian approach takes into account both previous knowledge and the inherent plausibility of the hypothesis, but meta-analysis is concerned only with the former. However, it is possible to combine both meta-analytical and Bayesian methods in the same analysis. There are Bayesian models for meta-analysis that allow a more complete accounting of uncertainty than a standard meta-analysis based on a random-effects model—see Cornell and Mulrow (1999) for more information. See also G. Howard et al. (2000) for a discussion of the relative strengths of traditional statistical tests in primary studies versus meta-analysis and Bayesian analysis for research synthesis.

Evaluation

There are too many other possible applications of Bayesian analysis to describe in detail, so only a few are mentioned. There are Bayesian versions of many standard statistical techniques. For example, there are Bayesian models for regression, ANOVA, and multivariate analyses, among others (e.g., Gelman et al., 1995). Unlike traditional applications of these methods, their Bayesian counterparts take account of prior knowledge about hypotheses and evaluate sample results in light of it. There are also ways to test point null hypotheses against range alternative hypotheses (P. Lee, 1997), but it seems rather silly to use Bayesian methods in so narrow a way as traditional statistical tests.

Although Bayesian methods are flexible and can evaluate kinds of questions that we would really like answered, there are two significant hurdles to their wider use in the behavioral sciences. The first is the relative paucity of Bayesian software tools for social scientists. Modules for Bayesian estimation are not generally available for statistical software packages used by many behavioral researchers. Commercial Bayesian software packages tend to be oriented toward other disciplines, such as computer science. There are a few freely available software tools for Bayesian analysis, including WinBUGS (Bayesian Inference Using Gibbs Sampling) for personal computers (BUGS Project, 2003),[4] a set of demonstration programs by P. Lee (2002) for the C++ programming language,[5] and First Bayes (O'Hagan, 1996), a program for personal computers that assists the learning of Bayesian methods.[6]

The second major obstacle is that many reference works for Bayesian statistics are quite technical. For example, they often require familiarity with integral notation for probability distributions and estimation techniques

---

[4] See http://www.mrc-bsu.cam.ac.uk/bugs/winbugs/contents.shtml
[5] See http://www-users.york.ac.uk/~pml1/bayes/book.htm
[6] See http://www.shef.ac.uk/~st1ao/1b.html

for the parameters of different kinds of probability distributions. These presentations are not accessible for applied researchers without strong quantitative backgrounds. However, there are some less technical introductions to Bayesian methods for behavioral researchers, including a book by Iversen (1984) and chapters by Pitz (1982) and Winkler (1982). Overall, behavioral researchers comfortable with structural equation modeling or related types of model-fitting techniques should be able to manage the basics of Bayesian estimation. The investment of time to learn these methods by those looking to free themselves from the constraints of traditional statistical tests is worthwhile.

CONCLUSION

There are even more methods that could be considered as alternatives to traditional statistical tests, including the families of robust statistics (Wilcox, 1998) and exploratory data analysis (Tukey, 1977), to name just two. There is no need to avoid moving beyond traditional statistical tests. The best time for change is now. Let us begin by making that better future for behavioral research.

RECOMMENDED READINGS

Diaconis, P., & Efron, B. (1983). Computer-intensive methods in statistics. *Scientific American, 248*(5), 116–130.

Dixon, P., & O'Reilly, T. (1999). Scientific versus statistical inference. *Canadian Journal of Experimental Psychology, 53,* 133–149.

Howard, G. S., Maxwell, S. E., & Fleming, K. J. (2000). The proof of the pudding: An illustration of the relative strengths of null hypothesis, meta-analysis, and Bayesian analysis. *Psychological Methods, 5,* 315–332.

Lunneborg, C. E. (2001). Random assignment of available cases: Bootstrap standard errors and confidence intervals. *Psychological Methods, 6,* 402–412.

REFERENCES

Abelson, R. P. (1997a). A retrospective on the significance test ban of 1999 (If there were no significance tests, they would be invented). In L. L. Harlow, S. A. Mulaik, & J. H. Steiger (Eds.), *What if there were no significance tests?* (pp. 117–141). Mahwah, NJ: Erlbaum.

Abelson, R. P. (1997b). The surprising longevity of flogged horses: Why there is a case for the significance test. *Psychological Science, 8,* 12–15.

Abelson, R. P., & Prentice, D. A. (1997). Contrast tests of interaction hypotheses. *Psychological Methods, 2,* 315–328.

Achenbach, T. M., McConaughy, S. H., Howell, C. T. (1987). Child/adolescent behavioral and emotional problems: Implications of cross-informant correlations for situational specificity. *Psychological Bulletin, 101,* 213–232.

Aiken, L. S., West, S. G., Sechrest, L., & Reno, R. (1990). Graduate training in statistics, methodology, and measurement in psychology: A Survey of Ph.D. programs in North America. *American Psychologist, 45,* 721–734.

American Psychological Association. (1994). *Publication manual of the American Psychological Association* (4th ed.). Washington, DC: Author.

American Psychological Association. (1999). *Standards for educational and psychological testing* (Rev. ed.). Washington, DC: Author.

American Psychological Association. (2001). *Publication manual of the American Psychological Association* (5th ed.). Washington, DC: Author.

Anderson, D. R., Burnham, K. P., & Thompson, W. L. (2000). Null hypothesis testing: Problems, prevalence, and an alternative. *Journal of Wildlife Management, 64,* 912–923.

Anderson, J. L. (1998, June). Embracing uncertainty: The interface of Bayesian statistics and cognitive psychology. *Conservation Ecology, 2*(1), Retrieved July 2, 2001, from http://www.consecol.org/vol2/iss1/art2/index.html

Arbuthnot, J. (1710). An argument for Divine Providence, taken from the constant regularity observ'd in the births of both sexes. *Philosophical Transactions of the Royal Society of London, 27,* 186–190.

Avery, R. D., Cole, D. A., Hazucha, J., & Hartanto, F. (1985). Statistical power of training evaluation designs. *Personnel Psychology, 38,* 493–507.

Bakan, D. (1966). The test of significance in psychological research. *Psychological Bulletin, 66,* 423–437.

Bangert-Drowns, R. L. (1986). Review of developments in meta-analytic method. *Psychological Bulletin, 99,* 388–399.

Baugh, F. (2002). Correcting effect sizes for score reliability: A reminder that measurement and substantive issues are linked inextricably. *Educational and Psychological Measurement, 62,* 254–263.

Becker, B. J., & Schram, C. M. (1994). Examining explanatory models through research synthesis. In H. Cooper & L. V. Hedges (Eds.), *The handbook of research synthesis* (pp. 357–381). New York: Russell Sage Foundation.

Berkovits, I., Hancock, G. R., & Nevitt, J. (2000). Bootstrap resampling approaches for repeated measures designs: Relative robustness to sphericity and normality violations. *Educational and Psychological Measurement, 60,* 877–892.

Berkson, J. (1942). Tests of significance considered as evidence. *Journal of the American Statistical Association, 37,* 325–335.

Bester, A. (1979). 5,271,009. In M. H. Greenberg & J. Olander (Eds.), *Science fiction of the fifties* (pp. 187–221). New York: Avon Books. (Original work published 1954)

Beutler, L. E., Williams, R. E., Wakefield, P. J., & Entwistle, S. R. (1995). Bridging scientist and practitioner perspectives in clinical psychology. *American Psychologist, 50,* 984–994.

Bird, K. D. (2002). Confidence intervals for effect sizes in analysis of variance. *Educational and Psychological Measurement, 62,* 197–226.

Bird, K. D., Hadzi-Pavlovic, D., & Isaac, A. P. (2000). PSY [Computer software]. Retrieved from http://www.psy.unsw.edu.au/research/psy.htm

Blalock, H. M. (1964). *Causal inference in nonexperimental research.* Chapel Hill: University of North Carolina Press.

Borenstein, M. (1998). The shift from significance testing to effect size estimation. In A. S. Bellack & M. Hersen (Series Eds.) & N. R. Schooler (Volume Ed.), *Comprehensive clinical psychology: Vol. 3. Research methods* (pp. 313–349). New York: Pergamon Press.

Boring, E. G. (1919). Mathematical vs. scientific importance. *Psychological Bulletin, 16,* 335–338.

Bracken, B. A., & McCallum, R. S. (Eds.). (1993). *Journal of Psychoeducational Assessment monograph series, Advances' in psychological assessment: Wechsler Intelligence Scale for Children—Third Edition.* German Town, TN: Psychological Corporation.

Brown, T. G., Seraganian, P., Tremblay, J., & Annis, H. (2002). Matching substance abuse aftercare treatments to client characteristics. *Addictive Behaviors, 27,* 585–604.

Browne, M. W., & Du Toit, S. H. C. (1991). Models for learning data. In L. M. Collins & J. L. Horn (Eds.), *Best methods for the analysis of change* (pp. 47–68). Washington, DC: American Psychological Association.

Bruce, C. R., Anderson, M. E., Fraser, S. F., Stepko, N. K., Klein, R., Hopkins, W. G., et al. (2000). Enhancement of 2000-m rowing performance after caffeine ingestion. *Medicine and Science in Sports and Exercise, 32,* 1958–1963.

BUGS project. (2003). WinBUGS (Version 1.4) [Computer software]. Retrieved from http://www.mrc-bsu.cam.ac.uk/bugs/winbugs/contents.shtml

Burdick, R. K., & Graybill, F. A. (1992). *Confidence intervals for variance components.* New York: Marcel Dekker.

Bushman, B. (1994). Vote-counting procedures in meta-analysis. In H. Cooper & L. V. Hedges (Eds.), *The handbook of research synthesis* (pp. 193–214). New York: Russell Sage Foundation.

Cahill, S. P., Carrigan, M. H., & Frueh, B. C. (1999). Does EMDR work? And if so, why?: A critical review of controlled outcome and dismantling research. *Journal of Anxiety Disorders, 13*, 5–33.

Campbell, D. T., & Erlebacher, A. (1975). How regression artifacts in quasi-experimental evaluations can mistakenly make compensatory education look harmful. In M. Guttentag & E. L. Struening (Eds.), *Handbook of evaluation research* (Vol. 1, pp. 597–617). Beverly Hills, CA: Sage.

Capraro, R. M., & Capraro, M. (2002). Treatments of effect sizes and statistical significance in textbooks. *Educational and Psychological Measurement, 62*, 771–782.

Carlsmith, J., M., Ellsworth, P. C., & Aronson, E. (1976). *Methods of research in social psychology*. Reading, MA: Addison-Wesley.

Cartwright, D. (1973). Determinants of scientific progress: The case of research on risky shift. *American Psychologist, 28*, 222–231.

Carver, R. P. (1978). The case against significance testing. *Harvard Educational Review, 48*, 378–399.

Chalmers, T. C., & Lau, J. (1994). What is meta-analysis? *Emergency Care Research Institute, 12*, 1–5.

Chow, S. L. (1996). *Statistical significance*. Thousand Oaks, CA: Sage.

Chow, S. L. (1998a). Précis of statistical significance: Rationale, validity, and utility. *Behavioral and Brain Sciences, 21*, 169–239.

Chow, S. L. (1998b). What statistical significance means. *Theory and Psychology, 8*, 323–330.

Clark, H. H. (1976). Reply to Wike and Church. *Journal of Verbal Learning and Verbal Behavior, 15*, 257–261.

Cohen, J. (1988). *Statistical power analysis for the behavioral sciences* (2nd ed.). New York: Academic Press.

Cohen, J. (1994). The earth is round ($p < .05$). *American Psychologist, 49*, 997–1003.

Collins, L. M., & Sayer, A. G. (2001). *New methods for the analysis of change*. Washington, DC: American Psychological Association.

Cook, S., & Wilding, J. (1997). Earwitness testimony 2: Voice, faces, and context. *Applied Cognitive Psychology, 11*, 527–541.

Cook, S., & Wilding, J. (2001). Earwitness testimony: Effects of exposure and attention on the Face Overshadowing Effect. *British Journal of Psychology, 92*, 617–629.

Cook, T. D., & Campbell, D. T. (1979). *Quasi-experimentation*. Chicago: Rand McNally.

Cook, T. D., Cooper, H., Corday, D. S., Hartmann, H., Hedges, L. V., Light, R. J., et al. (1992). *Meta-analysis for explanation*. New York: Russell Sage Foundation.

Cooper, H., M., & Hedges, L. V. (1994a). Research synthesis as a scientific enterprise. In H. Cooper & L. V. Hedges (Eds.), *The handbook of research synthesis* (pp. 3–14). New York: Russell Sage Foundation.

Cooper, H., & Hedges, L. V. (Eds.). (1994b). *The handbook of research synthesis.* New York: Russell Sage Foundation.

Cornell, J., & Mulrow, C. (1999). Meta-analysis. In H. J. Adler & G. J. Mellenbergh (Eds.), *Research methodology in the social, behavioral, and life sciences* (pp. 285–323). Thousand Oaks, CA: Sage.

Cortina, J. M., & Dunlap, W. P. (1997). On the logic and purpose of significance testing. *Psychological Methods, 2,* 161–172.

Cortina, J. M., & Nouri, H. (2000). *Effect size for ANOVA designs.* Thousand Oaks, CA: Sage.

Cowles, M., & Davis, C. (1982). On the origins of the .05 level of statistical significance. *American Psychologist, 37,* 553–558.

Cronbach, L. J., Rogosa. D. R., Floden, R. E., & Price, G. G. (1977). *Analysis of covariance in nonrandomized experiments: Parameters affecting bias.* Occasional Paper, Stanford Evaluation Consortium, Stanford University.

Cumming, G. (2002). Exploratory Software for Confidence Intervals [Computer software]. Retrieved from http://www.latrobe.edu.au/psy/esci

Cumming, G., & Finch, S. (2001). A primer on the understanding, use, and calculation of confidence intervals that are based on central and noncentral distributions. *Educational and Psychological Measurement, 61,* 532–574.

Dar, R., Serlin, R. C., & Omer, H. (1994). Misuse of statistical tests in three decades of psychotherapy research. *Journal of Consulting and Clinical Psychology, 62,* 75–82.

Darlington, R. B. (1996). *Measures for ordered categories.* Retrieved January 9, 2002, from http://comp9.psyc.cornell.edu/Darlington/crosstab/table5.htm

Diaconis, P., & Efron, B. (1983). Computer-intensive methods in statistics. *Scientific American, 248*(5), 116–130.

Dixon, P. M. (1998). Assessing effect and no effect with equivalence tests. In M. C. Newman & C. L. Strojan (Eds.), *Risk assessment* (pp. 257–301). Chelsea, MI: Ann Arbor Press.

Dixon, P., & O'Reilly, T. (1999). Scientific versus statistical inference. *Canadian Journal of Experimental Psychology, 53,* 133–149.

Dodd, D. H., & Schultz, R. F. (1973). Computational procedures for estimating magnitude of effect for some analysis of variance designs. *Psychological Bulletin, 79,* 391–395.

Dunlap, W. P., Cortina, J. M., Vaslow, J. B., & Burke, M. J. (1996). Meta-analysis of experiments with matched groups or repeated measures designs. *Psychological Methods, 1,* 170–177.

Eagley, A. H., & Carli, L. L. (1981). Sex of researchers and sex-types communications as determinants of sex differences in influenceability: A meta-analysis of social influence studies. *Psychological Bulletin, 90,* 1–20.

Edwards, W., Lindman, H., & Savage, L. J. (1963). Bayesian statistical inference for psychological research. *Psychological Review, 70*, 193–242.

Efron, B., & Tibshirani, R. J. (1993). *An introduction to the bootstrap*. New York: Chapman & Hall.

Einstein, A. (1973). *Ideas and opinions*. New York: Dell.

Eliason, S. R. (1993). *Maximum likelihood estimation*. Newberry Park, CA: Sage.

Ellis, M. V. (1999). Repeated measures designs. *Counseling Psychologist, 27*, 552–578.

Eysenck, H. J. (1995). Meta-analysis squared—Does it make sense? *American Psychologist, 50*, 110–111.

Feingold, A. (1994). Gender differences in personality: A meta-analysis. *Psychological Bulletin, 116*, 429–456.

Feingold, A. (1995). The additive effects of differences in central tendency and variability are important in comparisons between groups. *American Psychologist, 50*, 5–13.

Fern, E. F., & Monroe, K. B. (1996). Effect-size estimates: Issues and problems. *Journal of Consumer Research, 23*, 89–105.

Fidler, F. (2002). The fifth edition of the APA *Publication Manual*: Why its statistics recommendations are so controversial. *Educational and Psychological Measurement, 62*, 749–770.

Fidler, F., & Thompson, B. (2001). Computing correct confidence intervals for ANOVA fixed- and random-effects effect sizes. *Educational and Psychological Measurement, 61*, 575–604.

Finch, S., Cummings, G., & Thomason, N. (2001). Reporting of statistical inference in the *Journal of Applied Psychology*: Little evidence of reform. *Educational and Psychological Measurement, 61*, 181–210.

Fisher, R. (1925). *Statistical methods for research workers*. Edinburgh: Oliver & Boyd.

Fleiss, J. L. (1994). Measures of effect size for categorical data. In H. Cooper & L. V. Hedges (Eds.), *The handbook of research synthesis* (pp. 245–260). New York: Russell Sage Foundation.

Frederich, J., Buday, E., & Kerr, D. (2000). Statistical training in psychology: A national survey and commentary on undergraduate programs. *Teaching of Psychology, 27*, 248–257.

Frederick, B. N. (1999). Fixed-, random-, and mixed-effects ANOVA models: A user-friendly guide for increasing the generalizability of ANOVA results. In B. Thompson (Ed.), *Advanced in social science methodology* (Vol. 5, pp. 111–122). Stamford, CT: JAI Press.

Frick, R. W. (1995). Accepting the null hypothesis. *Memory and Cognition, 23*, 132–138.

Gage, N. L. (1978). *The scientific basis of the art of teaching*. New York: Teachers College Press.

Gatsonis, C., Kass, R. E., Carling, B., Carriquiry, A., Gelman, A., Verdinelli, I., et al. (Eds.). (2001). *Case studies on Bayesian statistics* (Vol. 5). New York: Springer-Verlag.

Gelman, A., Carlin, J. B., Stern, H. S., & Rubin, D. B. (1995). *Bayesian data analysis*. London: Chapman & Hall.

Gigerenzer, G. (1993). The superego, the ego, and the id in statistical reasoning. In G. Keren & C. Lewis (Eds.), *A handbook for data analysis in the behavioral sciences: Vol. 1. Methodological issues* (pp. 311–339). Hillsdale, NJ: Erlbaum.

Gigerenzer, G. (1998a). Surrogates for theories. *Theory and Psychology, 8,* 195–204.

Gigerenzer, G. (1998b). We need statistical thinking, not statistical rituals. *Behavioral and Brain Sciences, 21,* 199–200.

Gigerenzer, G., & Murray, D. (1987). *Cognition as intuitive statistics*. Hillsdale, NJ: Erlbaum.

Glaros, A. G., & Kline, R. B. (1988). Understanding the accuracy of tests with cutting scores: The sensitivity, specificity, and predictive value model. *Journal of Clinical Psychology, 44,* 1013–1023.

Glass, G. V. (1976). Primary, secondary, and meta-analysis of research. *Educational Researcher, 10,* 3–8.

Glass, G. V., & Hopkins, K. D. (1996). *Statistical methods in education and psychology* (3rd ed.). Boston: Allyn & Bacon.

Glass, G. V., McGaw, B., & Smith, M. L. (1981). *Meta-analysis in social research*. Newbury Park, CA: Sage.

Glass, G. V., Peckham, P. D., & Sanders, J. R. (1972). Consequences of failure to meet assumptions underlying the fixed effects analysis of variance and covariance. *Review of Educational Research, 42,* 237–288.

Gleick, J. (1988). *Chaos*. New York: Penguin.

Gleser, L. J., & Olkin, I. (1994). Stochastically dependent effect sizes. In H. Cooper & L. V. Hedges (Eds.), *The handbook of research synthesis* (pp. 339–355). New York: Russell Sage Foundation.

Gliner, J. A., Morgan, G. A., Leech, N. L., & Harmon, R. J. (2001). Problems with null hypothesis significance testing. *Journal of the American Academy of Child and Adolescent Psychiatry, 40,* 250–252.

Good, P. (2000). *Permutation tests*. New York: Springer-Verlag.

Gouzoulis-Mayfrank, E., Daumann, J., Tuchtenhagen, F., Pelz, S., Becker, S., Kunert, H.-J., et al. (2000). Impaired cognitive performance in drug free users of recreational ecstasy (MDMA). *Journal of Neurology, Neurosurgery, and Psychiatry, 68,* 719–725.

Greenwald, A. G. (1975). Consequences of prejudice against the null hypothesis. *Psychological Bulletin, 82,* 1–20.

Greenwald, A. G., Gonzalez, R., Harris, R. J., & Guthrie, D. (1996). Effect sizes and *p* values: What should be reported and what should be replicated? *Psychophysiology, 33,* 175–183.

Grimm, L., & Yarnold, P. R. (Eds.). (1995). *Reading and understanding multivariate statistics*. Washington, DC: American Psychological Association.

Grimm, L., & Yarnold, P. R. (Eds.). (2000). *Reading and understanding more multivariate statistics*. Washington, DC: American Psychological Association.

Griner, P. F., Mayewski, R. J., Mushlin, A. I., & Greenlan, P. (1981). Selection and interpretation of diagnostic tests and procedures: Principles and applications. *Annals of Internal Medicine, 94,* 557–592.

Haddock, C. K., Rindskopf, D., & Shadish, W. R. (1998). Using odds ratios as effect sizes for meta-analysis of dichotomous data: A primer on methods and issues. *Psychological Methods, 3,* 339–353.

Hagenaars, J. A., & McCutcheon, A. L. (Eds.). (2002). *Applied latent class analysis.* Cambridge, MA: Cambridge University Press.

Hall, J. A., Tickle-Degnen, L., Rosenthal, R., & Mosteller, F. (1994). Hypotheses and problems in research synthesis. In H. Cooper & L. V. Hedges (Eds.), *The handbook of research synthesis* (pp. 17–28). New York: Russell Sage Foundation.

Hardy, T. (1978). *Far from the madding crowd.* New York: Penguin Books. (Original work published in 1874)

Harlow, L. L., Mulaik, S. A., & Steiger, J. H. (Eds.). (1997). *What if there were no significance tests?* Mahwah, NJ: Erlbaum.

Harris, R. J. (1997a). Ban the significance test? [Special section]. *Psychological Science, 8*(1).

Harris, R. J. (1997b). Reforming significance testing via three-valued logic. In L. L. Harlow, S. A. Mulaik, & J. H. Steiger (Eds.), *What if there were no significance tests?* (pp. 145–174). Mahwah, NJ: Erlbaum.

Harris, R. J. (1997c). Significance tests have their place. *Psychological Science, 8,* 8–11.

Harsanyi, J. C. (1983). Bayesian decision theory, subjective and objective probabilities, and acceptance of empirical hypotheses. *Synthese, 57,* 341–365.

Hedges, L. V. (1982). *Statistical methodology in meta-analysis.* Princeton, NJ: Educational Testing Service.

Hedges, L. V. (1987). How hard is hard science, how soft is soft science? *American Psychologist, 42,* 443–455.

Hedges, L. V. (1994). Fixed effects models. In H. Cooper & L. V. Hedges (Eds.), *The handbook of research synthesis* (pp. 285–299). New York: Russell Sage Foundation.

Hess, B., Olejnik, S., & Huberty, C. J. (2001). The efficacy of two-improvement over chance effect sizes for two-group univariate comparisons under variance heterogeneity and nonnormality. *Educational and Psychological Measurement, 61,* 909–936.

Hogben, L. T. (1957). *Statistical theory.* London: Allen & Unwin.

Howard, G. S., Maxwell, S. E., & Fleming, K. J. (2000). The proof of the pudding: An illustration of the relative strengths of null hypothesis, meta-analysis, and Bayesian analysis. *Psychological Methods, 5,* 315–332.

Howell, D. C. (2001). Resampling Procedures (Version 1.3) [Computer software]. Retrieved from http://www.uvm.edu/~dhowell/StatPages/Resampling/Resampling.html

Hubbard, R., & Ryan, P. A. (2000). The historical growth of statistical significance testing in psychology—And its future prospects. *Educational and Psychological Measurement, 60,* 661–681.

Huberty, C. J. (1993). Historical origins of statistical testing practices: The treatment of Fisher versus Neyman–Pearson views in textbooks. *Journal of Experimental Education, 61,* 317–333.

Huberty, C. J. (2002). A history of effect size indices. *Educational and Psychological Measurement, 62,* 227–240.

Huberty, C. J., & Lowman, L. L. (2000). Group overlap as the basis for effect size. *Educational and Psychological Measurement, 60,* 543–563.

Huberty, C. J., & Pike, C. J. (1999). On some history regarding statistical testing. In B. Thompson (Ed.), *Advances in social science methodology* (Vol. 5, pp. 1–22). Stamford, CT: JAI Press.

Hunt, M. (1997). *How science takes stock.* New York: Russell Sage Foundation.

Hunter, J. E. (1997). Needed: A ban on the significance test. *Psychological Science, 8,* 3–7.

Hunter, J. E., & Schmidt, F. L. (1990). *Methods of meta-analysis.* Newbury Park, CA: Sage.

Hunter, J. E., & Schmidt, F. L. (1994). Correcting for sources of artificial variation across studies. In H. Cooper & L. V. Hedges (Eds.), *The handbook of research synthesis* (pp. 323–336). New York: Russell Sage Foundation.

Hunter, J. E., Schmidt, F. L., & Jackson, G. B. (1982). *Meta-analysis.* Beverly Hills, CA.

Hyde, J. S. (2001). Reporting effect sizes: The role of editors, textbook authors, and publication manuals. *Educational and Psychological Measurement, 61,* 225–228.

Hyde, J. S., Fennema, E., & Lamon, S. J. (1990). Gender differences in mathematics performance: A meta-analysis. *Psychological Bulletin, 107,* 139–155.

International Committee of Medical Journal Editors. (1997). Uniform requirements for manuscripts submitted to biomedical journals. *Journal of the American Medical Association, 277,* 927–934.

Iversen, G. R. (1984). *Bayesian statistical inference.* Newbury Park, CA: Sage.

Johnson, D. H. (1999). The insignificance of statistical significance testing. *Journal of Wildlife Management, 63,* 763–772.

Kaiser, H. F. (1960). Directional statistical decisions. *Psychological Review, 67,* 160–167.

Kanfer, R., & Ackerman, P. L. (1989). Motivation and cognitive abilities: An integrative/aptitude-treatment interaction approach to skill acquisition. *Journal of Applied Psychology, 74,* 657–690.

Kaplan, D. (2000). *Structural equation modeling: Foundations and extensions.* Thousand Oaks, CA: Sage.

Kaufman, A. S. (1994). *Intelligent testing with the WISC–III.* New York: Wiley.

Kaufman, A. S. (1998). Introduction to the special issue on statistical significance testing. *Research in the Schools, 5,* 1.

Kendall, P. C., & Grove, W. M. (1988). Normative comparisons in therapy outcome. *Behavioral Assessment, 10,* 147–158.

Kennedy, M. L., Willis, W. G., & Faust, D. (1997). The base-rate fallacy in school psychology. *Journal of Psychoeducational Assessment, 15,* 292–307.

Keppel, G. (1991). *Design and analysis* (3rd ed.). Englewood Cliffs, NJ: Prentice Hall.

Keppel, G., & Zedeck, S. (1989). *Data analysis for research designs.* New York: W. H. Freeman.

Keren, G. (1993). A balanced approach to unbalanced designs. In G. Keren & C. Lewis (Eds.), *A handbook for data analysis in the behavioral sciences: Vol. 2. Statistical issues* (pp. 155–186). Hillsdale, NJ: Erlbaum.

Keselman, H. J., Algina, J., & Kowalchuk, R. K. (2001). The analysis of repeated measures designs: A review. *British Journal of Mathematical and Statistical Psychology, 54,* 1–20.

Keselman, H. J., Huberty, C. J., Lix, L. M., Olejnik, S., Cribbie, R. A., Donahue, B., et al. (1998). Statistical practices of education researchers: An analysis of the ANOVA, MANOVA, and ANCOVA analyses. *Review of Educational Research, 68,* 350–386.

Kirk, R. E. (Ed.). (1972). *Statistical issues.* Monterey, CA: Brooks/Cole.

Kirk, R. E. (1995). *Experimental design* (3rd ed.). Pacific Grove, CA: Brooks/Cole.

Kirk, R. E. (1996). Practical significance: A concept whose time has come. *Educational and Psychological Measurement, 56,* 746–759.

Kirk, R. E. (2001). Promoting good statistical practices: Some suggestions. *Educational and Psychological Measurement, 61,* 213–218.

Kline, R. B. (1998). *Principles and practice of structural equation modeling.* New York: Guilford Press.

Kline, R. B., & Canter, W. A. (1994). Can educational programs affect teenage drinking? A multivariate perspective. *Journal of Drug Education, 24,* 139–149.

Kmetz, J. L. (1998). *The information processing theory of organization.* Aldershot, UK: Ashgate.

Kmetz, J. L. (2000). *A handbook for business and management research.* Retrieved October 3, 2001, from http://www.buec.udel.edu/kmetzj/Handbook.htm

Knight, G. P., Fabes, R. A., & Higgins, D. A. (1996). Concerns about drawing causal inferences from meta-analyses: An example in the study of gender differences in aggression. *Psychological Bulletin, 119,* 410–421.

Krantz, D. H. (1999). The null hypothesis testing controversy in psychology. *Journal of the American Statistical Association, 44,* 1372–1381.

Kruegar, J. (2001). Null hypothesis significance testing: On the survival of a flawed method. *American Psychologist, 56,* 16–26.

Kuhn, T. S. (1996). *The structure of scientific revolutions* (3rd ed.) Chicago: University of Chicago Press.

Kupfersmid, J. (1988). Improving what is published. *American Psychologist, 43*, 635–642.

Lachar, D., Wingenfeld, S., Kline, R. B., & Gruber, C. P. (2000). *Student behavior survey*. Los Angeles: Western Psychological Services.

Larman, C. (2002). *Applying UML and patterns*. New York: Prentice-Hall.

Lau, J., Ioannidis, J. P. A., & Schmid, C. H. (1997). Quantitative synthesis in systematic reviews. *Annals of Internal Medicine, 127*, 820–826.

Lee, P. M. (1997). *Bayesian statistics* (2nd ed.). New York: Oxford University Press.

Lee, P. M. (2002). Bayesian statistics: An introduction: C++ programs. Retrieved November 24, 2002, from http://www-users.york.ac.uk/~pml1/bayes/book.htm

Lenth, R. V. (2001). Some practical guidelines for effective sample size determination. *American Statistician, 55*, 187–193.

Lipsey, M. W. (1994). Identifying potentially interesting variables and analysis opportunities. In H. Cooper & L. V. Hedges (Eds.), *The handbook of research synthesis* (pp. 111–124). New York: Russell Sage Foundation.

Lipsey, M. W., & Wilson, D. B. (2000). *Practical meta-analysis*. Thousand Oaks, CA: Sage.

Lix, L. M., Keselman, J. C., & Keselman, H. J. (1996). Consequences of assumptions violations revisited: A quantitative review of alternatives to the one-way analysis of variance *F* test. *Review of Educational Research, 66*, 579–620.

Lunneborg, C. E. (1994). *Modeling experimental and observational data*. Belmont, CA: Duxbury Press.

Lunneborg, C. E. (2000). *Data analysis by resampling*. Pacific Grove, CA: Brooks/Cole.

Lunneborg, C. E. (2001). Random assignment of available cases: Bootstrap standard errors and confidence intervals. *Psychological Methods, 6*, 402–412.

Lykken, D. T. (1968). Statistical significance in psychological research. *Psychological Bulletin, 70*, 151–159.

Lytton, H., & Romney, D. M. (1991). Parents' differential socialization of boys and girls: A meta-analysis. *Psychological Bulletin, 109*, 267–296.

MacCallum, R. C., Zhang, S., Preacher, K. J., & Rucker, D. O. (2002). On the practice of dichotomization of quantitative variables. *Psychological Methods, 7*, 19–40.

Maccoby, E. E., & Jacklin, C. N. (1974). *The psychology of sex differences*. Stanford, CA: Stanford University Press.

Matthews, R. A. J. (2000). Facts versus factions: The use and abuse of subjectivity in scientific research. In J. Morris (Ed.), *Rethinking risk and the precautionary principle* (pp. 247–282). Woburn, MA: Butterworth-Heinemann.

Max, L., & Onghena, P. (1999). Some issues in the statistical analysis of completely randomized and repeated measures designs for speech, language, and hearing research. *Journal of Speech, Language, and Hearing Research, 42*, 261–270.

Maxwell, S. E., Camp, C. J., & Arvey, R. D. (1981). Measures of strength of association: A comparative examination. *Journal of Applied Psychology, 66*, 525–534.

Maxwell, S. E., & Delaney, H. D. (1990). *Designing experiments and analyzing data.* Belmont, CA: Wadsworth.

May, R. (1975). *The courage to create.* New York: W. W. Norton.

McBride, G. B. (1999). Equivalence testing can enhance environmental science and management. *Australian and New Zealand Journal of Statistics, 41*, 19–29.

McCartney, K., & Rosenthal, R. (2000). Effect size, practical importance, and social policy for children. *Child Development, 71*, 173–180.

McGraw, K. O., & Wong, S. P. (1992). A common language effect-size statistic. *Psychological Bulletin, 111*, 361–365.

McLean, J., & Kaufman, A. S. (Eds.). (1998). Statistical significance testing [Special issue]. *Research in the Schools, 5*(2).

McWhaw, K., & Abrami, P. C. (2001). Student goal orientation and interest: Effects on students' use of self-regulated learning strategies. *Contemporary Educational Psychology, 26*, 311–329.

Medin, D. L., & Edelson, S. M. (1988). Problem structure and the use of base-rate information from experience. *Journal of Experimental Psychology: General, 117*, 68–85.

Meehl, P. E. (1990). Why summaries on research on psychological theories are often uninterpretable. *Psychological Reports, 66* (Monograph Suppl. 1-V66), 195–244.

Melton, A. W. (1962). Editorial. *Journal of Experimental Psychology, 64*, 553–557.

Miller, D. W. (1999, Aug. 6). The black hole of education research: Why do academic studies play such a minimal role in efforts to improve the schools? *Chronicle of Higher Education, 45*(48), A17–A18.

Mittag, K. C., & Thompson, B. (2000). A national survey of AERA members' perceptions of statistical significance tests and other statistical issues. *Educational Researcher, 29*, 14–20.

Morris, S. B. (2000). Distribution of standardized mean change effect size for meta-analysis on repeated measures. *British Journal of Mathematical and Statistical Psychology, 53*, 17–29.

Morris, S. B., & DeShon, R. P. (1997). Correcting effect sizes computed with factorial analyses of variance for use in meta-analysis. *Psychological Methods, 2*, 192–199.

Morrison, D. E., & Henkel, R. E. (Eds.). (1970). *The significance test controversy.* Chicago: Aldine.

Mulaik, S. A., Raju, N. S., & Harshman, R. A. (1997). There is a time and place for significance testing. In L. L. Harlow, S. A. Mulaik, & J. H. Steiger (Eds.), *What if there were no significance tests?* (pp. 65–115). Mahwah, NJ: Erlbaum.

Myers, J. L., & Well, A. D. (2002). *Research design and statistical analysis* (2nd ed.). Mahwah, NJ: Erlbaum.

Nelson, N., Rosenthal, R., & Rosnow, R. L. (1986). Interpretation of significance levels and effect sizes by psychological researchers. *American Psychologist, 41,* 1299–1301.

Neyman, J., & Pearson, E. S. (1933). On the problem of the most efficient tests of statistical hypotheses. *Philosophical Transactions of the Royal Society of London, Series A, 231,* 289–337.

Nickerson, R. S. (2000). Null hypothesis significance testing: A review of an old and continuing controversy. *Psychological Methods, 5,* 241–301.

Nix, T. W., & Barnette, J. J. (1998). The data analysis dilemma: Ban or abandon. A review of null hypothesis significance testing. *Research in the Schools, 5,* 3–14.

Nunnally, J. C., & Bernstein, I. H. (1994). *Psychometric theory* (3rd ed.). New York: McGraw-Hill.

Oakes, M. (1986). *Statistical inference.* New York: Wiley.

Ogles, B. M., Lambert, M. J., & Masters, K. S. (1996). *Assessing outcome in clinical practice.* Boston: Allyn & Bacon.

O'Hagan, A. (1996). First Bayes (Version 1.3) [Computer software]. Retrieved from http://www.shef.ac.uk/~st1ao/1b.html

Olejnik, S., & Algina, J. (2000). Measures of effect size for comparative studies: Applications, interpretations, and limitations. *Contemporary Educational Psychology, 25,* 241–286.

Overall, J. E., & Spiegel, D. K. (1969). Concerning least-squares analysis of experimental data. *Psychological Bulletin, 72,* 311–322.

Pitz, G. F. (1982). Applications of Bayesian statistics in psychology research. In G. Keren (Ed.), *Statistical and methodological issues in psychology and social sciences research* (pp. 245–281). Hillsdale, NJ: Lawrence Erlbaum.

Platt, J. R. (1964). Strong inference. *Science, 146* (October 16), 347–353.

Polich, J., Pollock, V. E., & Bloom, F. E. (1994). Meta-analysis of P300 amplitude from males at risk for alcoholism. *Psychological Bulletin, 115,* 55–73.

Pollard, P. (1993). How significant is "significance"? In G. Keren & C. Lewis (Eds.), *A handbook for data analysis in the behavioral sciences: Vol. 1. Methodological issues* (pp. 449–460). Hillsdale, NJ: Erlbaum.

Prentice, D. A., & Miller, D. T. (1992). When small effects are impressive. *Psychological Bulletin, 112,* 160–164.

Prifitiera, A., & Dersh, J. (1993). Base rates of WISC–III diagnostic subtest patterns among normal, learning-disabled, and ADHD samples. In B. A. Bracken & R. S. McCallum (Eds.), *Journal of Psychoeducational Assessment monograph series, Advances in psychological assessment: Wechsler Intelligence Scale for Children* (3rd ed.; pp. 43–55). Germantown, TN: Psychological Corporation.

Provalis Research. (1996). Simstat for Windows (Version 2.04) [Computer software]. Montréal, Quebec, Canada: Author.

Raudenbush, S. W. (1994). Random effects models. In H. Cooper & L. V. Hedges (Eds.), *The handbook of research synthesis* (pp. 301–321). New York: Russell Sage Foundation.

Raudenbush, S. W., & Bryk, A.S. (2002). *Hierarchical linear models* (2nd ed.). Thousand Oaks, CA: Sage.

Reichardt, C. S., & Gollob, H. F. (1997). When confidence intervals should be used instead of statistical tests, and vice versa. In L. L. Harlow, S. A. Mulaik, & J. H. Steiger (Eds.), *What if there were no significance tests?* (pp. 37–64). Mahwah, NJ: Erlbaum.

Reichardt, C. S., & Gollob, H. F. (1999). Justifying the use and increasing the power of a *t* test for a randomized experiment with a convenience sample. *Psychological Methods, 4,* 117–128.

Rencher, A. C. (1998). *Methods of multivariate analysis: Vol. 2. Multivariate statistical inference and applications.* New York: Wiley.

Resampling Stats. (1999). Resampling Stats (Version 5.0.2) [Computer software]. Arlington, VA: Author.

Robinson, D. H., & Levin, J. R. (1997). Reflections on statistical and substantive significance, with a slice of replication. *Educational Researcher, 26,* 21–26.

Robinson, D. H., & Wainer, H. (2002). On the past and future of null hypothesis significance testing. *Journal of Wildlife Management, 66,* 263–271.

Rodgers, J. L. (1999). The bootstrap, the jackknife, and the randomization test: A sampling taxonomy. *Multivariate Behavioral Research, 34,* 441–456.

Rodgers, W. (1995). Analysis of cross-classified data. In L. G. Grimm & P. R. Yarnold (Eds.), *Reading and understanding multivariate statistics* (pp. 169–215). Washington, DC: American Psychological Association.

Rogers, J. L., Howard, K. I., & Vessey, J. T. (1993). Using significance tests to evaluate equivalence between two experimental groups. *Psychological Bulletin, 113,* 553–565.

Rosenthal, M. C. (1994). The fugitive literature. In H. Cooper & L. V. Hedges (Eds.), *The handbook of research synthesis* (pp. 85–94). New York: Russell Sage Foundation.

Rosenthal, R. (1976). *Experimenter effects in behavioral research.* New York: Halstead Press.

Rosenthal, R. (1979). The "file drawer problem" and tolerance for null results. *Psychological Bulletin, 86,* 638–641.

Rosenthal, R. (1994). Parametric measures of effect size. In H. Cooper & L. V. Hedges (Eds.), *The handbook of research synthesis* (pp. 231–244). New York: Russell Sage Foundation.

Rosenthal, R. (1995). Writing meta-analytic reviews. *Psychological Bulletin, 118,* 183–192.

Rosenthal, R., Rosnow, R. L., & Rubin, D. B. (2000). *Contrasts and effect sizes in behavioral research.* New York: Cambridge University Press.

Rosnow, R. L., & Rosenthal, R. (1989). Statistical procedures and the justification of knowledge in psychological science. *American Psychologist, 44,* 1276–1284.

Rossi, J. S. (1997). A case study in the failure of psychology as a cumulative science: The spontaneous recovery of verbal learning. In L. L. Harlow, S. A. Mulaik, & J. H. Steiger (Eds.), *What if there were no significance tests?* (pp. 175–197). Mahwah, NJ: Erlbaum.

Rozeboom, W. W. (1960). The fallacy of the null hypothesis significance test. *Psychological Bulletin, 57,* 416–428.

Sagan, C. (1996). *The demon-haunted world.* New York: Random House.

SAS Institute. (2000). The SAS System for Windows (Release 8.01) [Computer software]. Cary, NC: Author.

Schmidt, F. L. (1992). What do data really mean? Research findings, meta-analysis, and cumulative knowledge in psychology. *American Psychologist, 47,* 1173–1181.

Schmidt, F. L. (1996). Statistical significance testing and cumulative knowledge in psychology: Implications for the training of researchers. *Psychological Methods, 1,* 115–129.

Schmidt, F. L., & Hunter, J. E. (1997). Eight common but false objections to the discontinuation of significance testing in the analysis of research data. In L. L. Harlow, S. A. Mulaik, & J. H. Steiger (Eds.), *What if there were no significance tests?* (pp. 37–64). Mahwah, NJ: Erlbaum.

Schultz, K, F., & Grimes, D. A. (2002). Unequal group sizes in randomised trials: Guarding against guessing. *Lancet, 359,* 966–970.

Schuster, C., & von Eye, A. (2001). The relationship of ANOVA models with random effects and repeated measurement designs. *Journal of Adolescent Research, 16,* 205–220.

Sedlmeier, P., & Gigerenzer, G. (1989). Do studies of statistical power have an effect on the power of studies? *Psychological Bulletin, 105,* 309–315.

Serlin, R. C. (1993). Confidence intervals and the scientific method: A case for the Holm on the range. *Journal of Experimental Education, 61,* 350–360.

Shadish, W. R., & Haddock, C. K. (1994). Combining estimates of effect size. In H. Cooper & L. V. Hedges (Eds.), *The handbook of research synthesis* (pp. 261–281). New York: Russell Sage Foundation.

Shadish, W. R., Robinson, L., & Lu, C. (1999). *ES.* St. Paul, MN: Assessment Systems.

Shaver, J. P., & Norton, R. S. (1980). Randomness and replication in ten years of the *American Educational Research Journal. Educational Researcher, 9,* 9–15.

Shrout, P. E., & Bolger, N. (2002). Mediation in experimental and nonexperimental studies: New procedures and recommendations. *Psychological Methods, 7,* 422–445.

Siegel, S., & Castellan, N. J. (1988). *Nonparametric statistics for the behavioral sciences* (2nd ed.). New York: McGraw-Hill.

Silva, A. P. D., & Stam, A. (1995). Discriminant analysis. In L. Grimm & P. R. Yarnold (Eds.), *Reading and understanding multivariate statistics* (pp. 277–318). Washington, DC: American Psychological Association.

Smith, M. L., & Glass, G. V. (1977). Meta-analysis of psychotherapy outcome studies. *American Psychologist, 32*, 752–760.

Smithson, M. J. (2000). *Statistics with confidence: An introduction for psychologists.* Thousand Oaks, CA: Sage.

Smithson, M. (2001). Correct confidence intervals for various regression effect sizes and parameters: The importance of noncentral distributions in computing intervals. *Educational and Psychological Measurement, 61*, 605–632.

Snyder, P., & Lawson, S. (1993). Evaluating results using corrected and uncorrected effect size estimates. *Journal of Experimental Education, 61*, 334–349.

Sohn, D. (1995). Meta-analysis as a means of discovery. *American Psychologist, 50*, 108–110.

Sohn, D. (2000). Significance testing and the science. *American Psychologist, 55*, 964–965.

Sprent, P. (1998). *Data driven statistical methods.* London: Chapman & Hall/CRC.

SPSS. (1999). *SPSS Advanced models 10.0.* Chicago: Author.

StatSoft. (2003). STATISTICA (Version 6.1) [Computer software]. Tulsa, OK: Author.

Steiger, J. H., & Fouladi, R. T. (1992). R2: A computer program for interval estimation, power calculation, and hypothesis testing for the squared multiple correlation. *Behavior Research Methods, Instruments, and Computers, 24*, 581–582.

Steiger, J. H., & Fouladi, R. T. (1997). Noncentrality interval estimation and the evaluation of statistical models. In L. L. Harlow, S. A. Mulaik, & J. H. Steiger (Eds.), *What if there were no significance tests?* (pp. 221–257). Mahwah, NJ: Erlbaum.

Stevens, J. (1992). *Applied multivariate statistics for the social sciences* (2nd ed.). Hillsdale, NJ: Erlbaum.

Stigler, S. M. (1986). *The history of statistics.* Cambridge, MA: Belknap.

Strube, M. J., & Hartmann, D. P. (1983). Meta-analysis: Techniques, applications, and functions. *Journal of Consulting and Clinical Psychology, 51*, 14–27.

Sulloway, F. J. (1997). *Born to rebel.* New York: Vintage Books.

Tabachnick, B. G., & Fidell, L. S. (2001). *Computer-assisted research design and analysis.* Boston: Allyn & Bacon.

Task Force on Statistical Inference. (2000). Narrow and shallow. *American Psychologist, 55*, 965–966.

Taubes, G. (1993). *Bad science.* New York: Random House.

Thompson, B. (1992). Two and one-half decades of leadership in measurement and evaluation. *Journal of Counseling and Development, 70*, 434–438.

Thompson, B. (1993a). Statistical significance testing in contemporary practice: Some proposed alternatives with comments from journal editors [Special issue]. *Journal of Special Education, 61*(4).

Thompson, B. (1993b). The use of statistical significance tests in research: Bootstrap and other alternatives. *Journal of Experimental Education, 61*, 361–377.

Thompson, B. (1994). Planned versus unplanned and orthogonal versus nonorthogonal contrasts: The neo-classical perspective. In B. Thompson (Ed.), *Advances in social science methodology* (Vol. 3, pp. 3–27). Greenwich, CT: JAI Press.

Thompson, B. (1996). AERA editorial policies regarding statistical significance testing: Three suggested reforms. *Educational Researcher, 25*, 26–30.

Thompson, B. (1997). Editorial policies regarding statistical significance tests: Further comments. *Educational Researcher, 26*, 29–32.

Thompson, B. (1999). Journal editorial policies regarding statistical significance tests: Heat is to fire as p is to importance. *Educational Psychology Review, 11*, 157–169.

Thompson, B. (2002a). "Statistical," "practical," and "clinical": How many kinds of significance do counselors need to consider? *Journal of Counseling and Development, 80*, 64–71.

Thompson, B. (2002b). What future quantitative social science research could look like: Confidence intervals for effect sizes. *Educational Researcher, 31*, 25–32.

Thompson, B. (Ed.). (2003). *Score reliability: Contemporary thinking on reliability issues.* Thousand Oaks, CA: Sage.

Thompson, B., & Snyder, P. A. (1998). Statistical significance and reliability analyses in recent *Journal of Counseling & Development* research articles. *Journal of Counseling & Development, 76*, 436–441.

Thompson, W. L. (2001). 402 citations questioning the indiscriminate use of null hypothesis significance tests in observational studies. Retrieved November 11, 2001, from http://biology.uark.edu/Coop/Courses/thompson5.html

Tryon, W. W. (2001). Evaluating statistical difference, equivalence, and indeterminacy using inferential confidence intervals: An integrated alternative method of conducting null hypothesis statistical tests. *Psychological Methods, 6*, 371–386.

Tukey, J. W. (1977). *Exploratory data analysis.* Reading, MA: Addison-Wesley.

Tversky, A., & Kahneman, D. (1971). Belief in the law of small numbers. *Psychological Bulletin, 76*, 105–110.

U.S. Census Bureau. (2002). *Census 2000 news releases.* Retrieved December 10, 2000, from http://www.census.gov/Press-Release/www/2000.html

Vacha-Haase, T. (2001). Statistical significance should not be considered one of life's guarantees: Effect sizes are needed. *Educational and Psychological Measurement, 61*, 219–224.

Vacha-Haase, T., & Ness, C. N. (1999). Statistical significance testing as it relates to practice: Use within *Professional Psychology: Research and Practice. Professional Psychology: Research and Practice, 30*(1), 104–105.

Vacha-Haase, T., Nilsson, J. E., Reetz, D. R., Lance, T. S., & Thompson, B. (2000). Reporting practices and APA editorial policies regarding statistical significance and effect size. *Theory and Psychology, 10*, 413–425.

Vaughn, G. M., & Corballis, M. C. (1969). Beyond tests of significance: Estimating strength of effects in selected ANOVA designs. *Psychological Bulletin, 72,* 204–213.

Wayne, J. H., Riordan, C. M., & Thomas, K. M. (2001). Is all sexual harassment viewed the same? Mock juror decisions in same- and cross-gender cases. *Journal of Applied Psychology, 86,* 179–187.

Wechsler, D. (1991). *Wechsler Intelligence Scale for Children–Third edition (WISC–III).* San Antonio, TX: Psychological Corporation.

West, S. G. (2001). New approaches to missing data in psychological research [Special section]. *Psychological Methods, 6*(4).

Wilcox, R. R. (1987). New designs in analysis of variance. *Annual Review of Psychology, 38,* 29–60.

Wilcox, R. R. (1998). How many discoveries have been lost by ignoring modern statistical methods? *American Psychologist, 53,* 300–314.

Wilkinson, L., & the Task Force on Statistical Inference. (1999). Statistical methods in psychology journals: Guidelines and explanations. *American Psychologist, 54,* 594–604.

Winer, B. J., Brown, D. R., & Michels, K. M. (1991). *Statistical principles in experimental design* (3rd ed.) Boston: McGraw-Hill.

Wingenfeld, S. A., Lachar, D., Gruber, C. P., & Kline, R. B. (1998). Development of the teacher-informant Student Behavior Survey. *Journal of Psychoeducational Assessment, 16,* 226–249.

Winkler, R. L. (1982). The Bayesian approach: A general review. In G. Keren (Ed.), *Statistical and methodological issues in psychology and social sciences research* (pp. 217–244). Hillsdale, NJ: Erlbaum.

Woodward, L. J., Fergusson, D. M., & Horwood, L. J. (2000). Driving outcomes of young people with attentional difficulties in adolescence. *Journal of the American Academy of Child and Adolescent Psychiatry, 39,* 627–634.

Wortman, P. M. (1994). Judging research quality. In H. Cooper & L. V. Hedges (Eds.), *The handbook of research synthesis* (pp. 97–123). New York: Russell Sage Foundation.

Wright, R. E. (1995). Logistic regression. In L. G. Grimm & P. R. Yarnold (Eds.), *Reading and understanding multivariate statistics* (pp. 217–244). Washington, DC: American Psychological Association.

INDEX

Page numbers followed by *t*, *f*, or n. indicate tables, figures, or notes.

Accept–support (AS), 36, 39
Accidental samples, 24
Additive model, 52
Ad hoc samples, 24
Agnostic priors, 284
Ambient correlational noise, 71
Analysis of variance (ANOVA), 44
    alternative to estimation of variance components, 189
    compared with ANCOVA for one-way designs, 191–195, 193*t*
    confidence intervals for ψ and, 171
    factorial, 205–221. *See also* Factorial designs
    fixed-effects, 51
    inferential measures of association and, 183, 185
    meta-analysis and, 261
    mixed model or mixed-effect model, 204, 231n.
    standardized contrasts and independent samples, 172
ANCOVA (analysis of covariance), 23
    compared with ANOVA for one-way designs, 191–195, 193*t*
    correlation ratio and, 99–100
    dependent samples and, 118
    multiple regression and, 56
    one-way design with single covariate, 191
Anomalies, 248
APA's *Publication Manual* (5th ed.), 13–14
Approximate confidence intervals for δψ, 175–177
A priori power analysis, 42, 96
Asymptotic standard error, 34
Automated reasoning process as result of NHST, 76–77

Balanced designs, 20–22
    effects in balanced two-way designs, 208–213, 208*t*–209*t*

tests in two-way designs, 214–216, 215*t*–216*t*
Balanced replication, 249
Ban on statistical tests, proposal for, 3–4
Base rate, 154
Bayesian confidence interval, 288, 291
Bayesian estimation, 30, 280–293
    continuous random variables, 287–292, 290*t*
    discrete hypotheses, 283–286
    evaluation and limitations of, 292–293
    rarity in behavioral sciences, 280–282
    statement of, 282–283
Bayesian Id's wishful thinking error, 64
Bayes's factor, 285
Belief in law of small numbers, 69
Bias-corrected bootstrapped confidence intervals, 274–275
Biased sample statistics, 25
Blocking designs, 22
Board of Scientific Affairs' Task Force. *See* Task Force on Statistical Inference (TFSI)
Bonferroni correction, 40, 71
Bootstrapping, 274–276, 277–279, 279*f*
Box-score method, 251

Capitalization on chance, 99
Cause size vs. effect size, 97
Cell means model, 183n.
Central test distribution, 28
Change scores, 32
χ^2 test of association, 56–58
    results for same proportions at different group sizes, 57*t*
Circularity. *See* Sphericity
Classification analysis and error rates, 128–129
Clinical significance, 135

Common language effect size, 127–128
Completely between-subjects factorial
    design, 204
    equations for direct computation of
        intraclass correlation for, 233t
    equations for variance components
        estimators in, 232t
    single-factor contrasts in, 223–227
    values of descriptive and inferential
        measures of association for, 233t
Completely randomized design, 20
Completely within-subjects factorial
    design, 204
Complex interaction contrast, 212
Computer-intensive methods. See Resam-
    pling techniques
Conceptual validity, 257
Conditional model, 260
Conditional probability, 282
Conditional variance, 27
Confidence intervals, 26–27
    as alternative to NHST, 80
    Bayesian, 288, 291
    bootstrapped, 274–275
    for δ
        exact interval, 109–113, 112t
        traditional interval, 108–109
    for δψ
        approximate intervals, 175–177
        exact intervals, 177–178
    inferential, 84
    joint, 171
    for measures of association, 118–121,
        120t
    for μ, 28–30
    for $\mu_1 - \mu_2$, 30–34
    for other types of statistics, 34–35
    for ψ, 170–171
    recommendation on reporting, 88
    simultaneous, 171
    software for calculating, 137
Confidence interval transformation, 34
Construct replication, 249–250
Continuous independent variables, dichot-
    omizing of, 115
Continuous random variables, 287–292,
    290t
Contrast. See also Contrast specification
    and tests
    complex interaction contrast, 212
    criterion contrast effect size, 135

interaction contrast, 210, 213
    in completely between-subjects
        designs, 227–228
    normative contrast, 135
    observed group contrast on a
        dichotomy, 146t
    pairwise interaction contrast, 211
    single-factor contrast, 210
    in completely between-subjects
        designs, 223–227
    standardized contrasts, 171–179
    standardized mean differences
        interaction contrasts in com-
            pletely between-subjects
            designs, 227–228
        single-factor contrasts in com-
            pletely between-subjects
            designs, 223–227
    trends or polynomials, 167
Contrast specification and tests, 163–178
    confidence intervals for ψ, 170–171
    control of Type I error, 169–170,
        170t
    specification, 164–167
        orthogonal, 165–167, 166t
    statistical tests, 168–169
Contrast weights or coefficients, 164
    orthogonal vs. nonorthogonal
        contrasts, 164–165
Control factors, 23
Controversy over statistical significance
    tests, 3–4, 5
    historical background, 6–14
        criticism of statistical tests
            (1940–present), 8–11
        failure of early suggestions to
            report effect sizes (1994–
            present), 11–12
        hybrid logic of statistical tests
            (1920–1960), 6–7
        institutionalization of "Intro
            Stats" method (1940–1960),
            7–8
        rise of meta-analysis, 12
        TFSI report and APA's Publica-
            tion Manual (5th ed.), 13–14
    prospective view, 14–16
Correlated design, 20
    matched-groups design, 20
    repeated-measures design, 20
Correlational studies, 20

Correlation ratio, 99
Covariate analyses
    in comparative studies, 23
    effect size estimation in, 191–195,
        193t
Criterion contrast effect size, 135
Crossed factors, 204
Cross-validation sample, 249

Dependent samples, 20
    F test, 52–54
        assumptions of, 54–56
    measures of association, 116–118
    standardized contrasts, 174–177,
        175t
    standardized mean differences,
        104–107
Derivation sample, 249
Descriptive measures of association
    in factorial designs, 230–231
    in one-way designs, 180–183
Dichotomizing of continuous indepen-
    dent variables, 115
Dichotomous thinking as result of
    NHST, 76–77, 81
Difference scaling, 165
Difference score, 32, 169
Directional alternative hypothesis, 37–38
Dismantling research, 249
Doubly centered weights, 210, 211
Dunn–Bonferroni method, 169, 171

Education in statistics, recommendation
    to make less NHST-centric,
    89–90
Effect Size (ES) (software program), 137,
    148, 230
Effect size estimation. See also Parametric
    effect size indexes
    contexts for, 95–96
    examples of, 137–142
        caffeine effect on 2000-meter row-
            ing performance, 141–142,
            141t
        demographic and referral status
            effects on teacher ratings,
            137–138, 137t
        gender differences in basic math
            skills, 138–141, 139t

examples with dichotomous
    outcomes, 155–161
    driving records of youth with at-
        tentional difficulties, 157–158,
        158t
    predictive values of cognitive test
        profile, 158–161, 159t–161t
    smoking and coronary heart
        disease, 155–157, 156t
    guidelines for interpreting, 132–136,
        133t
    misleading effects of, 136
    in multifactor designs, 203–243. See
        also Factorial designs
    in one-way designs, 163–202. See
        also One-way designs
    recommendation on reporting, 88
    research journals requiring, 4
    software for, 136–137
    for tables 2 × 2, 144–151
        definitions of statistics for, 147t
        interval estimation, 149–151
        for observed group contrast on a
            dichotomy, 146t
        parameters, 144–146
        statistics and evaluation,
            146–149
    for tables larger than 2 × 2, 151–152
    terms used for, 96–100
        effect size vs. cause size, 97
        families of effect sizes, 97–100
Empirical cumulativeness, 248
Equivalence testing, 83–84
Error bars, 27
Error rates in classification analysis,
    128–129
Error term of F, 49
ES. See Effect Size
ESCI (computer program), 137
Estimated eta-squared, 99
Estimation. See also Effect size estimation
    in multifactor designs, 203–243. See
        also Factorial designs
    in one-way designs, 163–202. See
        also One-way designs
Exact confidence intervals
    for δ, 109–113, 112t
    for δψ, 177–178
Exact level of significance (p), 41
Exact replication, 249, 252
Experimental variables, 20

Experimentwise probability of Type I error, 39, 171
Explanatory meta-analysis, 255
Exploratory research as proper realm for NHST, 86–87
Exploratory Software for Confidence Intervals (ESCI), 178
External replication, 249
Extrinsic factors, 253–254

Factorial designs, 22, 203–243
    ANOVA and, 205–221
        basic distinctions, 205–206
        complete vs. reduced structural models, 216–217
        effects in balanced two-way designs, 208–213
        extensions to designs with three or more factors, 218–219
        nonorthogonal designs, 206, 219–221, 219t
        orthogonal designs, 205
        pseudo-orthogonal designs, 206
        tests in balanced two-way designs, 214–216, 215t–216t
        variability, sources of, 206–208
    completely between-subjects, 204
        equations for direct computation of intraclass correlation for, 233t
        equations for variance components estimators in, 232t
        single-factor contrasts in, 223–227
        values of descriptive and inferential measures of association for, 233t
    completely within-subjects, 204
    examples of, 234–242
        alcohol education's effect on recent drinking quantity, 240–242, 241t
        differential effectiveness of aftercare programs for substance abuse, 234–237, 235t
        earwitness testimony and face overshadowing effect, 238–240, 239t
        interpersonal problem-solving skills as function of gender

and alcohol use, 237–238, 238t
    measures of association, 230–234
        descriptive, 230–231
        inferential, 231–233
        interval estimation, 234
    mixed within-subjects, 204, 214, 229
    partial or incomplete, 204
    randomized groups, 204
    repeated-measures factors, 204, 228–229
    standardized mean differences, 221–230
        interaction contrasts in completely between-subjects designs, 227–228
        interval estimation, 229–230
        repeated-measures factors, 228–229
        single-factor contrasts in completely between-subjects designs, 223–227
    types of, 203–204
Factors of interest, 223
Fail-safe number, 261
Families of effect sizes, 97–100
    standardized mean differences, 98t
Familywise probability of Type I error, 39
"File drawer problem," 73
First Bayes (software program), 292
Fisher model, 6–7, 70
Fixed-effects factors, 22–23
Fixed-p approach, 7
Focused comparisons, 47
Fourfold tables, 143, 144–151
    definitions of statistics for, 147t
    for observed group contrast on a dichotomy, 146t
F tests for means, 44, 47–56
    assumptions of independent samples F test, 51–52
    dependent samples F test, 52–54
    assumptions of, 54–56
    independent samples F test, 48–50
    means and variances for three independent samples, 50t
    raw scores for three dependent samples, 54t
    results of independent sample F test, 50t

compared to results of dependent
samples F test, 54t
weighted vs. unweighted-means
analysis, 50–51
Fundamental concepts of statistical
testing, 19–59
χ^2 test of association, 56–58
comparative studies, 19–23
balanced and unbalanced designs,
20–22
covariate analyses, 23
fixed-effects and random-effects
factors, 22–23
independent samples designs and
correlated designs, 19–20
multiple independent or dependent variables, 22
F tests for means, 44, 47–56
assumptions of dependent
samples F test, 54–56
assumptions of independent
samples F test, 51–52
dependent samples F test, 52–54
independent samples F test,
48–50
weighted vs. unweighted-means
analysis, 50–51
logic of statistical significance
testing, 36–41
alternative hypotheses, 37–38
contexts and steps, 36
level of Type I error, 38–40
null hypotheses, 36–37
statistical tests, 40–41
power, 41–43
sampling and estimation, 24–35
confidence intervals, 28–35. *See
also* Confidence intervals
point and interval estimation,
26–28
sample statistics as estimators,
25–26
types of samples, 24–25
statistical tests and replication, 58
t tests for means, 44–47

Gain scores, 32
Garbage in, garbage out problem, 257
Group difference indexes, 97
case-level analyses of, 122–129

common language effect size,
127–128
error rates in classification
analysis, 128–129
measures of overlap, 122–124,
123f
tail ratios, 125–127
relation of group-level to case-level,
130–131, 131f, 131t
Group overlap indexes, 101
graphical display of group means,
124f
measures of overlap, 122–124, 123f

Hierarchical design, 204
Higher order designs, 22
Highest density region, 288
Homogeneity of regression, 192
Homogeneity of variance, 51, 171, 172,
214
Hybrid logic of statistical tests (1920–
1960), 6–7

Improvement over chance classification,
129
Incomplete factorial designs, 204
Independent samples, 19–20, 22
F test, 48–50
assumptions of, 51–52
measures of association, 114–116
standardized contrasts, 171–173,
173t
standardized mean differences,
101–104
Individual-difference variables, 20
Inference revolution, 8
Inferential confidence intervals, 84
Inferential measures of association
in factorial designs, 231–233
in one-way designs, 183–190, 187t,
189t, 190t
Informative priors, 284
Interaction contrast, 210, 213
in completely between-subjects
designs, 227–228
Interaction trend, 212
Internal replication, 249
International Committee of Medical Journal Editors, 14

Interval estimation, 26, 80, 149–151
    asymptotic standard errors for sample
        proportions, 150t
    in factorial designs, 229–230, 234
    in one-way designs, 190–191
"Intro Stats" method, 7
    institutionalization of (1940–1960),
        7–8
    trend showing adoption of, 8, 9f
Inverse probability error, 64

Jackknife, 274
Joint confidence intervals, 171
Journals and published research
    biases of journal editors, 73–74
        recommendation to discard, 87
    NHST making interpretation
        difficult, 74–75
    requiring effect size to be reported, 4

Lack of objectivity in NHST, 78
Latin-Squares design, 204
Law of large numbers, 25
Left-tail ratio (LTR), 125
Likelihood, 282
Literal replication, 249, 252
Locally available samples, 24
Logic of statistical significance testing,
    36–41
    alternative hypotheses, 37–38
    contexts and steps, 36
    level of Type I error, 38–40
    null hypotheses, 36–37
    statistical tests, 40–41
Logit d, 147
Long-run relative-frequency view of
    probability, 29

Magnitude fallacy, 66
Main comparisons, 210
Main effects model, 217
Manipulated variables, 20
Marginal probability, 282
Margin-bound measure of association,
    149
Matched-groups design, 20
Maximum likelihood estimation, 189
Maximum probable difference, 84

May, Rollo, 62
Meaningfulness fallacy, 66
Mean square, 25
Measures of association, 98, 114–122
    confidence intervals, 118–121
    dependent samples, 116–118
    in factorial designs, 230–234
        descriptive, 230–231
        inferential, 231–233
        interval estimation, 234
    independent samples, 114–116
    limitations, 121–122
    margin-bound, 149
    in one-way designs, 179–191
        descriptive, 180–183
        inferential, 183–190, 187t, 189t,
            190t
        interval estimation, 190–191
Measures of overlap and group
    differences, 122–124, 123f–124f
Mediator effects, 209, 255
Meta-analysis, 96, 133, 247–271
    examples of, 266–270
        amplitudes of event-related
            potentials from males at risk
            for alcoholism, 267–269,
            268f
        cross-informant consistency in
            reports about children's adjust-
            ment status, 270
        gender differences in personality
            characteristics, 269–270
    historical background (1976–
        present), 12
    mini meta-analysis, 262–265, 263t–
        264t
    research synthesis, 250–255
        goals, 250–251
        models of explanation, 254–255
        qualitative research reviews, 251
        quantitative research synthesis,
            251–254, 253t
    software for, 137
    steps of, 255–262
        analyze data, 258–262
        collect data, 256
        describe, interpret, report results,
            262
        evaluate data quality, 257
        formulate research question,
            255–256

measure predictors and criterion, 257–258
threats to validity of, 265–266
Method 1 (regression-based technique), 220, 221, 222t
Method 2 (regression-based technique), 220–221, 222t
Method 3 (regression-based technique), 221, 222t
Method factors, 253–254
Methodological validity, 257
Metric-free effect sizes, 97
Misinterpretation of null hypothesis. *See* Null hypothesis significance testing (NHST)
Mixed design, 204
Mixed-effects model or mixed model, 204, 231n., 260–261
Mixed within-subjects factorial design, 204, 214, 229
Model-driven analysis, 255
Moderator effects, 209
Moderator variable, 254
Monotonic relation of p values, 65
Multifactor designs. *See* Factorial designs
Multilevel ordinal categories, 144
Multiple-endpoint studies, 258
Multiple regression, 56
Multiple-treatment studies, 258

Narrative literature review, 251
Negatively biased estimators, 26
Negative predictive value, 154, 154t
Newman–Keuls procedure, 170
Neyman–Pearson model, 6–7, 70
NHST. *See* Null hypothesis significance testing
Nil hypotheses, 36–37
appropriateness of, 81
falsity of, 70–71
Nonadditive model, 5e
Noncentrality interval estimation, 35
Noncentral test distributions, 35
Nondirectional alternative hypothesis, 37
Nonexperimental studies, 20
Nonexperimental variables, 20
Nonindependence of study results, 258
Non-nil hypotheses, 36–37
Nonorthogonal contrasts, 165
Nonorthogonal designs, 206, 219–221

raw scores and descriptive statistics for, 219t
Nonparametric bootstrapping, 274
Nonparametric effect size indexes, 143–162. *See also* Effect size estimation
categorical outcomes, 143–144
examples of, 155–161
driving records of youth with attentional difficulties, 157–158, 158t
predictive values of cognitive test profile, 158–161, 159t, 161t
smoking and coronary heart disease, 155–157, 156t
sensitivity, specificity, and predictive value, 152–155
definitions of, 153t
distributions of groups with and without disorder on continuous screening test, 153f
estimated for score differences on visual-spatial and short-term memory tasks, 160t, 161t
predictive values of cognitive test profile, 158–161, 159t, 161t
Normal science, 247
Normative contrast, 135
Null hypotheses, 36–37
range null hypotheses, 82
Null hypothesis significance testing (NHST), 6, 8–9
automated reasoning process as result of, 76–77
basic rationale and steps of, 36–41. *See also* Logic of statistical significance testing
bias in research literature toward, 73–74, 87
bias toward groups over individuals, 78
continued use of vs. discarding, 79
criticisms of, 9, 10f, 16, 61–62
fallacies about testing outcomes, 70
framework for change, 85–90
lack of objectivity in, 78
misinterpretations, 62–70, 80
mistaken conclusions on null hypothesis, 66–68
of p values, 62–66
widespread nature of, 68–70, 69t

NHST, *continued*
    nil hypotheses found false, 70–71
    positive aspects of, 79–82
    probabilities and, 78
    problems with, 61–91
    random sampling assumed in sampling distributions, 71–72
    recommendations, 86–90
        educational changes, 89–90
        effect sizes and confidence intervals, 88
        exploratory research as realm for NHST, 86–87
        journal editors' bias, 87
        power, how to report, 87
        replication requirement, 89–90
        statistical software programs, 90
        substantive significance of results to be demonstrated, 88–89
        use of word "significant," 87–88
    replication and, 75–76, 89–90
    research literature problems caused by, 74–75
    statistical assumptions infrequently verified, 72
    variations on, 82–85
        equivalence testing, 83–84
        inferential confidence intervals, 84
        range null hypotheses and good-enough belts, 82
        three-valued logic, 84–85

Observational studies, 20
Odds-against chance fantasy, 63
Odds ratio, 145
Off-factors, 223
Omnibus comparisons, 47–48
One-variable bootstrap methods, 274
One-way designs, 163–202
    contrast specification and tests, 163–178
        confidence intervals for ψ, 170–171
        control of Type I error, 169–170, 170t
        specification, 164–167
        statistical tests, 168–169
    covariate analyses and effect size estimation, 191–195, 193t

defined, 22
examples of, 195–201
    basic math skills in introductory statistics, 197–199, 198t–199t
    cognitive status of recreational ecstasy (MDMA) users, 196, 197t
    learning curve data, analysis of, 199–201, 200t–201t
measures of association, 179–191
    descriptive, 180–183
    inferential, 183–190
    interval estimation, 190–191
standardized contrasts, 171–179
    dependent samples, 174–177, 175t
    exact confidence intervals for $\delta\psi$, 177–178
    independent samples, 171–173, 173t
Operational replication, 249
Ordered categories, 144
Orthogonal contrasts, 165–167, 166t, 172
Orthogonal designs, 205
Orthogonal polynomials, 167
Orthogonal sums of squares, 224

Pairwise comparison, 164
Pairwise interaction contrast, 211
Paradigm, 248
Parametric bootstrapping, 275
Parametric effect size indexes, 95–142.
    See also Effect size estimation
    case-level analyses of group differences, 122–129
        common language effect size, 127–128
        error rates in classification analysis, 128–129
        graphical display of group means, 124f
        measures of overlap, 122–124, 123f
        tail ratios, 125–127
    guidelines for interpreting, 132–136
        cautions, 132–133, 133t
        questions, 132
        substantive effect, 133–136
    levels of analysis, 101
    measures of association, 114–122

confidence intervals, 118–121
dependent samples, 116–118
independent samples, 114–116
limitations, 121–122
relation of group-level to case-level, 130–131, 131*f*, 131*t*
standardized mean differences, 101–114
dependent samples, 104–107
exact confidence intervals for δ, 109–113
independent samples, 101–104
limitations, 113–114
traditional confidence intervals for δ, 108–109
Partial factorial designs, 204
p as exact level of significance, 41
Person x treatment interaction, 52–53
Planned comparisons, 169
Point estimation, 26
Polynomials, 167
Population effect sizes, overestimated in published studies, 73–74, 74*t*
Population inference model, 71
Population parameters, 25, 256
estimated by sample standardized mean difference, 96–97, 97*f*
Population variance components, 115
Positive bias, 51
Positive predictive value, 154, 154*t*
Posterior probability, 282
Post hoc power analysis, 43
Power, 41–43
recommendation on how to report, 87
Predictive value, 154–155
example of cognitive test profile, 158–161, 159*t*–161*t*
negative, 154, 154*t*
positive, 154, 154*t*
positive and negative for screening test, 153*t*
Preliminary testing and pooling, 218
Primary analysis, 251
Principle of indifference, 284
Prior probabilities, 129, 282
Probabilistic revolution, 8
Proportional chance criterion, 129
Proportion difference, 145
Pseudo-orthogonal designs, 206
PSY (computer program), 137, 177, 230

Publication Manual (5th ed., APA), 13–14
Puzzle solving, 248
p values, 7, 9, 41
associated with null hypotheses not plausible, 71
criticisms of approach, 9–10
from *F* test, 9–10
misinterpretations of, 62–66
monotonic relation of, 65

Qualitative literature review, 251
Quantitative research synthesis, 251–254, 253*t*
Quasi-*F* ratios, 218

R^2 (correlation ratio), 11
Random-effects factors, 22–23
Randomization model, 72
Randomization procedures, 276
Randomized-blocks designs, 22, 204
Randomized-groups, 20
Randomized groups factorial design, 204
Random samples, 24
Random sampling assumed in sampling distributions, 71–72
Range hypotheses, 37
Range null hypotheses, 82
Rate ratio, 145
Reduced cross-classification method, 224
Reduced structural model, 217
Reification Fallacy, 68
Reject–support (RS), 36, 39
NHST in context of, 62
Relationship indexes, 97
Repeatability fallacy, 65
Repeated-measures design, 20
factorial designs, 228–229
intrinsically vs. nonintrinsically, 20
Replicability, 65
Replicated experiments, 204
Replication, 247–260
balanced, 249
in behavioral sciences, 247, 248
construct, 249–250
discouraged by NHST, 75–76
exact or literal, 249, 252
external, 249
internal, 249

Replication, *continued*
operational, 249
as random factor, 204
recommendation to require, 89–90
statistical tests and, 58
types of replication, 249–250

Rerandomization, 276
Resampling Procedures (RP) (computer
software), 277
Resampling Stats (computer program),
278
Resampling techniques, 273–280. *See also*
Bayesian estimation
evaluation and limitations of,
278–280
techniques, 274–278
Research. *See* Journals and published
research
Research synthesis, 250–255
Right-tail ratio (RTR), 125, 126*f*
Risk difference, 145
Risk ratio, 145
Root Mean Square Standardized Effect
Size (RMSSE), 234
RP (Resampling Procedures) (computer
software), 277
R2 program, 137, 234

S^2 = SS/N, 26
Sagan, Carl, 27, 62
Samples of convenience, 24
Sampling and estimation, 24–35
confidence intervals, 28–35. *See also*
Confidence intervals
point and interval estimation,
26–28
sample statistics as estimators, 25–26
types of samples, 24–25
Sampling distribution, 27–28
random sampling assumed in, 71–72
Sampling error and NHST, 79, 89
SAS/STAT, 111–112, 112*t*, 120, 120*t*,
178, 179*t*, 198. *See also*
STATISTICA
Secondary analysis, 251
Sensitivity, specificity, and predictive
value, 152–155
definitions of, 153*t*

distributions of groups with and
without disorder on continuous
screening test, 153*f*
positive and negative predictive
values for screening test,
153*t*
Sensitivity analysis, 262
Simple comparisons, 210
Simultaneous confidence intervals, 171
Single-*df*, 47, 210
Single-factor contrast, 210
in completely between-subjects
designs, 223–227
Single-factor designs. *See* One-way
designs
Smithson scripts for SPSS, 137, 190,
191, 234
Software. *See also specific types by name*
for Bayesian analysis, 292
for effect size estimation, 136–137
recommendations for statistical
software, 90
Specificity, 152–155
definition of, 153*t*
distributions of groups with and
without disorder on continuous
screening test, 153*f*
Sphericity, 54–56, 72, 168
Split-plot design, 204, 214, 229
SPSS. *See* Smithson scripts for SPSS
Standard error, 27
asymptotic standard errors for
sample proportions, 150*t*
Standardized contrasts, 171–179
Standardized mean changes, 105
Standardized mean differences,
101–114
confidence intervals for δ
exact, 109–113, 112*t*
traditional, 108–109
dependent samples, 104–107
in factorial designs, 221–230. *See
also* Factorial designs
independent samples, 101–104
limitations, 113–114
Standardized mean gains, 105
Standardizers, 98
Standard set, 165
STATISTICA, 43, 111, 112, 119, 120,
137, 178, 190, 234
Statistical decision theory, 82

Statistical significance testing, 36–41.
    See also Logic of statistical
    significance testing
Statistical tests, 40–41, 96
    in one-way design, 168–169
Statistical validity, 257
Subjective degree-of-belief view of
    probability, 29
Subjects effect, 32
Subjects factors, 23
Substantive factors, 253–254

Tables. *See also* Effect size estimation
    fourfold tables, 143, 144–151
        definitions of statistics for, 147*t*
        for observed group contrast on a
            dichotomy, 146*t*
        larger than 2 × 2, 151–152
Tail ratios, 125–127, 126*f*
Task Force on Statistical Inference
    (TFSI)
    graphical display of group means,
        124*f*
    purpose of, 3, 4
    report of, 13
    Type I error and pairwise
        comparisons, 170
Terminology in reporting statistical test
    results, 80–81
    effect size estimation and, 96–100
    recommendation to stop using word
        "significant," 87–88
TFSI. *See* Task Force on Statistical
    Inference
Theoretical cumulativeness, 248
Three-valued logic, 84–85
TNONCT, 111–112
Total sums of squares, 49
Traditional confidence intervals for δ,
    108–109

Transformation-based methods, 34
t tests for means, 44–47, 46*t*–47*t*
Two-variable bootstrap methods, 275
Type I errors, 38–40, 64, 68, 71
    control in one-way design, 169–170,
        170*t*
    equivalence testing and, 83
    rate in published studies, 73
    weighted by estimated costs of error,
        82
Type II errors, 41–42, 67, 68, 71
    weighted by estimated costs of error,
        82

Unbiased sample statistics, 25
Unconditional model, 260
Unconditional probability, 282
Uninformative priors, 284
Univariate designs, 22
Universe, 256
Unordered categories, 144
Unplanned comparisons, 169
Unweighted vs. weighted-means analysis,
    50–51
Upper confidence limit, 27

Validity fallacy, 65
Valid research hypothesis fantasy, 65
Variance-accounted-for effect size, 100
Vote counting, 251

Web site for supplemental readings,
    exercises, etc., 3
Weighted vs. unweighted-means analysis,
    50–51
WinBUGS (Bayesian Inference Using
    Gibbs Sampling), 292
Within-study variance, 259
Within-subjects design, 20

ABOUT THE AUTHOR

Rex B. Kline is an associate professor of psychology at Concordia University in Montréal, Canada. Since earning a PhD in psychology, his areas of research and writing have included the psychometric evaluation of cognitive abilities, child clinical assessment, structural equation modeling, and usability engineering in computer science. He lives with his wife and two children in Montréal.